In memoriam Henry Nash Smith

Contents

Preface

This is a collection of pieces concerning a variety of topics in American literature. They include essays, introductions, lectures, and a radio talk, along with some unpublished papers. There is no continuity or binding theme: they simply represent aspects of my interest in American literature over some twenty-five years. The earliest (on Henry Adams and Mark Twain) dates from 1961, while the first and last essays in the collection (previously unpublished) represent comparatively recent work. Inevitably, differences in approach and method will be detectable, and these may reflect changing attitudes to American literature through the period covered. If anything unites the pieces it is one person's uninterrupted and ongoing interest and pleasure in the distinguishing features and singular achievements of American writers and writing. From this point of view it is at once something of an act of homage and a small repayment of a debt of gratitude. As my method relies extensively on allusions and numerous short quotations it seemed undesirable to burden, lengthen, or interrupt the texts with numerous footnotes. This may seem unscholarly – indeed it is. I can only say that the pieces are offered exactly as essays – meditations, interpretations, explorations – and not as contributions to scholarship.

Thanks are due to the following periodicals and publishers for permission to reprint material: *Journal of American Studies*; *Modern Age*; *London Magazine*; *TriQuarterly*; *Salmagundi*; Oxford University Press; the British Academy; Macmillan.

This collection is dedicated to the memory of Henry Nash Smith, who guided and oversaw my first very faltering steps in the field of American studies. He did this, as he did everything, with extraordinary patience, unfailing courtesy, and considerate wisdom. In his scrupulousness, dedication, disinterested generosity, and humane care he was an

exemplary figure and an inspiration – both as man and scholar. My debt
to him is immeasurable as is that of many, many others. He can fairly be
regarded as the father of modern American studies. They could hardly
have had a more benign or responsible one.

TONY TANNER

King's College
Cambridge

1

Scenes of nature, signs of men

In this manner, they proceeded along the margin of the precipice, catching glimpses of the placid Otsego, or pausing to listen to the rattling of wheels and the sounds of hammers, that rose from the valley, to mingle the signs of men with the scenes of nature. (*The Pioneers*)

The distinction between scenes and signs is made very clearly here, and it is invariably clear in the work of James Fenimore Cooper. The opposition is static, even dichotomous, for although the scenes and signs 'mingle' they so not merge into a new unity or a third term. Nor do they problematize each other as they do in later American writers for whom it is often not clear to what extent scenes have become signs, and vice versa, if indeed the two can be distinguished and differentiated. In Cooper the opposition is not without attendant ambiguities and it is often these ambiguities which give thematic energy to Cooper's work; but the terms do not lose their distinctness. The scene may succumb to the sign, or it may outlast it, but it is always clear which is which; there is no peripheral contamination of the categories. Scenes are, primarily, to be seen – appreciated by the non-intervening eye – and there are many passages in Cooper where the narrative effectively comes to a halt while a static scene is ec-statically seen. A landscape, like a picture, if properly submitted to visually, may engender high feelings, a sense of the nobility of creation, of the aesthetic benevolence of God. The eye, in all its modes of operation, from the responsive–passive, appreciative–reverent, to the utilitarian–active, assessive–aggressive, is everywhere in evidence in Cooper. Let us consider Deerslayer's first visual experience of Lake Glimmerglass (in *The Deerslayer*). Deerslayer is travelling with the aptly named Hurry Harry, whose 'hurry' indeed precludes any appreciative response to scenes, which never induce in him the moods and responses of a decorous attention to the moral and aesthetic lessons to be imbibed from the scenes of nature. Deerslayer is different.

An exclamation of surprise broke from the lips of Deerslayer, an exclamation that was low, and guardedly made, however, for his habits were much more thoughtful and regulated than those of the reckless Hurry, when, on reaching

1

> the margin of the lake, he beheld the view that unexpectedly met his gaze. It was, in truth, sufficiently striking to merit a brief description.

And here the narrative is suspended while Cooper evokes the scene. It is seen entirely through his educated and Europeanized eyes, as such references as 'dark Rembrandt-looking hemlocks' sufficiently indicate. This is not a native American eye, not Deerslayer, taking possession of America's primal beauty. It is what might now be called a 'colonizing' eye. Cooper concludes this description in this way.

> In a word, the hand of man had never yet defaced or deformed any part of this native scene, which lay bathed in sunlight, a glorious picture of affluent forest grandeur, softened by the balminess of June and relieved by the beautiful variety afforded by the presence of so broad an expanse of water.
>
> 'This is grand! – 'Tis solemn! – 'Tis an edification of itself to look upon!' exclaimed Deerslayer, as he stood leaning on his rifle . . . 'Not a tree disturbed even by redskin hand, as I can discover, but everything left in the ordering of the Lord to live and die according to his own designs and laws!'

Deerslayer, in this mood, calls the scene a 'school' (which is already an oxymoron – nature praised as culture) which will set the mind to rights. He asks, later: 'Have the Governor's or the King's people given this lake a name ... If they've not begun to blaze their trails, and set up their compasses, and line off their maps, it's likely that they've not bethought them to disturb natur' with a name.' The idea of disturbing nature, even with a 'name', is an extension of Deerslayer's suspicion of maps and compasses and surveyors: the various ways of imposing a taxonomic nomenclature on nature, the attempt to master (and appropriate) it with measuring machines, the misguided idea that the mysteries of the 'ground' can be transplanted into the cartographic signs of the 'map'. He is, as always, against the idea of man's intervention into, interruption of, super-imposition on, nature with whatever kinds of sign. He indeed prefers an unmediated contact with the thing itself. This hostility to the presumptuous and imperialistic intrusions of language into the American scene is made a matter of comedy and burlesque in *The Prairie*, in which Cooper presents us with the absurd figure of Dr Obed Battius, who is the ultimate out-of-place pedant. He does, however, represent in exaggerated form both a threat and a problem. He is a verbal predator: he wants to classify everything, see everything 'enumerated and classed'. He cannot bear the idea of animals which might have remained 'unknown and undescribed'. He speaks in taxonomic. Thus, of an animal he has seen which he thinks is a monster:

> *Quadruped*; seen by star-light . . . see Journal for latitude and meridian. *Genus* – unknown; therefore named after the discoverer, and from the happy coincidence of being seen in the evening – *Verspertilio Horribiles, Americanus.*

Dimensions (by estimation) – *Greatest Length*, eleven feet; *height*, six feet, *head*, erect, *nostrils*, expansive ...

and so on. By a rather uncharacteristically broad piece of humour, it turns out to be his own ass.

But the problem and threat are real, and absolutely central to all American literature, if not America itself. Battius represents language in its most nakedly (here foolishly) imperialistic, which is to say cannibalistic, guise and manifestation. His passion for classification is voracious. Even in danger he will reach for some hitherto unclassified plant, 'devouring it with delighted, and certainly not unskilled eyes'. Tellingly, Esther says of his speech: 'There is a drug in every word he utters.' Leatherstocking, one of Deerslayer's many names, mocks classification and this misdirected concern for nomination. He laughs at Battius for thinking that 'a name could change the natur' of the beast' since 'The creatur' is the same, call it by what name you will.' He is, ultimately, not only against 'bookish knowledge' which 'smothers' nature, but against the 'drug' of language itself. For of course, in the most profound sense, it is just language itself which disturbs nature. Cooper wrote in *The American Democrat* that 'Men are the constant dupes of names, while their happiness and well-being mainly depend on things.' This separation and possible confusion of names and things has a particular urgency and importance in America and I will have more to say about it. But we may note that one of the most convulsive and far-reaching disturbances of nature with a name in the history of the world was that disturbance, that invasion and appropriation, which names itself 'America'. What happened and continues to happen to the continent, the 'thing' which is smothered under that name, continues to exercise if not obsess American writers. As it most certainly obsessed Cooper. Naming – to spell it out – pins things down: it fragments and atomizes the flowing totality of nature into static appellations (which is why Melville regarded most literature as consisting of a series of 'guide books' while reality went on flowing by). There is always a danger of reality's ebbing from the thing into the name so that a primary reality is lost in exchange for a fixed, arbitrary secondary reality of nominations and signs – of which men may indeed be 'dupes'. Yet a man can hardly avoid having, or getting, a name – usually of course that of the father. And in this connection Deerslayer/ Leatherstocking's evasiveness is particularly significant. It is always very hard to, as it were, get his name out of him. And he never uses the name of his father. In *The Prairie* when he is urgently pushed for his name he will not in fact pronounce it. He refers to his given name as 'beginning with an N and ending with an L', which anyway refers only, with puzzling mystification, to his first name. He adds: 'Lord, lad, I've been called in my time by as many names as there are people among whom I've dwelt ...

but little will it matter when the time shall come that all are to be mustered, face to face, by what titles a mortal has played his part!' He is elusive under nomination, in a sense continually dodging the whole naming process and the illusory permanence of identity that it imposes. Ideally he wants to stay clear of the realm of names. Of course, to the extent that he gets caught up in narrative, history, and society (whether tribal or settlement), he cannot. And by the same token, and *a fortiori*, nor could America. Itself a name, its self-securing, its maintenance, its extension, its 'progress' were all, in a very important sense, a naming process. In this matter, as in many others, Deerslayer both articulates and embodies an impossible nostalgia, an unrealizable dream, and an ineradicable discomfort which can take the form of guilt – all in relation to the unavoidable necessity, which was at the same time a potentially damaging and destructive disturbance, of naming.

In America, of course, the whole matter of names and naming had profoundly important political as well as cultural aspects. The fore-doomed gestures by Webster and others towards a wholly new American language, purged of the imperialism inherent in the hegemonic English which had ruled the colony, autonomous and independent as befitted the Adamic American in his liberated paradise, indicate that people in the early years of the Republic were very aware of this political dimension. The preoccupation with naming in the Lewis and Clark *Journals* also gives some indication of the awareness of the significance of the act of naming in America. Thus, they do at times respect and attempt to transcribe local Indian names. But that of course both indicates that there has been a previous and indigenous population, and takes away from their claims to discovery and its attendant rights – indeed you cannot really 'discover' the already named, any more than you should 'settle' (or take) the already domesticated or inhabited. So for the most part they impose hundreds of names of their own, sometimes merely literal and *ad hoc* ('Travellers Rest'), sometimes invoking the legitimating authorities and politicians of white America ('Jefferson's River'). Most of the names did not take hold – but the whole venture can be seen as an exercise of territorial annexation by nomination. A disturbance indeed, particularly for the Indians.

Whitman – one of the most notable of self-styled American Adams – was very aware of the importance and problematics of naming. Thus: 'Names are the turning point of who shall be master. There is so much virtue in names that a nation which produces its own names, haughtily adheres to them, and subordinates others to them, leads all the rest of the nations of the earth.' He wants to both resist and emulate the imperious and imperial power of the dominant language. Yet he also, somewhat like Deerslayer, can betray an apprehension about names, an instinct not to let himself be bound or defined by them. Discussing the possible title for the collection which became *Specimen Days*, he writes this:

> Then reader dear, in conclusion, as to the point of the name for the present collection, let us be satisfied to *have* a name – something to identify and bind it together, to concrete all its vegetable, mineral, personal memoranda, abrupt raids of criticsm, crude gossip of philosophy, varied sand clumps – without bothering ourselves because certain pages do not present themselves to you or me as coming under their own name with entire fitness, or amiability. (It is a profound, vexatious, never-explicable matter – this of names. I have been exercised deeply about it my whole life.)

Of course it is, and no doubt always has been, particularly vexatious for a writer, since his whole concern is to disturb nature with names, though of course the activity can be described in countless less pejorative ways. But it has been exceptionally troubling and problematic for the American writer, since there is so much in the mythology and ideology and iconography which grew up in and around America which privileges silence and suspects language and signification in general – even while there is much in the history which reveals a maximum reliance on and exploitation of language, America itself being a linguistic construct and a legal fiction. (There is a Puritan dimension to this deep ambivalence towards signs and signification, but I will come back to that.) Not surprisingly, we can find a clear demonstration of the problem, the ambivalence, in Emerson. In 'The Poet' he seems on the one hand to stress the passivity, which can become the redundancy, of the poet in his relation to nature. 'What we call nature is a certain self-regulated motion or change; and nature does all things by her own hands, and does not leave another to baptize her but baptizes herself': if nature is indeed self-baptizing this leaves the American Academic poet with little to do. 'The condition of true naming, on the poet's part, is his resigning himself to the divine *aura* which breathes through forms, and accompanying that.' In his relations with nature the poet should be like the traveller who 'throws his reins on his horse's neck and trusts to the instinctions of the animal to find his road'. The initiative is all with nature. Yet, shortly after, Emerson writes: 'We have yet had no genius with tyrannous eye, which knew the value of our incompatible materials . . .' If a 'tyrannous' eye is needed to perceive and discover, valorize and celebrate the 'incomparable' values and beauties of America, then it will require a 'tyrannous' tongue to articulate the perceptions and valorizations. Which is exactly contrary to throwing the reins on the beast's neck. This is not to attempt to catch Emerson out in a self-contradiction, which he anyway, and rightly, would not mind. The relationship of any writer both to nature and to language is an unfathomably inextricable mixture of activity and passivity, leading and following, initiative and resignation, tyranny and servitude. But I do think that the American writer, after the War of Independence, experienced the ambiguities, the ambivalences, the anguishes, involved in the relation between nature and language, thing and name, scene and sign, with a quite unprecedented acuteness. It is why it can be said that almost from the start American (i.e. post-colonial) literature was unavoidably 'modern' — whatever we care to mean by that term — in that it encountered and confronted the cultural, political, and ontological problematics of language in a way which was quite new, certainly in the history of the western world. Let me conclude this short excursus into the peculiarly American involvement with, and concern for, the 'true condition of naming', by quoting a poem by Hart Crane entitled 'A Name for All'.

> Moonmoth and grasshopper that flee our page
> And still wing on, untarnished of the name
> We pinion to your bodies to assuage
> Our envy of your freedom — we must maim
>
> Because we are usurpers, and chagrined —
> And take the wing and scar it in the hand.
> Names we have, even, to clap on the wind;
> But we must die, as you, to understand.
>
> I dreamed that all men dropped their names, and sang
> As only they can praise, who build their days
> With fin and hoof, with wind and sweetened fang
> Struck free and holy in one Name always.

There, indeed, is an American Dream!

I want to return to Deerslayer reverently, and almost silently, appreciating the 'innate loveliness' of the scene around Lake Glimmerglass and feeling 'thoroughly pervaded by the holy calm of nature'. Cooper tells us that ' he felt, though unconsciously, like a poet'. But all this time, note, Deerslayer is 'leaning on his rifle'. As already stressed, he is suspicious of names, even wishing to disavow the enculteration process which starts by imprinting a name on the new-born body. But this disaffiliation from the aggressive fixings of naming and discourse must be set against his rifle, which is most notably a 'sign of man'. The poet-appreciator (passive), and the hunting sharp-shooter (active) meet in Deerslayer, who incarnates the irresolvably ambiguous position of man — white man — in the American wilderness.

So the scene of nature becomes, in quite another way, the scene of 'action', and indeed it is in this book that Deerslayer slays his first human being. And the static 'scene' so picturesquely described by the educated narrator becomes the topography of adventure as the various possibilities of the lake are exploited by Indians and white men alike. Yet, after all the action – which makes for the narrative pace of the book – 'Glimmerglass' remains essentially undisturbed. Fifteen years later Deerslayer revisits Glimmerglass: the castle and the ark are diminished ruins, the principal actors or agents have effectively disappeared in one way or another. There are one or two signs of men – a canoe, a piece of ribbon – but mainly there is just the natural scene. The action which has taken place seems to have little or nothing to do with history, but was rather a brief, ephemeral episode which seems to leave little trace, on the mind of the reader, on the page of the author, on the undisturbable surface of Glimmerglass. 'From all these signs, it was probable the lake had not been visited since the occurrence of the final scene of our tale. Accident or tradition had rendered it again a spot sacred to nature; the frequent wars, and the feeble population of the Colonies, still confining the settlements within narrow boundaries.' It is the characters, not the lake, who disappear, dismissed under a narrative shroud (or killed off by the author). 'They lived, erred, died, and are forgotten.' The scene is temporarily, stronger than the sign. But – we remember Deerslayer and his rifle, and his delight in being a great shot and hunter. Commenting on one of his displays of his hunting skill, Cooper notes 'At that distant day when so few men were present to derange the harmony of the wilderness, all the smaller lakes with which the interior of New York abounds were places of resort for the migratory aquatic birds ...' The effect of Deerslayer's ambiguous presence in the wilderness is muffled. He is the 'poet' who appreciates the scene; but he is also the gun-man who violates the stillness of the scene – albeit he is always on the right side, trying to mediate. But even he is, necessarily, a 'deranger of the harmony of the wilderness' (as opposed to cultural 'arranging'), part of the forces of defacement and deformation. How far that process of 'derangement' can go is a crucial part of Cooper's fiction. For what is ultimately deranged is the static beauty of the scene as it is marked and marred, deranged and deformed, by the very visible and aggressive signs of men. For bullets, even more than names, are 'disturbances' of nature. And no amount of passive poetic wonder at nature's scenes can either conceal, or compensate, for that. The 'poet' leans on his rifle: the rifle deranges the poetry.

With reference to the rifle, it is worth remembering that in the first sixty years of the nineteenth century, America built up an extraordinarily powerful war machine. West Point military academy was founded in 1802 and it grew, thriving on the wars of 1812 and 1845. By 1859 Samuel Colt was manufacturing 60,000 weapons a year.

By 1860 American production of armaments was on a scale unsurpassed by previous European efforts. During the Civil War new machines were used for the first time as a practical demonstration of Yankee ingenuity. There were ironclads and repeating rifles with metallic cartridges. The telegraph and railways 'improved' strategy and logistics. Submarine warfare claimed its first victims, sharpshooters more effectively isolated their objects in space by the use of telescopic sights. Artillery using balloons for observational purposes became accurate to a hitherto unheard-of degree. The death toll was the triumph of the American industrial and political machine, with the inefficient rather than the immoral slaveocracy of the South superseded by a more progressive civilization.   (Clive Bush, *The Dream of Reason*, London, 1977)

All this, while the myths of freedom, minimum state interference, the rights of the individual to sing of himself, establish his own way of life, and cut his own path into the west, prevailed. It would not be the first time that the dreams of the imagination and legitimating official mythologies continued, quite at odds with the actual politico-economic-militaristic conditions of the state. Natty Bumppo/Deerslayer leaning on his rifle is, simply and impossibly, a myth leaning on a fact.

Tools are, precisely, the signs of culture, its unmistakable insignia, the very mode of its implementation, as Benjamin Franklin's autobiography – and life – everywhere attest. And more basic to Cooper's work, and more radically ambiguous than the rifle, is the axe. The ambiguity which surrounds the axe like an aura is very clear in *The Prairie*, where the opposition between the discourse of the author, privileged in this case, and the discourse of his main character, embedded in the action, is absolutely clear. Thus Cooper speaks:

The *march of civilization* with us, has a strong analogy to that of all coming events, which are known to 'cast their shadows before'. The gradations of society, from that state which is called refined to that which approaches as near barbarity as connection with an intelligent people will readily allow, are to be traced from the bosom of the States, where wealth, luxury and the arts are beginning to seat themselves, to those distant and ever-receding borders which mark the skirts and announce the approach of the nation, as moving mists precede the signs of the day.   (my italics)

As opposed to this cultural optimism in the eighteenth-century Enlightenment mode, consider the pessimism of Leatherstocking (as he is here called):

Look around you, men; what will the Yankee choppers say, when they have cut their path from the eastern to the western waters, and find that a hand, which can lay the 'arth bare at a blow, has been here and swept the country, in very mockery of their wickedness. They will turn on their tracks like a fox that doubles, and then the rank smell of their own footsteps will show them *the madness of their waste*.   (my italics)

'Waste' was to become a key word in American literature as writers tried
to trace out what America has made of its unparalleled resources, and
from Henry Adams through Scott Fitzgerald up to Norman Mailer,
Thomas Pynchon, Saul Bellow, Richard Brautigan, Don Delillo and
many others, you can hear a doomed sense of America transforming its
God-given plenitude to a heap of 'waste' which can neither be recycled
nor disposed of. The March of Civilization leads to the great Dust Bowl
if not further, to a state of total entropy. In *The Prairie* the family of
Ishmael Bush, ruthless frontier figures with no respect either for the laws
of the settlement or the divinity of nature, attack the land with an
aggressive delight and almost sadistic savagery which foretells the
ruthless spoliation of the 'scenes of nature' which Cooper valued so
highly. Thus we read how Ishmael's son

> buried his axe to the eye in the soft body of a cotton-wood tree. He stood for a
> moment regarding the effect of the blow, with that sort of contempt which a
> giant might be supposed to contemplate the resistance of a dwarf . . . he quickly
> severed the trunk of the tree, bringing its tall top crashing to the earth in
> submission to his prowess.

It is a rape; and we might remember what William Carlos Williams said
in many contexts, particularly envisaging America as an endlessly
brutalized female body waiting for the proper relationship – 'there must
be a new wedding'. The signs of the axe are signs of desecration and
violation. As Natty Bumppo says:

> and yet the wind seldom blows from the east, but I conceit the sound of axes,
> and the crash of falling trees, are in my ears . . . They scourge the very 'arth with
> their axes. Such hills and hunting grounds as I have seen stripped of the gifts of
> the Lord, without remorse or shame! I tarried till the mouths of my hounds
> were deafened by the blows of the chopper, and then I came west in search of
> quiet . . . I have come into these plains to escape the sound of the axe; for here
> surely, the chopper can never follow.

But the axe can, and will, and did penetrate everywhere, and the 'gifts
of the Lord' were quickly changed or trans(de)formed into the
commodities of man. The sign of the axe most decisively destroys the
scene of nature. It is the opposite of passive wonder; it posits and
presupposes man against nature, a 'mingling' which is a violent attack,
not a 'merging' of consciousness and object (as positioned and preached
by Emerson, for example). It points not to a relationship but to an
opposition. It may, indeed must, represent culture and building, but
while bringing civilized structure to the shapeless wilderness (good), it
callously and wantonly destroys great natural beauties and pre-existing
ecological harmonies (bad). It brings civilization and creates waste-lands.
The sign of the axe cannot 'mingle' with the scene of nature; it must

deface and then destroy it. It remains, in every sense, the leading edge of civilization. And yet, in a later novel by Cooper (*The Chainbearer*, 1845) – and we must recognize him for the great cultural ventriloquist and schizophrenic that he is – he can write as though he had never heard Natty Bumppo's words, much less penned them:

> The American axe. It has made more real and lasting conquests than the sword of any warlike people that ever lived; but they have been conquests that have left civilization in their train instead of havoc and desolation. More than a million square miles of territory have been opened up from the shade of the virgin forest, to admit the warmth of the sun; and culture and abundance have been spread where the beast of the forest so lately roamed hunted by savages . . . A brief quarter of a century has seen these wonderful changes wrought; and at the bottom of them all lies this beautiful, well-prized, ready, and efficient implement, the American axe.

This indeed is the triumph of the sign over the scene, here celebrated unambiguously as a radiant and efficient bringer of civilization, completely obscuring the fate of the scene deformed into 'waste'.

> Weapon shapely, naked, wan,
> Head from the mother's bowels drawn,
> Wooded flesh and metal bone, limb only one and lip only one
> Gray-blue leaf by red-heat grown, helve produced from a little seed sown
> Resting the grass amid and upon, To be lean'd and to lean on.

That is the opening of Walt Whitman's 'Song of the Broad-Axe', a poem which contains but hardly confronts some of the deep ambiguities and ironies to be detected in Cooper. It ends:

> The main shapes arise!
> Shapes of Democracy total, result of centuries,
> Shapes ever projecting other shapes,
> Shapes of turbulent manly cities,
> Shapes of the friends and home-givers of the whole earth,
> Shapes bracing the earth and braced with the whole earth.

The 'main shape', or sign, to 'arise' from, or be inscribed upon, the great continent discovered by Columbus, was simply 'America' itself. And, as one American writer after another was to ask, what did *that* mean?

The harpoon is as ambiguous a cultural tool as the axe. On the one hand, it is the Promethean weapon, killing the whale to bring back the oil to make light possible. On the other hand, it can be converted, or diverted, or indeed perverted, into an instrument of personal vengeance on nature itself, as Melville's Captain Ahab reveals. I will come to *Moby-Dick* later. At this point I want to make some comments on the tension between scene and sign in Hawthorne, and for this purpose I will refer to his short story called 'Endicott and the Red Cross'. The story concerns

two signs. First, there is the English banner 'with the Red Cross in its
field'. This flag flies over a band of colonial Puritans who are engaged in
military exercises under their leader, Endicott, who is wearing a
breastplate. 'This piece of armor was so highly polished that the whole
surrounding scene had its image in the glittering steel.' (I will come back
to this idea of the image-in-the-armour.) The scene for the exercise
includes a range of people suffering the devices of Puritan punishment.
There is the whipping-post, the pillory, the stocks; a woman with a cleft
stick on her tongue ('for having wagged that unruly member against the
elders of the church'); and a number of other people whose bodies are
being variously deformed to register their inner faults or contraventions
of Puritan law.

> And among the crowd there were several whose punishment would be life-
> long; some, whose ears had been cropped, like those of puppy dogs; others,
> whose cheeks had been branded with the initials of their misdemeanors; one,
> with his nose slit and seared; and another with a halter about his neck, which he
> was forbidden ever to take off, or to conceal beneath his garments.

Thus in various ways the body has been mutilated to carry the sign of the
victim's deviance or transgression; the body is treated as a script on which
can be inscribed or imprinted the 'letter' of the law. The idea of the
legible body was very important for the Puritans. But there is another
notable transgressor in the crowd, bearing the sign of her sin, which is the
second important sign in the story. Thus:

> there was likewise a young woman, with no mean share of beauty, whose
> doom it was to wear the letter A on the breast of her gown, in the eyes of all the
> world and her own children. And even her children knew what that initial
> signified. *Sporting with her infamy*, the lost and desperate creature had
> embroidered the fatal token in scarlet cloth, with golden thread and the nicest
> art of needlework; so that the capital A might have been thought to mean
> Admirable, or anything rather than adultress ... It was the policy of our
> ancestors to search out even the most secret sins, and expose them to shame,
> without fear or favour, in the broadest light of the noonday sun.

(my italics)

As Hawthorne here indicates, the Puritans were forever seeking to 'read'
people, to find out or interpret signs or rather symptoms, not so much of
their grace but of their sins. Thus the whole community lived in an
atmosphere of sadistic semiology, everybody looking for the bad signs in
everybody else. Once discerned, these could be translated into more
enduring, more visible, signs, tokens, badges: as it were, extracting the
sin *out of* the body and making it into a concrete sign which could be
imposed *on* the body. Whether one conceals one's sin or reveals it – and
just what concealment and revelation mean and entail – is part of the
story of *The Scarlet Letter*, in which Dimmsdale conceals his symptoms

and dies of his self-alienation and bad faith, while Hester Prynne is forced to wear her symptom-transformed-into-a sign and lives through taking positive efforts to transform its significations. Hester is of course anticipated here by the young woman wearing the scarlet A who, by 'sporting with her infamy', has rendered the fixed sign of adultress imposed on her by Puritan law multivalent, polysemic – irreducibly ambiguous. Sport/art thus become the revenge of the living, complex individual on the inert simplification of the sign. Such signs, like a second order of names, seek to hold, fix, pin down the individual once and for all in the permanent secondary identity of his or her transgression. Only art can contest the aggressive tyranny of such unitary readings and labellings of the individual.

How far such imposed labellings can go is revealed in the chapter in *The Scarlet Letter* entitled 'The Governor's Hall', where we again encounter the image in the armour. And note, first, the description of the outside – or skin – of the Governor's house, the central edifice of authority. It is covered with stucco and broken glass which make it sparkle and glitter in the sun.

> The brilliancy might have befitted Aladdin's palace, rather than the mansion of a grave old Puritan ruler. It was further decorated with strange and seemingly cabalistic figures and diagrams, suitable to the quaint taste of the age, which had been drawn in the stucco when newly laid on, and had now grown hard and durable, for the admiration of after times.

The outer, world-facing, covering is thus a tissue of fantastic and misleading – and uninterpretable – signs, a kind of parody of signification which reveals nothing about the nature of the 'interior', except inasmuch as it bespeaks just such a taste for the inscription of weird, indecipherable, but hard and durable, signs on the outside of the body of the house. It also glances at the elitist mixture of secrecy and mystification which is often both the face and instrument of power. Inside the house, in the hall, there is a gleaming suit of armour

> and little Pearl – who was as greatly pleased with the gleaming armor as she had been with the glittering frontispiece [sic] of the house – spent some time looking into the polished mirror of the breastplate.
>
> 'Mother' cried she, 'I see you here. Look! Look!'
>
> Hester looked, by way of humoring the child; and she saw that, owing to the peculiar effect of this convex mirror, the scarlet letter was represented in exaggerated and gigantic proportions, so as greatly to be the most prominent feature of her appearance. In truth, she seemed absolutely hidden behind it.

The multiple implications of this moment are marvellously compressed. The convexity of the armour is analagous to the convexity of the eye: the armoured Puritan eye is a distorting mirror. Thus Hester, who as a beautiful and sensual woman may here be taken as a 'scene of nature', in this distorting mirror disappears completely behind the letter A, the imposed 'sign of men'. Her physical creaturely uniqueness and otherness has been pre-empted, annulled, cancelled by the ever-expanding proportions of the rigid alphabetic sign. To the extent that she accepts the sign of man, and colludes with and consents to the sentence of the legislators, she ceases to be a woman and becomes a marble statue, self-reified according to the judgement of the community. Her 'Oriental' and 'voluptuous' qualities are effaced, and, explicitly, her sexuality is annihilated: 'There seemed no longer any thing in Hester's face for Love to dwell upon; nothing in Hester's form, though majestic and statue-like, that Passion would ever dream of clasping in its embrace; nothing in Hester's bosom, to make it again the pillow of affection.' To the extent that she 'sports' with the sign and even, on one occasion, rejects it, she goes some way to re-achieving and rediscovering her full femininity, her 'nature'. The Puritans owned the dominant discourse, they owned the signs. They could thus reify people according to how they read and inscribed them.

It is Pearl who most totally eludes this process of sadistic interpretation and inscription. Many versions of her are offered, even by her mother; but in a very profound sense she cannot be 'read'. Even when dressed to look like the scarlet letter 'it was the scarlet letter in another form; the scarlet letter endowed with life'. She thus naturalizes and absorbs the sign into her own iridescent, unpredictable, full human variousness, which cannot be 'held', either by the monochrome of the Puritan sign or by the hand of the pirate who tries to grasp her in the last scene. She escapes all the prevailing signs of the community, eludes the discourse, and leaves for Europe. Whereas Hester, though she tries to escape back into nature, the forest, the sea, anywhere outside the settlement, finally returns to it — she is too inscribed with it, we may say. Pearl gets away completely: as we read — 'she would grow up amid human joy and sorrow, nor forever do battle with the world, but be a woman in it'. The powerful simplicity of that last phrase indicates a kind of existence where the woman is not obscured and annihilated by the sign. Pearl enters a place free of that sadistic semiology of the Puritans where she does not have to do battle with the world, living in tense half-opposition, half-submission to the imposed sign like her mother, but where she will, simply, 'be a woman in it'. Which might be another American dream, a crucial one.

One word now about Endicott, aggressive male Puritan *par excellence*. While drilling his soldiers he receives news that the English are planning to impose their religious orthodoxy on America, 'to impose the idolatrous forms of English episcopacy'. Endicott grows increasingly angry: 'Who shall enslave us here? What have we to do with this mitred prelate, – with this crowned king? What have we to do with England?' And so saying, he takes his sword and slashes the flag and 'rent the Red Cross completely out of the banner'. It can be seen as a first gesture towards Independence. But we note that it is a crude attack on the sign: not a fine exercise of a transforming embroidery, but a direct act of *découpage* done in angry hostility – presaging not sport or art but war.

The American writer who plays most conspicuously with signs is of course Poe. In his work there is not really any presence of 'nature', but rather a series of cryptograms or clues which have to be de-coded, interpreted, translated. Another way of putting it would be to say that the scenes are composed of signs of varying orders of intelligibility – or even, we could say, the scenes are composed of signs overlayed on one another, so that the reader has to be a cryptographer and a detective. (Quite apart from Poe's importance for Baudelaire, it is significant that two of his stories have been key documents for two major contemporary European writers both deeply concerned with language and 'traces': 'The Man in the Crowd' for Walter Benjamin, and 'The Purloined Letter' for Jacques Lacan.) In 'A Few Words on Secret Writing' (1841) Poe wrote: 'As we can scarcely imagine a time when there did not exist a necessity, or at least a desire, of transmitting information from one individual to another in such a manner as to elude general comprehension so we may well suppose the practice of writing in cipher to be of great antiquity.' So that much of his work is a series of cyphers upon cyphers, and we must in turn become de-cipherers to detect and discern the truly significant signs. And these signs may not be found in mysterious depths. It may be, as in 'The Purloined Letter', that the key signs are imperceptible to the conventionalized eye because of their excessive and unexpected obviousness. Thus Dupin fastens on 'the hyperobtrusiveness' of a document and solves a case which the police, with their official eyes seeking stereotyped clues, cannot penetrate. Dupin alone can see that in order to conceal the vital letter, 'the minister had resorted to the comprehensive and sagacious expedient of not attempting to conceal it at all'. It is an expedient to which Poe himself resorts, perhaps more often than we think. Again, when Dupin solves the problems of 'The Murders in the Rue Morgue', he closes with these rather patronizing words about the Prefect of Police. He is 'too cunning to be profound ... I like him especially for one master stroke of cant, by which he has attained his reputation for ingenuity. I mean the way he has "de nier ce qui est, et d'expliquer ce qui n'est pas".' Official vision, obfusacting and self-mystifying, can lead to an avoidance, a denial, a non-perception of the actual, legible signs of things as they actually, legibly are.

Paradoxically, or not so paradoxically, it takes an artist/detective/true reader truly to see and read the obvious – blindingly obvious, as we say – signs of the world. As Poe shows in other stories (e.g. 'Mystification'), man is not only an under-interpreter; he can be a very gullible over-interpreter as well. The crucial document or parchment in 'The Gold-bug', which is all written in numbers, asterisks, brackets, and so on, again teases and provokes the human ability – and compulsion – not just to read but to decipher. But looking at the manuscript Legrand says: 'And yet . . . the solution is by no means as difficult as you might be led to imagine from the first hasty inspection of the characters.' The general point is that man is an animal who covers/conceals nature with riddles, enigmas, cryptograms. Because he is uniquely a creature of language he can overlay any one given scene with an infinity of increasingly mystifying signs. Such a proliferation of signs inviting and defying decipherment is indeed the human game and Poe plays it to the hilt. But he also – or thereby – shows the element of futile self-mystification which may be inextricably involved in this impulse, so that while generating more signs to be deciphered we lose all sense of the scene which is simply to be seen.

Perhaps the most striking example of Poe at play in this area occurs in chapter 23 of *The Narrative of Arthur Gordon Pym*. Amid the incredible topography of the island here described, there are five very strange 'figures', reproduced in the narrative because Pym 'luckily' had with him 'a pocketbook and pencil'(!). Pym calls them, scrupulously and equivocally, 'indentures in the surface', for it is a question whether they are part of the scene of nature, or the signs of men – formations or inscriptions.

> With a very slight exertion of the imagination, the left, or most northerly of these indentures might have been taken for the intentional, though rude, representation of a human figure standing erect, with outstretched arm. The rest of them bore also some little resemblance to alphabetical characters, and Peters was willing, at all events, to adopt the idle opinion that they were really such.

Pym, on the other hand, is convinced that they are 'the work of nature'. At which point the scenes of nature and the signs of men do really seem to merge in an irresolvable ambiguity. Or even an identity. Does nature really have its own language of signs; or do we alphabetize and 'figure' nature even in the act of looking at it? Do we, perhaps, only ever see signs, nature being always already 'indentured' or inscribed? Among other things, Poe can show us that it may well be a fond illusion, or self-deception, to think we can ever gain unmediated accesss to the scene.

The end of *Gordon Pym* is swallowed in a terminal whiteness which is of some importance for American literature. 'And now we rushed into the embraces of the cataract, where a chasm threw itself open to receive us. But there arose in our pathway a shrouded human figure, very far larger in its proportions than any dweller among men. And the hue of skin of the figure was of the perfect whiteness of snow.' The Prince, in Henry James's *The Golden Bowl*, is to remember this narrative image as he moves towards his own somewhat different kind of terminal embrace. But arguably no American writer remembered it more vividly than Melville: 'Nor even in our superstitions do we fail to throw the same snowy mantle round our phantoms; all ghosts rising in a milk-white fog – Yea, while these terrors seize us, let us add that even the king of terrors, when personified by the evangelist, rides on his pallid horse.' This of course is from 'The Whiteness of the Whale' in *Moby-Dick*, in which Ishmael examines his 'nameless horror' concerning that phenomenon: 'It was the whiteness of the whale that above all things appalled me.' 'Whiteness' relates to 'namelessness' and featurelessness: the front of the whale is a white blank (albeit wrinkled). A blank has no features, no distinguishing signs, and hence no 'name'. By the same token, *any* 'name' or 'sign' can be 'inscribed' ('indentured'?) on that blankness by the projective imagination of man. It is a black-board, or rather a white-board, on which anything can be written. There is nothing to check, constrain, or counter the most egotistical script being imposed on it. (Compare the place in *The Scarlet Letter* where Dimmsdale thinks he sees an 'A' in the sky and Hawthorne comments: it 'could only be the symptom of a highly disordered state when a man ... had extended his egotism over the whole expanse of nature until the firmament itself should appear no more than a fitting page for his soul's history and fate'.) The firmament, the whale's front, as 'page' – not to be read but to be written on. Melville's white whale is in fact very close to that 'human figure' whose skin 'was of the perfect whiteness of snow' which concludes – and eludes – Poe's narrative. And if Poe saw the world as in some sense an entire multi-layered sign-system, we may remember that C.S. Peirce, the great American semiologist who was to have such an influence on the work of contemporary semiologists, contended that 'the entire universe is perfused with signs, if it is not composed exclusively of signs'. This, if you like, is the complete secularization of the Puritan emphasis on the universe as a tissue of God's signs, and no writer realized this more profoundly, and explored the implications more extensively and effectively, than Melville. In *Moby-Dick* at one point Stubb says jeeringly: 'Signs and wonders, eh? Pity if there is nothing wonderful in signs and significant in wonders.' The attempt to keep wonder and signification together, indeed identical, is very manifest in Puritanism (arguably it must be at the centre of any religious conviction), and Emerson and the Transcendentalists also strived to keep them merged. What Melville is acutely aware of is the possibility of a world in which there has been a separation of wonder and significance – a terrible falling apart of the mute scenes of nature and the voluble signs of men, and thus no sure ground for any kind of meaning or revelation.

Umberto Eco distinguishes between the Dictionary (abstract) and the Encyclopaedia (concrete) as two basic ways in which western man has tried to contain and arrange knowledge. What the former excludes, and the latter (like the novel) necessarily includes, is references to setting, context, circumstance. Melville's novel indeed starts like a dictionary and ends like an encyclopaedia. A dictionary attempts to fix the meaning of a word abstractly, atemporally, without context, whereas a good encyclopaedia will provide various settings to suggest and explain the aura of connotations and associations round a word. Melville's novel is more like many encyclopaedias, parts of encyclopaedias, overlaid, imbricated, each transparent to the other but none having any final privileged status. There is nothing veridical in the novel. Melville continually unstabilizes both the denotations and the connotations of the word, the whale. He inserts it into many semantic fields, only to extract it to place it in others. It is not just that he exploits and explores both the mediaeval and modern notions of the whale. The text is literally in-terminable, since there is no final point of complete definition, no point of rest, no principle of closure available as the whale-word plunges in and out of different semantic fields, around chains of references which lead off into labyrinthine interconnections. To de-fine the identity, and fix the meaning, of the whale-word is a task which cannot be completed, as Ishmael realizes. 'God keep me from completing anything. This whole book is but a draught – nay, but the draught of a draught.' And, of course, the draft of a draft. Even while writing and putting out endless nets of linguistic sub-codes – from myths to measurements, sermons to sciences, scripture to maritime reports – Ishmael knows that the whale is endlessly escaping, as it escapes the *Pequod* which can finally only go down in the vortex left by what it may hunt but never hold. The nets of language, meanwhile, finally bring up only more language.

The signs of men – taken in the most extensive sense – cannot hold, detain, in any way catch or fix, the moving scene of nature (in this case it is the white whale, not the whale-word but the thing itself). The signs simply lead you on to other signs – as indeed Peirce was to show. That is why, for example, it is often said that the book seems to make and unmake itself as it goes along. Ishmael does not deify, reify, or codify the whale; he does not interpret or offer single 'readings'. Rather, he speculates endlessly: all his utterances are accented with provisionality. Thus his discourse is completely open – though it contains the closed discourses of such figures as Ahab who are trapped within fixed interpretations and monocular readings of reality.

This is one reason why Melville starts his book with 'Etymology'

provided by a 'late consumptive usher to a Grammar School' who 'loved
to dust his old grammars' and lexicons 'with a queer handkerchief,
mockingly embellished with all the gay flags of all the known nations of
the world'. The mocking embellishments on the white surface may
remind us of Hawthorne and Hester Prynne's 'mocking embellishment'
of the letter 'A' on her Puritan dress; it certainly anticipates a recurrent
activity in the book, in which we read of many different ways in which
man embellishes the blank surfaces of the world – from handkerchiefs to
the front of whales; from cathedrals to coffins; from maps to human skin
(there is a lot of tattooing in the book) to paper itself. Following
'Etymology' there are the 'Extracts' supplied by a 'Sub-sub-librarian'.
Where Etymology proceeds like a dictionary, seeking to cover the
lexical names for the whale, the Extracts are more like a mini-
encyclopaedia, offering examples of different contexts and types of
discourse in which the whale has appeared. Both are clearly inadequate to
what Melville has in hand; the usher is dead and the librarian is 'sub-sub'.
They diminish or pass away among the stillness of their books. There
could be no clearer warning, or jocular reminder, that the book and the
whale are forever mutually exclusive, that the scene forever eludes the
sign. 'Has the Sperm Whale ever written a book, spoken a speech? No,
his great genius is declared in his doing nothing particular to prove it. It is
moreover declared in his pyramidical silence.' Thus Ishmael, who
proceeds to attempt to transcribe the whale's 'brow' for us. 'I put but that
brow before you. Read it if you can.' We can read the book, but the book
cannot read the brow. So it is, and so Ishmael knows it to be.

This is why Melville, through Ishmael, developed a narrative
technique of hesitation, tentativity, dubiety, uncertainty – and play. It
absconds from judgement while offering a plurality of possible
interpretations. It abounds in approximations, speculations, and tentative readings, but it does not pretend to offer any privileged interpretative view-point. It asserts only to retreat. It moves through modulations
of moods. It ponders and puns, jokes and wonders. It is at home in
language – indeed it *is* the home of languages – but it knows that, by the
same token, it is hermeneutically exiled from nature. There are, in fact,
all too many signs, and no available principle of assortment or
hierarchization. This is a narrative mode that knows that it does not
know. It moves endlessly around in the space between signs and scenes,
knowing that ultimately there is no way to bridge that gap. The signs
point hopelessly in the direction of wonders they can never have. Or be.

(Some strikingly appropriate comments on the relationship of
language to nature, given the above comments on Melville, are to be
found in Alexander Bryan Johnson's *A Treatise on Language* of 1836. One
section starts: 'We confound theories with the realities of nature';

another, 'Words are sometimes the ultimate meanings of words'; and, notably, 'We mistake words for things . . . words are deemed the cement in the reasoning of philosophers who, while they are investigating the relation of words to each other, seem to believe that they are investigating the realities of the external creation.' All these comments come from Johnson's Lecture XII.)

At this point it would be possible to continue the story by looking at the work of novelists from Henry James to Thomas Pynchon, or more theoretical semiological work by writers from Charles Peirce to Charles Norris. But at this point I want, as it were, to go back to the beginning and consider briefly some aspects and implications of the Puritans' obsession with signs. For the elect and the saved, the scene of the world was composed entirely of signs and the signs were fixed and interpretable – stabilized, as it were, by God. But, declared Jonathan Edwards, for the unsaved and unregenerate, 'living with words or signs alone interposes a distance between them and reality'. And so such people make use of signs, becoming unaware or unmindful of what the signs refer to (namely, 'ideas'; supremely, God). And this is to be in a 'lost' state indeed. For it was particularly important for the American Puritans that the scene should be a sign and the sign should reveal the intention, and thus the attention, of God who thus, among other things, authorized and legitimated their 'errand into the wilderness'. The Puritan poet Edward Taylor writes of 'The glory of the world slickt out in types'. Types, or more accurately anti-types, referred, of course, to the perception of an analogy, or the fulfilment of a prefiguration, which a person, object, or event represented – particularly with reference to the Old Testament, which was full of types which prefigured their anti-types in the New Testament. Or beyond. This practice was not of course exclusive to the Puritans but it became of particular importance in America as a way of linking the Puritans and their 'errand' with a larger prefigural pattern. The practice of perceiving types and anti-types in the Bible spread out to the discerning of them everywhere and in (potentially) every saved Puritan. Similarly the original prefiguring type was not confined to the Bible but could extend to include saints, historical figures, even figures from classical literature. This could and did lead to a rampant hermeneutic activity, and when you add the consideration that the Puritans were continually searching for signs of grace or damnation in themselves and everybody else, you can see that you have the conditions for an unchecked (even paranoid or megalomaniac) semiology. Crudely speaking, everything could be a type or anti-type, could signify, something else. The Puritans lived in a hopelessly over-interpretable world. There was a continuous excess of significance and signification. Everything meant too much. Nothing was simply what it was. The

quickest way to get some sense of this state of mind is to consider
Jonathan Edwards's work 'Images or Shadows of Divine Things'. For
Edwards of course the excessive significance of all things pointed to or
revealed some aspect of God. But consider the state of mind which could
perceive portentous signifiers everywhere but which did not have an
assured belief in the fixed and anchoring transcendent signified – God.
You would then have writers like Hawthorne and Melville. I will simply
run together some of Edwards's words and phrases, to convey some sense
of what I mean by the Puritan sense of – or quest for – excessive
significance. Here are some of the words he uses, often over and over
again: image, imitation, shadow, resemblance, represents, representation, type, analogy, significations, antitype, typify, a showing forth,
emblem, parallel, parable, vein, scheme, signified. For Edwards, of
course, all these 'significations ... seem to be chiefly intended by the
author of nature, because He thought that great and glorious mystery of
Christ's incarnation and union with mankind most worthy to be much
showed forth and observed'. But it would not be hard to imagine from
his essay a secular 'author' both creating and perceiving all these
'significations'. Creating by perceiving them. With the secularization,
splitting and dissemination of the single divine author it would be, and
proved to be, impossible to put any check on this sign–detecting activity.
Bear this in mind while considering some statements by Edwards.

> It is apparent that there is a great and remarkable analogy in God's works.
> There is a wonderful resemblance in the effects which God produces, and
> consentaneity in His manner of working in one thing and another throughout
> all nature ... why is it not reasonable to suppose he makes the whole as a
> shadow of the spiritual world? ... By mystery can be meant nothing but a type
> of what is spiritual. And if God designed this for a type of what is spiritual why
> not many other things in the constitution and ordinary state of human society
> and the world of mankind?

Why not indeed!

Vegetables, fruit, plants, animals, the weather, trees, the parts of the
body, the sea, storms, flowers, names of persons, metals, love, lightning,
silk–worms, clothes, birds, mountains, the traveller, cats, rivers ... they
all show forth, represent, emblematize, typify, signify various aspects of
God's (or the Devil's) working and powers. Two things are worth
remarking on. First, the relative interchangeability of the terms so that
there is a somewhat chaotic flow of imperfectly differentiated words all
pointing to various modes of representation, typification, analogy, etc.
Secondly, material things not only represent aspects of non-material
things; they can represent, or be analogies for, each other. 'So it is God's
way in the natural world to make inferior things in conformity and
analogy to the superior, so as to be in images of them.' Beasts are made

like men, plants are made in imitation of animals, 'the earth answers to the womb'. 'The time of blossoming is as it were the time of love and pleasure.' *As it were* – not assured identification but, rather, a tentative metaphor. It is a phrase he uses more than once. Similarly, he often hedges his assertions with 'seems' – as in 'seems to represent' and 'seems to typifie' and 'this signification of ingrafting seems to be chiefly intended by the author of nature . . .' Significations discerned by Edwards seem to be intended by God. The very word leaves, or creates, room for doubt, uncertainty, anxiety – which of course are always present as the underside of Puritan assurance. Edwards assures his readers that 'The material world and all things pertaining to it, is by the Creator wholly subordinated to the spiritual and moral world.' This means that every visible thing or phenomenon 'subserves the purpose of the moral and spiritual world'. So one thing can always be the image of another thing. And – it can always represent some spiritual or moral meaning. Take away the divinely sanctioned hierarchy, whereby 'the less perfect is as it were a figure or image of the more perfect', and you could have a hermeneutic anarchy, an interpretative *laissez-faire* situation, in which anyone can suggest that anything is an image, figure, analogy – as it were – for anything else, either concrete or abstract. The whole world could become a network, or a circuit, of endless analogies and images, everything 'showing forth' something else. Or, at least, seeming to do so. The suggestion is made in Melville's work that some hidden meaning or significance 'lurks' in all things, or else things are 'little worth'. From this point of view the world means nothing in and for itself. It must always mean, signify, something else. Without certain belief in the transcendental signifier/signified – God – this way of looking at the world must produce great interpretative anxiety, as in Hawthorne.

It could also produce, as it certainly did in America, symbolism. Here again we can see that Puritan modes of thought and perception laid the ground for what became a dominant mode in American literature. Hawthorne provides a key moment, while he is looking at the material letter 'A' in the Custom House. 'My eyes fastened themselves upon the old scarlet letter. Certainly there was *some deep meaning* in it, *most worthy of interpretation*, and which, *as it were*, streamed forth from the mystic symbol, subtly *communicating* itself to my sensibilities, but *evading* the analysis of my mind' (my italics). Some deep meaning . . . most worthy of interpretation . . . as it were . . . communicating . . . evading . . . but communicating what? It is all hesitation, dubiety, tentativity – a reluctance to assert meaning, an unwillingness to deny it. Thomas Pynchon's character Oedipa Maas is in more dire hermeneutical straits by the end of *The Crying of Lot 49*, but they relate her to Hawthorne and Jonathan Edwards. 'Behind the hieroglyphic streets there would either be a transcendent meaning, or only the earth ... For there either was some Tristero beyond the appearance of the legacy of America, or there was just America. And if there was just America then it seemed the only way to be at all relevant to it was as an alien, unfurrowed, assumed full circle into some paranoia.' Only the earth ... just America ... irrelevant ... this was the Puritan's nightmare. But the Puritan believed (or desperately tried to) in a 'transcendent meaning', not the Tristero as such but some hidden scheme of meaning and significance which operated like the Tristero, a secret, second order of communication, constantly delivering mysterious messages. And all the Puritan did was relevant to that scheme, to God. The Puritan was a paranoid who could, or thought or hoped he could, correctly interpret the meanings of all the signs – the mysterious 'letters' – he saw around him. Oedipa is a Puritan without a key to the signs, without a certainty about God – or the Tristero. She feels, thus, irrelevant – herself and the earth signifying nothing. In desperation she must become a paranoid without any assurance about either the significance or even the existence of the signs – all those types, tropes, emblems, images, analogies, figures, re-presentations which were so ubiquitous and clear for Jonathan Edwards. But in her mental stance, her need and quest, she remains a child of the Puritans. As so many American writers and fictional characters are. Because if there is 'only earth', 'just America', and no sacred mission, no manifest destiny, no chosen people, no promised land, than there is indeed only 'the wilderness' and an 'errand' on nobody's behalf going nowhere, carrying and signifying nothing. A signless scene. And then, for a Puritan-influenced imagination, America is only a horrible mistake and you arrive at that extreme pessimism which is so inseparable from euphoric, optative American optimism and which says with Melville:

> To Terminus build Fanes! Columbus ended earth's romance;
> No New World to mankind remains.

There is of course another tradition in American writing which seeks to stress the sufficiency of the scene as sign in itself, uninterpreted, uninscribed. We might take William Carlos Williams as the representative on this non-Puritan, or indeed anti-Puritan, line in American literature which celebrates 'just America', 'only earth'. But I want to conclude with a different kind of story concerning another kind of attempt to impose signs on the American scene. It is told by Frank Rowsome in a book entitled *The Verse by the Side of the Road*. A man named Leonard Odell, who was broke, picked up an idea from his brother:

> One day on the road between Aurora and Joliet he saw a set of small serial signs advertising a gas station: Gas, Oil, Restrooms, things like that ... and then at the end a sign would point to a gas station. Al thought 'Every time I see one of

those setups, I read every one of the signs. So why can't we sell a product that way?'

So they bought some boards, bought locations at road sides, and spaced out the sign boards with advertisements for Burma-Shave on them, appearing serially, phrase by phrase. Rowsome describes their impact on the world of advertising:

> It was upon this advertising scene – a lapel grabbing, intensely hard-sell – that the Odells arrived with their distinctive, often ironic humour. HE PLAYED / A SAX / HAD NO B.O. / BUT HIS WHISKERS SCRATCHED / SO SHE LET HIM GO. The little signs first startled, then delighted, the highway traveler. Their unwillingness to be portentous, their amiable iconoclasm, pleased people. There was an unexpectedness about these flippant new signs; one would cruise a familiar highway and come upon, newly installed, a series such as: THE ANSWER TO / A MAIDEN'S PRAYER / IS NOT A CHIN / OF STUBBLY HAIR.

And there were commercial advantages to the road sign.

> At 35 miles an hour it took almost three seconds to proceed from sign to sign, or eighteen seconds to march through the whole series. This was far more time and attention than a newspaper or magazine advertiser could realistically expect to win from casual viewers. Yet Burma-Shave almost automatically exacted this attention from virtually every literate passer-by ... Another advantage lay hidden in spaced-out signs: they established a controlled reading space and even added an element of suspense.

The most successful run apparently was: HE HAD THE RING / HE HAD THE FLAT / BUT SHE FELT HIS CHIN / AND THAT WAS THAT. Their success was very great, and earnings for the company ran into millions of dollars a year. The signs spread all over the country; the farmers who usually owned the requisite land became 'proud of these signs'. 'The signs themselves underwent continuous evolution.' 'Then it was noticed that signs had a way of disappearing completely on dark nights if they were located near college towns.' Here we have the beginning of the depradation of the sign. But it was not only college boys: cows often 'ruminatively rubbed the posts to a bright shine, tilting the set slightly askew in the process'. Of course, people also used the signs for shooting practice. But

> in the first decades the strangest natural enemies of Burma-Shave signs were horses. Although several jingles referred pejoratively to horses (e.g. OLD DOBBIN READS / THESE SIGNS EACH DAY / YOU SEE HE GETS / HIS CORN THAT WAY), the broken signs did not represent literary criticism. Study by Kam and his crew revealed that the signs were being installed at a perfect height to serve as horse back-scratchers.

Finally, all the signs disappeared. There are various explanations.

> People were driving too fast to read small signs. Or it was the fault of the superhighways with their sprawling rights-of-way and frequent exclusion of all

commercial signs. Or home-made corny little signs, produced without benefit of agency commision, were no longer enough; now it was vital to portray graphically why the product was superior to its competitors, as by TV demonstrations.

And so, down came all the road signs. Most of them found their way into museums, or antique shops.

> More meaningful, perhaps, is the fact that the little red signs still exist, very much alive, in thousands of memories. The setting in each case is individual, although the memories have much in common. It may be that you are en route to Shady Grove by Pine Lake, driving a spunky red Ford V-8 or a delightful Packard with bright red hexagons on its hubcaps. The sun is high, the sky blue, and drifting into the open car there is the warm tar smell from the road, blended with the new honeysuckle. Then along the roadside this cadenced message unfolds: IF YOU / DON'T KNOW / WHOSE SIGNS / THESE ARE / YOU CAN'T HAVE / DRIVEN VERY FAR.

But effectively the old signs have disappeared – superseded by other media methods to be sure, but parabolically we may think of them being eroded, erased – as it were dismantled and devoured – by the cows and horses, as the whale drew the *Pequod* down to destruction. It is the ultimate – and, as we might think, inevitable – revenge of the scene on the sign.

2

Notes for a comparison between American and European Romanticism

I

Animals have often provided Romantic writers with important images. Blake's tiger and Melville's whale are both used to focus on the awesome and ambiguous energies at the heart of creation. Insects, too, have often been invoked for the purposes of emulation or identification. Wordsworth gathers visual pleasures 'like a bee among the flowers'; Emerson admires the 'Humble-Bee' in his 'sunny solitudes':

> Sailor of the atmosphere;
> Swimmer through the waves of air;
> Voyager of light and noon;

Emily Dickinson cries 'Oh, for a bee's experience / Of clovers and of noon'; Rilke writes 'We are the bees of the Invisible. Nous butinons éperdument le miel du Visible pour l'accumuler dans la grande ruche d'or de l'invisible.' It is an attractive and understandable image for any Romantic writer who seeks to assimilate the pollen of perception in order to transmute it into the honey of his art. But more unusual perhaps is the attraction which the spider has held for American writers from Jonathan Edwards to Robert Lowell. Thus Edwards starts one of his earliest pieces of writing, 'Of Insects': 'Of all Insects no one is more wonderfull than the Spider especially with Respect to their sagacity and admirable way of working.' Edwards was particularly struck to see spiders apparently 'swimming in the air' (like Emerson's bee), and he describes how he watched and experimented to see how they managed to sustain themselves in space. The secret, the marvel, was the way they 'put out a web at their tails' which was so light that the wind took it, and held up the spider at the same time; then

25

> If the further End Of it happens to catch by a tree or anything, why there's a
> web for him to Go over upon and the Spider immediately perceives it and feels
> when it touches, much after the same manner as the soul in the brain
> immediately Perceives when any of those little nervous strings that Proceed
> from it are in the Least Jarrd by External things.

Pausing to notice how the Puritan imagination effortlessly makes the
external fact emblematic of an inner process, I want to juxtapose
Whitman's poem on 'A Noiseless Patient Spider' where the spider's
emblematic significance is fully developed:

> A Noiseless patient spider,
> I mark'd where on a little promontory it stood isolated,
> Mark'd how to explore the vacant vast surrounding,
> It launched forth filament, filament, filament, out of itself,
> Ever unreeling them, ever tirelessly speeding them.
>
> And you O my soul where you stand,
> Surrounded, detached, in measureless oceans of space,
> Ceaselessly musing, venturing, throwing, seeking the spheres to connect
> them,
> Till the bridge you will need be form'd, till the ductile anchor hold,
> Till the gossamer thread you fling catch somewhere, O my soul.

We could scarcely hope to find a better image of the American Romantic
writer, which is almost to say the American writer, than this. Isolated and
secreting filament, filament, filament (think of Whitman's constantly
renewed stream of notations and enumerations) to explore, to relate to,
and to fill 'the vacant vast surrounding'. America is the 'measureless
oceans of space'; the web is the private creation of the writer, constructed
with a view of attaching himself somehow to reality, a world of his own
making in which he can live on his own terms, assimilating and
transforming what the outside world brings his way. Emily Dickinson,
too, obviously saw something of her own poetic activity in the
movements of the spider, as in the famous poem which starts:

> A spider sewed at night
> Without a light
> Upon an arc of white.

And in other poems, for example, 'The spider ... – dancing softly to
Himself / His Coil of Pearl – unwinds.' She elsewhere calls the spider an
artist of 'surpassing merit' whose tapestries, wrought in an hour, are
'Continents of Light'; but also very ephemeral. 'He plies from Nought to
Nought / In insubstantial Trade.' A not dissimilar image occurs to Henry
Adams in the crucial chapter in his *Education* on 'A Dynamic Theory of
History':

> For convenience as an image, the theory may liken man to a spider in its web, watching for chance prey. Forces of nature dance like flies before the new, and the spider pounces on them when it can . . . The spider-mind acquires a faculty of the memory, and, with it, a singular skill of analysis and synthesis, taking apart and putting together in different relations the meshes of its trap.

And in a comparably important statement in Henry James's essay 'The Art of Fiction' the work of the spider receives perhaps its finest transformation:

> Experience is never limited, and it is never complete; it is an immense sensibility, a kind of huge spider-web of the finest silken threads suspended in the chamber of consciousness, and catching every air-borne particle in its tissue. It is the very atmosphere of the mind; and when the mind is imaginative . . . it takes to itself the faintest hints of life, it converts the very pulses of the air into revelations.

The emblem has become a metaphor; the web has been internalized and experience has become the atmosphere of the mind.

Now it is a truism that one of the recurrent features of Romantic art is the elevation of inner activity over external reality. Hegel's is only the most sweeping of many such generalizations, when he says in the Introduction to the *Philosophy of Art*:

> In brief, the essence of Romantic art lies in the artistic object's being free, concrete, and the spiritual idea in its very essence – all this revealed to the inner rather than to the outer eye . . . This inner world is the content of Romantic art; Romantic art must seek its embodiment in precisely such an inner life or some reflection of it. Thus the inner life shall triumph over the outer world . . .

But since for Hegel Romantic art included nearly everything since Classical art, this panoramic view of the internalization or subject-ivization of reality (examined brilliantly and at length by Erich Heller in *The Artist's Journey into the Interior*) will not help us very much in an attempt to suggest some of the differences between American and European Romanticism. This analogy between the American writer and the spider may at least provide a specific point of departure.

II

One of the formative experiences of all those early American writers was of a sense of space, of vast unpeopled solitudes such as no European Romantic could have imagined. As the hero of Chateaubriand's *René* says to his American auditors: 'Europeans constantly in a turmoil are forced to build their own solitudes.' The reverse was true for the American Romantic. Solitude was all but imposed on him. Nothing seemed easier for him than to take a few steps to find himself confronting and caught up in those measureless oceans of space where Whitman found his soul both surrounded and detached. This gravitation towards empty space is a constant in American literature, even if it appears only in glimpses, as for instance when the narrator of *The Sacred Fount* turns away from the crowded house of Newmarch and staring up at the sky finds the night air 'a sudden corrective to the grossness of our lustres and the thickness of our medium'; or when the narrator of *The Last Tycoon* says 'It's startling to you sometimes — just air, unobstructed, uncomplicated air.' Charles Olson is justified in starting his book on Melville (*Call me Ishmael*) with the emphatic announcement: 'I take SPACE to be the central fact to man born in America, from Folsom cave to now. I spell it large because it comes large here. Large, and without mercy.' But like those spiders who came under Jonathan Edwards's formidable scrutiny, the American artist, once he found himself at sea in space, had to do something to maintain himself, and one instinctive response was to expand into the surrounding space. William Cullen Bryant writes of 'The Prairies': 'I behold them from the first, / And my heart swells, while the dilated sight / Takes in the encircling vastness'; Whitman claims 'I chant the chant of dilation'; Emerson records how 'the heart refuses to be imprisoned; in its first and narrowest pulses it already tends outward with a vast force and to immense and innumerable expansions . . . there is no outside, no inclosing wall, no circumference to us'. Emerson's eye, and his mind after it, was continually drawn to the remotest horizons; the only true encirclement to a man obsessed with circles was earth's vanishing point, the very perimeter of the visible world where sight lost itself in space. When he writes about 'The Poet' and his attraction to narcotics of all kinds Emerson says: 'These are auxiliaries to the centrifugal tendency of a man, to his passage out into free space, and they help him to escape the custody of that body in which he is pent up, and of that jail-yard of individual relations in which he is enclosed.' Near the end of *Walden* Thoreau has some marvellous lines about the 'ethereal flight' of a hawk which sported alone 'in the fields of air'. 'It appeared to have no companion in the universe . . . and to need none but the morning and the ether with which it played.' Thoreau ends the book, appropriately enough, with the parable of the bug which hatches out in an old table and breaks free into 'beautiful and winged life', and Whitman at the end of *Song of Myself* literally feels himself diffused back into the elements: 'I depart as air . . .' In these three seminal American Romantics we find a similar 'centrifugal tendency'; a dilation of self, which can become an abandoning of self, into the surrounding vastness. But of course if this were all we would have had no record of the movement since words are not carefully strung together by a man in the process of being metamorphosed into the circumambient air, as Emerson seems to recognize in a letter to Samuel Gray Ward: 'Can you not save me, dip me into ice water, find me some girding belt, that I glide not away into a stream or a gas, and decease in infinite diffusion?' Like those spiders swimming in the air, the American writer throws out filament, filament, filament, and weaves a web to sustain himself in the vastness. Paradoxically these webs are often notable for being composed of many very concrete particulars and empirically perceived facts (thus Thoreau is also one of the earthiest of writers); it is as though these solid details offered some anchoring attachment. When Frost described a poem as a stay against confusion, he might have more accurately phrased it, for the American writer, as a stay against diffusion.

The web is the writer's style; the concrete details are the nourishing particles which the web ensnares and transforms. And what extraordinary webs the American Romantics (and indeed post-Romantics) have spun: Emerson's essays for instance, which often seem to tremble and blur with the very vertigo they were written to counteract, or *Walden* and *Moby-Dick* which, although they seem to repeat stock Romantic themes – the return to nature, the voyage – are of a stylistic idiosyncrasy which can scarcely be paralleled in European writing. And much of that style is not being used to explore self or environment so much as to fill in the spaces between self and environment. Again, *Song of Myself* might at first glance appear to have much in common with *The Prelude*, and the phrase 'egotistical sublime' which Keats applied to Wordsworth could certainly be extended to Whitman. And yet the sense of harmonious reciprocities between mind and landscape, that 'intimate communion' which, says Wordsworth, 'our hearts / Maintain with the minuter properties / Of objects which already are belov'd', is absent from Whitman's more desperate and sometimes hysterical ecstasies. 'My voice goes after what my eyes cannot reach, / With the twirl of my tongue I encompass worlds and volumes of worlds.' This verbal and visual pursuit of objects and worlds to fill up his void is somewhat different from the serene stealth with which, for Wordsworth, 'the visible scene / Would enter unawares into his mind / With all its solemn imagery'.

Among American Romantics there is an unusual stress on a visual relationship with nature. 'I am becoming a transparent eyeball; I am nothing; I see all' – Emerson's famous formulation is relevant for much subsequent American writing. Thoreau, whose other senses were active enough, puts the emphasis on sight: 'We are as much as we see.' Whitman asks himself 'What do you see Walt Whitman?' in 'Salut au Monde' and answers literally and copiously, using the phrase 'I see' eighty-three times. Obviously new habits of attention, recovered visual intimacies with nature, were crucial for European Romantics as well (and Ruskin was to make of sight an instrument arguably more sensitive than anything to be found in American writing). But more often than in America, the English Romantic's response was also auditory. Keats listening darkling to his nightingale is only one of the many English Romantic poets whose ears were highly receptive to any vibrations or music that reached them. 'With what strange utterance did the loud dry wind / Blow through my ears', 'I heard among the solitary hills / . . . sounds / of undistinguishable motion', 'Then sometime, in that silence, while he hung / Listening, a gentle shock of mild surprise / Has carried far into the heart the voice / Of mountain torrents' – these examples from Wordsworth of the voice and utterances of landscape may be readily multiplied, perhaps the most famous being 'The Solitary Reaper', where the sound of the woman's song provides lasting nourishment for the poet:

> The music in my heart I bore,
> Long after it was heard no more.

The American Romantics do not give the impression of valuing auditory responses in quite this way. More to the point, for the English Romantics a purely visual relationship to the outside world betokened a state of deprivation, a loss of intimacy, a failure of poetic vision. Coleridge's 'Dejection: an Ode' hinges on this severance between self and surrounding things: 'I see them all so excellently fair, / I see, not feel, how beautiful they are!' And Shelley's 'Stanzas Written in Dejection', by lamenting the absence of some other 'heart' to 'share in my emotion' as he looks at the scene in front of him, is also asserting the insufficiency of mere sight. A purely or predominantly visual relationship with nature in fact can indicate a state of alienation or detachment from it. An auditory response suggests that the sounds of the environment mean something to the hearer, something within becomes alert to something without which seems to speak a comprehensible language. This suggests at least the possibility of communication, of significant relationship, perhaps even of a kind of dialogue. To be linked to a thing only by sight is at the same time to be severed from it, if only because the act of purely visual appropriation implies a definite space between the eye and the object. And American writers have been predominantly watchers. Thoreau, supposedly so immersed in his environment, can still use this strange image: 'I enter some glade in the woods . . . and it is as if I had come to an open window. I see out and around myself.' Having left man-made dwellings behind him, he reintroduces part of their architecture to describe his feelings. To be in the midst of nature and yet to see it as through an open window is surely in some way also to feel cut off from it. Emerson often refers to the world as 'spectacle' and is extremely sensitive to all shades of visual experience, as when he says it is enough to take a coach ride to have the surrounding world 'wholly detached from all relation to the observer'. He said of the soul: 'It is a watcher more than a doer, and it is a doer, only that it may the better watch.' This in turn anticipates James, whose central figures are all great watchers, thereby excluded from participation in the world they survey – like James himself, leaning intently out of one of the many windows in his house of fiction. Again, in Hemingway's characters their visual alertness and acuity is in part a symptom of their alienation.

Those American writers we associate with the New England Renaissance (and many subsequently) most typically felt themselves to be swimming in space; not, certainly, tied fast into any society, nor really attached very firmly to the vast natural environment. In many ways this state was cherished and preferred; to sport in fields of air could be the ultimate ecstasy. On the other hand there was the danger of, as it were, vanishing or diffusing altogether. The emergent strategy, variously developed by different writers, was to spin out a web which could hold them in place, which would occupy the space around them, and from which they could look out into the world. But even when they scrutinized their environment with extreme care, and took over many of its details to weave into their webs of art, they were seldom in any genuine communion with nature. European Romantics, on the other hand, do seem to have enjoyed moments of reciprocal relationship with nature and could speak truly of what they 'half perceive and half create'. With Wordsworth they could consider 'man and nature as essentially adapted to each other'. In discovering nature they were at the same time discovering themselves; in internalizing what was around them they were at the same time externalizing what was within, as Coleridge often described. 'The forms / Of Nature have a passion in themselves / That intermingles with those works of man / To which she summons him.' That is Wordsworth, and it is just that sort of fruitful *intermingling* of Nature's and Man's creative potencies that is absent from American Romantic writing, which tends, rather, to testify that Nature holds off from man's approaches. Nature is indeed seen, seen with intense clarity through the intervening air, but it leaves precisely that intervening space to be filled by the writer's own filament. That marriage between subject and object, mind and nature, which is an abiding Romantic dream, is seldom consummated in the work of the American Romantics. When Emerson speaks of 'the cool disengaged air of natural objects' he is pointing to a perceptual experience which makes for important differences in American Romanticism.

Of course it would be an unacceptable simplification of Emerson's strangely fluid writing to fix on any one of his descriptions of nature as his definitive attitude. But in his first famous essay on 'Nature' we find a conception of nature markedly different from any to be found in any comparable European documents. Above all it is the fluidity, the insubstantiality, the transparency of nature which is stressed. Emerson may sound like Wordsworth when he talks of 'that wonderful congruity which subsists between man and the world' – so much was a stock Romantic piety, or hope. But what a strange congruity Emerson's is. To the poet, he says, 'the refractory world is ductile and flexible'. When a poetic mind contemplates nature, matter is 'dissolved by a thought'. The Transcendentalist, says Emerson (and Transcendentalism was pertinently described as 'that outbreak of Romanticism on Puritan ground' by James Elliot Cabot)[1] has only to ask certain questions 'to find his solid universe growing dim and impalpable'. The 'poet turns the world to glass'; when he looks at nature he sees 'the flowing or the Metamorphosis'. 'The Universe is fluid and volatile': 'this surface on which we now stand is not fixed, but sliding'. If there is any 'fixture or stability' in all this sliding, dissolving, melting world, it is 'in the soul'. 'We are not built like a ship to be tossed, but like a house to stand', says Emerson. Since his Nature is distinctly watery, and the 'ethereal tides' seem at times almost to inundate him as he opens himself to them, we may wonder what will be the origin of this stable house of self which can stand firm in the flowing flux of Existence.

Although Emerson is sometimes very specific about individual facts and perceptions, the nature he refers to has no autonomy and very little local identity. It is a mental fabrication. We look in vain for the specificity of all those place-names which are so common in European Romanticism, whether it is Tintern Abbey or Mont Blanc or 'Lines Composed while Climbing the Left Ascent of Brockley Coome, Somersetshire, May 1795' (Coleridge). Emerson says that America's 'ample geography. dazzles the imagination' and a dazzled imagination may respond in unusual ways. His own response, more often than not, is to treat nature as a flimsy, flowing tissue of appearances. He is concerned either to see through it, or withdraw from it. It is indeed a source of emblems, but he tends only to assert this emblematical quality. Perhaps the difference between an emblem and a metaphor is that an emblem is a sign existing at a definite remove from what it signifies and composed of different material; while a metaphor merges the sign and the thing signified. For Emerson Nature was more a matter of emblems than metaphors; it provided no final resting place, no home, for the mind. Here, perhaps, we can detect vestiges of the old Puritan suspicion of matter as fallen, flawed, and misleading – despite Emerson's programmatic optimism about the essential benevolence of all creation. However it is, Emerson's Nature lacks the substantiality, the local external reality, to be found in

[1] Quoted by Henry James in his essay 'Emerson', reprinted in *The American Essays of Henry James*, ed. Leon Edel (New York, 1956), p. 70.

many European Romantic writers. In Emerson Nature may be a symbol
for the mind, or a manifestation of the invisible Over-Soul. What it tends
not to be is its own solid self. Children, said Emerson, 'believe in the
external world'. When we grow older we realize that it 'appears only'.
Perhaps Emerson found no more dramatic phrase for his concept of
Nature than when he suggested it might be 'the apocalypse of the mind'.

What Emerson has done is to interpose his version of a ductile,
transparent, fluid, apparitional nature between himself and the hard,
opaque, refractory (and dazzling) otherness of the real American
landscape. This way he makes Nature amenable to himself and his
purposes. It is notable how often he talks of playing with Nature as if it
were a collection of baubles and toys. The genius, he writes in his journal,
'can upheave and balance and toss every object in Nature for his
metaphor'; we must be like Shakespeare, he says, who 'tosses the creation
like a bauble from hand to hand'. Anything less tossable fom hand to
hand, less bauble-like, than the American landscape in the mid-
nineteenth century would be hard to think of. But Emerson is swimming
in air; and this Nature, this flowing stream of soft transparent playthings,
is the web he has created to keep himself afloat. By contrast Wordsworth's or Keats's poetic Nature is, if not the apocalypse of reality, at least
its consecration. More recent American writers have not found
themselves in exactly the same vast otherness as the mid-nineteenth-
century writers. If anything they have to deal with a congestion which
would squash them rather than an emptiness which might swallow
them, though of course there is a kind of crowdedness which feels like a
vacancy. But when Wallace Stevens says that 'resistance to the pressure
of ominous and destructive circumstance consists of its conversion, so far
as possible, into a different, an explicable, an amenable circumstance', he
seems to be placing the emphasis in a way which is typical of the
American Romantic attitude, which has so often 'converted' the given
environment into something amenable, not necessarily benevolent if we
think of Poe, Hawthorne, Melville, but amenable – ductile to the
weavings of their art.

III

Emerson tells his American poet-figure 'Thou shalt leave the world',
adding: 'the impressions of the actual world shall fall like summer rain,
copious, but not troublesome to thy invulnerable essence'. Reality
becomes something like a light shower, easily disregarded. In its place, as
he says at the end of 'Nature', 'Every spirit builds itself a house'. This is
the house (or the web) which we have already seen the American artist
constructing for his own stability, sustenance and unhindered develop-

ment. 'Build therefore your own world', Emerson goes on to admonish his readers in a phrase which has given Richard Poirier a starting-point for his exciting book *A World Elsewhere*. Poirier's more fully developed ideas, as in such a passage as the following, corroborate my suggestion that the creation of a verbal web, safe for habitation and the expansion of consciousness, is a major characteristic of American Romanticism:

> The books which in my view constitute a distinctive American tradition within English literature are early, very often clumsy examples of a modernist impulse in fiction: they resist within their pages the forces of environment that otherwise dominate the world. Their styles have an eccentricity of defiance, even if the defiance shows sometimes as carelessness. Cooper, Emerson, Thoreau, Melville, Hawthorne, Mark Twain, James – they both resemble and serve their heroes by trying to create an environment of 'freedom', though as writers their efforts must be wholly in language. American books are often written as if historical forces cannot possibly provide such environment, as if history can give no life to 'freedom', and as if only language can create the liberated place.

Elaborating on the Emersonian image of the house, Poirier comments: '*Walden* is only one of the examples of something like an obsession in American literature with plans and efforts to build houses, to appropriate space to one's desires'; he mentions the houses in Cooper, Mark Twain, *The House of the Seven Gables*, Fawns in *The Golden Bowl*, Sutpen's Hundred, Silas Lapham's house, Gatsby's estate, even Herzog's country house, and of course the work of crucial architects like Frank Lloyd Wright, and he adds 'the building of a house is an extension and an expansion of the self, an act by which the self possesses environment otherwise dominated by nature'. It is certainly a way of interposing your world between yourself and the given world and obviously of particular importance in America where the unparalleled freedom, and need, to erect habitations of one's own design has produced unique architectural and literary structures alike. Poirier could have developed his point further. When Emily Dickinson says 'I dwell in Possibility – a Fairer House than Prose' we can see that it is also the house of her own style. Similarly all those extremely ornate and cunningly decorated, coloured, and upholstered interiors in Poe's stories (which Baudelaire commented on enthusiastically), are surely images of his own pure art style which he so defiantly opposed to the unpoetical barrenness of contemporary America. (One might note in passing Edith Wharton's enthusiastic writing on house decoration which preceded her fictional works.) The opening stanza of Wallace Stevens's 'Architecture' (in *Opus Posthumous*) admirably evokes this whole attitude:

> What manner of building shall we build?
> Let us design a chastel de chasteté.

De pensée ...
Never cease to deploy the structure.
Keep the laborers shouldering plinths.
Pass the whole of life hearing the clink of the
Chisels of the stone-cutters cutting the stones.

Let us build a castle of thought (just as James speaks of 'a palace of thought'); what is more, let us build it of any materials we please, arranged in any fashion that pleases us. The suggestion is that for these and comparable writers, art is a continuous building of a private edifice; and the process of building – of playing with the available materials, as Emerson's poet plays with the baubles of nature, as Stevens plays with rare exotic things and words (like 'chastel') – is perhaps more important than the product. Build therefore your own world, or weave your own web – here is a key cry of the American writer, particularly those writers we designate as being in one way or another Romantic. The same sort of idea is of course also to be found in Europe, in Coleridge's 'stately pleasure-dome' and Tennyson's 'Palace of Art', for instance. But these are different sorts of building, built for a different purpose (to explore the world of the creative unconscious among other things), and in both cases the edifices represent dreams from which there has to be a waking.

A good visual example of this sort of private 'architecture' in American art is provided by an amazing picture by Erastus Field called 'Historical Monument of the American Republic'. It shows the most extraordinary mélange of heterogeneous architectural styles of building from various cultures and various ages, all connected up at the top by tenuous little bridges – filaments, really, of the painter's fantasy. The result is that although the various specific contents of the work are public and historical, the over-all effect is private and fanciful. Field is building his own world and its relation to the actual world is more apparent than real. Among poets, Stevens can be such an architect. Pound and Eliot likewise use fragments of the world's past and disparate cultures to build their own private worlds. This sort of relatively unfettered eclecticism when dealing with the past is peculiarly American and an utterly different thing from the European writer's sense of the past. If anything it negates the historical sense – Pound plays with the cultures of the past, tossing pieces from hand to hand, just as Emerson played with images of Nature. The results and new juxtapositions can be brilliant, breath-takingly original, and very un-European. As in Field's painting, images of the real past are dislodged and reassembled at the whim of the poet as he spins out his web. And there is another aspect to this almost forceful gathering together of human culture into one web through the sheer effort of style. Faulkner often repeats a sentiment that 'I'm trying to say it all in one sentence, between one Cap and one period ... I don't know how to do it. All I know is to keep on trying in a new way.' This ambition to 'put all mankind's history in one sentence' partly explains some of the Gargantuan qualities to be found in many American writers – for example, an unprecedented omnivorousness which affects syntax as well as length. Wallace Stevens reveals his own tendency towards this when he writes in a letter, 'for me the important thing is to realize poetry . . . it is simply the desire to contain the world wholly within one's own perception of it'. This pre-empting of the world and history, this making it over on your own terms, is necessarily a condition of much art anywhere. But nowhere do you find this will to reconstitute and contain the world and the past in the web of an individual style more strong than in certain American writers.

A final point about this private house of the American Romantic, again from Emerson: 'It is awful to look into the mind of man and see how free we are . . . Outside, among your fellows, among strangers, you must preserve appearances, a hundred things you cannot do; but inside, the terrible freedom.' The notion that the house which the spirit builds for itself may become a place of terror is deftly conceded by Emily Dickinson with her trenchant economy:

> One need not be a chamber to be haunted,
> One need not be a house;
> The brain has corridors surpassing
> Material place.

Robert Frost's 'Bereft' suggests similar terrors, when the wind turns threatening and the leaves hiss at him:

> Something sinister in the tone,
> Told me my secret must be known:
> Word I was in the house alone
> Somehow must have gotten abroad,
> Word I was in my life alone,
> Word I had no one left but God.

The horrors which take place in Poe's secluded rooms also emphasize how often the American writer is to be found sitting alone in the house which his soul has made for him and which is so often and so singularly haunted.

Alone in his house or sporting in fields of air alone, the American writer seems to have taken his cue from Emerson's axiom, 'Alone is heaven.' The word, and the aspiration, recur constantly, and it is most apt that the first sentence of Emerson's first major essay should define the conditions for the procurement of solitude: 'To go into solitude, a man needs to retire as much from his chamber as from society.' As Emily Dickinson puts it, 'the soul selects her own society/Then shuts the door.'

No single sentence differentiates Emerson more clearly from a writer like Wordsworth than this (it follows after Emerson has been discussing the grandeur of nature): 'Yet this may show us what discord is between man and nature, for you cannot freely admire a noble landscape if laborers are digging in the field hard by. The poet finds something ridiculous in his delight until he is out of the sight of men.' But Wordsworth does not. For Wordsworth to encounter the shepherd, the leech-gatherer, the reaper, or anyone else living in intimacy with nature, could be the occasion of an epiphany, a visionary gleam. Emerson reveals a more Oriental streak in the American response to landscape when he emphasizes the discrepancy between tiny man and the vast dissolving grandeur of nature. Indeed, he would even banish those tiny figures which Oriental painters include to remind one of that discrepancy. For Emerson the ideal landscape was the unpeopled landscape. Thoreau does meet people in the woods, yet his instinct is for solitude. 'It would be sweet to deal with men more, I imagine, but where dwell they? Not in the fields which I traverse.' Whitman seems to reach out to embrace the whole continent; his imagination is crowded with electric, tactile contacts. Yet it seems to be more a dream of contact; for the most part he is 'out of the game', 'apart from the pulling and hauling', looking, peering, beholding, watching – one of those great lonely voyeurs who recur in American literature. At the end of the poem it is his evasive solitariness which we feel as he promises to 'stop somewhere waiting for you' and then vanishes without even waiting to close off his poem with a full stop. Carlyle's warning to Emerson could be extended to cover other American writers: 'We find you a Speaker indeed, but as it were a Soliloquizer on the eternal mountain-tops only, in vast solitudes where men and their affairs all lie hushed in a very dim remoteness...' By contrast, 'The Prelude' starts and ends with an address to 'my Friend' (Coleridge, of course).

All Romantics are supposed to be soliloquizers, enraptured by their own potency, yet a good deal of European, certainly of English, Romantic poetry is addressed to friends, or presupposes or involves them. These Romantics cherished company, even if it had to be very select, just as they seem more interested in women than were their American counterparts. And the implications of this go beyond the relatively trivial question of whether the European Romantic had more friends than the American. It involves a difference in their relative conceptions of their own role in relation to their societies. 'The poet', says Wordsworth, 'binds together by passion and knowledge the vast empire of human society'; poets, says Shelley, 'are the unacknowledged legislators of the world', Wordsworth's poet is a 'man speaking to men'; by contrast the American Romantic seems more to be a man speaking to himself. William Cullen Bryant stands in the American woods and dreams of a future civilization: [I] 'think I hear / The sound of that advancing multitude / Which soon shall fill these deserts'; but his poem ends, 'A fresher wind sweeps by, and breaks my dream, / And I am in the wilderness alone.' The European Romantic did not have to dream of crowds and societies and civilizations, they were everywhere he turned; and despite the fixed image of the European Romantics as escapists, most of them were very politically minded and concerned with the development of society. Ever since Rousseau had shown that society was an arbitrary, man–made structure, the idea had been gaining ground that man could reshape society according to the demands and dictates of his imagination. Mental structures might precede and ordain political structures. The French Revolution demonstrated both the will and the ability of men to actively reshape their society. In a rich and authoritative article on 'English Romanticism: The Spirit of the Age', M. H. Abrams demonstrates conclusively that for the English Romantics the French Revolution was the single most formative experience of their lives. The great outburst of social or anti-social energy provoked and encouraged a similar release of personal creative energy. Millennial hopes and apocalyptic expectations ran high. The advent of the New Jerusalem or Paradise on Earth was prophesied. English Romantics argued from the French Revolution to the Book of Revelation, and prophesied liberating changes in the 'vast empire of human society'. The poet's role was to offer the shaping vision, to produce imaginative constructs which would provide models for social constructs. Acknowledged or not, they felt themselves to be, or potentially to be, the legislators of the world. Most European Romantics were implicitly if not explicitly revolutionary; as Hazlitt shrewdly commented on the Lake School, 'regular metre was abolished with regular government'. Of course, disillusion with the French Revolution set in, and it is precisely a part of Professor Abrams's story to show how the English Romantics experienced a loss of hope, gave up their expectations of a specific historical revolution in the near future, and concentrated on what Abrams calls 'the apocalypse of imagination'. I quote one of his conclusions, concerning this shift of emphasis. 'The hope has been shifted from the history of mankind to the mind of a single individual, from militant external action to an imaginative act; and the marriage between the Lamb and the New Jerusalem has been converted into a marriage between subject and object, mind and nature, which creates a new world out of the old world of sense.'

In America, the writing of the Transcendentalists, and all those we may wish to consider as Romantics, did not have this revolutionary social dimension. It was not rooted in the energizing conviction that the poet's imaginative visions, in one way or another, could vitally influence and enhance the conditions of life of their fellow men. Whitman certainly talks of the great 'en-masse' and has dreams of a harmonious collectivity, yet even here the strongest emphasis is on 'the centripetal isolation of a human being in himself'. Between that centrifugal tendency into space I mentioned earlier, and this centripetal isolation of the human being in himself, the American artist spins his self-sustaining web, with society usually excluded, ignored, or unenvisaged. Appropriately enough the most famous use of the image of the spider's web in nineteenth-century English literature is in George Eliot's *Middlemarch*, where she uses it to illustrate the complex and ramifying inter-relatedness of all human relationships, that 'stealthy convergence of human lots'. What in English literature has here provided an image of our unavoidable involvement in the lives of other people, in American literature has typically been the image for the patterns and strategies with which the American artist both fills and preserves his radical solitude. The contrast has at least some parabolic aptness.

IV

While dealing with attitudes towards society and civilization, another point is worth making, which is put clearly in the poem written by Bryant for the painter Thomas Cole as the latter was about to leave for Europe. First Bryant reminds Cole of the wonderful wild and savage landscapes which he has painted (and which indeed he loved), then he warns him of what he will see in Europe:

> Fair scenes shall greet thee where thou goest – fair,
> But different – everywhere the trace of men,
> Paths, homes, graves, ruins, from the lowest glen
> To where life shrinks from the fierce Alpine air –
> Gaze on them, till the tears shall dim thy sight.
> But keep that earlier, wilder image bright.

In Europe, 'everywhere the trace of men': in America, 'that wilder image'. Bryant himself is clearly appreciative of both, but he more particularly wants to retain 'that wilder image' which the as-yet uncivilized landscape of America can provide. The wildness of this landscape was felt to have values and provide spiritual nourishment not available in Europe. 'We need the tonic of wildness', says Thoreau, while Cole, in his 'Essay on American Scenery' (1835), insists that 'the wilderness is YET a fitting place to speak of God'. Against those who prefer Europe, Cole argues that 'the most impressive characteristic of American scenery is its wildness', while in 'civilized Europe the primitive features of scenery have long since been destroyed or modified'. He instances some of the splendid wildnesses of America, for example

Niagara: 'in gazing on it we feel as though a great void had been filled in our mind – our conceptions expand – we become a part of what we behold'. (It is amusing to recall that when Chateaubriand first saw Niagara he was so overwhelmed that he wanted to throw himself in, and indeed did nearly fall over the edge – a pregnant Romantic anecdote. And it was in the wild American woods, Chateaubriand says, a new, an 'unknown muse appeared to me'. Such wildness, he felt, would provoke a new poetry.) At the same time anyone writing in America then was aware that the rapid 'improvements of cultivation' were inevitably replacing 'the sublimity of the wilderness'. Here was a difficulty. The American wilderness was a source of visionary exaltation. Unlike Europe, the land was not scarred and stained by the intolerable crimes of history: 'You see no ruined tower to tell of outrage – no gorgeous temple to speak of ostentation.' But if American landscape was not suffused with a sense of the past it was full of what Cole calls 'associations ... of the present and future'. 'And in looking over the yet uncultivated scene, the mind's eye shall see far into futurity. Where the wolf roams, the plough shall glisten; on the gray crag shall rise temple and tower ...' There is a problem for the American Romantic. Blessedly, there are no man-made towers marring the American landscape; but happily there will soon be towers springing up. The wonder and richness of America is its wildness, but wonderfully, the wildness will soon be put to the plough. As soon as Cole has outlined his optimistic vision of a civilized society living in a domesticated landscape, he goes on 'yet I cannot but express my sorrow that the beauties of such landscapes are quickly passing away – the ravages of the axe are daily increasing – the most noble scenes are made desolate and oftentimes with a wantonness and barbarism scarcely credible in a civilized nation'. Where the European Romantic, used to the 'traces of men', might look forward to an imagined millennium for human society, the American was very aware of increasing depredations of the precious wildness. He might cling to images of idealized pastoral domesticity, or indulge in pieties about manifest destiny or the melting-pot, but his strategy on the whole was to seek out that solitude, those unpeopled landscapes, prescribed by Emerson – in reality, or in art. That is why while European Romanticism characteristically looks to the past and to the future, American Romanticism seeks to move out of time altogether, out of time and into some sort of space. For time means history, and history means 'traces of men' and society, and society means not only the loss of 'that wilder image' but also the spaces it provided and the limitless freedom to sport in air.

'The great discovery of the eighteenth century is the phenomenon of memory,' says Georges Poulet, and certainly the attempt to renew contact with one's individual past and the past of society is a decisive

factor in the literature of Europe we call Romantic. Chateaubriand's
René, who laid down so many of the behaviour patterns for subsequent
Romantic poets and heroes, is exemplary in this. Accounting for his
melancholy in the depths of the American woods, René recalls his
European past. In one early phrase he anticipates many subsequent
works: 'Memories of these childhood adventures still fill my soul with
delight.' Another key word is introduced when he describes how the
sound of bells in his native land awakens the happiest associations in later
life. 'All is contained in these delicious reveries into which we are
plunged by the sound of our native bells.' Revery, first eulogized by
Rousseau, is a word which appears very frequently in European
nineteenth-century literature, and René's sentiment is echoed by
Wordsworth and Proust to mention only the most obvious. To cope
with his misery – caused by that favourite Romantic frustration, hopeless
incestuous love – René has recourse to the Romantic antidote of travel. 'I
went and sat among the ruins of Rome and Greece: countries of strong
and productive memory.' In particular he favours moon-lit meditations:
'Often, by the rays of this star which nourishes our reveries, I thought I
saw the Spirit of Memory seated in deep thought by my side.' I need
hardly point out what a wealth of Romantic iconography is here
assembled. And when René cries out, 'Is it my fault, if I find limits
everywhere, if what is finite has no value for me?', and 'I lacked
something that could fill the emptiness of my existence', he articulates
archetypal Romantic feelings. Having left Europe after the death of his
sister and come to the depths of the American woods, he does not find
anything to fill that emptiness and indeed he is said to die shortly after
completing his tale, his recollection. A recollection, not quite in
tranquillity, but one which suggests that what meaning and content
there was to his life is all in the past. There is nothing emptier than the
present. René also affords us an excellent picture of a typical European
Romantic as he sits at the edge of the sea when his sister has immolated
herself in a convent after confessing her illicit love. René is awaiting his
ship, knowing that his life henceforward will always be incomplete,
unfilled. As he describes the contrast between the convent behind him
and the ocean in front, we can see him hanging between two worlds. On
the one side there is the place, the symbol, of infinity, calm, refuge,
timeless knowledge, and unfaltering motionless light; on the other, the
unceasing tides of Time, the place of storm, of shipwreck, of uncertain
navigation, and moving beacon lights which shift and sway with the
swell of the sea. And in between, drawn to both, full inhabitant of
neither, is the unappeasable, the European, René.

René, it is true, does not find something to fill his inner emptiness in
past, present, or future. He perhaps qualifies as one of those who, as

Georges Poulet puts it, in an effort to create their identities out of the past and present or future time, risk a 'double tearing of the self' by finally feeling themselves cut off from both. But if nearly all Romantics have felt what Poulet calls 'the infinite deficiency of the present moment', some of them have indeed managed to reconstitute a more lasting self out of remembrance. For memory proved to be one of the major defences against the disintegration of the self and its endless diffusion into innumerable unrelated moments. As Poulet puts it, 'all at once the mind is able to feel an entire past reborn within itself. This past, together with the whole train of its emotions, surges up in the moment and endows it with a life that is not momentary.' Instead of being a mere creature of intermittent and discrete sensations, the writer, through this remembering, recapturing, re-experiencing of the past, discovers the miracle of his own duration. It would be out of place and unnecessary to embark on any sketch of the role of memory in European Romanticism; but this deliberate cultivation of an awareness and a sense both of society's historical past and the past of the individual provided the European Romantic with one of his main themes and activities. Let Wordsworth suffice as an obvious example:

> But a sense
> Of what had been here done, and suffer'd here
> Through ages, and was doing, suffering, still
> Weigh'd with me, could support the test of thought,
> Was like the enduring majesty and power
> Of independent nature; and not seldom
> Even individual remembrances,
> By working on the Shapes before my eyes,
> Became like vital functions of the soul;   (*Prelude*, VIII, 781–9)

and again:

> There are in our existence spots of time,
> Which with distinct pre-eminence retain
> A vivifying Virtue, whence . . .
>   our minds
> Are nourished and invisibly repair'd . . .   (*Prelude*, XI, 258–65)

In the rediscovery of the Middle Ages in German Romanticism, or in the Hellenism of poets like Shelley and Byron, European Romanticism was as retrospective as it was revolutionary.

A few quotations from Emerson will suggest how radically different was the American Romantic's attitude towards memory and the past. 'But why should you keep your head over your shoulder? Why drag about this corpse of your memory . . ?'; 'In nature every moment is new; the past is swallowed and forgotten; the coming only is sacred'; 'how easily we might walk onward into the opening landscape . . . until by

degrees the recollection of home was crowded out of the mind, all
memory obliterated by the tyranny of the present, and we are led in
triumph by nature'. Emerson described himself as 'an endless seeker with
no Past at my back', and in his funeral address on Thoreau he said of him,
'he lived for the day, not cumbered and mortified by his memory'. This
antipathy to memory, the resolute rejection of the past, is of course
connected to America's national growth. For the past was Europe, that
old world whose influence America had to escape if it was to discover
itself. It is part of the American genius not to be dominated and held back
by the inertia of the past, to feel that the future is still full of infinite
possibilities, that, as Stevens put it, 'the vegetation still abounds with
forms' – new forms, not copies of the old forms of the past. However,
this denial of memory seems to rob most American writers of any
experience of duration. Henry Miller is only an extreme form of the
many American writers, Romantic and otherwise, who seem to
experience life as an unrelated series of spasmodic 'nows'. 'There is
nothing else than now', says the Hemingway hero to himself. The past
can certainly be every kind of burden, a real load of nightmare and
repression. But to lack any sense of the past can be impoverishing, and to
live in a pure present can have its terrors. Certainly it must lead to a much
less stable sense of self. As I suggested earlier, the tendency of certain
American writers to dilate into the space around them, even to dissolve
into their environment, is related to this flight from the past which is a
flight out of time.'WHAT SCARED YOU ALL INTO TIME?, . . . COME
OUT OF TIME AND INTO SPACE. FOREVER. THERE IS NO THING TO
FEAR. THERE IS NO THING IN SPACE.' William Burroughs's message
to Allen Ginsberg effectively sums up a position held intermittently by
American writers over the last hundred years. Of course if the American
artist did manage to vanish out of time and into space he would not write
anything. First, because, as Burroughs points out, there is no thing in
space and you cannot have art without things any more than you can
have consciousness without things. Secondly, because it is doubtful
whether the pure present, a series of spatial moments utterly cut off from
the past, can mean anything at all. Needless to say, Emerson, Whitman,
and Thoreau did not vanish in this way, and even Burroughs is still
writing. But Emerson and Whitman, for example, get very repetitive;
indeed at times it seems as if Emerson's prose loses inner direction, as if the
words at least had got out of time and into space where they are sporting
in air. And the American novelist had to turn to the past before he could
find any subjects productive of drama and significance. Hawthorne
sitting in the customs house sifting through those old papers is the precise
image of the American artist looking for some sort of American past
which will provide the dynamic for his art. Mark Twain and Melville

both looked back for the material of their greatest works, while James's fiction begins and ends with the introduction of an American sense of the present into European territories drenched with the past. Today, young American poets like Ed Dorn are trying to isolate and imaginatively use the figure of the Indian and his culture – the true historic past of America.

For good or bad the American Romantic writers do not have that sense of the past which was so important for their European counterparts. Of course, they faced a landscape devoid of 'traces of men': clean, 'dazzling', but humanly speaking empty – potentially alien in a way that the European landscape, so saturated with history, legend, myth, could never be. This perhaps partially explains why the European writer can seem to be more genuinely intimate with his landscape than the American with his, why it offers him so much in the way of suggestions, associations, and consolations, while the American landscape, 'that wilder image', tends to hold off from its watcher as pure obdurate fact. Of course there is a whole tradition of sublime writing celebrating nature in American Romantic poetry. Josephine Miles has described it in her excellent *Eras and Modes in English Poetry* (London, 1977), but she also, most interestingly, notes that the whole vocabulary of subtle 'psychological discriminations' which was developed by the English Romantics was not adopted or developed in America. This corresponds to my sense that the American Romantic feels nature to be something so vast as to be almost beyond him; he does not feel that sort of psychological intimacy with his environment, that sense of reciprocities between man and man, man and nature, which marks much European Romantic writing. For Emerson, despite his celebratory euphoria, the actual surrounding world could often seem 'an Iceland of negations' from which he would habitually escape into his visions of 'infinitude'. Similarly, Wallace Stevens uses the image of a barren wintry landscape to describe his sense of a world which has not been supplemented and illuminated by some imaginary construct invented by the poet himself. The world unmediated or unmodified by Imagination is perhaps a cold and empty place for most Romantics. But whereas the European seems to draw help from history, legend, memory, from friends (and lovers), from visions of future societies, from the landscape itself, as he strives to fill that emptiness, the American Romantic seems to be thrown back much more on his own resources, the devices and designs of his own style. To consider American Romantic literature from Emerson to Wallace Stevens in this light is to realize anew how very remarkable and inventive those resources are.

That recurrent image of the spider, drawing the filament out of himself alone, weaving his private web, provides an illuminating analogy for the situation, and secretion, of the American writer. His delight (or is it sometimes his desperation?) is to put together his own unique verbal structure; and in this activity, the ingredients which go into the making of each piece of filament are perhaps less important than the fact of the web itself which sustains the writer in the real and imagined spaces of America. The visions of the European Romantic interpenetrated on all sides with their natural and human surroundings. It is just this feeling of *interpenetration* that seems to me to be missing in the work of the American Romantic. If we seek him out we are most likely to find him as Emily Dickinson found her spider – dancing softly to himself, unwinding his coil of Pearl. The wonder is what 'continents of light' he thus manages to summon into being.

3

Problems and roles of the American artist as portrayed by the American novelist

It is truism that from the start the American writer has been on the defensive about his vocation. When Martin Chuzzlewit, on his arrival in America, tries to find out something about the state of American literature, he is sharply told: 'We are a busy people, sir, . . . and have no time for reading mere notions. We don't mind 'em if they come to us in newspapers along with almighty strong stuff of another sort, but darn your books.' Darn your books – very often that seems to be the public response that the American writer dreads in advance, and it seems to induce not only a vague sense of guilt about his calling, but on occasions more self-destructive feelings. Whether he sets about evoking a romance of the past, or attempts to address himself to contemporary realities, the American novelist usually betrays an apprehension that his role will somehow set him at odds with his society. This is, of course, no new position for the artist to find himself in. The difference seems to be the degree of anxiety and vulnerability experienced by the American artist: European artists may be equally alienated from their societies, but they seem able to draw confidence from the artistic traditions behind them. It is this sort of confidence which seems unavailable to many American writers.

Why this should be so is a fair matter for speculations, and these have not been lacking. So it is my intention to be as specific as possible. Poets can be rhapsodic and exhortatory, critics can be theoretic and prescriptive, when discussing the role of the American artist. But the novelist deals with concrete situations, a specific environment, a totality of objects, an ongoing set of interrelationships. He shows the growth and fate of the individual in place and time. And so it is with the portrayal of the American artist by the American novelist on which I will be concentrating.

46

One of the first artists in American fiction is Owen Warland in Hawthorne's 'The Artist of the Beautiful' (1844). Warland has received a severe Freudian going over at the hands of Professor Frederick Crews in his book *The Sins of the Fathers* (New York, 1966), but I would like to recall some of his characteristics and his plight. He is small, nervous, delicate. He dislikes the processes of ordinary machinery, indeed the sight of a steam engine makes him sick. He is an apprentice to a watchmaker, but when left to himself he shows no interest in mending clocks – he is indifferent to society's time – and he devotes himself to a secret activity, dedicating himself, as he sees it, to the spiritual and the beautiful. He is scorned by the community whose hard utilitarianism and materiality bruise him at every turn (his surname suggests an embattled rather than a peaceful life), and he loses Annie, the one girl who might have shown him some understanding, to the local blacksmith, whose virility and social usefulness make him an obvious contrast to the rather effeminate Warland. For a while Warland becomes a drunkard; he is considered mad, and, adds Hawthorne, 'the lack of sympathy . . . was enough to make him so'. When he hears that Annie is engaged to the blacksmith he relapses into 'a sort of vegetable existence' which Professor Crews suggests is eunuch-like. His one consoling activity is a prolonged attempt to realize the 'ideal butterfly' by making a perfect mechanical one. When it is completed he gives it to Annie and the blacksmith as a toy for their child. They find it a 'pretty plaything', but the child soon crushes it with one quick grasp. The story hardly suggests a very confident role for the artist in the community, nor does it really say much for either the value or durability of his products. And if the community is depressingly harsh and philistine, the artist is himself alarmingly feeble. It was perhaps with this story in mind that William Dean Howells made use of a particular image in his essay 'Criticism and Fiction'. He suggests that the plight of the would-be realist writer is like that of a young scientist being told by his elders not to bother examining a grasshopper he has just found in the grass. Instead he is advised to study an artificial wire-and-cardboard grasshopper which represents 'the ideal', as opposed to the merely 'photographic'. Howells was asking for real books with real grasshoppers in them; and indeed, Owen Warland's ideal butterfly had proved to be far from indestructible in the rude fist of the infant republic.

In discussing his own sense of severance from his community in the 'Custom-House' chapter of *The Scarlet Letter*, Hawthorne compares his ejection from a rather unexacting public office to a beheading. He strongly implies by this rather excessive metaphor that it was only by dying from public life and withdrawing into his private 'sunless fantasies' that he could become a 'literary man'. The ordinary world, he says, has ceased to be reality for him. 'I am a citizen of somewhere else.' This defection into art was obviously not unattended by guilt. Hawthorne was very aware of his ancestors as great law-makers, and in breaking from this tradition he is apt to appear to himself as a law-breaker. In a very legalistic society the artist is always likely to appear as some sort of antinomian. It is apt that William Wetmore Story, whose works Hawthorne used in his novel *The Marble Faun* and whose biography was written by Henry James, gave up the legal profession for art – a significant step to be re-enacted in fiction by James's first American artist, Roderick Hudson.

In the 'Custom-House' chapter Hawthorne indeed imagines his ancestors passing judgement on him. ' "What is he?" murmurs one gray shadow of my forefathers to the other. "A writer of story-books! What kind of business in life, – what mode of glorifying God, or of being serviceable to mankind in his day and generation, – may that be? Why, the degenerate fellow might as well have been a fiddler!" ' This self-indictment welling up from Hawthorne's ancestral conscience is tolerably complete. But over against this – the case for the prosecution, we might call it – Hawthorne reveals another sense of guilt, which implicitly makes up the case for the defence. While he was a good public servant, working for the community, giving up his time to 'Uncle Sam', he found that he was being overtaken by a 'wretched numbness' and entering a state of prolonged intellectual 'torpor'. He recalls how he had a vague sense of the characters who might make up his novel, but they contemptuously rejected him. ' "What have you to do with us?" that expression seemed to say. "The little power you might once have possessed over the tribe of unrealities is gone! You have bartered it for a pittance of the public gold. Go then, and earn your wages!" ' Thus the voice of his creative conscience berates him in precisely opposite terms from the voice of his ancestral conscience. Working for the public gold, and working from the private imagination, are, it seems, mutually incompatible, indeed mutually exclusive, activities. It was perhaps with some similar sense of the distance between possession of public gold and mastery over the tribe of unrealities that Melville wrote in a letter of 1849: 'So far as I am individually concerned, & independent of my pocket, it is my earnest desire to write those sort of books which are said to "fail".'

I am really touching on two very large problems here, for before considering those of the fictional artist I am commenting briefly on those experienced by the American writer himself. At any time in the nineteenth century the American writer might have worried that his practice of writing fiction should be considered irreligious (as presuming to emulate the creative work of God), or undemocratic (as issuing from, and appealing to, a highly developed individual sensibility), or unprofitable or useless (when compared with the manual and mercantile work which was building America), or degenerate or effeminate (when measured against some vague but strong notion of virility nourished by both the Puritan's and the pioneer's idea of what a man's work consisted of. In both cases some kind of mastery was believed in, mastery over the wilderness, over the community, over impulse, over the wayward fantasies of the imagination). In addition the American novelist faced another problem, that of what kind of art was suitable in America. There were problems here both of avoiding inappropriate European stylistic conventions and of discovering authentic American subjects, but these are familiar topics. Perhaps rather cryptically, I want to suggest that one major problem for the American writer was whether to regard the world as transparent or opaque. Hawthorne, conveniently for my purposes, uses both words in an important sentence in the 'Custom-House' chapter. He is, as so often, in his rather defensive apologetic mood, and he is all but upbraiding himself for his folly in going back to the past for the subject for his novel 'with the materiality of this daily life pressing so intrusively upon me'. What he deprecatingly refers to as the 'soap bubble' of his romance of the past was constantly being broken by 'the rude contact of some actual circumstance'.

> The wiser effort would have been, to diffuse thought and imagination through the opaque substance of to-day, and thus make it a bright transparency; to spiritualize the burden that began to weigh so heavily; to seek, resolutely, the true and indestructible value that lay hidden in the petty and wearisome incidents, and ordinary characters, with which I was now conversant.

In that opaque substance of today there was, he says 'a better book than I shall ever write'. Notice here two opposed groups of words. On the one hand, there is the material, the actual, the circumstantial, the contemporary, the opaque. It is affirmed that this area of reality is full of concealed value, but there is also the expressed feeling that it is burdensome, wearisome, intrusive, harsh in its contact. On the other hand there is the spiritual, the romantic, the imaginary, and this is, or should be, capable of turning the opaque outer world into a 'bright transparency'.

Hawthorne, it seems, feels that he ought to have addressed himself to the opaque contemporary world; at the same time he makes it abundantly clear that in this case it was the inaccessible but deeply suggestive past which awakened in him that sense of romance which for him was an indispensable spur to the writing of a novel. Romance, we should remind ourselves, was a particularly slippery word in the nineteenth century; and in America at least it was used to refer, not just to an exotic story, but to the spiritual, the ideal, the imaginary, any realm not directly accessible to the senses. Taking the word 'romance' in its widest connotations it becomes abundantly clear that much of the best of American fiction has been written out of a tension between the empirically 'real' and a sense of the romantic – a proposition which has been very profitably examined by such critics as Richard Chase and Daniel Hoffman. I want to try to approach the matter from a slightly different angle by positing a tension, felt by the novelist or artist, between an opaque and a transparent treatment of his material.

I would call it opaque treatment to stress the factuality of life. Americans are known to have a genius for respecting and mastering facts, whether in their factories or their philosophies, and it does not desert them in their fiction. However, it seems that there has always been that tug away towards that more transparent treatment of the world which went under the vague name of Romance. Melville offers a good example of this. While writing *Mardi* he wrote in a letter:

> Well: proceeding in my narrative of *facts* I began to feel an incurible [*sic*] distaste for the same; & a longing to plume my pinions for a flight, & felt irked, cramped & fettered by plodding along with dull common places, – So suddenly standing [abandoning?] the thing altogether, I went to work heart & soul at a romance which is now in fair progress. . . . It opens like a true narrative . . . & the romance & poetry of the thing thence grow continually, till it becomes a story wild enough I assure you & with a meaning too . . . My instinct is to out with the *Romance*.

The constriction, at times the tedium of dealing with the opaque world have led many American writers to 'out with the romance', which, as I have suggested, can involve taking the liberty of dealing with things as transparencies.

When you treat a thing as transparent then it follows that you expect to see something hidden behind it, or to see something else through it. Now here I think we should make ourselves aware of different possible kinds of hidden or anterior things. You may, like the Transcendentalists, look through the visible world to see the Oversoul, or God, or some mystical revelation or metaphysical truth. Or you may look under the surface of people and things and detect all the dark propensities and deceits which may linger under a fair surface. We could perhaps differentiate here between Ascendentalists and Descendentalists, for the positional metaphors employed by writers are nearly always revealing. Emerson tends to be an Ascendentalist – 'show me the highest spiritual cause lurking, as it always does lurk, in these suburbs and extremities of nature' ('The American Scholar'). Melville is more of a Descendentalist. Thus in a letter of 1849: 'I love all men who *dive*. Any fish can swim near the surface, but it takes a great whale to go down stairs five miles or more . . . I'm not talking of Mr. Emerson now – but of the whole corps of thought-divers, that have been diving & coming up again with bloodshot eyes since the world began.' The distinction is worth making, albeit in this very crude form, because while it is one thing to claim to be able to see through objects to some higher spiritual law or principle, it is rather another to treat people as transparencies and claim to be able to detect all sorts of dark impulses swimming around well below the surface. It is quite clear that Hawthorne felt some guilt at presuming, as it were, to penetrate the inviolable and sacred interiority of other people. Perhaps people should only be transparent to God, and for a mere fellow mortal to tamper with the ultimately unknowable otherness of another individual might be a form of blasphemy. The role of the detached observer has always been potentially fraught with guilt for the American writer, just as, in another vein, Scott Fitzgerald could write 'We had run through a lot, though we had retained an almost theatrical innocence by preferring the role of the observed to that of the observer' ('My Lost City'). Yet any novelist interested in the psychological dimension of human conduct must perforce become an observer and make this act of penetration and claim to be able to see down into his fellow men and women. Melville, Hawthorne, and James are all great 'divers' of this kind, and I shall now consider novels by each of them.

What I intend to do is offer a brief glance at six novels written between 1850 and 1915 which depict the life, and often the death, of American artists, and consider what they show of the ontogenesis of the artist, the kind of art he attempts to create, and his fate in the society of his time. From the first three, Melville, Hawthorne, and James, we might expect portraits of artists given to a more transparent treatment of the world; while from the latter three, Crane, London, and Dreiser, we might expect portraits of artists more committed to the opaque. This distinction for the most part holds, though as we shall see it is by no means an absolute one. But more interesting, I think, is to note from the outset that whatever treatment of the world these fictional artists go in for, it seems inevitably and inexorably to isolate them from society, often inducing a self-destructive drive which causes morbid illnesses and in some cases leads to a premature death. I shall start with Melville's *Pierre* (1852). Pierre Glendinning comes from an old aristocratic family. He lives very contentedly in the country with his mother – whom he calls sister – and he is set fair to inherit vast estates and marry the beautiful and pure Lucy. Nature is thus seen to smile on Pierre, but we are warned that she will prove 'ambiguous to him in the end'. In terms of the plot what happens is that he discovers that he has a real sister, Isabel, illegitimately begotten by his father, and now living in poverty and anonymity in Pierre's own neighbourhood. This discovery that the apparently secure reality of his life and social position has another level, on which illicit passions produce unacknowledged relationships suppressed to maintain the conventional structure of society, completely undermines Pierre. His world is inverted; its morality vanishes; the sanctions and ordinances prescribed by convention, principle, and propriety come to seem a tissue of shams and lies. Finding the smiling surface of life to be false, Pierre becomes a 'diver'.

He abandons his mother and Lucy, and takes his sister Isabel to the city where he promises to maintain them by his writing. (It is notable that to maintain a certain necessary appearance of legality he calls his sister his wife – it is a 'fictitious alliance', but the fluidity and ambiguity of those relationships which society regards as so fixed and clearly demarcated, is something that becomes clear to him. Society is maintained by 'fictitious alliances'.) They live in a run-down building called the House of the Apostles, and there Pierre embarks on what is to be his great work in which he will lay bare the truth of things. He intends to 'gospelize the world anew, and show them deeper secrets than the Apocalypse!' But as Melville wrote in a letter to Hawthorne in 1851: 'Though I wrote the Gospels in this century, I should die in the gutter.' Pierre's health is undermined, his eyesight starts to fail, and as he writes on and on Melville asks: 'Is it creation, or destruction? Builds Pierre the noble world of a new book? or does the Pale Haggardness unbuild the lungs and life of him?' Certainly his life as a writer brings him neither health nor happiness, and even though Lucy comes to join their strange ménage, Pierre is in a state of total isolation. 'Pierre, nevertheless, in his deepest, highest part, was utterly without sympathy from anything divine, human, brute, or vegetable. One in a city of hundreds of thousands of human beings, Pierre was solitary as at the Pole.' Succumbing to inanition, blindness, and vertigo, he collapses in the city streets one night. The plot terminates when his cousin Glen, having first refused to recognize him as a relation, now accuses him of seducing Lucy and attacks him. Pierre shoots him dead. In his prison cell he and Isabel commit suicide while Lucy appears to die of shock and grief. And thus, fairly gruesomely, ends the life of one of the earliest American writers in fiction.

It is the discovery of the existence of his sister Isabel which starts Pierre on the road to art – and social ruin. She comes, as it were, from the underside of society, and once perceived calls into question all surface truth and accepted names. Throughout she remains a completely mysterious, ambiguous figure for Pierre, and in her person she is like Truth itself in all its elusiveness. From the first glimpse of her face Pierre finds that the world is losing its solidity; the phenomenon is repeatedly referred to. 'On all sides, the physical world of solid objects displaced itself from around him, and he floated into an ether of visions.' Isabel herself finds that the phantasmal and the evidential, to use James's terms, do not occupy their usual separate places in her life. 'Always in me, the

solidest things melt into dreams, and dreams into solidities.' She herself
strikes Pierre as a 'fluid' phenomenon; she seems to his 'dilated senses' to
'swim in an electric fluid', she exists in 'an ever-creeping and condensing
haze of ambiguities'. If you see Isabel as an incarnation of the Reality
under the social surface and its language, then the following two
statements are important. Pierre 'strove to condense her mysterious haze
into some definite and comprehensible shape'. And near the end Isabel
says to him: 'Thy hand is the caster's ladle, Pierre, which holds me
entirely fluid. Into thy forms and slightest moods of thought, thou
pourest me; and I there solidify to that form, and take it on, and
thenceforth wear it, till once more thou mouldest me anew.' This is the
mysterious fluid essence of life itself, telling the artist that it is up to him to
attempt to arrest that fluidity into some temporary form, with the covert
warning that no form *can* ever truly hold that fluidity or solidify and
shape that haze. Paradoxically, Isabel draws Pierre towards serious
literature at the same time as she reveals to him the invalidity of the whole
naming process – she represents 'vital realness' as opposed to 'empty
nominalness'. She is that which must, and cannot, be uttered.

Thus when Pierre takes to writing, and starts to rip off the layers of
deceit which make up the world, he finds only 'surface stratified on
surface. To its axis, the world being nothing but superinduced
superficies'. Writing itself, even at its most sincere, is a doomed pursuit.
'For the more and the more that he wrote, and the deeper and the deeper
that he dived, Pierre saw the everlasting elusiveness of Truth; the
universal lurking insincerity of even the greatest and purest written
thoughts.' Pierre's attempt to write a great modern Inferno is rejected as a
'blasphemous parody' by his publishers, who had wanted a 'popular
novel'. His writing costs Pierre his family, his happiness, his health, and
he becomes a victim, alienated and despised. Nevertheless there is
obviously something daring as well as doomed in Pierre's attempt to
pursue Truth down to its deepest core, and write a literature which
refuses to accept the comfortable surface of things. In a letter to
Hawthorne Melville refers to his delight in 'ontological heroics'; in a less
jocular mood his novel *Pierre* explores just where 'ontological heroics'
will take the contemporary artist who insists on attempting them in his
art. He becomes an exile in his own land, hemmed in by 'ambiguities' as
constricting as the walls of the actual prison where Pierre ends his life,
dispossessed of the solidities of life but not in possession of the fluidity of
Truth.

At one point Pierre reads a strange pamphlet called 'Chronometricals
and Horologicals' by an enigmatic philosopher named Plotinus
Plinlimmon. Chronometrical time is always kept in accordance with the
Greenwich standard, no matter how far afield the ship travels; while

Horological time is the local time scheme which varies from place to place. In terms of the pamphlet, a chronometrical soul – like Christ's – in its intuitions of right and wrong, is always in line with Heavenly truth; but, by the same token, it will 'always be contradicting the mere local standards and watchmaker's brains of this earth'. The pamphlet warns that 'he who finding in himself a chronometrical soul, seeks practically to force that heavenly time upon the earth; in such an attempt he can never succeed . . . he will but array all men's earthly time-keepers against him'. The lesson seems to be 'That in things terrestrial (horological) a man must not be governed by ideas celestial (chronometrical)'. With his ontological heroics, and his 'chronometrical' attempts to reveal absolute truth on earth, Pierre it would seem fails to learn that lesson. On the other hand, for a novelist to capitulate to horological standards is to limit himself to surface appearances and become a monger of lies, as Pierre discovers by reading the popular fiction of his day. (Remember Owen Warland's indifference to his job of clock repairing.) In between the impossible chronometrical and the debased horological it would seem, from Melville's novel, that there is no satisfactory role for a novelist aiming somehow to convey truth to his contemporaries. Notice that at no time does Pierre consider writing the sort of stable analysis of society that Stendhal or George Eliot undertook. His book, we gather, is a long soliloquy, by an 'apparent author-hero' who says such things as: 'Now I drop all humerous or indifferent disguises, and all philosophical pretentions. I own myself a brother of the clod, a child of the Primeval Gloom.' This preferred mode or genre has a prophetic aptness, since American writers have shown a greater liking for the metaphysical monologue than have their European counterparts.

The Marble Faun (1860) is not only Hawthorne's most ambiguous book, but one of the most problem-ridden books ever produced by an American. It reveals ambiguous attitudes towards art, nature, law, religion, passion, Europe, and America – to go no further. Here I just want to consider the uncertain attitude towards art contained in the book. It opens in a sculpture gallery and introduces the four main characters, three of whom are artists. Miriam, of some exotic European descent, is a painter whose pictures lack technical merit but are full of passion and colour. In her own person she is an ungraspable mystery, like those 'images of light' of 'apparent tangibility' which prove to be forever out of reach. In this she is somewhat like Melville's Isabel – the incarnation of some elusive and enigmatic essence of experience. Her works are of two kinds. Those depicting terrible female passions released – Jael driving the nail through the temples of Sisera, Judith and Holofernes, Herodias receiving the head of John the Baptist; and sketches of 'domestic and common scenes' – an infant's shoe, for instance – in all of which she has included a figure 'apart', an observer excluded from the felicity he or she gazes on. This we know to be in line with Hawthorne's own feelings about the isolating apartness of the artist. Miriam's studio is almost totally curtained off from daylight and is seen as the 'outward type of a poet's haunted imagination'. She is indeed an artist of the interiority of the human mind and heart. Hilda, an innocent young American girl, is by contrast an expert copyist. One day she shows Miriam a very felicitous copy of Guido's Beatrice Cenci. She has caught the outward expression perfectly; but Miriam says: 'if I could only get within her consciousness! if I could but clasp Beatrice Cenci's ghost, and draw it into myself!' Such an act of dangerous empathy horrifies Hilda, and this helps to explain her rather strange mid-way position between religion and art.

Hawthorne explains that when Hilda came to Europe she 'lost the impulse of original design' and 'ceased to aim at original achievement'. Hawthorne explains that this is out of a sense of reverence for the great religious paintings of the past; her copying work is thus akin to a religious activity as in all humility she attempts to recapture the religious feeling which produced the originals. But we may note that by restricting herself to copying Hilda safely removes herself from any of the possible dangers involved in the process of artistic creation. Just as she is somehow both in Rome but not touched by it, just so she wants some contact with art, without any of the contamination which to her delicate senses often seems to hover around it. In the geography of the book Rome is often associated with graves, catacombs, cellars, labyrinths, darkness, depths both of time and space, decay, a contagious mistiness, and so on, even while its great beauties are also referred to. Hilda, by contrast, is all too obviously a creature of the upper air, living at the top of a tower, associated with doves and the pure white light, a believer in 'ideality' who disdains all commerce with problematical human passions. She specifically repudiates any belief in the existence of the subterranean when they are discussing the story of Curtius, who reputedly leaped into a chasm which opened in ancient Rome. Thus it is that she simply refuses to have any contact with Miriam after she has unintentionally glimpsed the murder committed by Donatello and Miriam. Hilda stays at the surface and thus produces no original art. If she does not produce any pictures of Judith or Jael, neither does she produce any new pictures of the Madonna or other holy figures. She maintains her 'maiden elevation', and one feels that her resolute virginity, of mind as of body, really cuts her off, or defends her – Hawthorne cannot make up his mind – from any deep appreciation of Rome. She is innocent, cold, pitiless, and to us priggish. For good or bad reasons she effectively abstains from art even while practising it. This is the significance of her being a copyist.

Kenyon may seem to be rather different and more open to Rome. He too believes in the ideality of art – for him everything is an emblem, a symbol, or contains a meaning, a moral, and so on. But the main work he is engaged on is a sculpture of Cleopatra (taken, as Hawthorne admits, from a work done by William Wetmore Story at the time), and this suggests a degree of recognition of the passionate, the carnal, the exotic in human experience. Another of his pieces is of a pearl diver who has become entangled in the weeds at the bottom of the sea, and lies dead among the rare shells he sought. Such a subject might suggest that Kenyon himself might be something of a 'diver' in Melville's terms. But Kenyon is more deceptive than Hilda. At a crucial moment Miriam comes to Kenyon's studio. Her solitude and the miserable secret of her past are weighing so heavily on her that she effectively appeals to him to act as her confidant. Arguably, the desperate act which she implicitly incites Donatello to commit might have been averted if Kenyon had agreed to listen to her, to open himself to her disburdening with full sympathy. But he draws back, and she detects this sudden contraction, his unwillingness to become implicated in her secret past. It is hard to estimate how much irony is intended, but it is fairly devasting. The American artist is there in Rome, working on a large figure of the most voluptuous, passionate, sexually wilful female in history or legend; yet when a real live passionate woman comes to him as if in request of some contact and recognition, he closes himself off. For this artist it is one thing to mould dead images of mythical, legendary, emblematical figures; it is, apparently, quite another to open himself to the disturbing complexities and intensities of actual experience. It is notable that whereas Hilda, in her time of distress, finds a sympathetic confessor in the figure of a Catholic priest though she is not a Catholic, Miriam in her time of distress fails to find a sympathetic confessor in the figure of an American artist, although he is currently engaged in evoking an image of the serpent of old Nile. As Miriam notes, Kenyon's image of the dead pearl diver is 'cold and stern in its moral lesson', and Kenyon himself takes care not to plunge into any depths of human experience. He is no more of a diver than Hilda, and arguably as cold, as moralistic, and as much of a virgin as she. Whereas Donatello and Miriam go beyond the law, and thus enter a whole new dimension of human experience, suffering, insight, atonement, and so on, Kenyon and Hilda stay very securely within what Hawthorne himself refers to as the 'iron rules' which dominate their contemporary life. I would imagine that Kenyon's best piece might have been his bust of Milton.

And yet, of course, Hawthorne is not by any means wholly endorsing this self-protective Puritan kind of artist. He himself refers to 'those dark caverns, into which all men must descend, if they would know anything beneath the surface and illusive pleasures of existence', and clearly he seems to have felt that if an artist was to establish contact with any reality beyond the surface illusions of life he would have to become some kind of Descendantalist. But Kenyon and Hilda will finally have nothing to do with Descendentalism. They remain impermeable to Europe, to a full sense of the darker depths of human experience, and it is fitting that by the end they plan to return home and marry. On the other hand, when Hawthorne wants to justify the role of the artist he does so in terms of idealities rather than depths. 'Yet we love the artists, in every kind . . . They were not wholly confined within the sordid compass of practical life; they had a pursuit which, if followed faithfully out, would lead them to the beautiful . . . Their actual business . . . necessarily illuminated their conversation with something akin to the ideal.' When Hilda is going through her state of depression she all but loses faith in art altogether. The key chapter is called 'The Emptiness of Art Galleries': as she wanders through the galleries of Rome she is touched 'by the icy demon of weariness'. The great Italian religious paintings now seem to her to be repetitive and dead, a lifeless substitution of the artificial for the natural. She looks at them and sees 'but a crust of paint over an emptiness'. Interestingly, only the Flemish masters of domestic realism survive this disenchanted gaze. Their pictures of simple things, offered in all their secular opacity just as things, seem preferable to the false transparencies of those paintings which invite the viewer to look through them to a higher, ideal, religious world. For Hawthorne this preference for the opaque over the transparent is a temporary aberration; for later realists like William Dean Howells it could be the basis of a new aesthetic.

Where Hawthorne is visibly somewhat nervous about introducing his American artists into a Europe in which it was difficult to tell the richness from the rottenness, Henry James found in the situation the perfect theme for the first full release of his genius, *Roderick Hudson* (1876). This novel traces the short career of an American artist who opens himself up fully, indeed greedily, to European experience, with fatal results. Indeed so short is the time between Hudson's first eager impressions of Rome and his fall, which must be considered a suicide, in the Swiss Alps, that James felt he had to apologize for the implausible rapidity of his deterioration. Hudson's 'disintegration', says James in a later preface, occurs too quickly: 'at the rate at which he falls to pieces, he seems to place himself beyond our understanding and sympathy'. Aesthetically, the point is debatable. But the picture of an American artist rather quickly 'falling to pieces' after an initial burst of great creative power is perhaps more appropriate than James realized. It was Scott Fitzgerald who said that the lives of American writers contained no second acts, and there is something almost prophetic in James's picture of an American artist moving at such a pace that he would have no energy left after the crowded first act of his artistic life.

From the beginning, when he is seen as a discontented student of Law in a provincial American town, Hudson is seen as doing 'everything too fast', and he characterizes himself as being driven by a 'demon of unrest'. Upon seeing one of his statues, Rowland Mallett, a rich friend who appreciates art but cannot produce any himself, offers to take Hudson to Europe and become his patron. Mallett is one of James's 'observers' and it is worth noting that James made, thus early, a clear distinction between the artist and the observer. Roderick is depicted as having genius, 'the sacred fire', and it takes him into regions well outside the boundaries of the social law of which he was so imperfect a student. Rowland Mallett has no genius and so, while capable of appreciating art and Italy, he can remain safely within the moral law. There is no doubt that James felt that genius could take a person into dangerous areas in which all conscience might be lost. As Rowland Mallett comes to realize, although genius is divine, it can be 'capricious, sinister, cruel'; and he comes to think of Roderick as a fairly ruthless egotist. His worry about Roderick is that 'the values in such a spirit' might not be 'much larger than the voids', and in the event in this book the voids swallow up the values. The inflamed genius who set out from America ends his life as a hollow husk, burnt out, eclipsed, in a catatonic torpor. His fall from the mountain only completes the process of dying which has completely overtaken his inner life.

To illuminate some aspects of Roderick's doomed career it is helpful to notice the changing subjects of his sculpture. His first piece seen by Rowland is of a youth, standing naked, drinking deeply from a gourd, and it is called 'Thirst'. Rowland asks if the drinker represents an 'idea' or is a 'pointed symbol' and Hudson agrees that his work represents innocence, youth, curiosity, drinking deeply of knowledge, pleasure, and experience. The one thing that Roderick does not mention as being represented by his symbolic work is any actual drink, such as wine. Yet when he gets to Europe he soon discovers the pleasures of real champagne as well as the inspiration of high ideals. Indeed his downfall might be ascribed to a mixture of intoxications in which it becomes impossible for him to separate the ideal from the actual. Roderick's first successes as a sculptor in Italy are his monumental Adam and his Eve – appropriate enough for an American artist. He speaks of going on to do David and 'a ripping Christ' who will be 'the perfection of form . . . to symbolise the perfection of spirit'. In these early days his talk is always about ideas or ideal forms, including a prospective 'magnificent image of my Native Land'. However, at this time he first sees Christina Light, who is for him 'a glimpse of ideal beauty'. If such beauty is wrong, he says, then he is happy to see her as 'the incarnation of evil'. Christina, although nominally American, has been brought up in Europe, and she is another of those disturbingly ambiguous females, such as Melville's Isabel and Hawthorne's Miriam, who seem ultimately as elusive as life itself. She is a mixture of passions while presenting a totally indifferent face to the world; she may be the epitome of corruption, as she herself says, or the finest bloom of a fusion of cultures; she is capable of unpredictable metamorphoses. Roderick is 'intoxicated' by her, while Rowland Mallett thinks her 'unsafe': 'she was a complex, wilful, passionate creature who might easily draw down a too confiding spirit into some strange underworld of unworthy sacrifices, not unfurnished with traces of others lost'. Roderick's idealizing aspirations are discussed in terms of flight and gained altitudes of spirit, but once he has been intoxicated by the sight of Christina, his movement is irreversibly downwards. Rowland sees this happening and has 'a vision of the wondrous youth, graceful and beautiful as he passed, plunging like a diver into a misty gulf. The gulf was destruction, annihilation, death . . .'

After getting to know Christina, Roderick's art changes. He does a sculpture of a woman leaning back in a languid pose. Rowland, still the good New Englander, asks 'What does it mean?' Roderick for the first time disdains the notion of some extra dimension of ideal meaning. 'Anything you please,' he says, 'A "Lady conversing affably with a Gentleman".' It is a totally secular piece, opaque to higher meanings, and not surprisingly Rowland is not sure that he likes it. Roderick's bust of Christina Light has more depth, but it reminds another artist, the perceptive Gloriani, of Salome. Roderick's art is now penetrating into the mystery of the dangerous and destructive female. He is beginning to dive. At this point a pompous American named Mr Leavenworth comes to him and asks him to do a representation of the idea of Intellectual Refinement. To be fair, the younger Roderick would have seen nothing ridiculous in so abstract a commission, but Mr Leavenworth becomes for him a stifling and tedious presence chattering on about 'spiritual art'. One of Roderick's next pieces is of 'a *lazzarone* lounging in the sun' (i.e. one of the lowest class of beggars in Naples). Mr Leavenworth happens to come in and ask if it is something in the style of the Dying Gladiator. ' "Oh no," said Roderick seriously, "he's not dying, he's only drunk." ' The righteous Mr Leavenworth reproves him. 'Ah, but intoxication, you know . . . is not a proper subject for sculpture. Sculpture shouldn't deal with transitory attitudes.' Roderick has the better of the exchange, but a potentially serious point is being made. In a way Roderick has turned his attention from the eternal to the transitory, and the difference in his statues between the upstanding unfallen Adam and the prone drunken beggar (even though the figure is 'subtly idealised') does offer an analogue for his own artistic life. Gloriani more than once speaks of Roderick's coming down to earth, and in truth Roderick is more and more often seen lying down. More seriously, he is now totally 'intoxicated' with things of this world. His eye is no longer on Platonic ideas or eternal types; it is turned earthwards, into the bedevilling compounds of actual life. It is perhaps this which enables him to do such a touching and truthful bust of his mother for what is his last-mentioned work. Not Adam and Eve, our biblical or mythical parents, but his actual individual parent – this again indicates the change which has come over Roderick's art.

In his feeling of adoration for Christina Roderick goes beyond socially recognized good and evil; when she withdraws from him he cannot return to a form of life governed by those categories. He can only collapse into apathy and die. Where Kenyon closed himself off to the dangers of Miriam and was able to return intact to America, Roderick opens himself up to the ambivalence of Christina and ends up dead at the bottom of a Swiss gorge. One general point made about Roderick summarizes something important about the American artist. As Rowland sees Roderick: 'the great and characteristic point with him was the perfect separateness of his sensibility. He never saw himself as part of a whole; only as the clear-cut, sharp-edged, isolated individual, rejoicing or raging, as the case might be, but needing in any case absolutely to affirm himself.' A perfectly separate sensibility is one which cannot truly be socialized; the affirmation of the artist self is inseparable from its isolation, perhaps finally from its destruction – these are two propositions which James's novel may fairly be said to bear out. The difficulty for the artist to see himself as 'part of a whole' is not restricted to Americans, but it seems to have remained for American artists a more constant problem. It is relevant to note that a perfectly separate self is unlikely to be in harmony with the democratic *en masse*.

I will mention more briefly three American artists as they are depicted by novelists associated with the decades of American realism, and in each case I want to point to the element of unease, if not sickness and self-destructiveness, that seems to be inextricably associated with the practice of their art. Stephen Crane's painter Hawker, in his slight novella *The Third Violet* (1897), is at odds with everyone and everything – himself, his friends, his art, his world. His trouble may simply be frustrated love. Still, consider this description of him painting one of his contemporary landscapes.

> He seemed engaged in some kind of a duel. His hair dishevelled, his eyes gleaming, he was in a deadly scuffle. In the sketches was the landscape of heavy blue, as if seen through powder-smoke, and all the skies burned red. There was in these notes a sinister quality of hopelessness, eloquent of defeat, as if the scene

represented the last hour on a field of disastrous battle. Hawker seemed
attacking with this picture something fair and beautiful of his own life, a
possession of his mind, and he did it fiercely, mercilessly, formidably. His arm
moved with the energy of a strange wrath. He might have been thrusting with
a sword.

He paints 'like a man who is killing'. Allowing that Crane was obsessed
by man's aggressive and destructive impulses, it is interesting that when
he came to depict an American artist, he showed those impulses at work
in and through his art.

Turning to Jack London's *Martin Eden* (1909), it is perhaps surprising
to find that in London's fictionalized account of his own struggle to
successful authorship and its result, we discover a conclusion quite similar
to that of *Roderick Hudson*. Martin Eden is a man whose artistic
aspirations are mixed up with his social aspirations. The book opens with
his stumbling, awed entry into a cultured middle-class home: he longs to
be admitted to this world. But at dinner his memory takes him back to
the world of fighting and drinking in which he spent his youth. As
Martin rises socially, he keeps 'seeing himself down all his past', a violent
past of raw struggles and basic satisfactions. Believing vaguely in
evolution, he regards those early days as a regression to the primordial
slime in which he and his companions were 'animals, brute-beasts'. But
although he enjoys the struggle to break into cultured society, once
successful he finds that he has lost reality somewhere along the way and
he becomes totally alienated. His vitality ebbs and, as with Roderick
Hudson, a great torpor settles over him, and he commits suicide. But
there are significant things to note about his work and his terminal
sickness. 'His work was realism, though he had endeavoured to fuse it
with the fancies and beauties of imagination. What he sought was an
impassioned realism, shot through with human aspiration and faith.
What he wanted was life as it was, with all its spirit-groping and soul-
searching left in.' He starts by writing about his own experience of
whaling, and interestingly enough he does a piece on 'pearl diving'. In his
essay on the theory of the novel entitled 'God and Clod' he attacks the
God school of writers for denying man's earthly origin, and the Clod
school for denying man's 'heaven-sent dreams and divine possibilities'.
He himself attempts to combine these extremes in a new form of realism
– another version of the attempt to mediate between the romantic and
the real, the transparent and the opaque. If some of his writing is clumsy
then it is 'the clumsiness of too great strength'. A lot of this immense
personal strength goes into his art, but a lot also goes into his ferocious
'individualism'. This fierce individuality, like Roderick Hudson's,
produces the need 'absolutely to affirm himself', and it brings him social
success: but it also finally brings him isolation and alienation from

everything. At the end he knows he is 'sick', mentally not physically. 'All the life that was in him was fading, fainting, making towards death.' Finding himself increasingly desirous of sleep, he takes one more sea voyage in an attempt to bestir himself. However, his great will-power, which had been the driving force behind his artistic and social success, now turns on itself: 'he had will, – ay, will strong enough that with one last exertion it could destroy itself and cease to be'. His values have become voids, and, having spent a life aspiring in art and climbing in society, he suddenly reverses the whole process by jumping overboard and swimming downwards to his death – another ambiguous and fatal dive by an American artist.

Theodore Dreiser's Eugene Witla in *The Genius* (1915) also struggles to escape or avoid the limitations of society and the circumscriptions of convention. 'For a given order of society no doubt he was out of place – for life in general, he could not say.' Like Martin Eden, he has a boundless energy which struggles to break out of a narrow social background and achieve success through art. For Eugene, artistic, sexual, and business success are all intertwined and confused. Different periods of success in each activity alternate with periods of failure and sickness, nervous breakdowns and torpor being the other side of his determined energy of expansion and achievement. One result of the energy of expansion he possesses is that he feels that he is somehow beyond, or exempt from, the common versions of values and ideas. 'With Eugene convention meant nothing at all, and his sense of evil and good was something which the ordinary person would not have comprehended.' 'He was always thinking in his private conscience that life was somehow bigger and subtler and darker than any given theory or order of living.' In his art this takes him forward to a vivid appreciation of the hidden beauty and power of apparent urban ugliness. One of his early successes is a brutal picture of an ugly negro emptying garbage into an ash cart (probably an allusion to the so-called Ash Can School of painting), and his pictures seem positively to attack conventional people with the realities they have ignored. Thus another of his pictures 'fairly shouted its facts . . . And there was no apologising for anything in it, no glossing anything over. Bang! Smash! Crack! came the facts one after another, with a bitter brutal insistence on their so-ness.' This is opaque art at its most extreme, and yet even here we read that 'everything he touched seemed to have romance and beauty, and yet it was real and mostly grim and shabby'. The Clod school will not renounce all dealings with the God outlook. In his life this energy to drive beyond conventions and accepted structures takes Eugene, after many affairs, the death of his wife, business failures, and bouts of morbidity and sickness, to a final isolation – seemingly beyond all his earlier heated engagements with society. He is finally recognized as a great artist, though considered strange and eccentric. In the last scene he is brooding over a passage in Herbert Spencer about the overwhelming thought of 'infinite space'. After seeing his little daughter to bed, he goes outside and gazes up into 'the sparkling deeps of space'. It is an appropriate posture for the American artist, even one who is nominally a social realist. For the American artist has ever felt more at home in unsocialized space than within any social order, just as he has usually preferred to feel himself to be working according to chronometrical rather than horological time.

This has been of necessity only a preliminary exploration and, as such, it will hardly justify any grand generalized conclusions. It does seem, going by the American novelist's own fictional version of the situation of the American artist, that whether the artist embarks on romantic or realistic work, he inevitably ends up isolated; any pursuit of reality and truth through art seems inexorably to take him beyond the laws and conventions of his contemporaries and forces him to abandon the communal structure of consciousness. It seems that from the start the American novelist has betrayed an instinct that there can finally be no such thing as socialized art, and thus perhaps no such person as a socialized artist. At the same time there is no sign from his fictional artists that the practice of their art affords any lasting compensatory consolations or confidence. To conclude we may return to Hawthorne. At the end of the 'Custom-House' chapter, Hawthorne, ever defensive, leaves the reader with this rather odd speculation. 'It may be, however, – O, transporting and triumphant thought! – that the great-grand-children of the present race may sometimes think kindly of the scribbler of bygone days, when the antiquary of days to come, among the sites memorable in the town's history, shall point out the locality of THE TOWN-PUMP.' When Mark Twain was at his most popular he wrote to William Dean Howells: 'Yes, high and fine literature is wine, and mine is only water; but everybody likes water.' Yet there is strong evidence that he disliked the public which applauded him and required him, as he said, 'to paint himself striped and stand on his head every fifteen minutes'. By the end of his life this one-time demotic hero had become a bitter misanthropist, as alienated from his society as many of the fictional artists we have considered. Looking at the solitude and fate of figures like Pierre Glendinning, Roderick Hudson, Martin Eden, Eugene Witla, we may perhaps feel that the American novelist has often wondered whether the American artist can ever be so socially central, so obviously indispensable, as the town pump; or whether, scorning to be simply a supplier of popular water, his own higher outpourings will make him forever 'a citizen of somewhere else'.

4

James on Hawthorne

'Exposed late in life to European influences, Mr. Hawthorne was but superficially affected by them – far less so than would be the case with a mind of the same temper growing up among us today. We seem to see him strolling through churches and galleries as the last pure American – attesting by his shy responses to dark canvas and cold marble his loyalty to a simpler and less encumbered civilization.' That was how James concluded his first piece of writing on Hawthorne – a review of his *French and Italian Note-Books* which appeared in 1872. James was twenty-eight at the time and was very eager to return to Europe and pursue the vocation of novelist which he had already decided on. A month before writing this review he had written a letter to Charles Eliot Norton stressing his desire to get back to Europe, at the same time admitting that he might well be exaggerating 'the merits of Europe'. To quote some now famous lines: 'It's the same world there after all and Italy isn't the absolute any more than Massachusetts. It's a complex fate, being an American, and one of the responsibilities it entails is fighting against a superstitious valuation of Europe.'

This self-cautioning note is fairly prophetic if you consider that, at the time, James had written nothing more probing than *Watch and Ward*. But caution was not uppermost in his mind in 1872 and he was desperately keen to immerse himself in the almost inexhaustible wealth of material which Europe offered. This determination really to expose himself to Europe explains the rather patronizing tone of his review of Hawthorne. 'Excessively detached Mr. Hawthorne remains, from the first, from Continental life, touching it throughout mistrustfully, shrinkingly, and at the rare points at which he had, for the time, unlearned his nationality . . . He walks about bending a puzzled, ineffective gaze at things . . . There seems from the first to have been nothing inflammable in his perception of things; there was a comfortable want of *eagerness* in his mind.' One can see James forming his own resolutions in these somewhat condescending comments on Hawthorne's limited capacities of response. He, James, would not be mistrustful, shrinking, puzzled and ineffective; on the contrary, *he* intended to be open, eager, 'inflammable in his perceptions'. It is as though by 'placing' his great predecessor James was tentatively marking out the territory he intended to claim as his own. Hawthorne had not explored the 'complex fate' of being an American in Europe: James already leaves the readers of his review with the intimation that he would. And of course he did. But by distinguishing between himself and Hawthorne thus early in his career James by no means severed his connections either with the man or his work. It is entirely appropriate that his first important short story on the international theme and the first novel he wrote about an American in Europe both show a very clear debt to Hawthorne. The short story, 'The Passionate Pilgrim', was based on an incident that Hawthorne had related in 'Consular Experiences', one of the essays in *Our Old Home*. There he tells how a penniless American had entered the consular office in Liverpool one day, and adds: 'Like a great many other Americans he had long cherished a fantastic notion that he was one of the rightful heirs of a rich English estate.' James's story explores just such a case. Similarly, *Roderick Hudson* owes its setting – Rome – and the rudiments of its theme – the expatriate American artist – to Hawthorne's last novel, *The Marble Faun*. And James's debt to Hawthorne did not diminish with the years: in matters of subject, theme, and even technique (particularly with regard to the symbolism in James's late work) the influence of Hawthorne is pervasive. It is quite arguable, indeed, that no other writer influenced James more. And so far from putting the figure of Hawthorne behind him once and for all when he went to live in Europe, James constantly returned to him, revaluing his works, reassessing his significance, rewording his own interpretation of the man. For it was only part of the truth for James to describe Hawthorne as 'the last pure American': he was also something rather more complex – the first American novelist. And in turning to reconsider the example of Hawthorne so often (I have in mind at least five more important references, which I will mention), James reveals his life-long preoccupation with the problem, not just of being an artist in America, but of being an American artist.

In every one of his redefinitions of Hawthorne, James is making, indirectly or implicitly, a further essay in self-definition. It is one of these rare felicities of literary history that in 1878 James was invited to write a critical biography of Hawthorne, for the resulting work not only remains one of the most brilliant short studies of Hawthorne we have, it

also affords us an invaluable insight into the mind and feelings of Henry
James at the very moment when he was about to embark on twenty-five
years of fiction writing in Europe which would establish him as one of
the greatest of modern novelists. In looking back at Hawthorne, James is
at the same time looking forward to the great works he was already
confident of writing; the book is vibrant with a sense of achievements to
come. Less than two years later James published *The Portrait of a Lady*.

Considering how little James had actually written at the time (1878), it
is rather remarkable that he should have been invited to contribute to
what was a distinguished series, namely *English Men of Letters*. The series
was being run by John Morley, who had already secured contributions
from such famous people as Anthony Trollope, Leslie Stephen, Edmund
Gosse, and J. A. Symonds; and although he had met James socially it must
have seemed a rather singular step to invite this relatively unknown
American into such company. Perhaps the reason was that Hawthorne
was the only American writer to be included in the twenty-nine titles and
Morley felt that James's intimate and recent knowledge of New England
admirably qualified him to evoke and assess his famous fellow
countryman. In any event, he could not have made a happier choice, and
James's contribution to the series will surely outlive all the others.
However, it is worth bearing in mind when reading the book the
circumstances in which it was written. James had only recently (1876)
decided to settle permanently in London; he was still very keen to gain
some sort of recognition and prestige in English society and John
Morley's invitation must have struck him not only as a great honour but
as a fine opportunity. An opportunity, above all perhaps, to reveal and
demonstrate his own superior understanding of, and sympathy with, the
mysteries of European society, the traditions of European art. Put it this
way: if James could 'place' Hawthorne and Hawthorne's America as
'provincial', then, by the same token he, James, must have transcended
that provinciality. Not, I am convinced, that James adopted attitudes
which were not at the same time his most sincere convictions; but it *is*
worth remembering that the book was addressed primarily to an English
audience.

The point is worth making with some care because one of the main
American criticisms of the book – understandably enough – was that it
went too far in overstressing the provinciality of Hawthorne and
America. In a famous review of the book William Dean Howells made
some fair objections in his usual temperate way:

> If it is not provincial for an Englishman to be English, or a Frenchman French,
> then it is not so for an American to be American; and if Hawthorne was
> 'exquisitely provincial', one had better take one's chance of universality with
> him than with almost any Londoner or Parisian of the time. Provinciality, we

> understand it, is a thing of the mind or soul; but if it is a thing of the experiences, then that is another matter.

James certainly goes out of his way to assert the provinciality not only of Hawthorne but of almost every other American writer mentioned in his book – Poe, Emerson, Thoreau, for example; and when he makes his famous list of all that American writers lack, which ends with 'no sporting class – no Epsom or Ascot!', any present-day reader will feel a good deal of sympathy with Howells's objections. Howells's answer is worth quoting at length, since it serves to bring into focus a crucial issue in the history of American fiction.

> After leaving out all those novelistic 'properties', as sovereigns, courts, aristocracy, gentry, castles, cottages, cathedrals, abbeys, universities, museums, political class, Epsoms, and Ascots, by the absence of which Mr. James suggests our poverty to the English conception, we have the whole of human life remaining, and a social structure presenting the only fresh and novel opportunities left to fiction, opportunities manifold and inexhaustible. No man would have known less what to do with that dreary and worn-out paraphernalia than Hawthorne.

Howells is here adopting a classic American stance in insisting that wherever there is human life art can flourish and that, so far from nourishing literature, the burdens of an old society and the accretions of a long history may well hamper and depress it. James had adopted an entirely opposite point of view by affirming at the very outset of his book on Hawthorne that 'the moral is that the flower of art blooms only where the soil is deep, that it takes a great deal of history to produce a little literature, that it needs a complex machinery to set a writer in motion'. Implicitly, indeed almost explicitly, this suggested that America was all but incapable of producing major literature as yet. Howells, the great encourager of and spokesman for an emerging American literature, could scarcely be expected to accept James's axioms. In replying to Howells's review James made his position, if anything, clearer, and it is worth quoting at length from the letter (31 January 1880) since it makes an interesting supplement to what he says in the book.

> Your review of my book is very handsome and friendly and commands my liveliest gratitude. Of course your graceful strictures seem to yourself more valid than they do to me. The little book was a tolerably deliberate and meditated performance, and I should be prepared to do battle for most of the convictions expressed. It is quite true I use the word provincial too many times – I hated myself for't, even while I did it (just as I overdo the epithet 'dusky'). But I don't at all agree with you in thinking that 'if it is not provincial for an Englishman to be English, a Frenchman French, etc. so it is not provincial for an American to be American'. So it is not provincial for a Russian, an Australian, a Portugese, a Dane, a Laplander, to savour of their respective

countries: that would be where the argument would land you. I think it is extremely provincial for a Russian to be very Russian, a Portugese very Portugese; for the simple reason that certain national types are essentially and intrinsically provincial. I sympathize even less with your protest against the idea that it takes an old civilization to set a novelist in motion – a proposition that seems to me so true as to be a truism. It is on manners, usages, habits, forms, upon all these things matured and established, that a novelist lives – they are the very stuff his work is made of; and in saying that in the absence of those 'dreary and worn-out paraphernalia' which I enumerate as being wanted in American society, 'we have simply the whole of human life left', you beg (to my sense) the question. I should say we had just so much less of it as these same 'paraphernalia' represent, and I think they represent an enormous quantity of it. I shall feel refuted only when we have produced (setting the present high company – yourself and me – for obvious reasons apart) a gentleman who strikes me as a novelist – as belonging to the company of Balzac and Thackeray.

James's ambition at the time was to be a novelist in the European manner – hence his reference to Balzac and Thackeray – and his high claims for European society were based on a feeling, not that it was morally superior to America, but that it was more complex, more stimulating, and thus more nutritive for the aspiring novelist. He did not believe that 'human life' was some abstract essence which could be seen and grasped in separation from the diverse forms in which it manifested itself. And those forms were, simply, society. 'We know a man imperfectly until we know his society', he said in a later essay on Emerson. The richer and denser the society, the greater the number of potential sources of knowledge. James's case against America was not based on any notion that it was somehow intellectually backward or morally inferior to Europe (quite the contrary indeed); it was rather that, as a novelist, he found it comparatively empty. In that same essay on Emerson (published 1887) James spoke of the curious fate of 'the primitive New England character' and 'its queer search for something to expend itself upon'. If you consider that character and the thin society in which it had its being, James went on, you get 'the impression of a conscience gasping in the void, panting for sensations, with something of the movement of a landed fish'. Where America was a void, Europe was a plentitude, or, to follow his own imagery, it was an ocean in which the gasping American conscience could at least find an element to swim in. That a person, particularly an American, might well drown in those deep and dangerous waters was a part of James's sense of the complexity of the American fate. But as a novelist he clearly felt that there was more to be learned from a swimming fish than from a landed one.

I have stressed this matter because in order to appreciate the full significance of James's little book on Hawthorne one must see it in the light of James's own recent decision. He was an aspiring American novelist who had decided that he must seek his stimuli and material in Europe; and he was writing about the one manifestly great American novelist to date who had operated on quite contrary convictions and who had, in fact, not even visited Europe until he was forty-nine, when his major works were already written. More than that, he was writing about the one American writer for whom he had a great respect. Emerson, Thoreau, even Poe had, he felt, comparatively little to give him no matter how benevolently he regarded them; and it was only years later that he came to love the work of Walt Whitman. Hawthorne was the one man above all others with whom he had to come to terms. And if there is something a little patronizing and condescending at times in his remarks about Hawthorne – and there is – we should see this as, in part, an indirect attempt to justify the different path he had elected to follow as a young American novelist.

Thus it is that he continually stresses the 'dreariness' and 'aridity' of Hawthorne's environment, and he starts his book by insisting that Hawthorne's own life was 'deficient in incident', 'simple', 'unagitated', 'provincial'. To establish this image of a genius starved of adequate material to work on, James quotes passages in which Hawthorne depicts himself in this very light. Thus: 'No author, without a trial, can conceive of the difficulty of writing a romance about a country where there is no shadow, no antiquity, no mystery, no picturesque and gloomy wrong, nor anything but a commonplace prosperity, in broad and simple daylight, as is happily the case in my dear native land.' And again: 'I have another great difficulty in the lack of materials; for I have seen so little of the world that I have nothing but thin air to concoct my stories of . . .' And having established the picture of a genius starved in America, James goes on to imply that when Hawthorne did finally get to Europe he was too old to take advantage of what it offered. Thus, commenting on Hawthorne's book on England (*Our Old Home*) James says: 'It is the work of an outsider, of a stranger, of a man who remains to the end a mere spectator (something less even than an observer), and always lacks the final initiation into the manners and nature of a people of whom it may be said, among all the people of the earth, that to know them is to make discoveries.' The implication is clear: James himself had come to an early realization of the paucity of material in America and had removed himself to Europe at the right age to partake of what he later called 'the banquet of initiation'. In such ways do we see James quietly justifying himself while sympathetically outlining the difficulties Hawthorne faced as an artist in America.

But if the book were merely a covert *apologia pro vita sua* it would be far less interesting and profound than in fact it is. For one thing, James blatantly contradicts himself as to the value of Europe for an American artist, as when he says: 'Hawthorne forfeited a precious advantage in ceasing to tread his native soil. Half the virtue in *The Scarlet Letter* and *The House of the Seven Gables* is in their local quality; they are impregnated with the New England air.' Perhaps then Hawthorne was at his best when he was most 'provincial'? Another interesting oscillation can be detected in James's assessment of Hawthorne's work as a whole. On the one hand he effectively deprecates it by continually attaching to it such epithets as 'charming', 'exquisite', 'soft', 'simple', 'pure', 'natural', 'spontaneous', 'childlike', and so on – as though to emphasize that Hawthorne's work was as innocent and simple as the land it emerged from. On the other hand many of his most brilliant comments reveal that he was far from unaware of the troubling depths in Hawthorne's work; as when he says of his imagination that it was 'always engaged in a game of hide-and-seek in the region in which it seemed to him that the game could best be played – among the shadows and substructions, the dark-based pillars and supports of our moral nature'. He credits Hawthorne, rightly, with 'a haunting care for moral problems' and sums up by saying, 'Man's conscience was his theme.' Such insights as these reveal that James was at least half aware of those elements in Hawthorne's work which were carried over into his own; for surely the above remarks would perfectly fit much of James's own fiction. To mention only one more interesting contradiction, James at one point speaks disparagingly of allegory and the use of symbols – we must not forget that at the time he was trying to emulate the great European Realists; and yet he can go on to praise some of Hawthorne's allegorical works with the following penetrating words: 'The charm is that they are glimpses of a great field, of the whole deep mystery of man's soul and conscience. They are moral, and their interest is moral; they deal with something more than the mere accidents and conventionalities, the surface occurrences of life. The fine thing in Hawthorne is that he cared for the deeper psychology.' It is surely no very 'childlike' writer who has 'a haunting care for moral problems' and 'the deeper psychology'. It is, rather, a writer very like James himself, whose own major novels were attempts to fathom 'the whole deep mystery of man's soul and conscience'. It is worth remembering that James's own late work tended increasingly towards allegory, and a use of symbols very close to the manner in which he said Hawthorne used them, namely, as 'images which shall place themselves in picturesque correspondence with the spiritual facts with which he is concerned'. It is not the least remarkable thing about this book that while it seeks to establish the limitations of Hawthorne's art, it provides us with brilliantly appropriate terms in which to discuss James's own subsequent achievement. When James finally emerged as a great novelist, it was as a novelist much more in the manner of Hawthorne than of Balzac or Thackeray.

What James was really doing in this book was attempting to explore and articulate three matters of urgent interest to him: roughly, the status of America, the peculiar psychology of the American individual, and the problems of the American artist. America he saw, as many other writers did in the nineteenth century, as a new Eden. It was 'nature' unscarred – or unenriched – by history and the deposits of time. And even American nature is seen by him as crude, immature, and juvenile. This idea is reinforced by constant use of images drawn from agriculture and horticulture. Even Hawthorne's most complex works are repeatedly referred to as 'flowers' springing from such unlikely places as 'Salem puddles' or 'the blossomless garden of American journalism'. The feeling James conveys is that nothing happens according to the dictates of human art and artifice in America; whatever crops up is a spontaneous eruption from innocent old mother earth. The force and relevance of all these images become apparent when James considers the Civil War. If America had been a paradise, this was when the American Adam fell. The passage is justly famous:

> The subsidence of that great convulsion has left a different tone from the tone it found, and one may say that the Civil War marks an era in the history of the American mind. It introduced into the national consciousness a certain sense of proportion and relation, of the world being a more complicated place than it had hitherto seemed, the future more treacherous, success more difficult . . . the good American, in days to come, will be a more critical person than his complacent and confident grandfather. He has eaten of the tree of knowledge. He will not, I think, be a sceptic, and still less, of course, a cynic; but he will be, without discredit to his well known capacity for action, an observer.

One of the reasons why James continually plays down the sombre and tragic aspects of Hawthorne's work was this semi-mythic view of America. If pre-Civil-War America was innocent and simple then even its greatest artist, Hawthorne, must have been basically innocent and simple too. Not that James ever proposes such a crude piece of pseudo-logic, but some such hidden feeling is surely behind such designations of Hawthorne as 'childlike' and the last of 'the more primitive type of man of letters', 'the last pure American'. That James knew very well, or at least felt very well, that he was something else a good deal more profound, we have already seen. But when we are surprised by James's continual insistence on the sportive, playful, and essentially light-hearted nature of Hawthorne's work we should bear in mind this prevailing notion of the almost prelapsarian status enjoyed by pre-Civil-War America.

If this was America, what was the American? Here James fastens on two very important keys – self-consciousness and individualism. It might seem like one of the many wonderfully witty turns of phrase in the book when James remarks that Hawthorne was born on that very day when 'the great Republic enjoys her acutest fit of self-consciousness' (i.e.

Independence Day, 4 July), but, whether deliberately or not, he is adumbrating one of the main themes of the book. Thus near the very end he returns to a serious consideration of Hawthorne's 'exaggerated, painful, morbid national consciousness' and goes on to generalize: 'It is, I think, an indisputable fact that Americans are, as Americans, the most self-conscious people in the world . . . They are conscious of being the youngest of the great nations, of not being in the European family, of being placed on the circumference of civilisation rather than at the centre, of the experimental element not having as yet entirely dropped out of their great political undertaking.' That is to say that for the American a rather disturbing sense of 'relativity' has replaced 'that quiet and comfortable sense of the absolute' enjoyed, for example, by the English. The same point is made when he is discussing 'the importance of the individual in the American world'. Here again James can be seen to be clarifying a clue to the national differences which he was keenly pursuing. 'The individual counts for more, as it were, and, thanks to the absence of a variety of social types and of settled heads under which he may be easily and conveniently pigeon-holed, he is to a certain extent a wonder and a mystery.' People in Europe, he goes on, have their 'standards fixed by the general consent of the society' in which they live: they are comfortable and assured because when they must judge something they have only to consult the prevailing standards of the society around them. But the American has not this advantage – hence his 'agitated conscience', hence his 'isolated sense of moral responsibility'. One may note in passing how perfectly appropriate those terms would be in any discussion of James's main American protagonists, from Isabel Archer to Lambert Stretcher and Maggie Verver. This is what I meant by suggesting that within the compass of this small book James is in fact exploring his feelings about his country and his countrymen (and women) with a cogency, a freshness, a directness (and a wit) which are extremely illuminating when we turn back to the greater complexity and impersonality of his major novels.

But of course above all James is fascinated by the figure of Hawthorne as the American artist. Given that great empty innocent country, how did an artist of Hawthorne's calibre emerge? In an attempt to get at what I think is the most important thing in Hawthorne for James, let me just mention again the letter he wrote to Howells in which he admitted using the word 'provincial' to excess (I have counted eight occasions), but added in parenthesis that he also overdid the epithet 'dusky'. He does indeed use it at least eleven times and this is of particular interest because 'dusky' was in fact one of Hawthorne's key words (indeed, the word first appears in this book in a quotation from Hawthorne, which is most apt). I single this out as a clue to James's feelings about Hawthorne, because

James habitually described America as being, as it were, *all* light – bright, glaring, and unsubtle. 'In the light, fresh American air, unthickened and undarkened by customs and institutions . . .' – there are many such phrases. More to the point, he extended this image of shadowless light to the minds of many American writers and thinkers, particularly the Transcendentalists. But not to Hawthorne: for Hawthorne was more at his ease in darkness. One example: when James imagines Hawthorne's reaction to Margaret Fuller, a woman 'in whose intellect high noon seemed ever to reign, as twilight did in his own. He must have been struck with the glare of her understanding, and, mentally speaking, have scowled and blinked a good deal in conversation with her.' (Interestingly enough Henry James Senior uses much the same image for Hawthorne in one of his letters describing Hawthorne in society with other New England writers: 'it was so pathetic to see him, contented sprawling Concord owl that he was and always has been, brought blindfold into that brilliant daylight and expected to wink and be lively'.) Art of course cannot be made out of unclouded, unrefracted light; it must have contrast, darkness, chiaroscuro. And Hawthorne had found the necessary darkness, found it in his Puritan heritage. So James remarks on

> how the imagination, in this capital son of the old Puritans, reflected the hue of the more purely moral part, of the *dusky, overshadowed* conscience. The conscience, by no fault of its own, in every genuine offshoot of that *sombre* lineage, lay under the *shadow* of the sense of *sin*. This *darkening* cloud was no essential part of the nature of the individual; it stood fixed in the general moral heaven under which he grew up and looked at life. It projected from above, from outside, a *black* patch over his spirit, and it was for him to do what he could with the *black* patch.

James himself italicized 'sin' but I have taken the liberty of adding the others to point out that James traced Hawthorne's achievement back to the fact that he had capitalized on the darkness latent in America's Puritan history and heritage.

It is true that James continually tries to deny Hawthorne an ultimate seriousness, refusing to see him as a tragic writer or a pessimist or even a writer of gloomy stories. Instead he suggests that Hawthorne, as it were, played with darkness, and made the 'heavy moral burden' of the past 'evaporate in the light and charming fumes of artistic fiction'. One reason for this attitude is that James, at the time, considered allegory and symbolism as comparatively light sport compared with the laborious and meticulous social soundings of the great Realists. I have already tried to suggest some others. The important fact remains that in trying to account for Hawthorne's emergence as the first major American novelist James fastened on his sense of moral guilt, his awareness of evil knowledge, his feeling for all the darkness in people and places and things. And it was just such a feeling that made James himself a great novelist. His 'overdoing' of the word 'dusky' is merely symptomatic of a more interesting and significant aspect of this book – that whenever James thinks of Hawthorne he sees him as a man with a sense of darkness in a country of too much light.

Let me make what seems to me the most important point about the book once more. James at the time not only wanted to justify his move to Europe; he was genuinely aspiring to become a novelist of concrete social detail like the great Realists he mentions, Balzac and Thackeray. This accounts for some of his rather odd comments in the book, as for instance when he compares *The Scarlet Letter* with a very minor English novel, *Adam Blair*, by John Gibson Lockhart. Note the terms he uses: 'Lockhart was a dense, substantial Briton, with a taste for the concrete, and Hawthorne was a thin New Englander, with a miasmatic conscience.' James had 'British' ambitions at the time, and indeed much of his work is far more concrete than Hawthorne's. But James knew even then that it was Hawthorne's 'miasmatic conscience' that made him a great writer. What he could not perhaps foresee was that he too would be praised, not for his handling of the concrete, but for his knowledge of the conscience: 'the historian of fine consciences' Conrad was to call him. Even at this time James admired Hawthorne more perhaps than he implies, and he certainly had deep temperamental affinities with him which we can sense even when James is apparently most detached and critical. And sometimes, indeed, the deeply understanding sympathy reveals itself in memorable words, as when he compares Hawthorne to Emerson, a writer with whom James had little affinity. 'Emerson, as a sort of spiritual sun-worshipper, could have attached but a moderate value to Hawthorne's cat-like faculty of seeing in the dark.' It was just such a faculty, more than any 'British' mastery of the concretions of society, that would make James what he was to become – an unmistakably great, and an unmistakably American, novelist. A novelist who, as this little book beautifully if unconsciously reveals, owed his greatest debt not to Balzac but to Nathaniel Hawthorne.

This is not the place to go into a full account of James's debt to Hawthorne. One may note, however, one or two of the more obvious points where James's comments on Hawthorne's work seem especially relevant to his own fiction. For example when he describes the figure of Coverdale in *The Blithedale Romance*: 'Coverdale is a picture of the contemplative, observant, analytic nature, nursing its fancies . . . a portrait of a man, in a word, whose passions are slender, whose imagination is active, and whose happiness lies, not in doing, but in perceiving – half a poet, half a critic, and all a spectator.' How many Jamesian figures those words could apply to; they are relevant even to

James himself! Then again, when he praises *The Marble Faun* for its close study of the moral relationships between 'four people' and says about Hilda: 'She has done no wrong, and yet wrong-doing has become a part of her experience, and she carries the weight of her detested knowledge upon her heart' – is it not possible to discern the outlines of the situation in *The Golden Bowl* and the plight of Maggie Verver? Other critics have noted significant thematic resemblances between the work of the two men; thus James's famous 'Beast in the Jungle' may be compared with Hawthorne's 'The Christmas Banquet', for both are studies of men whose tragedy is that they never suffer because they are incapable of genuine human feeling. More generally, James's most basic theme – the evil of manipulating, exploiting, and appropriating other people – is certainly adumbrated in Hawthorne's suggestion that 'the Unpardonable Sin might consist in a want of love and reverence for the Human Soul'. But for the remainder of this chapter I think it will be more useful if I draw attention to some of James's subsequent statements about Hawthorne, if only to show how constantly the figure of Hawthorne recurred in James's thinking.

In 1897 Charles Dudley Warner asked James to contribute an introduction to Volume XII of an anthology, *Library of the World's Best Literature*, which included some extracts from Hawthorne. And in the essay which James submitted there was a notable change of emphasis in his attitude to Hawthorne. There is little or no reference to all the material that Hawthorne lacked by being in America: on the contrary he was 'happy in an appetite that could often find a feast in meagre materials'. The note of condescension has all but vanished (though he manages to imply that ultimately there was something of a 'dilettante' about Hawthorne), and James goes much more directly to the dark sources of Hawthorne's genius. The Puritan imagination, he says, was able to make a great deal 'of the spiritual contortions, the darkened outlook, of the ingrained sense of sin, of evil, and of responsibility'. So Hawthorne could find his subject in 'the pressing moral anxiety, the restless individual conscience'. If American society was still simple, there was 'a life of the spirit more complex than anything that met the mere eye of sense', and Hawthorne had sufficient ingenuity to probe that life. 'This ingenuity grew alert and irrepressible as it manoeuvred for the back view and turned up the under side of common aspects – the laws secretly broken, the impulses secretly felt, the hidden passions, the double lives, the dark corners, the closed rooms, the skeletons in the cupboard and at the feast.' We hear much less of the 'charming' and 'childlike' Hawthorne in such paragraphs. Similarly when he speaks of Hawthorne's European experience there is a marked change of tone. No longer does James patronize 'poor Hawthorne' for his lack of initiation and failures of response. On the contrary he commends the way in which Hawthorne 'surrendered himself to the charm of Italy' and finds in his travel writings 'the mixture of sensibility and reluctance, of response and dissent, the strife between his sense of beauty and his sense of banishment'. It is impossible not to feel that James's years in Europe had brought him to a much more sympathetic understanding of Hawthorne's complex responses. In adopting a different attitude to Hawthorne, James is also revealing changes in himself. And nowhere more so than at the end of the essay when, instead of calling Hawthorne an outsider in Europe, he now treats him as the universal alienated writer. 'He is outside of everything, and an alien everywhere. He is an aesthetic solitary. His beautiful, light imagination is the wing that on the autumn evening just brushes the dusky window. It was a faculty that gave him much more a terrible sense of human abysses than a desire rashly to sound them and rise to the surface with his report.' James probably felt that he could and would venture deeper into those 'human abysses' than Hawthorne had dared, but nevertheless he clearly now feels much closer to Hawthorne. For James, too, often felt himself to be 'an alien everywhere', and what he says of Hawthorne's method fits his own. 'He never intermeddled; he was divertedly and discreetly contemplative, pausing oftenest wherever, amid prosaic aspects, there seemed most of an appeal to a sense of subtleties.' It is worth remembering that it was around this time that James wrote such stories as 'In the Cage', *What Maisie Knew, The Awkward Age, The Sacred Fount* – works which, in varying ways, concentrate on individual figures who are excluded, apart, 'outside everything'.

The fact is that towards the end of the century James was feeling that it could be a bad thing for any artist to be alienated from his native land. Hamlin Garland reports that in 1899 James said to him: 'If I were to live my life over again, I would be an American. I would steep myself in America, I would know no other land.' In the same year he wrote to his brother William stressing how important it was for young Americans 'to contract local saturations and attachments in respect to their *own* great and glorious country' and only a short time later he wrote to a friend of Edith Wharton's with the advice – 'She *must* be tethered in native pastures.' This was not his final word on the matter, but it helps to explain the particular tone of his next piece of writing about Hawthorne, a letter written for Hawthorne's centenary and published in 1904. For here James ascribes Hawthorne's success as a writer precisely to the fact that he stayed at home and exposed himself to his local environment. 'Salem had the good fortune to assist him, betimes, to this charming discrimination – that of *looking for romance near at hand, and where it grows thick and true, rather than on the other side of the globe and in the Dictionary of Dates.*' I have italicized those last words to draw attention to what a reversal of attitude they imply on James's part. The majority of the letter is taken up with a loving evocation of Hawthorne's New England – 'the old sunny and shady Salem, the blissfully homogenous community of the forties and fifties' – and with praise for Hawthorne's sense of 'man's relation to his environment'. Having once rather patronized Hawthorne for not having derived very much from coming abroad, James now seems almost to envy him for having extracted so much out of staying at home.

But this nostalgic feeling could not survive another contact with the actual America of the present. Shortly after writing this letter James revisited America for the first time in over twenty years and the Salem he saw could not sustain the role he had claimed for it in the evolution of Hawthorne's genius. Particularly interesting are his reactions when he is shown the actual House of the Seven Gables which was supposed to be the inspiration of Hawthorne's novel.

> The weak, vague domiciliary presence at the end of the lane may have 'been' (in our poor parlance) the idea of the admirable book – though even here we take a leap into dense darkness; but the idea that is the inner force of the admirable book so vividly forgets, before our eyes, any such origin or reference, 'cutting' it dead as a low acquaintance and outsoaring the shadow of its night, that the connection has turned a somersault into space, repudiated like a ladder kicked back from the top of a wall. Hawthorne's ladder at Salem, in fine, has now quite gone, and we but tread the air if we attempt to set our critical feet on its steps and its rounds, learning thus as we do, and with infinite interest as I think, how merely 'subjective' in us are our discoveries about genius.

James had gone back to look at the environment which he thought had produced and been responsible for Hawthorne's particular genius. What he found was totally disillusioning. Not only was there a new Salem of foreigners and business and industry which had obliterated much of Hawthorne's world; such bits of that earlier environment and world which did remain were too weak and trivial to produce or explain the particular power of Hawthorne's work. It is as though James had looked at the actual house, then thought about the book Hawthorne had written, and decided once and for all that you can never account for art in terms of the environment from which it emerged. James repudiated the connection just as the book, for him, utterly repudiated the house which had supposedly spawned it. The full extent of James's disillusion with America, his horror at what was happening to his country, can be found in *The American Scene*. It is enough here to remember that when James returned to Europe he felt with renewed conviction that his decision to leave America for Europe had been a wise one; that whatever the drawbacks of expatriation, what he had gained, as an artist, was well worth the price. The old James, just like the young James, left America feeling once again that his native country was inimical to all forms of art.

It is fitting, then, that his last reference to Hawthorne should echo his earliest comments on that writer – though this time, instead of the condescension and superiority of youth, we find the mellow sympathy and understanding of age. It is in *Notes of a Son and Brother*, the first of James's autobiographical volumes, that he recalls his desolation on hearing of the death of Hawthorne. This leads him to a memory and recollection of all the joy he had derived from his work (as a youth), which in turn leads him to one final retrospective comment on the special, the unique tone of Hawthorne's work.

> And the tone had been, in its beauty – for me at least – ever so appreciably American; which proved to what a use American matter could be put by an American hand: a consummation involving, it appeared, the happiest moral. For the moral was that an American could be an artist, one of the finest, without 'going outside' about it, as I liked to say; quite in fact as if Hawthorne had become one just by being American *enough*, by the felicity of how the artist in him missed nothing, suspected nothing, that the ambient air didn't affect him as containing. Thus he was at once so clear and so entire – clear without thinness, for he might have seemed underfed, it was his danger; and entire without heterogeneity, which might, with less luck and to the discredit of our sufficing manners, have had to be his help.

James's first remarks about Hawthorne referred to him as 'the last pure American' and now, once again, at the end of his life James looks back at Hawthorne, seeing him not as the total outsider but as the essential artist of an earlier America. He, James, *had* 'gone outside', left America for Europe, with every justification as it now seemed to him; for Hawthorne, in his more innocent America, that had not been necessary. But however James changed and qualified and expanded his views on Hawthorne, he never put him out of his mind, never failed to think and think again about him. For, seen from whatever angle, the life and works of Nathaniel Hawthorne held one supreme and enduringly valuable moral for Henry James – 'the moral was that an American could be an artist'.

5

The lost America – the despair of Henry Adams and Mark Twain

Henry Adams and Samuel Clemens are often considered to represent the polar extremes of their age. Yet, however divergent their careers seem to be, it is absorbing to watch them approaching, each in his different way, a final mood of total despair that argues concurrence rather than coincidence. Personal tragedies might be adduced to explain this: the heart-breaking death of Susy Clemens and the long-drawn-out agony of Livy, the suicide of Adams's wife Clover, even the humiliation of bankruptcy, which Clemens suffered personally and Adams witnessed in his family – these certainly are contributory causes. But as one examines the conspicuous modes of this despair – a compound of comminatory denunciation and brooding, intense pessimism – one is compelled to search further afield for the prime causes. Such an investigation reveals that this despair is in a slow process of incubation from their earliest work, and that it is finally hatched by the growing discords, conflicts, and problems of the age. It is not a despair of personal bereavement but of country – ultimately of man.

Much of Adams's despair, to say nothing of his wounded pride, is the negative residue of a constantly diminishing faith in American politics, which seemed progressively to abandon all the moral idealism that he felt that he and his family preeminently represented. His bitterness grows as it becomes increasingly apparent that such a person as himself has no part to play in the politics of his age: that such a state of affairs should have come about clearly indicated an intolerable debasement of the whole political scene. His two early novels and the nine-volume history really have a common theme; they ask the questions: What is the fate of idealism in American politics? Is there any longer any meaning in the way things are going? Is life moving towards any ideal end?

Adams's *The Life of Albert Gallatin*, as well as being a simple biography, is also an examination of political aspiration that results in failure, and it points out the fact that republican idealism failed to establish its ideally conceived society. *Democracy*, written almost immediately after 1879, is an excoriating analysis of contemporary American democratic administration. The heroine, Mrs Madeline Lee, sets out to understand Senator Radcliffe, who is made to represent the contemporary American politician in all his naked power. He proves to be selfish, hypocritical, and unscrupulous, 'a naked will operating under convictions of moral lunacy'. Mrs Lee comes to consider him 'diseased' and the disease is diagnosed as 'atrophy of the moral sense'. She had been searching for some meaning in life and had focused on the senator as a possible provider of an ideal end for which she could work. His failure to furnish her with such an ideal induces in Mrs Lee a mood of complete despair: for her, life is 'emptier than ever now that this dream was over'. She decides to 'quit the masquerade' and sets out on a voyage to the Mediterranean and the Nile. The voyage, we feel, is but the first of many meaningless meanderings, and it aptly prefigures Adams's own restless existence. These two novels about the futile search for some form of idealism were written while Adams was engaged in research for his great *History*. This work, published between 1889 and 1891, is a massive demonstration of the inevitable failure of idealism. The ideals governing Jeffersonian republicanism are set out in the chapter called 'American Ideals', and the rest of the work records the attempt to achieve these ideal goals. As George Hochfield observes in *Henry Adams: An Introduction and Interpretation*, 'The failure of that attempt – for failure it obviously was – is thus the conclusion to which the whole work tends.' The attempt to establish an ideal society leads eventually to the horrors of war: this is the mute, sinister portent of the work. To phrase it thus is to slight its greatness but for our purpose it is interesting to note that Adams chose to study exactly that portion of history which would provide him with a pessimistic conclusion. Even here, long before *The Education*, there are hints of an incipient determinism, a determinism justified by this great failure of the past. As Hochfield writes: 'the necessitarianism that tinctures the *History* is a response to the failure of idealism; it signifies Adams' conclusion that idealism must have been doomed from the start by the very nature of history'. It is as though Adams unconsciously chose just that period in American history which would most warrant his inchoate pessimism. The odd thing is that Clemens chose to do exactly the same.

Clemens of course was not so articulate or painstaking in his political opinions. He was an admirer and later a friend of Grant, and Grant's regime did not fill him with the same deep disgust that afflicted the more perspicacious Adams. Nevertheless, he is far from being blithely unaware of an unpleasant drop in the tone of American politics after the Civil War. In *The Curious Republic of Gondour*, written in 1871, he satirizes an aspect of American politics that we might have expected to annoy Adams rather than Clemens, for the curious thing about Gondour is that 'for the first time in the history of the republic, property, character, and intellect were able to wield a political influence'. In this strange land an education entitles a man to more votes than the unlettered hod-carrier, and the ignorant are not allowed to swamp the intelligent with their greater numbers. The tone is more that of an alienated aristocrat than that of a supporter of the great American dream of government by the people. Three years later Clemens gave the definitive title to his times with *The Gilded Age*. The book is by no means the unrelieved attack on democracy that Adams's novel was to be, but the satirical intent is clear and Senator Dilworthy invites comparison with Senator Radcliffe. Clemens was no stranger to Washington, and his stay there during the winter of 1867 was sufficient to give him as low an opinion of American politics as Adams held. However, it is in that strangely confused book *A Connecticut Yankee*, published just before the *History*, that Clemens comes so close to echoing Adams's despairing conclusions. The book actually starts out from a point of view very distant from the omniscient retrospection of Adams the historian: the novel, as Professor Henry Nash Smith has shrewdly pointed out, is a *roman expérimental* and the question at issue is whether republican idealism and nineteenth-century tech-nology can redeem society. This in turn poses the question of whether or not man can improve his lot if offered an ideal opportunity – whether, indeed, man is perfectible. Thus, it is asking the same question answered negatively by the *History*, for the ideals that are tested in that book are man's natural capacity to develop morally and intellectually, and the possibility of intelligent economic expansion.

Frequently before the writing of this book Clemens exhibits a belief in natural goodness, the innately decent proclivities of the 'heart' that has not been corrupted by inherited prejudice and the coercions of established institutions. Huck Finn is his supreme assertion of such a belief, and Hank Morgan is in some ways a grown-up Huck who instead of being in passive flight *from* society is in aggressive conflict *with* it. To the dark ages of sixth-century England he brings these two great gifts – a theory of amelioration based on a belief in the goodness and perfectibility of man, and the economic principles and technological means to implement a beneficent alteration of the age. But all his efforts prove wasted: the initial philanthrope gradually becomes misanthropic; the idealistic democrat shades into a scornful tyrant; hoping to bring light he ends by concentrating on destruction: people are unapt for improvement – idealism is bound to fail. As the faith in man falls, so a savage authorial anger intrudes itself: the undertaken project of reconstruction ends in a foul holocaust just as the *History* shows idealism leading inevitably to the 'bloody arena' of war. Adams never had Clemens's belief in the perfectibility of man: he called it 'this doubtful and even improbable principle' and proved the point by his *History*. Clemens's anger and dismay are the greater for his having once believed, but the conclusions he reaches are identical. Yet we may note, as we noted of the *History*, that Clemens chose a situation in which idealism was bound to fail: established historical fact precludes all possibility of success, and surely it is not excessive to see in this choice of situation a lurking, if unacknowledged, pessimistic determinism such as we discerned in Adams. (A similar unconscious fatalism clearly dictates his preoccupation with the Joan of Arc story; she is another idealistic person who comes to redeem a 'sick age', and her ultimate rejection by society is even more inflexibly determined than Hank Morgan's.) It might here be argued that *A Connecticut Yankee* was an anti-English polemic stimulated by the patronizing contempt of America exhibited by Matthew Arnold, but the satiric barb of the book is aimed at contemporary America – the 'dark ages' become the corrupt post-Civil-War years in which the great American dream was so glaringly betrayed. The Round Table, for instance, comes to have an uncanny resemblance to the stock exchange, and the final civil war is precipitated by a shady deal reminiscent of the railroad frauds of the Seventies: the slavedriver in the illustrations, which were executed by the radical Dan Beard with Clemens's approval, is clearly meant to be Jay Gould; in a word, the degradation and misery of the sixth century is America's own.

The years from 1873 to 1879 were years of great economic distress; the small farmers were badly off and in the cities there was widespread unemployment, while in 1877 the first nation-wide strike led to a sinister outburst of labour rioting. In 1879 Henry George published his *Progress and Poverty*. The book opens with a statement of the expectations and opportunities of the early nineteenth century: its theme is 'disappointment has followed disappointment', a theme re-echoed in Adams's historical work and Clemens's novels. If the ideals on which America was founded were being rapidly stained by political practice, so also was the paradisaical surface of the continent suffering a comparable degradation from the rapid urbanization and industrialization of the period. One would not have expected a nostalgia for the unspoiled wildness of an earlier America to have had much effect on the urbane temperament of Adams, yet it clearly does. Several amazingly passionate passages in the *Education* reveal that for Adams 'the vast maternity of nature' always 'showed charms more voluptuous than the vast paternity of the United States senate'. And this is not to be discounted as the urban man's genteel indulgence in the country from a safe distance – this is not an age of pastoral poetry. It is definitely the profligate waywardness of an untamed nature that arouses his sympathies. When he first sees the South he is most distressed by the fact that it is 'unkempt, poverty-striken, ignorant, vicious', and yet certain aspects of it draw him as though he were hypnotized by them against his better, civilized, judgement. 'The want of barriers, of pavements, of forms; the looseness, the laziness; the indolent southern drawl; the pigs in the streets, the negro babies and their mothers with bandanas; the freedom, openness, swagger of nature and man soothed his Johnson blood' – a passage that Clemens would have applauded. What disappoints Adams in his later travels is that 'the sense of wildness had vanished'; and *Huckleberry Finn* embodies a similar lament, lyrically developed, for some lost 'wildness' that is Huck's natural element. We should remember that Adams, when talking of the visible nature of trees and mountains, never calls it a chaos: the wildness of this nature gratified some deep instinct in him and he was saddened to see it vanishing from the continent. The nature he came to consider as pure chaos was an intellectual system. To maintain the comparison with Clemens we may recall the passage in which he speaks of changes on the Mississippi. 'Ten years had passed since he last crossed the Mississippi, and he found everything new. In this great region from Pittsburgh through Ohio and Indiana, agriculture had made way for steam; tall chimneys reeked smoke on every horizon, and dirty suburbs filled with scrap iron, scrap paper and cinders, formed the setting of every town.' In *Life on the Mississippi* Clemens records his feelings as he witnesses the changes along the river he knew so well as a youth, and the great quality of the work is a controlled nostalgia for a lost era. And yet here we must point to a difference. Just as Clemens had believed in the perfectibility of man while Adams doubted, so he was initially optimistic about the beneficence of industrialization, an optimism never shared by Adams. When Clemens sees some of those tall chimneys on the horizon he expresses great delight at the 'changes uniformly evidencing progress, energy, prosperity': it was only later that, sickened by the corruptive powers of materialism, he gravitated to a mood of cynical despair.

More specifically let us cite the machine and the mob as two phenomena that served to alienate these men from their age. There is a significant moment when Adams visits the great Chicago Exposition in 1893. The extended exposure to mechanical novelties of which he has no understanding completely immobilizes him. Before the array of steam engines, electric batteries, telephones, etc., he 'had no choice but to sit down on the steps and brood as [he] had never brooded on the benches of Harvard College . . . The historical mind can only think in historical processes, and probably this was the first time since historians existed,

that any of them had sat down helpless before a mechanical sequence.'
The word 'mechanical', so neutral to us, should be noted, for it gradually
acquires an ominous weight of meaning as Adams discovers that the
world is being increasingly administered by mechanical forces of one
kind or another. (His attitude is comparable to that of the writer of the
Erewhonian 'Book of the Machines': 'Is it not plain that the machines are
gaining ground upon us, when we reflect on the increasing number of
those who are bound down to them as slaves, and of those who devote
their whole souls to the advancement of the mechanical kingdom?')
There is an irony in this, since the eighteenth-century rationalism that
was so dear to Adams was based on the Newtonian conception of Nature
as a divinely ordered machine. But the Great Watchmaker had decreed a
mechanistic universe which was rational and explicable. As the scrap
heaps and the cinders came increasingly into view mechanism gradually
ceased to exemplify a rational principle and seemed to become a hideous
principle of blind force. Mechanism had turned on the class and way of
life that initially upheld it. Adams talks of 'the whole mechanical
consolidation of force, which ruthlessly stamped out the life of the class
into which Adams was born'. Again in the Exposition: 'As he grew
accustomed to the great gallery of machines he began to feel the forty-
foot dynamo as a moral force, much as the early Christian felt the cross.'
But at least there had been a Christ on the cross: the dynamo is
completely impersonal in its divine power. It is non-human and
therefore inhuman, non-moral and therefore immoral, or rather amoral.
And it is that dynamo which really unfixes Adams's mind. Clemens's
career affords us a comparable symbol, although his antipathy to the
machine is the result of a long process of disillusionment rather than the
sudden bewilderment felt by Adams. His relationship with the Paige
typesetter symbolically foreshortens this disillusionment. An initial
enthusiasm gradually gives way to a profound despair as the machine
heartlessly robs him of a fortune and mockingly refuses to arrive at the
hoped-for perfection.

A concomitant of Adams's reaction to the dynamo is a feeling that just
as the world is coming to be dominated by impersonal forces so also are
the inhabitants of this world becoming as impersonal, mechanical, and
inhuman as the forces that guide them. The mob was making its
appearance in America and, although in many ways these people were
the victims of the machines that Adams deprecated, their impersonal
violence disturbed him as much as did the dynamo. In his youth, he
recalls, he was once involved in a snow-ball fight: the sides were the Latin
school versus the rest of the local boys. The account of the fight reads like
a parable. At first the Latin school dominates the others, but then as night
comes on the tide turns. 'A dark mass of figures could be seen below,

making ready for the last rush, and rumour said that a swarm of black-guards from the slums . . . was going to put an end to the Beacon Street cowards forever. Henry wanted to run away with the others, but his brother was too big to run away, so they stood still and waited immolation. The dark mass set up a shout, and rushed forward.' It ends as all children's games should, but throughout the extended description one feels the terrible threat of the dark forces who come swarming up against the Latin school (which very easily can be made to represent the aristocratic element in society) threatening total annihilation. In its way it is like a small Dunciad, and the idea that 'universal darkness' will eventually 'cover all' is a theme which grows throughout the book until that last apocalyptic description of New York in 1905, which ends:

> A traveler in the highways of history looked out of the club window on the turmoil of Fifth Avenue, and felt himself in Rome, under Diocletian, witnessing the anarchy, conscious of the compulsion, eager for the solution, but unable to conceive whence the next impulse was to come or how it was to act. The two-thousand-years failure of Christianity roared upward from Broadway, and no Constantine the Great was in sight.

Although Clemens had a ready sympathy for the strikers so brutally suppressed under President Cleveland, he also came to hate 'the mob'. Colonel Sherburn's scornful arraignment of the brutality, pusillanimity, and cowardice of the lynching crowd is an overt piece of authorial intrusion: Hank Morgan, who came to save the people, finds himself admiring their king and despising them as 'muck', and it is the ungrateful mob that allows Joan to be burned after she had devoted herself to their liberation. Adams's patrician heritage helped to enforce his antipathies on him and, although Clemens certainly enjoyed no comparably cultured environment as a child, yet he also recalls that 'the aristocratic taint was in the air'. His Virginian father, John Marshall Clemens, was a type of aristocrat in his insistence on the proud, austere, dignified bearing proper to 'a man'; an Andrew Jackson, perhaps, rather than a John Quincy Adams. If Adams inherited an aristocracy of class, then Clemens certainly inherited an aristocracy of character, and this must not be ignored in any attempt to account for their disaffiliation from the age of the common man. Mobocracy, like 'dollarocracy' and 'machineocracy' aroused bitterness, contempt, and despair in both men. It remains to examine this despair.

The *Education* is an account of a life dissolving into chaos. Adams construes his life as a series of false starts – a continual failure to learn anything. Everywhere he looks he can only see a world 'both unwise and ignorant' and full of contradictions among intelligent people: 'from such contradictions . . . what was a young man to learn'. Continually he says 'the horizon widened out in endless waves of confusion', and we should note that sea image: it is one that will recur. On the moral level he never finds anything he can trust. In London diplomatic circles he loses all confidence and when Russell, Gladstone, and Palmerston seem to be double-dealing he makes it a crucial test: 'could one afford to trust human nature in politics . . . for education the point was vital. If one could not trust a dozen of the most respected private characters in the world . . . one could trust no mortal man.' When they fall short of his idealistic standards he just gives up, blaming it all on 'the sheer chaos of human nature'. Such moments recur: as he makes his way through political life he seeks out something he can hold fast to, some one facet of human nature that will never let him down. He is almost adolescent, almost child-like in his search for goodness in the world. One can see him as conducting on an international urban level the search that Huck carried out down the Mississippi, and in the course of this search he confesses 'he had wholly lost his way'. He is always making another 'leap into the unknown' and after working near the Grant administration for a while he emerges with the comment by now only to be expected from him. He 'had made another total misconception of life – another inconceivable false start'. Like Huck he is lost and always passive. He 'drifted into the mental indolence of history' and wherever he goes he says that knowledge absorbs him – 'he was passive'. Like Huck he often appears as 'a helpless victim' with no defence or means of attack and he feels 'at the mercy of fools and cowards': even when he takes a job as a teacher his morbid comment is: 'he went on, submissive'. Again like Huck he is continually on the move. Feeling unfitted for Boston 'he had to go': shocked by McKinley's ways he says 'once more, one must go!' He is well aware of this nomadic aspect of his life since he adds: 'Nothing was easier! On and off, one had done the same thing since the year 1858, at frequent intervals.' Very early on in the book he recalls: 'Always he felt himself somewhere else . . . and he watched with vague unrest from the Quincy hills the smoke of the Cunard steamers stretching in a long line to the horizon . . . as though the steamers were offering to take him away, which was precisely what they were doing.' It is important to note how purposeless Adams makes all his voyaging seem – both the actual travel and the larger voyage towards knowledge. He is always 'drifting' with some unspecified current. The sea imagery is prolific throughout the book. It starts when he is writing of the Civil War: 'On April 13 the storm burst and rolled several hundred thousand young men like Henry Adams into the surf of a wild ocean, all helpless like himself, to be beaten about for four years by the waves of war.' But there was no ebb of the tide for Henry Adams. As the end of his first year in England approaches he writes: 'His old education was finished; his new one was not begun; he still loitered a year, feeling himself near the end of a very long, anxious tempestuous successful voyage, with another to follow, and a summer sea between.' Success would seem to consist merely in keeping afloat – a success not always permitted him since he elsewhere talks of 'sinking under the surface'. In 1871, he writes, 'his course had led him through oceans of ignorance' and the ocean seems limitless. In the chapter entitled 'The Abyss of Ignorance' the final stage of passivity is reached. 'After so many years of effort to find one's drift, the drift found the seeker and slowly swept him forward and back, with a steady progress oceanwards.' He doesn't let go of the image even when talking of smaller matters; of his attempt to study 'race and sex' he writes: 'Even within these narrow seas the navigator lost his bearings and followed the winds as they blew.' That he sometimes wishes this sea of ignorance to turn into something more soporific, something to rock him back to unconsciousness again, is shown by one remarkable passage. 'Adams would rather, as choice, have gone back to the east, if it were only to sleep forever in the trade-winds under the southern stars, wandering over the dark purple ocean, with its purple sense of solitude and void.' Images of the sea as a fearful void are supported by images of darkness. He refers to himself as being 'lost in the darkness of his own gropings' and after King's death 'Adams could only blunder back alone, helplessly, wearily, his eyes rather dim with tears, to his vague trail across the darkening prairie of education, without a motive, big or small, except curiosity to reach, before he too should drop, some point that would give him a far look ahead.' This 'darkening prairie' later becomes 'mountains of ignorance' where the 'weary pilgrim . . . could no longer see any path whatever and could not even understand a signpost'. One tends to forget the almost phantasmagoric nature of his accounts because of the tempered, elegant, detached tone, but the accounting voice is a neutral, almost blank, one and its purpose is to direct attention to the pitiful figure struggling down on earth. 'Never had the proportions of his ignorance looked so appalling. He seemed to know nothing – to be groping in darkness – to be falling forever in space.' The images of sea, space, and darkness blend for one moment when he tells of the significance for him of Karl Pearson's writing: 'At last their universe had been wrecked by rays, and Karl Pearson undertook to cut the wreck loose with an axe, leaving science adrift on a sensual raft in the midst of a supersensual chaos' and now Adams finds himself 'on the raft'. He might have found two companions on the raft – Huck Finn, and that hapless narrator of *The Mysterious Stranger*, Theodor Fischer. In one sense the voyages of these two boys complement each other. Huck is afloat in America in search of a destination. He is an Odysseus without an Ithaca. Like Odysseus he is 'never at a loss' and knows how to disguise himself or manufacture a tale in order to get himself out of trouble and continue on his way; but that way is no longer clear. The frontier to which he finally heads is too vague to be a definite destination – it is the geographical location of the great unknown. But still, there is a feeling that out there all things are possible. Huck, we feel, stands a chance. But not Theodor. The ending of *The Mysterious Stranger* reads like a more hysterical and total version of Adams's own despair. Here is a part of Satan's last speech.

> In a little while you will be alone in shoreless space, to wander its limitless solitudes without friend or comrade forever . . . It is true, that which I have revealed to you; there is no God, no universe, no human race, no earthly life, no heaven, no hell. It is all a dream – a grotesque and foolish dream. Nothing exists but you. And you are but a *thought* – a vagrant thought, a useless thought, a homeless thought, wandering forlorn among the empty eternities!

One can add comparable evidence from Clemens's last period that he became increasingly preoccupied with images of chaos, darkness, purposelessness, the passivity of man before the dark forces of the world, and the complete lostness of man. In some of his late, unfinished scraps of fiction there is a measure of unwarranted horror which one might expect from a writer more devoted to symbolism than Clemens at any time showed himself to be: there is a feeling of living in a symbolic universe to which man has lost the interpretive key, thus leaving the writer with an accumulating emotion that finds no satisfactory deciphering expression. Just to mention the three sea stories among these late papers will reveal something of this process, and the preoccupation with purposeless voyages which end in horror is one which seems to mirror something that was going on in Adams's mind. (It is interesting to recall that Emerson employed images of voyaging and water to enforce his optimistic view of man's effortless relationship with a benign nature. 'Place yourself in the middle of the stream of power and wisdom which animates all whom it floats, and you are without effort impelled to truth, to right and a perfect contentment.' And again: man 'is like a ship in a river . . . he sweeps serenely over a deepening channel into an infinite sea'.)

For Twain and Adams that 'infinite sea' turned into pure nightmare. *The Enchanted Sea Wilderness* is the story of a ship which wanders into a great area of the ocean where the compass suddenly goes beserk and loses all value as a means of steering and plotting direction. First it runs into a terrible nine-day storm which the sailors nickname 'the devil's race track' and then it emerges into a deadly calm or 'the everlasting Sunday'. Here they slowly drift until they see what they take to be a fleet on the horizon: full of hope they row towards it but it turns out to be a dead fleet which rotted away years ago leaving only the deceptive shells on the surface to mock all who find them with an image of their irrevocable fate. In all this 'universal paralysis of life and energy' the only active thing is the compass which is whirling around 'in a frenzy of fear'. Out of this morbid but pregnant predicament Clemens makes nothing and we are left to wonder how the narrator lived to tell the tale.

A more suggestive story is *An Adventure in Remote Seas*, where once again a ship gets lost but this time arrives at a strange island. Half the crew go ashore to catch penguins and find, implausibly enough, a vast hoard of gold: this turns the captain's mind and the men are employed in weighing and counting it. Strikes and labour disputes arise and there are some satirical references to the question of adopting the silver standard, on which William Jennings Bryan was campaigning at the time. All thought of the original purpose of the voyage is given up, and those on shore start to forget the ship and cease to worry about their location. Suddenly they realize the ship has gone – and here the story breaks off. This has all the inchoate lineaments of an allegory. The unknown island which they discover could be America and the penguins (who are so docile and friendly while the sailors cut their throats) might well be the original inhabitants, the Indians. The frenzy aroused by the money is Clemens's comment on what the Industrial Revolution was doing to men and the final situation seems to symbolize contemporary America: busy scrambling for money while the one chance of salvation, the ship, is finally lost, leaving the men abandoned in a nameless ocean with only a meaningless wealth for consolation. Again this is not brought to anything; it remains formless and crude, merely indicating a desire to express a bitter comment on the crisis of mankind.

The long story to which DeVoto applied Clemens's phrase 'The Great Dark' is a more prolonged, though scarcely more successful, attempt to find a fitting parable to carry his feelings. A man named Henry Edwards dreams that he embarks on a long trip across the drop of water that he had been studying under the microscope shortly before falling asleep. The 'blind voyage' across this unknown ocean moves from dream to nightmare. At first it is constantly dark: no one knows where they are but they try and conceal the fact from others; the charts and compass prove to be utterly useless since none of the expected landmarks seems to exist; fantastic animals flounder in the sea, occasionally attacking them, giving the impression of a Bosch-like apocalyptic chaos. Hideous surreal incidents multiply and the story spirals to a pitch of phantasmagoric insanity: the sea dries up, fighting and brawling (again over a useless treasure) gradually account for all the characters except Edwards who, like Theodor Fischer, is left alone in an arid eternity. The terrible dream turns out to be the true reality – a favourite theme of the aging Clemens.

This unrelenting vision of life as chaos is, in essence and conclusion, not very different from that of Henry Adams. Whence this similarity of vision? Both of them had ceased to believe in God but both retained something of that Calvinistic intensity of vision common to believers of previous ages. It is their inability to disburden themselves of the mental framework which accompanied belief that makes both determinists of one kind or another. God had either fled or been diminished to a thing – a *deus absconditum*, but the feeling of predestination lingered on just beneath the surface of the conscious mind. To this we can trace the persistent image of the voyage in so much nineteenth-century American literature, but now what was the destiny to which man had been predestined? The compasses were not functioning, the chart of infallible absolutes was completely useless on these novel seas of dissolving belief. It seems that without the one all-solving deity the world collapsed into an amorphous, inexplicable mess before which the only reaction was one of sterile horror. Not that either man wanted the old God back, but they were equally dismayed at America's failure to provide any substitute ideal purpose or explanation (they are both, at one time or another, extremely sardonic about evolutionary optimism).

At first both Clemens and Adams had credited man with some degree of free will: in the *History* there is such a thing as moral responsibility and decision, while Huck is a superb example of man's ability to argue with, challenge, and finally rebuff the circumpressure of environment and heredity. By the end of their lives they were both convinced that free will was completely illusory. In the *Education* Adams decides that people involved in politics are simply 'forces as dumb as their dynamos' and this interpretation gradually extends over all mankind. One sentence intimates the large shift in conviction. 'Adams never knew why, knowing nothing of Faraday, he began to mimic Faraday's trick of seeing lines of force all about him, where he had always seen lines of will.' Very quickly man becomes 'a feeble atom'.

1898 was a bad year for Clemens, a year in which he sought some relief from Susy's death and his bankruptcy, in a prolonged spell of uninterrupted work. He not only wrote *The Mysterious Stranger* but he also completed a work which he had been toying with for eighteen years – *What Is Man?* It is entirely apt that the very first sub-title should read: 'a. Man the Machine'. This book has been almost entirely ignored by subsequent generations and for good reason: yet Clemens was so apprehensive about the scandal he thought it would cause that he would only print it anonymously and privately for a few friends in 1906. It is a jumble of half-pursued thoughts and improperly defined terms the whole upshot of which is that man is 'an impersonal machine . . . he is moved, directed, COMMANDED by exterior influences – solely. He originates nothing, not even a thought.' And then there follows that notorious simile – Shakespeare is merely a 'Gobelin loom' compared with the sewing machine which is the average man. Of course it wasn't subsequent generations who were shocked – it was Clemens himself. He was terrified by his own conclusion (and note how his 'exterior influences' have taken over the imperious authoritarianism of the Calvinist God). There is something unnerved and frenzied about his insistence that man is a completely irresponsible object at the mercy of forces that he cannot understand and he is almost vengeful in his efforts to humiliate and degrade mankind.

It is interesting that he seeks out the most ignoble animals with which to compare man (in personal dignity, for instance, man is on the same level as a rat), for Adams continually chooses to compare himself to animals: and such animals – the small, the helpless, the ones that crawl. For example he likens himself at various times to a mosquito, a maggot, a worm, a firefly, and a horseshoe crab. More interesting is his simile for Jefferson, Madison, and Monroe. In a letter to Tilden in 1883 he wrote: 'they appear like mere grasshoppers kicking and gesticulating on the middle of the Mississippi River . . . they were carried along on a stream which floated them, after a fashion, without much regard to themselves'. One can see here an unconscious preparation for his later attitude toward the predicament of man: this image conjoins just those two themes which later he consciously exploited. Man is as helpless as a trivial animal: his life is a brief floating on the endless waters of chaos.

As a boy Adams was impregnated with truths that were rigid, absolute, and transcendent: it is only natural that when he embarks on his search for some new truth he should search for some inflexible, theoretic, and timelessly true principle. His search for unity is actually a yearning for some inviolable, transcendent principle of unification such as Aquinas had postulated. But along with everything else the philosophic climate was changing. Absolute systems of philosophy tended to be reactionary, to justify the old *status quo* that brought them into being; they inhibited reform, they imposed a mental vice on a world which was breaking its boundaries in every direction. A new philosophy was needed to control and discipline the new directions man was taking without closing off any avenues to him – the philosophy was pragmatism. Pragmatism kept truth open and searched for useful instruments rather than final answers; it turned away from 'a priori reasons, from fixed principles, closed systems, and pretended absolutes': it turned towards facts and was not dismayed by their improvident multiplicity.

William James, attacking a conservative professor, writes in a way that seems almost like a direct answer to the morbid despair of Adams and Clemens with all their images of oceans of chaos and fruitless voyages. He writes:

> These critics appear to suppose that, if left to itself, the rudderless craft of our experience must be ready to drift anywhere or nowhere. Even tho there were compasses on board, they seem to say, there would be no pole for them to point

to. There must be absolute sailing directions, they insist, decreed from outside, and an independent chart of the voyage added to the 'mere' voyage itself, if we are ever to make a port. But is it not obvious that even tho there be such absolute sailing-directions in the shape of pre-human standards of truth that we *ought* to follow, the only guarantee that we shall in fact follow them must lie in our human equipment . . . The only *real* guarantee we have against licentious thinking is the circumpressure of experience itself, which gets us sick of concrete errors, whether there be a trans-empirical reality or not.

As the recurrent imagery of their late work reveals, both Adams and Clemens felt profoundly uneasy without a set of 'absolute sailing directions'.

It is strange that Adams and Clemens never seem to have met. They had many mutual friends – Clarence King, John Hay, and most notably William Dean Howells, and they both spent many years in New England, yet we have no record of a meeting. There is a strange moment in *What Is Man?* when Clemens suddenly cites one 'Henry Adams' as a (presumably fictional) example of the unhappiest man he knows: he must certainly have known too much about Adams to have used the name quite innocently, and perhaps this is a covert way of intimating that he considers himself at an extreme temperamental remove from such a man. Had they met they would probably have found themselves at odds, yet they are two of the most notable alienated figures of their age. They never felt quite at home anywhere, never quite settled down, never really found themselves. At one point Adams imagines describing himself to his father and finds that all he could say of himself would be: 'Sir, I am a tourist', and when he later calls himself 'a historical tramp' we are reminded of that habitual tourist who punningly names himself in *A Tramp Abroad*. Both these international hobos spent many years of their lives wandering around the world and beneath the successful exterior of the one and the cultured veneer of the other one can indeed discern the lineaments of that recurrent American image – the tramp. Devious and unpremeditated as their wanderings may seem they were both on the same road, not *to* anywhere but *away from* a society with which they could no longer identify themselves and which seemed to offer no answering image to their own deepest hopes and ideals.

If these two were alone in their disillusion and despair one might be inclined to put it down to a personal perversity of vision. But the evidence is all the other way. One can trace a spectrum of complaint throughout the age. Whitman, although he had faith in democracy – 'the unyielding principle of the average' – conceded 'the appalling dangers of universal suffrage in the United States'. Committed to loving all men he was yet sufficiently offended by the progress of post-Civil-War America to write that 'society', despite or because of 'unprecedented materialistic advancement . . . is canker'd, crude, superstitious and rotten'. A man less like Adams than Whitman never lived and yet the former would have supported Whitman's complaint that 'the element of the moral conscience, the most important, the vertebrae to State or man, seems to me either entirely lacking, or seriously enfeebled or ungrown'.

Brooks Adams, in his significantly titled *The Law of Civilization and Decay*, developed an adventurous cyclical interpretation of history and the lesson he reads in the past is the inevitable disintegration of a society in which the economic type had gained total supremacy. As determinist as his brother Henry he maintained that Nature operates on the human mind 'according to immutable laws' – a theory which endorses pessimism but slights man's ability to learn from the past. Consequently he saw in the exaltation of the new materialistic middle class a portent of inevitable doom. Henry James fled to England to avert his eyes from the new generation of Americans dedicated to the 'great black ebony God of business': in the last scene of *The Bostonians* Basil Ransom dismisses the middle class mob at the lecture hall as 'senseless brutes' and it is difficult not to feel that he speaks with the author's approval.

Near the turn of the century Henry Adams, perspicacious enough to see that the future of society might lie in the direction of state-socialism, pronounced it a 'future with which I sincerely wish I may have nothing to do'. Clemens, more angry because more humane, composed this 'salutation speech from the 19th century to the 20th' (subsequently withdrawn) in which he bitterly arraigns the imperialistic greed of the West.

> I bring you the stately matron named Christendom, returning bedraggled, besmirched and dishonoured from pirate-raids in Kiao-Chow, Manchuria, South Africa and the Philippines, with her soul full of boodle, and her mouth full of pious hypocrisies. Give her soap and a towel, but hide the looking glass.

But middle-class America was to receive a more disturbing turn-of-the-century salutation. In 1899 Thorstein Veblen published *The Theory of the Leisure Class* in which the pecuniary fanaticism of the *nouveau riche* received its most mordant, sardonic analysis. His evidence must be taken as conclusive. It remained for later scholars such as Vernon Parrington to clarify the phenomenon which had so distressed men like Clemens and Adams: namely, 'the emergence of a new middle class' which in the second half of the nineteenth century subdued America 'to middle class ends'.

6

Henry James and Henry Adams

When Henry James sent Henry Adams a copy of *Notes of a Son and Brother* (the second volume of what is now referred to as his *Autobiographies* – the others being *A Small Boy and Others* and *The Middle Years*), Adams's response was rather extraordinary. The reminiscence, he wrote to Mrs Cameron, had reduced him to a pulp. Why idealize all that past life in a vanished nineteenth-century America, he wanted to know. 'Why did we live? Was that all? Why was I not born in Central Africa and died young? Poor Henry James thinks it all real, I believe, and actually still lives in that dreamy, stuffy Newport and Cambridge, with papa James and Charles Norton – and me! Yet, why?' To James himself he wrote what we can only infer was one of his pessimistic and melancholy outbursts. His letter is lost but we have James's marvellous reply, from which I want to quote at some length, if only to convey a sense of the rare poise in his tone.

> My dear Henry,
>
> I have your melancholy outpouring of the 7th, and I know not how better to acknowledge it than by the full recognition of its unmitigated blackness. *Of course* we are lone survivors, of course the past that was our lives is at the bottom of the abyss – if the abyss *has* any bottom; of course, too, there's no use talking unless one particularly *wants* to. But the purpose, almost, of my printed divagations was to show that one *can*, strange to say, still want to – or at least can behave as if one did. Behold me therefore so behaving – and apparently capable of continuing to do so. I still find my consciousness interesting – under *cultivation* of the interest . . . *Why* mine yields an interest I don't know that I can tell you, but I don't challenge or quarrel with it – I encourage it with a ghastly grin. You see I still, in the presence of life (or of what you deny to be such) have reactions – as many as possible – and the book I sent you is a proof of them. It's, I suppose, because I am that queer monster, the artist, an obstinate finality, an inexhaustible sensibility. Hence the reactions – appearances, memories, many things, go on playing upon it with consequences that I note and 'enjoy' (grim

word!) noting. It all takes doing – and I *do*. I believe I shall do it again – it is still an act of life. But you perform them yourself – and I don't know what keeps me from calling your letter a charming one! There we are, and it's a blessing that you understand – I admit indeed alone – your all-faithful . . . Henry James.

For James, as long as there was consciousness, there was life – life possessed of interest no matter how much gloom and desolation engulfed him. In 1910 his brother William had died and James was plunged into despair. 'I sit heavily stricken and in darkness', he wrote. But he did not remain mute and passive: he embarked on a positive testimony to William James which turned into his own autobiography. He confronted the fact of death with an act of life. And his charmingly delicate reproach to Adams was a just one; for Adams, too, in the bleak years which followed the suicide of his wife (in 1885), found his consciousness intrinsically interesting, and some ten years before James was writing his autobiographies, Adams too had cast far back into the past and written his *Education* which, like James's unfinished work, was essentially a history of the development of his particular mind. For Adams and for James the main, if not the sole guarantee of the reality of their own identities was the fact, the mystery, of that mixture of perception and retrospection, thought and memory, called consciousness. They were not defined by any public role because neither of them had one; no society conferred a dimension of social reality on them because although they moved through many societies, they were committed to none. Both were disengaged from America to some extent – emotionally, intellectually, physically – neither was fully assimilated into Europe (James's deathbed adoption of British nationality scarcely constitutes assimilation). Adams goes out of his way to call himself a 'tourist' and James refers to himself as an 'outsider'. Both terms apply to both men. They were, unquestionably, two of the most remarkable minds to emerge from New England, and they were homeless minds. They were like some other great modern writers in this respect; their minds achieved a degree of richness and complexity that made it impossible for them to be contained and circumscribed by any worldly profession, any particular culture or society, any one country. Their allegiances were internal. 'Everyone must bear his own universe', said Adams. True; but not everyone feels it and the majority, happily perhaps, live in a universe they believe is being carried by other people. But James and Adams knew that they carried their own universe; which was the mind and everything within it. Each was a supreme consciousness – a consciousness without a context. Consciousness operating in the absence of context is a not uncommon phenomenon among American writers – one feels something of it in Emerson, for example. But this absence is often welcomed and sought for. The consciousness liberated from the limitations of a context can start again – see it new, think it new, make it new. Thus one often finds in American writers – particularly outside of New England – the systematic emptying of consciousness to facilitate the accession of new perceptions and fresh notations. In emptying the mind such writers deny duration, immobilize memory, and thus attempt to rid themselves of the past. But the older part of America had a more complex relation to the past. Immigrants *from* Europe turned round and went on pilgrimages *to* Europe. So in many New England writers you find a more ambivalent attitude to the past; an instinct to flee it combined with a compulsion to seek it out; a fear *of* it which is at the same time a fascination *with* it. (This is as true, for instance, of Hawthorne as it is of Lowell.) James's last novel, *The Sense of the Past*, is about a man who dreams of making a visit to the past. Weirdly the dream comes true and he finds that he has indeed made the return. But he is trapped. He cannot escape back to the present. The dream darkens towards nightmare. So that in saying that Adams and James each embody a consciousness without a context I am not saying that it is a consciousness without a past. For both of them duration was a reality and a mystery to be explored, and memory was an amazing faculty to be exercised, or, for James, an inexhaustible treasure trove to be endlessly looted. Both men were historians. James was what Conrad called him 'the historian of fine consciences', and Adams was in effect the historian of America's conscience in his monumental work on *The Administrations of Jefferson and Madison*, as well as in *his* two novels. But as well, and this brings me to the subject of this paper, they were both superlative historians of themselves. And, given the many apparent similarities – similar dates of birth, common friends, comparable experiences of America and Europe during the same period; given, too, that they were both in their differing ways visionaries and artists; and given, finally, that in some ways they *were* lone survivors of a vanished America, it seemed to me it might be interesting to take a brief comparative look at the histories they wrote of their own memories, their own consciousnesses, their own selves.

What did they see when they looked back; or rather, what did they *do* with what they saw? For, of course, the retrospective vision can detect significances, discern patterns, or impose shapes which are scarcely available to the participating vision. For Adams (aged 67) and James (aged 70), most of the material was in when they wrote their autobiographies. It was up to them to select, omit, arrange as they pleased. Omissions there certainly are, and of a major order. Adams, for instance, never mentions his wife, nor her suicide in 1885; yet this had a shattering effect on him. James takes some 600 pages to reach the age of 26 and his first visit to Europe as an adult, and of these twenty-six years his chronological account is sketchy and apparently casual and random.

Both men, as a matter of fact, had a horror of biography. When Adams sent his *Education* to James he wrote: 'This volume is a mere shield of protection in the grave. I advise you to take your own life in the same way, in order to prevent biographers from taking it in theirs.' In a sense both books are shields, and it has taken the admirable scholarship of Ernest Samuels and the persistent labours of Leon Edel to reconstruct the lives in a more traditional biographical way. James and Adams did not write 'confessions' in any literal sense, and with reference to sheer factual information they conceal as much as they reveal. What, then, do they do with their lives seen in retrospect? One thing they did was to turn them into representative American lives; or rather, they made their own pilgrimages of consciousness into something approaching archetypes of the American mind in search of a role in the changing modern world. By suppressing what seemed to them irrelevant, or merely contingent, or untouchably private, they went some way towards generalizing their past experience, so that their books offer less in the way of personal reminiscence for its own sweet, nostalgic sake, and become recognizable national odysseys which contribute to the self-consciousness of America itself. Adams always refers to himself in the third person as though the author was a distant dispassionate observer; and although James uses the first person he handles his younger years with a very special kind of detachment. And although the usual thing to say is that the two books couldn't be more different, there are one or two similarities which make the differences even more interesting.

For instance, both books stress the failure of orthodox traditional education. Adams constructs his book as a series of failures to gain an education: his chapter on his years at Harvard ends, as do so many subsequent chapters, with the emphasis 'education had not begun'. James did not structure his book to this end but he, too, often describes the various attempts to give him the usual good education, whether in Europe or at Harvard Law School, and always he shows himself emerging as 'an obscure, a deeply hushed failure'. Either their educations are not adequate for them, or they are not adequate to their educations. Whichever way it is, the effect in both books is of a consciousness somehow at odds with, or out of step with, the environment in which it finds itself. These, then, are minds which refuse to be wholly shaped by the world around them; the customary ways of construing, assessing, and manipulating reality as taught by society's official educators are not for them. They cannot take reality for granted in quite the same way, nor do they find its meanings so stable as the tutors they are put to school with. Throughout both books there is manifest an inclination to disengage the mind from the accepted and accredited world pictures, or constructs or models, which are offered to them. As a result of this, both books depict minds striving to achieve their own vision of things, trying to draw up their own maps. Unlike many American writers they do not find anchorage in the certainties of the external world. They represent a different tradition from the one which leads to William Carlos Williams's saying 'no ideas but in things'. They would have said, no ideas but in consciousness. Things are endlessly dubious, capable of many different readings. Rather than let the world shape their minds, Adams and James, in different ways, dramatize the instinct of the mind to reshape the world. So, to sum up the similarities, we can say that both books show a detached and wandering consciousness (they were both rootless travellers bereft of any deep sense of anchorage); a lone consciousness beset by mysteries, wonders, problems, and horrors out of which it must somehow derive some nourishing or sustaining meaning. And both books outline the steps in a crucial inner transformation. For both books portray the incapacity of the two authors in the world of action, the world of politics, business, material success; but then both books show the emergence of a sort of superior sensitivity, a responsive spectator in quest of comprehension – in Adams's case the historian prophet, in James's case the novelist. So both books have a certain bare outline in common. The failure turns into the visionary. Out of the alien comes the artist.

And yet, of course, the difference between the two books is radical. James's work, we recall, reduced Adams to pulp and provoked a letter which we may assume contained some assertion as to the futility of his undertaking and a strong exhortation to silence, for James wrote back to defend the primary activities of reacting to things and articulating those reactions. As he grew older Adams grew more and more attached to the supreme value of silence and he ended his *Education* with an emphasis on death, silence, the cessation of interest, the final failure of motive power, the futility of further inquiry. The death of Hay is the occasion for this final commitment to silence. 'It was not even the suddenness of the shock, or the sense of void, that threw Adams into the depths of Hamlet's Shakespearian silence . . . it was only the quiet summons to follow – the assent to dismissal. It was time to go. The three friends had begun life together; and the last of the three had no motive – no attraction – to carry it on after the others had gone.' The end of Adams's book is an end indeed: it marks the termination of his interest in life. By way of contrast, it is entirely right that James's work remained unfinished. How could he have finished it? Every new day of consciousness would have extended the account. For James, interest in life was coextensive and coterminous with life itself. To be conscious was to be interested; only the final failure of consciousness would warrant the abandoning of his work. His autobiographies seem to anticipate no firm conclusion, just as he felt that experience itself had no certain limits, that properly speaking relations stop nowhere. But Adams was very interested in 'stoppage'. In a late letter (1912) he works out his 'date of stoppage' for the world, 1917 as it happens. And his famous 'Letter to American Teachers of History' reveals how attractive the notion of 'entropy' was to him, because it provided vivid metaphors for the conclusion of the world's history. He relished Kelvin's prediction 'that all nature's energies were slowly converting themselves into heat and vanishing in space, until at last nothing would be left except a dead ocean of energy at its lowest possible level' and his demonstration that 'the universe . . . was flattening steadily, and would in the end flatten out to a dead level where nothing could live'. He clearly preferred Kelvin's Law of Degradation to Darwin's Law of Elevation and something in his sombre imagination was moved by the notion of man as 'a bottomless sink of waste' and the picture of the world as an ever-increasing 'ash-heap'. Everything was sinking into dissolution and inertia. The title of his favourite book was *Decline and Fall*.

Now clearly there was some grim personal consolation in this attitude. After all, a world which did not require the service of an Adams in public office was clearly going downhill. For the offspring of presidents to be reduced to mere spectatorship and commentary clearly indicated that a radically new phase of history had commenced, and to Adams – the inheritor of eighteenth-century values, at sea in a twentieth-century world – that phase inevitably appeared as a step closer to chaos, rather than any move towards perfection or improvement. But Adams's pessimism is not solely a projection of a personal grudge. His ancestors *had* stood for important values and beliefs in the history of America, and if these values and beliefs were now dispensable then clearly something radical had happened. In his *Education* Adams generalizes himself into a mind brought up on older values trying and failing to comprehend the world that was coming into being. He starts by recalling the 'perfect poise' of Charles Francis Adams, a poise not incompatible with public leadership. But by the end of the book the only poise available to the modern Adams is an achieved and maintained private indifference. Adams's comic yet bitter image for the American author tells us something of the personal disappointment underlying the mask of indifference. 'My favourite figure of the American author is that of a man who breeds a favourite dog, which he throws into the Mississippi River for the pleasure of making a splash. The river does not splash, but it drowns the dog.' James, too, no doubt felt that he had thrown in some dogs who had been drowned without splashing. But for James the answer was never to commit himself to silence and indifference and forewarnings of a general stoppage. And it was presumably James's imperturbable persistence in his writing, through no matter what personal isolation and public disorder, that left Adams so aghast. Now whether Adams was correct in his pessimistic predictions it is not my immediate aim to discuss: 1917 has come and gone, but only just. I want rather to try to suggest the kind of mind Adams had and in what it differed so radically from James's.

Turning to the *Education* we notice that Adams recasts his life as an unremitting search for abstract meaning. He starts with a number of vivid childhood *impressions* but by the end he is desperately in quest of a *law*, a theory, some comprehensive intellectual system which will give coherence to the welter of his experience. 'From cradle to grave this problem of running order through chaos, direction through space, discipline through freedom, unity through multiplicity, has always been, and must always be, the task of education . . .' And what he demonstrates is that the task cannot be accomplished: 'In plain words, chaos was the law of nature; order was the dream of man.' Now in this quest for some law which could be intellectually formulated Adams dismisses a whole range of impressions which James himself found endlessly nourishing. Adams can recall all the random vivid sights and smells of boyhood summers. He clearly responded to the unkempt nature of the South, and the 'passionate depravity that marked the Maryland May' stirred him to the writing of a deeply sensuous passage (at the start of Chapter Eighteen) which T. S. Eliot found worthy of incorporating into his poetry almost unchanged. But such memories of sense impressions are excluded as soon as mentioned, because they did not *mean* anything. Similarly, when he is recalling the various places where he attempted to gain some education we find mere impressions are dismissed. For instance, Antwerp moved him at first: 'the taste of the town was thick, rich, ripe, like a sweet wine' – a Jamesian response; but Adams adds 'but he might as well have drunk out his excitement in old Malmsey, for all the education he got from it'. Again when he first really responds to Beethoven in Germany 'a new sense burst out like a flower in his life', but again the retraction follows 'he could not credit it, and watched it as something apart, accidental, and not to be trusted'. Note the word 'accidental' there. It recurs when Adams describes his reactions to Italy and Rome. Adams recalls being very moved: 'life had no richer impression to give', but he dwells no longer on these impressions because he cannot see 'what they teach'. So Italy too is dismissed as 'a piece of accidental education'. Rome provokes him to all sorts of questions – 'Why! Why!! Why!!!', but no one and nothing can tell him what it all 'means'. So he concludes: 'In spite of swarming impressions he knew no more when he left Rome than he did when he entered it.' Here is a crucial point. Impressions did not constitute knowledge for Adams; the exfoliation of the flowers of the senses was not to be trusted because it did not lead towards abstract formulations of meaning. But for James, impressions were the basis and perhaps the sum of knowledge. He preferred Europe to America mainly because it provided a richer, denser range of impressions. James cultivated and tended the very flowers that Adams distrusted. Those areas of experience which Adams rejected as accidental James embraced as essential.

If Adams disregarded mere impressions, what then did he concentrate on? In a word, the foredoomed failure of the human mind to comprehend a universe of power. 'Power' or what Adams also calls 'the eternal mystery of force' is a key concept in the book. A force like the Virgin of Chartres he can understand; it was a unifying force, a source of form. But as he said in an essay ('The Tendency of History') 'the old idea of form' has now been adapted to incorporate 'the idea of Energy'. Just so, in the *Education* he starts in the ordered and intelligible world of Quincy and ends in the unintelligible formlessness of modern New York. 'The outline of the city became frantic in its effort to explain something that defied meaning. Power seemed to have outgrown its servitude and to have asserted its freedom . . .' After the intelligible Virgin, the unintelligible dynamo, which he makes into a symbol of all the new impersonal generators of undreamt-of powers which were bursting on the world. It is this bewilderment in the face of new powers which leads him to seek for some 'law of acceleration', some 'dynamic theory of history' which will at least reduce to intellectual order the rate at which new powers are discovered and released in the world. But such is the rate of new inventions that the mind cannot keep pace with the forces appearing all around it. As he says succinctly in a letter, 'our power is always running ahead of our mind'. His valiance is in his attempt to keep up in this race for comprehension. His dread was that humans were inherently unstable and yet 'at the rate of progress since 1800, every American who lived into the year 2000 would know how to control unlimited power'. This is a dread we can all share: human unreason with unreasonable power at its fingertips. And Adams's pessimism went further, for in a strange anticipation of Freud's idea of the death-wish in *Beyond the Pleasure Principle* he projects the idea of some universal urge to death running through all nature. 'As Nature developed her hidden energies they tended to become destructive'; and, 'nature has educated herself to a singular sympathy for death'. Indeed his most profound experience was of nature as an 'insanity of force'. While watching his sister die in great agony, tortured by a freakish illness after a trivial fall, he says, 'the human mind felt itself stripped naked, vibrating in a void of shapeless energies, with resistless mass, colliding, crushing, wasting, and destroying what these same energies had created and labored from eternity to perfect'. In a universe reduced to a jungle of hostile energies and an accelerating wastage of things there is little education to be had, and Adams approaches his conclusion with the minimal discovery: 'he had learned his ignorance'. It is, of course, a moot point whether the greatest mind can learn more, and Adams was certainly a great mind. As the late R. P. Blackmur said of him:

> the greatness of the mind of Adams himself is in the imaginative reach of the effort to solve the problem of the meaning, the use, or the value of its own energy. The greatness is in the effort itself, in the variety of response deliberately made to every possible level of experience. It is in the acceptance, with all piety, of ignorance as the humbled form of knowledge . . . As it is a condition of life to die, it is a condition of thought, in the end, to fail.

The silence which Adams preached is only an anticipation of that silence to which all energy of mind must eventually succumb.

But in all Adams's apocalyptic foreboding we must notice the very high degree of contrivance and schematization in the *Education*. Adams minimizes the successes and deprecates the satisfactions of his own life to make the final emergence of the pessimistic visionary-philosopher more graphic. As Professor Samuels says, and demonstrates so well, 'each experience, appraised in terms of the philosophic calculus of 1905, is manipulated to demonstrate failure, mistake, misconception, ignorance, and futility'. Adams admits that 'he inherited dogma and *a priori* thought' and one becomes aware of a good deal of brilliant but inflexible *a priori* arrangement, juxtaposition, and conceptual opposition in the *Education*. Artistic license, we may say, and so it is. But the feeling of verdict preceding evidence, of experience being subtly deformed by dogma, is sometimes very strong. From the start one is aware of a strong disposition towards patterning and schematization – town life against rural life, school versus summer, convention against exoticism, tidy North opposed to ragged South, restraint versus liberty, form and wildness, theory and practice, force and freedom, heat and cold, and above all, unity and multiplicity: every new idealistic expectation is followed by a disillusioning event. In these ways the myriad details of a life are classified, divided, opposed, and arranged in a pattern of remorseless clarity. Each narrative event is disposed in such a way as to provoke a particular stage in his intellectual development. For example, he places the assassination of the Russian Minister Plehve just before the moment he develops his dynamic theory of history. Adams puts himself in France at the time, studying the church of the Virgin: the juxtaposition of modern news and ancient worship triggers off a crucial bout of questioning in his mind. 'Martyrs, murderers, Caesars, saints and assassins – half in glass and half in telegram; chaos of time, place, morals, forces and motive – gave him vertigo. Had one sat all one's life on the steps of Ara Coeli for this? Was assassination to be the last word of

Progress?' History here serves to set the scene for a visionary moment. Again, near the end Adams depicts himself looking out of his window on Fifth Avenue, 'witnessing the anarchy, and compares it to being in Rome under Diocletian. The two-thousand-years failure of Christianity roared upward from Broadway, and no Constantine the Great was in sight.' Autobiography here is the tenuous occasion for apocalypse. There is indeed a great deal of consummate art in the book and a gift for ironic observation and deprecation to which I have not begun to do justice. Nevertheless, it seems to me indisputable that much of the art and the irony goes into portraying and justifying Adams's final state of consciousness – pessimism and silent indifference.

This pessimism, I would like to stress, is directly related to Adams's search for a lucid pattern in things which could be intellectually formulated. In his essay on 'The Tendency of History' the aspirations of the historian are seen as being the discovery of a system, 'a great generalization that would reduce all history under a law'. The search is for a clear 'trail' in 'the thickset forests of history'. Adams would like to see a 'science of history' which 'must be absolute . . . and must fix with mathematical certainties the path which human society has got to follow'. His letters are full of such statements as 'It is mathematically certain to me that another thirty years of energy-development at the rate of the last century, must reach an *impasse*.' 'Logically we must strangulate and suffocate in just fifteen years.' And the more he insisted on patterns and systems and laws the more helpless man's position seemed to him. 'As I have measured the mass of our social movement, nothing can now deflect it, and it matters not a straw what anyone says or does.' This need for a clear path in history dominates the *Education*. Adams's mind insisted on 'a necessary sequence of human movement', at least 'a spool on which to wind the thread of history without breaking it'. But Adams can see quite clearly that the responsibility for 'unity' was not with history but the human mind. 'Without thought in the unit, there could be no unity; without unity no orderly sequence or ordered society. Thought alone was Form. Mind and Unity flourished or perished together.' But by a sort of tragic paradox, as man's consciousness expands, so does the complexity which it must try to order – 'as the mind of man enlarged its range, it enlarged the field of complexity, and must continue to do so, even into chaos, until the reservoirs of sensuous or supersensuous energies are exhausted, or cease to affect him, or until he succumbs to their excess'. For Adams, only the mind could bestow Unity, and he could foresee it drowning in its own confusion, ignorance, and chaos. He drives the final paradox home. If there is a unity in life 'the unity was chaos'. Such form as his mind can produce is really a glimpse of imminent formlessness and chaos.

Adams's pessimism finally extends to his own mind, and consciousness itself ceases to have any value for him. We find him in 'The Tendency of History' at least entertaining the notion that 'Consciousness is only a phase in the decline of vital energy', and in a late letter he specifically says, 'As I look back on our sixty years of conscious life, I have to search hard for a word of warm satisfaction.' All his mind does for him now is prove that all experience is 'failure'. This was another reason why he welcomed the Law of Entropy, because 'it imposes a servitude on all energies, including the mental'. The only law on which Adams would repose with any confidence was a law which denied human consciousness any autonomy or purpose and which predicted its final extinction. No wonder Adams preached silence. But we may confront him with one of his own notions here. He wrote in an essay: 'Always and everywhere the mind creates its own universe, and pursues its own phantoms.' Adams 'created' a notional universe of chaotic forces and meaningless multiplicity, but perhaps he was too single-minded in the phantom he pursued. He set out after a system, a distinct pattern, a law, and when he found that it was a phantom indeed, when it vanished before his closing hands, he returned the blackest verdict on human life. Chaos without, chaos within. Human consciousness, as he knows it, is stripped of all its pleasures, and compensations and possibilities, and reduced to the grim, bleak task of analysing and forecasting the doom to come. Such a narrowing of the scope of consciousness is impoverishing and unacceptably severe.

Compare, for instance, James's words to Grace Norton in that famous letter of consolation in which he spoke of the 'gift of life':

> Life is the most valuable thing we know anything about, and it is therefore a great mistake to surrender it while there is any yet left in the cup. In other words consciousness is an illimitable power, and though at times it may seem to be all consciousness of misery, yet in the way it propagates itself from wave to wave, so that we never cease to feel, and though at moments we appear to, try to, pray to, there is something that holds one in one's place, makes it a standpoint in the universe which it is probably good not to forsake.

My main point is simply that although James was also capable of many pessimistic perceptions of the world (he spoke of 'the Medusa face of life'), yet he never lost a sense of what he calls 'the wonder of consciousness in everything', meaning simply the wonder of *his* being conscious of the world. This phrase may serve as a fitting introduction to a few remarks about the distinguishing qualities of James's *Autobiographies*. For while he shows himself in many ways quite as confused in the world as Adams, he does not push on so remorselessly to the narrowest pessimistic conclusions. He held on to one value at least. 'I lived and

wriggled, floundered and failed, lost the clue of everything but a general
lucid consciousness . . . which I clutched with a sense of its value.' When
James looked back he reconstructed his past very differently from
Adams. On first reading, one has the impression that James's work is
much less patterned than Adams's; indeed it seems to flout the very
notion of arrangement. But I do not think this is senescent laziness on
James's part. His intention was different.

Adams set out to combine two histories: the history of his own efforts
to comprehend the world, and the history of the human race up to the
present and into the future. But James confines himself almost entirely to
the history of the development of his own consciousness – its confusions
and gratitudes, its bewilderments and wonders, its experience of the
strangeness of life and its intimations of the grace of art. He does not seek
for any containing system of ideas; he does not try to draw up a theory
which will unify the history of the world. Adams, we noted, organized a
lot of his material around symbolic opposites, the most important being
multiplicity and unity. There is nothing so schematic in James. And this is
not simply because he was less well equipped to handle abstract ideas than
Adams. His whole sense of how consciousness and memory worked was
different, and it is this which makes his account of his 'education' so
different from Adams's. Let me run together some of the ways he refers
to his relationship to the past. 'Remembrance steals on me . . . I woo it all
back . . . I turn round again to where I left myself gasping . . . Let me
hurry, however, to catch again that thread . . . I scarce know why, nor do
I much, I confess, distinguish occasions – but I see what I see . . . I lose
myself under the whole pressure of the spring of memory . . . I meet
another acute unguarded reminiscence . . .' James apologizes for leaving
'the straighter line of my narrative'. He 'gleans' memories from things
'not minding that later dates are involved'. He is totally indifferent to
external chronology, the unilinear history of physical events; he has a
rarely subtle sense of the mysterious commerce between present
consciousness and those vestiges of past states of consciousness preserved
in the intermittent brilliances of memory. Not for James the comparatively crude imposition of a narrative with a dogmatic intent. He uses
words like 'surrendering' and 'succumbing' to the past; thus 'I live back
of a sudden – for I insist on just yielding to it.' There is certainly no
ordering of the past according to a theory. It is rather as if James's mind
was wandering through the museum of his own memory, responding to
sudden gleams and forgotten echoes, alternatively wooing and yielding
to the still-vibrant impressions which are stored in the recesses of his
consciousness. He does not want to find a theory which will explain life:
he is content to recapture vibrant images of life. This is a crucial
distinction, for where Adams tends always to ideas, dismissing impres-

sions as merely accidental, James cherishes impressions and tends always to images as having an intrinsic value.

> I foresee moreover how little I shall be able to resist, through these Notes, the force of persuasion expressed in the individual *vivid* image of the past wherever encountered, these images having always such terms of their own, such subtle secrets and insidious arts for keeping us in relation with them, for bribing us by the beauty, the authority, the wonder of their saved intensity. They have saved it, they seem to say to us, from such a welter of death and darkness and ruin that this alone makes a value and a light and a dignity for them, something indeed of an argument that our story, since we attempt to tell one, has lapses and gaps without them.

The story *is*, indeed, the sequence of preserved images which furnished James's own consciousness. In actual life, all tends to death and darkness and ruin. The Past, in reality, is so much 'imponderable dust'. The human consciousness, as long as it still is conscious, performs a great act of salvage and rescue, simply by remembering, recalling the stored-up images. The human consciousness saves what life merely wastes.

I think it is no accident that at the end of the first two volumes of the autobiography (the only completed ones) James each time concludes with an unwelcome cessation of human consciousness. *A Small Boy and Others* ends with James recalling a time of illness when he was so feverish he passed out. The last words are, 'I fell into a lapse of consciousness that I shall conveniently here treat as a considerable gap.' *Notes of a Son and Brother* ends with a moving account of the life and death of Mary Temple, the young girl who played a major part in the evolution of James's fictional world. She became the very image of a generous but doomed consciousness which James explored and dramatized time and time again. 'She was absolutely afraid of nothing she might come to by living with enough sincerity and enough wonder . . . Life claimed her and used her and beset her – made her range in her groping, her naturally immature and unlighted way from end to end of the scale.' James writes of her beautifully, and at the end he speaks out with a directness which blinks no facts and glosses over none of the horrors of life. He describes Mary Temple's progressive weakening. 'None the less she did in fact cling to consciousness; death, at the last, was dreadful to her; she would have given anything to live – and the image of this, which was long to remain with me, appeared so of the essence of tragedy that I was in the far-off aftertime to seek to lay the ghost by wrapping it . . . in the beauty and dignity of art.' Here James ends his second volume; again with a lapsing from consciousness, and an intimation of the consolations of art and the value of the preserved image.

There are many other fine studies of characters in the book; James's father and his brother William in particular, of course, but even the most minor figures are addressed and recreated with James's full art. One tiny example which seems to me to be representatively fine. An unnamed uncle who 'was blank from whatever view, remaining so under the application of whatever acid or exposure to whatever heat; the one identity he could have was to be part of the consensus. Such a case is rare . . . that of a natural platitude that had never risen to the level of sensibility.' This 'ancient worthy', like so many characters in the Jamesian universe, came to an end on his first trip to Europe. He 'disembarked in England only to indulge in the last of his startled stares, only to look about him in vague deprecation and give it all up. He just landed and died.' In all this we can notice how different is James's way of treating characters from Adams's. Adams tends to make his characters figures in parable, representative of certain virtues or certain failings: they exist mainly in relation to Adams's quest for meanings and explanations. But for James each character is a single mystery, to be relished, respected, deprecated, or adored. Whatever his own feelings, the recalled characters are not stiffened into allegory, not adapted to a fixed schema. James is content to preserve them in art, recapture them in all their unique complexity. For their own sake – for the sake of mere life. They too are vivid images rescued from the imponderable dust. In this work of salvaging things from 'the limbo' of the past, James never succumbs to the too theoretic misanthropy which is evident in Adams's work. James's tone is distinctly generous and grateful. 'As I breathe all this hushed air again even the more broken things give out touching human values and faint sweet scents of character, flushes of old beauty and good-will.'

The main difference between the two men is that although James felt quite as much an outsider, an alien, 'a visiting consciousness' as Adams, although he was as uncertain as to ultimate meanings, James yet felt there was an intrinsic value in the recovered images of life, just as it was. His consciousness was prepared simply to appreciate these images, while Adams wanted to interpret, classify, systematize. That is why James refers so often to the 'recoverable picture'. He had the instinct of the artist, while Adams developed the drive of the philosopher. That is why consciousness was for James a consolation, whereas for Adams it became a torment. You never find James complaining of multiplicity or yearning for unity. On the contrary he delights in the multiple details he can recapture. He loves to evoke what he calls the 'tiny particles of history'; that is why he will spend pages recapturing a room, someone's clothes, a facial appearance, a sudden tremor of delight or fear; as he beautifully puts it, 'the passion, that may reside in a single pulse of time'. The myriad details which he draws into his net do not worry him by their unrelated scatteredness as they would Adams. On the contrary he refers even to the merest scrap of recollected detail as 'gold dust'. Such fragments did not need to be knit together into an intellectually coherent unity before they yielded a value. These images were valuable in themselves, and he allows them to come together and recongregate in involuntary constellations. Unity for Adams was, had to be, a matter of linear cause and effect. But for James the unity of the mind was a more subtle and mysterious thing – like a web, in which every caught particle (of 'gold dust') was related to every other particle through the infinite complexity of the tremulous filaments of consciousness. This is why he has such a degree of reverence for the apparently chance configurations of memory. As he says on the first page:

> To recover anything like the full treasure of scattered, wasted circumstance was at the same time to live over the spent experience itself, so deep and rich and rare, with whatever sadder and sorer intensities . . . and the effect of this in turn was to find discrimination among the parts of my subject again and again difficult – so inseparably and beautifully they seemed to hang together and the comprehensive case to decline mutilation or refuse to be treated otherwise than handsomely.

The mood is very remote from that of Adams's *Education*. It is much nearer the mood of that great autobiography which Proust knew by heart, Ruskin's *Praeterita*, in which Ruskin, at the end, reflects so movingly: 'How things bind and blend themselves together', and concludes with that marvellous picture of the fireflies fitfully glowing in the Italian dusk. '*How* they shone! moving like fine-broken starlight through the purple leaves . . . the fireflies everywhere in sky and cloud rising and falling, mixed with the lightning, and more intense than the stars.' The fireflies irradiate the night just as clusters of vivid images and impressions coruscate in the shadows of memory. With such celebratory words does human consciousness transcend the ravages inflicted by Time. Just so, for James an evocation of the past is always a 'fond evocation'. He is content to 'squeeze the sponge of memory' and watch 'the stored secretions flow'. He sought no 'necessary sequence' as Adams did. It was enough that memory, that 'mine of consciousness' in Hegel's phrase, should yield up its buried gems.

In connection with this generous appreciation of sheer life it is worth noting the large number of gustatory images employed by James. He frequently dwells on literal pleasures of the palate – jams, cream, peaches, savoury soups, and a memorable waffle ('the oblong farinaceous compound, faintly yet richly brown, stamped and smoking, not crisp nor brittle, but softly absorbent of the syrup dabbed upon it for a finish'). And these literal memories merge into metaphors. So we find such phrases as 'the wine of perception' (which Adams found so valueless in his education), and there are many passages referring to his storing up 'treasures of impression that might be gnawed, in seasons or places of want, like winter pears or a squirrel's hoard of nuts'. He even says things like 'wherever I dip, again, I pull out a plum from under the tooth of time'. Perhaps these images smack a little too much of the gourmet; yet in sum they aptly convey James's sense of the essentially positive relationship between consciousness and existence. Life *does* nourish the mind and feed the memory. The writer must first 'devour' the world perceptually; in due time he will 'distill' these perceptions into a work of art (another of James's images). James was surely trying to stress the assimilatory intimacy, the unmediated reciprocity, between mind and life. After all, neither is anything without the other. And as there are literal delights of the palate, so, for James, there is a subtler but no less real pleasure in the ability of the consciousness to savour its own contents, the impressions and images it has garnered and hoarded. Time and again James reveals himself as somehow excluded from participation in life: like his favourite character Strether he is constantly regarding life from the isolated vantage point of a balcony; but the compensation is that he can comprehend and appreciate and sympathize more than the actual immersed participants in life are able to do. He realizes early on that there are two ways of taking life: 'one way of taking life was to go in for everything and everyone, which kept you abundantly occupied, and the other way was to be occupied, quite as occupied, just with the sense and image of it all, and on only a fifth of the actual immersion'. The second way was James's way. He chose, he says, to 'live inwardly'. And he derives as much joy, perhaps more, from 'the secrets of the imaginative life' than other people derive from 'the actual concretions of existence'.

It is interesting to note that as he grew older, James, like Adams, found that life itself grew more complex as the perceiving mind develops in complexity: 'the limits of reality as I advanced upon them seemed ever to recede and recede'. The difference is that James does not mind. It is all scope and matter for wonder, food for consciousness. If life is larger and more mysterious than any human system, well, his consciousness can accept that. James, unlike Adams, did not seek to build a stable structure of knowledge; looking back he decided on a different subject matter altogether. He describes what he decided would be his subject in this way: 'the personal history as it were, of an imagination, a lively one of course . . . had always struck me as a task that a teller of tales might rejoice in, his advance through it conceivably causing at each step some rich precipitation'. Whom should he choose? 'He had been with me all the while, and only too obscurely and intimately . . . I had in a word to draw him forth from within rather than meet him in the world before me, the more convenient sphere of the objective, and to make him objective, in short had to turn nothing less than myself inside out.' So, in his *Autobiographies* James is turning his consciousness inside out, trying to recapture what went into it to turn it into the consciousness of a novelist, an artist. That is why he does not seek to worry the past into a sequence, or make it the basis for a prediction, or subsume it to a system. Whatever the past was, however it was, it was what went into the making and forming of his, James's consciousness – which was, as we have seen, the one value he believed in to the last. This is why he is so much gentler and more sensitive with the past than Adams. He is both fonder and more detached, seemingly incapable of derision:

> the beauty of the main truth as to any remembered matter looked at in due detachment, or in other words through the haze of time, is that comprehension has then become one with criticism, compassion as it may really be called one with musing vision, and the whole company of the anciently restless, with their elations and mistakes, their sincerities and fallacies and vanities and triumphs, embalmed for us in the mild essence of their collective submission to fate.

It is a twilight mood, but far from despair; a mood in which meditation, comprehension and compassion are at one. The past was imponderable dust; and the present (the First World War) was dark indeed; and James does not at all slight or mitigate the darkness, death, and ruin in life. But over against it he continued to hold up 'the wonder of consciousness'. Whereas Adams set out to unravel the secrets of nature, James set out to explore the mystery of his own consciousness. And it was James who rejected despair.

One final comment, this time from a contemporary artist, Naum Gabo; it catches the distinction I have been trying to make between these two great minds. Gabo writes:

> Once we put Nature outside us and embark on a voyage to catch up with its beginning and to touch its ceiling, we shall inevitably, sooner or later, come into a void of nothingness. It is imperative for us to know beforehand when we embark on a voyage into the infinite that wherever we may travel, whatever planet we may find on our way, our consciousness will be waiting for us there, and we shall never find anything save what that consciousness has prepared for us. And then it was clear to me that whatever secrets there are in Nature, I can unravel and understand them only through the images which my conscious-ness forms of my experiences. The images of our life, as well as of Nature, can only be understood when we take them for what they are in our experience, namely, as works of art created by our consciousness.

James was aware of this supreme value of consciousness and I think it helped him to negotiate that 'void of nothingness' out of which Adams, for all his theories, found no guide.

7

William Dean Howells and
A Hazard of New Fortunes

'The most vital of my fictions', wrote Howells of *A Hazard of New Fortunes*; and certainly this book, finished in 1889 when Howells was 52, represents the peak of his achievement as a novelist. It was also the full flowering of certain changes which had come about in his life (and hence in his fiction) since 1886; and to appreciate his achievement up to that date it is useful to turn to an essay by Henry James, summing up Howells's contribution to American literature, and written in 1886, just before the changes commenced. James praises Howells's 'unerring sentiment of the American character' and notes admiringly his capacity to 'feel' and respond to the quality of contemporary American life. 'I will not say that Mr. Howells feels it all equally, for are we not perpetually conscious how vast and deep it is? – but he is an authority upon many of those parts of it which are most representative.' He then stresses the strong documentary bias in Howells's work – 'I know of no English novelist of our hour whose work is so exclusively a matter of painting what he sees, and who is so sure of what he sees' – and welcomes it in these terms: 'His work is of a kind of which it is good that there should be much today – work of observation, of patient and definite notation.'

Howells's work does reveal a deep faith in a sort of positivism, a habit of scrupulous regard for the massed contingencies of one particular place at one particular time (he was indebted to both Comte and Taine), and his conviction as to the supreme value of sheer observation is responsible both for the limits and virtues of his work. 'The only secret of art is to observe with the naked eye', he wrote in 1871: he is surely wrong, for art has many more secrets than that, but it was just this singleness of concentration which enabled him to make his unique contribution to American literature. The American imagination, then as now, tended to express itself in romance, projecting its vision through symbol and myth,

111

rarely content to limit itself to what James called 'the fatal futility of Fact'. But Howells considered facts to be far from futile, and he made them the object of his patient concern.

As a novelist he started late, and he started cautiously. Before his first novel, written when he was 35 and largely autobiographical (*Their Wedding Journey*), he had published books on Italy and a collection of *Suburban Sketches* which addressed themselves to the task of objective description of specific localities. Gradually Howells enlarged his scenes, trying to assemble, as it were, a gallery of limited but complete pictures of American life as it was then being lived. He was giving America something that Hawthorne, Melville, Poe, Cooper, even James himself did not give and probably did not care to give – something, however, which America very much needed at that time: normative images of contemporary society. When Mark Twain and Henry Adams both praised the 'photographic' quality of Howells's early work, they were not simply paying a fashionable compliment. American society had very few photographs of itself, and in post-Civil-War America, with convulsive industrial and social changes making themselves felt, Howells did invaluable work in showing Americans to themselves in the *milieu* of the moment. As James pointed out, he concentrated on the representative places and people of America – Bartley Hubbard and Silas Lapham rather than Hester Prynne and Captain Ahab – but though there is much that is merely charming and innocent in his early comedies of manners, he can occasionally be as sharply perceptive as his beloved Jane Austen; and works like *A Modern Instance* were the reverse of flattering. He was in fact attacked for being cold, sceptical, analytic, scientific, and too concerned with commonplace things and people. So Howells made one of his characters in *The Rise of Silas Lapham* counter the sort of romantic idealism which produced such criticisms with the words: 'Commonplace? The commonplace is just that light, impalpable, aërial essence which they've never got into their confounded books yet.' Emerson had indeed asserted the 'worth of the vulgar' – 'I embrace the common, I explore and sit at the feet of the familiar, the low' – but for purely philosophical or mystical motives. His transcendentalism enabled him to intuit the divine unity of all things by meditating on the most trivial fact; but 'embracing the common' was more of a religious exercise than anything else. For Howells it was a crucial tenet in an aesthetic creed which was to produce an important period of social realism in American literature. James's description of Howells's qualities as a novelist gains added force if we realize that it was a description which, at that time, could not have been applied to any other American writer.

> He is animated by a love of the common, the immediate, the familiar and vulgar elements of life, and holds that in proportion as we move into the rare and strange we become vague and arbitrary; that truth of representation, in a

word, can be achieved only so long as it is in our power to test and measure it. He thinks scarcely anything too paltry to be interesting, that the small and vulgar have been terribly neglected, and would rather see an exact account of a sentiment of a character he stumbles against every day than a brilliant evocation of a passion or a type he has never seen and does not even particularly believe in. He adores the real, the natural, the colloquial, the moderate, the optimistic, the domestic, and the democratic; looking askance at exceptions and perversities and superiorities, at surprising and incongruous phenomena in general.

James appreciates Howells's 'art of imparting a palpitating interest to common things and unheroic lives', and finishes with a generous and accurate prediction about Howells's future work. 'It is hard to see how it can help being more and more fruitful, for his face is turned in the right direction, and his work is fed from sources which play us no tricks.' But, in passing, James also offers a serious criticism of Howells's novels. He suggests that they reveal the innocence of American life inasmuch as they 'exhibit so constant a study of the actual and so small a perception of evil'.

It was a fair comment. But on 4 May 1886 a bomb was thrown in Haymarket Square, Chicago, killing eight policemen: eight known anarchists were arrested, regardless of alibis, and in an atmosphere of brutal mob hysteria, one subsequently committed suicide and four were hanged. This was the turning-point in Howells's life. Hitherto he *had* thought that, on the whole, 'the more smiling aspects of life' were 'the more American'. Now, after this blatant and vicious miscarriage of justice, Howells lost his sanguine and complacent attitude towards American society, never fully to recapture it. To his father he wrote, 'the historical perspective is that this free Republic has killed five men for their opinions'; to a friend, 'it's all been an atrocious piece of frenzy and cruelty, for which we must stand ashamed forever before history'. Howells himself, with real courage, defended the men and protested against the sentences passed. This availed nothing for the victims – but much for his fiction. He wrote to Hamlin Garland: 'I did not bring myself to the point of openly befriending those men who were civically murdered in Chicago for their opinions without thinking and feeling much, and my horizons have been indefinitely widened by the process.' Those widening horizons ultimately resulted in *A Hazard of New Fortunes*, the first comprehensive attempt to anatomize the new emergent urban-industrial America.

Up to 1866 Howells had mainly focused on the failings and foibles of individuals seen against the accepted stabilities of some provincial setting: manners and morals were scrutinized, but the complexities of economics and politics did not intrude. After that he tried increasingly to explore and reveal the forces at work in American society at large, for the stability of society could no longer be taken for granted – something was wrong with it, rotten in it. In *Silas Lapham* the subject is the moral rise which accompanies the financial fall of the main character. In *A Hazard of New Fortunes* the real subject is the future of America. That gives some idea of how much the horizons had widened for Howells in a mere three years.

Several other events and influences combined with Howells's anguish over the Haymarket affair to produce the widened scope and deeper seriousness of *A Hazard of New Fortunes*. Since he was a writer who relied very largely on personal experiences and feelings in his writing – to ensure that verifiable authenticity of texture which was his aim in fiction – it is not surprising that his letters provide some clear hints on the direct relationship between his life at the time and the novel. In a letter to Mrs Achille Fréchette written in 1887 he describes his feelings about the execution of the anarchists and then goes on to ask: 'Have you read Tolstoi's heart-searching books? They're worth all the other novels ever written.' It was just at this time that Tolstoy became the major influence on Howells, not only encouraging him to attempt a new comprehensiveness in his coverage of society, but forcing him to re-examine his ideas on the relationship between individual morality and society. He wrote later: 'I can never again see life in the way I saw it before I knew him.' Tolstoy, as much as the Haymarket affair, determined the mood of the novel, a mood also influenced by the protracted illness and ultimate death in 1889 of his daughter Winifred, so that much of the sombre brooding in the book is charged with his own private sadness.

We have clues as well to the sources of some of the material used in the novel. Thus in 1887 he wrote to DeForest: 'I'm just back from my old home in Ohio, where I saw a town in full bloom from the discovery of natural gas. It was a wonderful spectacle gaseously, materially and morally. I believe I shall try to write a story about it. I saw lots of character, blowing off with almost as much noise as the gas wells themselves.' This provided him with a potent image of the terrifying, possibly infernal, powers which had been unleashed over a land hitherto almost completely rural and agrarian, producing people with new powers and new problems – like Dryfoos in the novel. In 1888 he wrote to James: 'I found your letter here when I came home this morning from a house-hunt in New York . . . I should hardly like to trust pen and ink with all the audacity of my social ideas; but after fifty years of optimistic content with "civilization" and its ability to come out all right in the end, I now abhor it, and feel that it is coming out all wrong in the end, unless it bases itself anew on a real equality . . . But at the bottom of our wicked hearts we all like New York, and I hope to use some of its vast, gay, shapeless life in my fiction.' The move to New York provided Howells with the initial impetus for the novel – he himself was hazarding new fortunes in New York at the time – and his house hunt occupied the first fifth of the finished book. This move away from Boston was as significant as his earlier infiltration of it had been. It meant that the literary centre of America had moved, for the first time, out of Brahmin New England. In focusing on the mixed turbulence of New York – from whence Boston seemed to be 'of another planet' – Howells effectively signalled the end of an epoch in American literature. As for his new social ideas, they were coming to him thick and fast in the late eighties: Edward Bellamy, Henry George, Laurence Gronlund, William Morris, the 'Fabian Essays', as well as Tolstoy, all contributed to the socialist ideas which increasingly occupied his mind, and influenced his fiction. In *The Minister's Charge* (1887) the Rev. Sewell preaches his last sermon on the theme of 'Complicity', a concept which became of major importance to Howells after the Haymarket affair. Then in *Annie Kilburn* (1888), bearing in mind the more than 10,000 strikes that had disrupted the economy in 1886, Howells turned his attention squarely to 'the relations of capital and labour'. *A Hazard of New Fortunes*, with its wide spectrum of social philosophies opposed and juxtaposed, is the result of these years of incessant troubled thinking by Howells; it is his definitive attempt to explore and express the variety of social theories which proliferated as the faults and horrors of a capitalist *laissez-faire* society became increasingly apparent.

More immediately, a prolonged traction strike which occurred in New York while he was finishing his novel gave Howells just the sort of documentary material he most liked to work from, and its occasional ugly incidents offered a precedent for the violent climax with which he brought the issues of his book to a head. Howells believed that if the structure of society was all wrong then the best way to get at that wrongness was, almost literally, to go out into the streets and pick up the evidence as it offered itself. Many of the tours which Basil March takes round the city come straight out of Howells's own notebooks, kept while he was engaged in similar wanderings, and the scattered street incidents which shock him had shocked Howells; even the restaurant 'Maraoni's', where March meets Lindau, was 'Moretti's', where Howells used to dine with a club of literary and theatrical people. Similarly many of the characters for the novel were recruited at least partially from people Howells had known: Lindau was based on a lonely German refugee called Limbeck who taught Howells German when he was twenty, and Fulkerson owes much of his being to a wild, free-wheeling, picaresque character, known to Howells and Mark Twain, named Ralph Keeler. The Marches are of course based on the Howells family: his favourite observers, they occur in seven novels, three times as major figures. Basil March, standing by Lindau against the capitalist Dryfoos and risking his job, is, in effect, Howells writing in defence of the

Haymarket anarchists – a gesture of principle which also could have put his employment in serious jeopardy. And Basil March, involved in a society which he knows is corrupt and unjust, feelingly aware of the inequalities and suffering around him, uncertain as to blame, uncertain as to cure, conscience-stricken but ineffectual – that too is Howells, 'theoretical Socialist, practical Aristocrat' as he called himself, the very image of the worried intellectual who sees many wrongs but has no solutions, who is himself concerned to maintain his high standard of living in the precarious society whose defects occupy his waking mind.

Before examining how Howells gathered these disparate materials together into a novel it will be helpful to consider some of his literary theories and economic ideas: we may then be in a better position to understand the form of the novel and the moral import of its action. Howells's realism, his love for 'the poetry that resides in facts and resides nowhere else', his stress on 'veritism' and 'the truthful treatment of material', were throughout moral. He himself contrasted the 'spiritual' realism of the Russians with the 'sensual' realism of the French, and in his own work he never attempted to emulate the unsparing and unremitting analytic candour of the French school. He thought that life should be looked at 'in the right American manner', a manner which will 'question the results with the last fineness for their meaning and value'. The moral meaning was out there in the facts if the novelist only observed honestly enough: 'Morality penetrates all things, it is the soul of things.' So he can assert, with no contradiction, first that 'the novel ends well that ends faithfully', and then that the most poisonous and mendacious of novels are those which 'imagine a world where the sins of sense are unvisited by the penalties following, swift or slow, but inexorably sure, in the real world'. His idea of objective truth never involved moral neutrality, simply because he did not believe that the truth could be morally neutral. A novelist must not be false to humanity, 'either in its facts or its duties' – the one was as apparent as the other. Similarly, he would ask of a novel: 'Is it true? – true to the motives, the impulses, the principles, that shape the life of actual men and women? This truth, which *necessarily* includes the highest morality and the highest artistry – this truth given, the book cannot be wicked and cannot be weak' (my italics). Art had a responsibility; it should help us 'to know and to understand, that we may deal justly with ourselves and one another': art which 'disdains the office of teacher is one of the last refuges of the aristocratic spirit which is disappearing from politics and society, and is now seeking to shelter itself in aesthetics'. After the Haymarket affair, as his sense of involvement and responsibility grew, he felt that art, though objective, should be committed – *engagé* as we should now say. 'Art, indeed, is beginning to find out that if it does not make friends with Need it must perish.' On the other hand realism should not be 'tendencious. It does not seek to grapple with human problems, but is richly content with portraying human experiences.' It should do justice to the insoluble complexities of real life and 'the God-given complexity of motive' in real people – no romantic gloss, no facile superadded sermons, no 'unreality'. He wanted to see characters as he saw them in Hardy, 'in the necessity of what they do and what they suffer', that is, 'really doing what they must while seeming to do what they will'.

This raises the complicated question of determinism. Howells thought it is 'our conditioning which determines our characters, even though it does not always determine our actions'. This is an uneasy compromise which leaves some scope for moral assessment and allows important possibilities to personal conduct: it keeps the full pessimism of naturalism at bay. On the other hand it leads to difficulties when it comes to the shaping of a novel: here Howells believed that 'the man does not result from the things he does, but the things he does result from the man, and so plot comes out of character'. That is – environment determines character, which in turn should determine the shape of the book. Believing this, Howells was consistent in his scorn for 'plot' and his lack of interest in 'novels of incident, of adventure'. A novelist should just 'put certain characters before you' and, as it were, leave the rest to them. His ideal of a novel was the 'free and simple design' of *Don Quixote*, in which 'event follows event without the fettering control of intrigue' and all 'grows naturally out of character and conditions'. He thought this 'loose, free and variable form' would be ideal for portraying the fluid life of America and, although in his own early work he favoured the economic and narrow focus of Turgenev, he moved on to wider, vaster books which could encompass the random comings and goings of many characters. As though trying to catch the very shapelessness of life itself he says: 'I don't know that you are bound to relate things strictly to each other in art, any more than they are related in life'; and he came to realize and assert that 'the more art resembles life, the less responsive it [is] to any hard and fast design'. Characters should not be constrained by a plot: the constraints of environment would suffice.

This faith that observation and ordinary life when brought together would produce a novel led Howells to undervalue style and composition: these latter sounded aristocratic and aesthetic, and Howells wanted art to be democratic and humanitarian. James saw this trend in his work. He wrote, in 1886, that Howells was wrong to say that 'style matters less and less', and he regretted that Howells 'should appear increasingly to hold composition cheap – by which I mean, should neglect the effect that comes from alternation, distribution, relief. He has an increasing tendency to tell his story altogether in conversations.' Clearly Howells's position involves grave formal difficulties since all art must depend on some selection and arrangement and Howells leaves himself few criteria to determine these. It is as though his ideal of fiction would be to capitulate to the profuse inclusiveness of life itself. We will not embark on the theoretical problems involved in his ideas, but just point to these difficulties in relation to *A Hazard of New Fortunes*. He wants to bring a number of people together to examine their various views and several fates. But how, in the absence of a plot? He himself saw the difficulty.

> There are few places, few occasions among us, in which a novelist can get a large number of polite people together . . . Perhaps it is for this reason that we excel in small pieces with three or four figures, or in studies of rustic communities, where there is propinquity if not society. Our grasp of more urbane life is feeble; most attempts to assemble it in our pictures are failures, possibly because it is too transitory, too intangible in its nature with us, to be truthfully represented as really existent.

So, refusing to bind his fluid material with a plot, he was left with an essentially episodic method of composition. As he said, somewhat defensively, 'a big book is necessarily a group of episodes more or less loosely connected by a thread of narrative, and there seems no reason why this thread must always be supplied'. Yet without this 'thread' he still wanted to show that all human lives are intertangled, to bear out his theory of 'complicity' – and the purely episodic book would have tended to demonstrate rather the opposite, the fragmentary unrelatedness of people. So instead of a plot he sets up a situation which will plausibly permit characters to come and go and talk to each other, even bringing them into occasional collisions and embraces. This situation is the editing of the magazine *Every Other Week* (based, of course, on his long experience as editor of the *Atlantic Monthly*). The contributors and their families can fairly be expected to come into contact with each other. But this is an external contrivance: how can he initiate any significant action? The answer is that he cannot, without having recourse to tiny bits of plot – extraordinary coincidences, unexpected meetings, sudden violence in the streets (the coming together of March and Lindau at the place of Conrad's death in the riot is a contrived and melodramatic chance beyond the bounds of pure realism): these are necessary to supplement the domestic gatherings, the office meetings, the conversational strolls which permit his characters to talk but not, really, to act. Say what he will, it is Howells who forces his characters together. Left alone, there is really nothing to combine all the people in the book; no significant action irresistibly draws them all in. They converge but never really congregate: they touch and jostle with no real engaging and relating. Their lives overlap but are in no way interlocked. When they walk out of a room, or out of a chapter, they walk out into a void; when they reappear it is

Howells who has summoned them. This is perhaps part of the unintentional truth of the book: that in the new world represented by the great conglomeration of New York, people are both responsible for each other and separated from each other. Alongside Howells's entirely acceptable theory of human complicity has to be set the undeniable fact of human isolation. People lead plotless lives: the writer must provide one if art is to display values and meanings not to be discerned in the blurred continuity of everyday life.

Yet Howells did want his work to do something more than display the fortuitous configurations of the commonplaces of life. What this 'more' was can best be suggested by some of his comments on the European writers he admired. Thus: 'The great and dreadful delight of Ibsen is from his power of dispersing the conventional acceptations by which men live on easy terms with themselves and obliging them to examine the grounds of their social and moral opinions.' Like Tolstoy he made it his business 'to make us look where we are standing, and see whether our feet are solidly planted or not. What is our religion, what is our society, what is our country, what is our civilization?' He welcomed the French realists because if the house of society is in disrepair we should know it, and also because 'it is extremely valuable to have the underpinnings of sentiment and opinion examined, from time to time'. The novelist cannot offer solutions ('the longer I live the more I am persuaded that the problems of life are to be solved elsewhere, or never'), but he can 'give us pause'. That is, he can and must 'make us take thought of ourselves, and look to it whether we have in us the making of this or that wrong, whether we are hypocrites, tyrants, pretenders, shams conscious or unconscious; whether our most unselfish motives are not really secret shapes of egotism; whether our convictions are not mere brute acceptations; whether we believe what we profess'. And Tolstoy's great achievement is to 'bring us back to the gospels as the fountain of righteousness'; he teaches 'the law and life of self-sacrifice'. A good novel may be sad 'because life is mainly sad everywhere', and it should not be final since finality is beyond us: but above all it should demonstrate that 'in the vast orphanage of nature we have no resource but love and union among ourselves'. This is what Howells wanted to show in his most ambitious novel.

Clearly we have gone beyond aesthetic considerations here, because for Howells ideas about art were inseparable from social and even religious convictions. His own were in fact very simple, despite all the social theorists he was reading so avidly. He had no flair for economic analysis, and his economics no less than his aesthetics were based on ethics. The most important of his ethical ideas can be traced back to his childhood, which he spent in rural Ohio under the strong influence of a father who was a benign and intense Swedenborgian. Much of what Howells found in Tolstoy was in fact a refinding of his childhood influences. As he realized: 'Tolstoi gave me new criterions, new principles, which, after all, were those taught us in our earliest childhood, before we came to the evil wisdom of the world.' The basic idea he learned from his father was that self-concern and love of this world are damning: only honest labour and selfless love can save – egotism is the root of all evil. All his later theories rest on this conviction. The other major influence was simply being brought up in rural America 'where all had enough and few too much': 'we are a village people' he later wrote, and what he meant, like any Populist, was that life in America deteriorated and grew more corrupt as it drew further from the small rural communities he grew up in. Silas Lapham is regenerated by renewed contact with rural America: Dryfoos cannot go back, any more than America could go back, and his fall seems unredeemable.

These two influences combined to make Howells detest the ferocious competitiveness involved in urban capitalism. This new economy seemed to produce 'insuperable inequalities' which effectively prevented 'the brotherhood' which was the avowed ideal of America. Howells never really understood what was happening, economically, in America. All he could see was a vicious predatory selfishness and a cruel indifference spreading among the population as the industrial revolution grew in power. At the same time the cities grew and the land was ravenously exploited and despoiled. Howells's anatomy of society went no further than a juxtaposition of these facts. In his Utopia of *Altruria* the economy tends everywhere to simplification, and the inhabitants prefer cities to shrink. Their major achievement is to have controlled the struggle for survival and to have passed from 'a civility in which people live *upon* each other to one in which they lived *for* each other'. Howells knew there was no going back, but he had no realistic notions of how to supervise and modify the growth of the society of his age, no proper concepts of the mechanics of control. He had instead a pious mystical faith (again Swedenborgian) that the new society would somehow appear. 'I look forward to the decay of both the old parties, and the growth of a new one that will mean true equality and real freedom.' He hated all violence (hence the criticism of Lindau in the book) and was convinced that 'every drop of blood shed for a good cause helps to make a bad cause'. He still believed that the labouring class 'has the majority of votes and can *vote* the laws it wants'. He was never a party man or an active reformer (a vote for Bryan in 1896 was about the limit of his partisanship): he simply had 'faith in the grand and absolute change', a faith, be it said, which was often darkend by moods of total pessimism. Letters of 1890 contain these sentiments – 'for the greater part of the time

I believe in nothing, though I am afraid of everything . . . Perhaps we can only suffer into the truth, and live along, in doubt whether it was worth the suffering. It may be an illusion, as so many things are (may be all things); but I sometimes feel that the only peace is in giving up one's own will.' There was always a mystical, quietistic side to Howells, a part of him which withdrew from the world of hard facts and brutal economics. (It is worth remembering that the next novel he wrote was *The Shadow of a Dream*, a novel that moves into the silent elusive domains of the private heart and soul.)

His economics thus appear naïve. But as a novelist he was more immediately concerned with individuals and he was able to show quite graphically the havoc and despair caused by the myriad forms of egotism and selfishness which people display. He saw America becoming a plutocracy and minced no words in proclaiming the fact; but the only remedy for social wrongs, indeed for all wrongs, as far as he could see, was 'love'. His idea that 'men are bound together so indissolubly that every advance must include the whole of society', his theory of 'complicity', his notion of 'the mystery of our human solidarity' – these are more religious than political, more Christian than Marxist. The dangers of 'self-hood', 'the distinction of self-forgetfulness', the idea that 'whenever we love, the truth is added unto us', the certainty that 'unselfish labour gives so much meaning to human life' – such beliefs have little to do with economics, but they are basic to Howells's fiction. His economic ideas, then, like his mature ideas about fiction, really come down to the one basic tenet: 'In the vast orphanage of nature we have no resource but love and union among ourselves.'

This brief summary of Howells's ideas at the time should help us to appreciate what he was trying to achieve in this novel. In it he manages to touch on most of the doubts and hesitations and worries that were bothering him, and a good deal of society, when he wrote. None of the characters is wholly right or completely evil, nor are they caricatured into mere ciphers for different theories. But they do represent the varying points of view which were shaping the America of that time. Basil March is basically the centre of consciousness, and one of his meditations about the 'frantic panorama' of New York leads up to the basic proposition of the book:

> Accident and then exigency seemed the forces at work to this extraordinary effect; the play of energies as free and planless as those that force the forest from the soil to the sky; and then the fierce struggle for survival, with the stronger life persisting over the deformity, the mutilation, the destruction, the decay of the weaker. The whole at moments seemed to him lawless, godless; the absence of intelligent, comprehensive purpose in the huge disorder, and the violent

struggle to subordinate the result to the greater good, penetrated with its dumb appeal the consciousness of a man who had always been too self-enwrapped to perceive *the chaos to which individual selfishness must always lead.* (my italics)

This is modern America, and Howells in the book tries to show the multiplicity of types of selfishness that are responsible, somehow, for the chaos of society; and the rarer types of selflessness which at present are helpless to redeem society – as things are, they can only die for it in the name of a better future. Conrad Dryfoos is a Tolstoyan figure of renunciation and good works, too saintly to live. Lindau, the socialist, is dismembered by the society for which he once gave a hand. He dies for his opinions, like the Haymarket anarchists, though his own theories are vitiated by the acceptance of violence and he is fatally wounded in a brawl he is actively encouraging. These two selfless extremists are foredoomed victims of a selfish society, and Howells gives them added dignity by hinting a comparison between Lindau and the Old Testament prophets, and between Conrad and Christ. Another impractical idealist is Woodburn, with his hatred of commercialism and his dream of a perfected agrarian feudal society, such as he thinks the South could have created (a prophetic touch by Howells – Woodburn's ideas live on!).

The two most selfish characters are Dryfoos and Beaton, and here Howells displays real insight. Dryfoos, the very incarnation of selfish individualism, is in many ways a victim of a change in society. In a rural community his ideals of self-help were valuable, as they had been for the pioneer: with the full release of the uncontrollable potential of the industrial revolution his old virtues become new vices, because of the terrible power at their disposal. 'His moral decay began with his perception of the opportunity of making money quickly and abundantly.' He is the supreme example of 'the men who have made money and do not yet know what money has made them'. All normal feelings dry up in him: he ends a hollow man, lost to all joy, shaken by remorse, a slightly bewildered victim of the 'dog eat dog' world in which he made his pile and lost his soul. Dryfoos is Howells's mordant parabolic representative of America itself. His wife is a more pathetic victim, utterly out of place in the world of commercial success, while his daughters represent a new type – shallow and crude but destined to be a disruptive influence in society because of the unanswerable force of their wealth. Beaton is in private what Dryfoos has been in public. (Howells suggests a link through Christine's intaglio ring – Beaton trifles with it on her hand, doubtless meditating whether to marry her for her money; while it is on Dryfoos's hand when he strikes his son – his wealth has thus soured his natural affections.) Beaton is a clever artist, and also a complete egotist, utterly insensitive to the needs and feelings of other people, a subtly drawn justification of Howells's insight that 'to do whatever one likes is finally to do nothing that one likes, even though one continues to do what one will'. Howells was acute enough to realize that 'a nature like Beaton's was chiefly a torment to itself', for Beaton is condemned to selfhood, and Howells manages to convey just what a wretched, empty life results from such a condition. Beaton finally seems to lose all volition entirely, too light and irresolute to go through with the suicide that he triflingly meditates, just as he has triflingly meditated a variety of personal relationships which he is too self-preoccupied to develop. He is a nasty and rather chilling example of the utterly selfish life, and one of Howells's most telling portraits.

Fulkerson, the gay, philistine, unscrupulous, entrepreneur type, can survive in society; while March himself starts the book as a 'self-enwrapped' man of average selfishness, who gradually learns to take a more engaged, less egotistical view of society. (Just before the end of the book he gets a new hat – in Jungian terms this indicates a new personality, but it is doubtful if Howells intended anything so symbolic.) This development reflects the metamorphosis Howells himself underwent, and is a particularly interesting comment on Howells's changing conception of the responsibilities of art. At first as March wanders round New York he sees only the 'picturesque' aspects of the various poverty-stricken 'phases of low-life' he encounters: they offer good, and profitable, copy for the magazine. It is Conrad who maintains that the city is really preaching a continual sermon and that art could serve an ethical purpose by making 'the comfortable people understand how the uncomfortable live'. When the strike is on, Fulkerson is still keen to exploit its 'aesthetic aspects' for the magazine, but March develops a broader awareness and subtler conscience and is in a position to act as a spokesman for Howells's own views. Somewhat like Howells's idol Tolstoy, he has 'replaced the artistic conscience by the human conscience'. He does very little, apart from objecting to Lindau's dismissal, but his early complacency has given way to heart-felt doubts and worries and his late musings are more social than artistic:

> Some one always has you by the throat, unless you have some one else in *your* grip. I wonder if that's the attitude the Almighty intended His respectable creatures to take toward one another! . . . what I object to is this economic chance-world in which we live and which we men seem to have created . . . At any time of life – at every time of life – a man ought to feel that if he will keep on doing his duty he shall not suffer in himself or those who are dear to him, except through natural causes. But no man can feel this as things are now; and so we go on, pushing and pulling, climbing and crawling, thrusting aside and trampling underfoot; lying, cheating, stealing; and when we get to the end, covered with blood and dirt and sin and shame, and look back over the way we've come to a palace of our own, or the poor-house . . . I don't think the retrospect can be pleasing.

It was in the late eighties that Howells's own art began to 'make friends with Need': more generally he felt that the American artist was not paying enough attention to the conditions and qualities of the life around him. Since, as he reiterates in this book, 'conditions *make* character', it followed that he should want American artists to turn their gifts to portraying the contemporary environment. He himself goes out of his way in this novel to include descriptions of the conditions of life all over New York: he is extremely observant about architecture and interior decorations; he devotes much time and attention to clothes and furniture; he describes with care different streets and various immigrant communities. As always he is fascinated by all means of transport (he himself was an early example of the rootless, semi-nomadic artist), and he is particularly brilliant in his evocation of the Elevated trains at night and the great railway stations of the city. Indeed, he seems to anticipate the Ash-can School of painters when he comments, reproachfully, on 'the superb spectacle' of the railway 'which in a city full of painters nightly works its unrecorded miracles'. Howells took it upon himself to record a great deal of what had hitherto been left unrecorded and, in contrast to the trivial aestheticism exemplified by Beaton, he encouraged American artists to come to grips with the surging, unexplored stuff which filled their daily lives.

Thus with its compendious variety – of character, of idea, of scenic detail – the novel attempts, as no other novel had previously attempted, to present an inclusive image of contemporary American life. It is an impressively honest book. All the characters, except the saints, live in 'enforced complicity with rapine'; they all 'respect money' and have to sell out, more or less, to survive; they all 'truckle and trick' to some degree, though some have more principles than others. March shares Howells's mystical hope that one day, somehow, 'the order of loving kindness, which our passion or our wilfulness has disturbed, will be restored', but meanwhile, as he says, 'we go on trembling before Dryfooses and living in gimcrackeries'. The book portrays a society in which people are insecure, bewildered, often alone, submerged or elevated by forces beyond their control, living in desperate poverty or surrounded by the vulgar 'gimcrackeries' which serve as the status symbols of the currently well-to-do (Howells wrote one of the most sympathetic reviews of Veblen's *Theory of the Leisure Class* when it appeared). While behind them all is the heartless teeming anonymity of the city, the new world that Dryfoos and all he stands for was all unconsciously, all inevitably, bringing into being. It was something to tremble before; and it was a remarkable feat to produce a novel which could adequately and forcefully communicate that profound apprehension.

Howells's importance for American literature transcends his actual achievement as a novelist. By the end of his life he had become the first – and hitherto the last – American Academician. It is not too much to say that for the last quarter of the nineteenth century Howells was responsible for educating and directing American literary taste. His lifelong fight was against the falsifying unreality of base romantic literature (he respected the genuine sort of romance such as Hawthorne wrote); he wanted to gain respect and attention for 'the phrase and carriage of everyday life'. He spoke for empirical observation and against facile idealism. In a famous passage he imagined the old-fashioned idealist complaining to the modern scientist in these terms:

> I see that you are looking at a grasshopper there which you have found in the grass and I suppose you intend to describe it. Now don't waste your time and sin against culture in that way. I've got a grasshopper here, which has been evolved at considerable pains and expense out of the grasshopper in general; in fact, it's a type. It's made up of wire and card-board, very prettily painted in a conventional tint, and it's perfectly indestructible. It isn't very much like a real grasshopper, but it's a great deal nicer, and it's served to represent the notion of a grasshopper ever since man emerged from barbarism. You may say that it's artificial. Well, it is artificial; but then it's ideal too; and what you want to do is to cultivate the ideal. You'll find the books full of my kind of grasshopper, and scarcely a trace of yours in any of them. The thing that you are proposing to do is commonplace; but if you say that it isn't commonplace. for the very reason that it hasn't been done before, you'll have to admit that it's photographic.

Howells made the real grasshopper his particular care and the upholders of the ideal grasshopper his particular enemies. When he wrote, in his first novel, 'Ah, poor Real Life, which I love, can I make others share the delight I find in thy foolish and insipid face' he was, in effect, announcing a programme. When he started to write, the sentimental tradition had a firm grip on American literature. These romancers (like Horace Courtenay, Caroline Lee Hentz, Rose Terry – but their name is legion) inculcated, wrote Howells, 'a varying doctrine of eager conscience, romanticized actuality, painful devotion, and bullied adoration, with auroral gleams of religious sentimentality'. However, in 1862 T. W. Higginson, in 'A Letter to the Young Contributor' (published in *Atlantic Monthly*), pleaded for an indigenous and contemporary American literature; and for the next forty years, mainly under the leadership of Howells, a school of realism grew up which was to have a lasting effect on the whole subsequent development of American literature.

Apart from his own work, which was very popular and influential in his own time (he was perhaps the first American writer to make a very good living by writing), Howells encouraged other American writers and introduced foreign authors, forcing them on the attention of his contemporaries as probably no other man could have done at that time. If ever a man tried to be in touch with the best that was being written and thought, that man was Howells: it is hard to imagine what would have happened to American taste and, indeed, American literature, without his ceaseless and untiring aid, his impassioned and judicious supervision. Here are some of the writers he either encouraged to write and first published, or effectively introduced to an American audience for the first time: Henry James, Mark Twain, John DeForest, Edward Eggleston, Sarah Orne Jowett, Mary Murfree, George Washington Cable, Bret Harte, Harold Frederic, Hamlin Garland, Frank Norris, Stephen Crane. Indeed, it was almost entirely due to Howells that by 1900 there were very few sections of America that had not been written about: he made Americans regard and respect their own land, their own kind. But he also turned their attention abroad, and with the help of the remarkable Thomas Sergeant Perry (who wrote some 427 items for Howells) he introduced or directed attention towards such people as: Gogol, Tolstoy, Dostoevsky, Turgenev, Baudelaire, Flaubert, Stendhal, Zola, Musset, the Goncourts, Mérimée, Gautier, Mistral, Bourget, Scribe, Dumas the elder, Saint-Beuve, Renan, Björnson, Ibsen, Shaw, Verga, Galdós, Valdés. As well as being a cultured editor he was a brave one: in 1881 he published a sensational exposé of big business, Henry D. Lloyd's 'The Story of a Great Monopoly', which was a telling indictment of Standard Oil and a forerunner of the Muckraking movement. This list alone reveals what a generous, sensitive, and intelligent critic Howells was. Apart from 'banging the babes of Romance about' as he called it (an activity which attracted to his work the labels 'atheism', 'poison', 'dirt'), he was, in Dreiser's words, 'the lookout on the watch tower straining for a glimpse of approaching genius'. He wrote, sincerely, 'nothing of my own which I thought fresh and true ever gave me more pleasure than I got from the like qualities in the work of some young writer revealing this power', and it was surely an open-minded critic who could start his career by encouraging the unknowns, Henry James and Mark Twain, and finish it by introducing and supporting Crane, Garland, and Norris.

By the end of his life Realism was threatened by two new movements. First, a recrudescence of romanticism. Frank Norris described it in these terms: 'Just as we had with *Lapham* and *A Modern Instance* laid the foundations of a fine, hardy literature that promised to be our very, very own . . . we commenced to build upon it a whole confused congeries of borrowed, faked, pilfered romanticisms'; while in his famous interview with Howells, Stephen Crane said: 'It seemed that realism was about to capture things, but then recently I have thought that I saw coming a sort of counter wave, a flood of the other – a reaction, in fact.' That was in

1894: by 1900 books like *The Prisoner of Zenda* were selling in millions, and in 1904 *Colliers Magazine* could announce that 'the popular novel of today is romantic – romantic in subject and effusively romantic in method . . . All this is far removed from the minute study of common-place people which Mr. Howells has made the basis for most of his fiction.' Howells could see what was happening. It was just after the Spanish war and, he wrote, being ashamed of our 'lust of gold and blood' we now welcomed 'the tarradiddles of the historical romancers as a relief from the facts of the odious present'. As he said to Crane, 'I suppose we shall have to wait.'

But there was another, more serious, change in fiction which he recognized without being able to adapt himself to it. He wrote with typical tolerance in 1903: 'A whole order of literature has arisen, calling itself psychological, as realism called itself scientific, and dealing with life on its mystical side . . . we have indeed, in our best fiction, gone back to mysticism, if indeed we were not always there in our best fiction, and the riddle of the painful earth is again engaging us with the old fascination.' Howells's realism was based on the premiss that the meaning of life could be gleaned from the observable surfaces of people and things: now writers were diving for private meanings dragged out from hidden depths. Howells's time was over. But not before he had done enough to earn the sort of praise lavished on him in *The Critic* in 1899.

> He is part of our literary climate. We breathe Howells, most of us . . . We cannot untangle him from ourselves. His art belongs to us. Our common American lives are the warp and woof of all that he has brought. In his large and sane and noiseless way he may be said to have done more for the self-respect of American fiction than any other living man.

Howells's work was admired by people as various as Mark Twain and Henry James in America, and Turgenev and Thomas Hardy abroad. When *A Hazard of New Fortunes* appeared it proved to be very popular, and it undoubtedly exerted a positive influence on the progressive thinking of the nineties. Howells's reputation reached its apogee in 1912 when President Taft made a special journey to attend his 75th birthday dinner, and praised his service to the ideals of 'refinement and morality', calling him 'a force for good'. By this time Howells had become a symbol of orthodoxy and the official culture, and as such he was soon under attack from the young writers of a new age. In 1915 he wrote to James: 'I am comparatively a dead cult with my statues cut down and the grass growing over them in the pale moonlight'; and soon he was to be jeered at as being the head of the 'sissy school' of literature. Gertrude Atherton blamed Howells for making American literature 'the most timid, the most anemic, the most lacking in individualities, the most bourgeois, that any country has ever known'. Mencken, having read

almost none of Howells's work, proclaimed: 'He had nothing to say . . .
His psychology was superficial, amateurish, often nonsensical; his irony
was scarcely more than a polite facetiousness; his characters simply
refused to live.' Sinclair Lewis spoke of him with patronizing contempt
in his Nobel Prize speech of 1930 ('he had the code of a pious old maid'),
and in the same year V. L. Parrington wrote that 'in elaboration of the
commonplace he evades the deeper and more tragic realities that reach to
the heart of life'. All rebels and innovators need a figure to tilt at, and
Howells, at least as a symbol, was all too obvious and available. Since
then there has been no great renewal of interest in his work, though
several discerning critics have found a lasting value in it. Lionel Trilling
has made a brilliant case for him (of which more later). Newton Arvin
pointed out that it was Howells who described the 'warped and stunted
and perverted lives' of Americans at the turn of the century, and added
that 'few writers have realised so keenly what happened to the old
dogmas of self-help and self-cultivation by the time the triumph of
individualism had taken its toll of them'. He found Howells's work still
'usable', particularly for its 'implicit criticism of an egocentric culture'.
Henry Steele Commager found in his novels a 'realism that does not
depend upon sensationalism or violence, a style that is subtle rather than
raucous, and a concern for values that are permanent rather than
transient'. Other critics, like Edwin Cady and Everett Carter, have
written systematic and sympathetic books on Howells and gradually a
more appreciative view is being taken of his total achievement. 'Your
really beautiful time will come', wrote James to Howells. It has not come
yet, but we are now perhaps in a good position to assess his peculiar
qualities as well as his undeniable limitations.

Again it is James who provides a fine note of just appreciation, this
time in a letter written to Howells on his 75th birthday. He stresses the
advantages Howells reaped by staying at home: 'You have piled up your
monument just by remaining at your post. For you have had the
advantage, after all, of breathing an air that has suited and nourished you;
of sitting up to your neck as I may say – or at least up to your waist – amid
the sources of your inspiration.' This gave Howells an increasing
authority of perception so that

> they make a great array, a literature in themselves, your studies of American
> life, so acute, so direct, so disinterested, so preoccupied but with the fine truth
> of the case . . . You saw your field with a rare lucidity; you saw all it had to give
> in the way of the romance of the real and the interest and the thrill and the
> charm of the common, as one may put it; the character and the comedy, the
> point, the pathos, the tragedy, the particular home-grown humanity under
> your eyes and your hand and with which the life all about you was closely

> interknitted. Your hand reached out to these things with a fondness that was in
> itself a literary gift.

It is a touching and generous piece of praise, the more so as one feels how different were James's own fictional interests from the democratic 'documentary' notation he approved in Howells. But occasionally he managed to suggest his reservations, implying not only that Howells wrote too much, too variously, and too facilely – which he did – but that he was leaving something out. In 1884, for example, he wrote: 'I don't think you go far enough, and you are haunted with romantic phantoms and a tendency to factitious glosses'; and in 1890: 'There's a whole quarter of heaven upon which, in the matter of composition, you seem consciously – *is* it consciously? – to turn your back.' Edith Wharton doubtless had the same thing in mind when she spoke of the 'incurable moral timidity' she felt in Howells's work. More outspokenly, Norris finally came to assert the limitations of Howells's realism, with its focus on 'the ordinary, the untroubled, the commonplace', and advocated a fiction which could reach down into 'the unplumbed depths of the human heart, and the mystery of sex, and the problems of life, and the black, unsearched penetralia of the soul of man'.

There is undeniable justice in the charges brought against Howells. There are certain passions his characters are never moved by; none of them ever gets out of hand; no black energy threatens the prevailingly decorous tone of his novels. Howells tended to keep any *radical* disorder out of his work. His characters appear in low relief. There are no baffling penumbras between them, no uncertain spaces and twilight recessions behind them. His novels are decidedly not 'fraught with background'. Yet he himself was far from being the 'incurable optimist' James thought him. Here, for instance, is a letter to Mark Twain about the latter's proposed autobiography:

> You always rather bewildered me by your veracity, and I fancy you may tell the truth about yourself. But *all* of it? The black truth, which we all know of our selves in our hearts, or only the whitey-brown truth of the pericardium, or the nice, whitened truth of the shirtfront? Even *you* wont tell the black heart's truth. The man who could do it would be famed to the last day the sun shone on.

If Howells kept the 'black heart's truth' out of his work it was not from ignorance.

He did practise exclusion, of course, despite his avowed reverence for all truth. He admitted that he preferred 'cleanly respectabilities' and would have no 'palpitating divans' in his own work. He responded to Whitman's work but complained: 'He has told too much . . . [the reader] goes through his book, like one in an ill-conditioned dream, perfectly naked, with his clothes over his arm.' Writers of our time have often found 'more enterprise in walking naked', but Howells had different ideals. He was writing to try and create a society in which people would be 'refined, humane, appreciative, sympathetic', and to that end 'always I strove for grace, distinctness, for light, and my soul detests obscurity still'. He believed that 'most of the good things come from the mean of life'. Not that he was unaware of the turbulent amoral life of the unconscious, the 'filmy shapes that haunt the dusk' (see for instance *Between the Dark and the Daylight*), but he preferred 'clear day'. Undoubtedly there were personal motives behind this preference: it was willed, even a little desperate. 'Man is a creature of light; tragedy is darkness. In its presence he stands before the unknown, before the night, and the result is not revelation, but impenetrable darkness.' It was better, therefore, to concentrate on 'the normal daily round, with its endless variety of revelation of traits and formative influences, its gentle humor and gentler pathos, its ills for which it ever has its uses and its cures'. Edwin Cady has described Howells's own psychic troubles and recurrent nightmares and depressions, and suggests that he adopted, as a strategy for survival, what William James called the religion of healthy-mindedness, by which 'the slaughter-houses and indecencies without end on which our life is founded are huddled out of sight and never mentioned, so that the world we recognize officially in literature and society is a poetic fiction far handsomer and cleaner and better than the world that really is'. Howells knew what he was keeping out, but it seems that there were some areas he dare not penetrate, some darknesses he dare not enter. He knew about them – after all he did admire Ibsen and Zola – but he had to hold back. He could have written, with the Goncourts, that his consuming interest was 'the passion for the study of reality', but he could not have gone on, as they did, to speak of a delight in penetrating to 'life itself, with its entrails still warm and its tripe still palpitating'. And if we do detect some failure of penetration, some slackness and thinness, some lack of real imaginative thrust in his work, it is at least partially because of our current conviction that, in William James's words, 'healthy-mindedness is inadequate as a philosophical doctrine, because the evil facts which it refuses positively to account for are a genuine portion of reality, and they may after all be the best keys to life's significance, and possibly the only openers of our eyes to the deepest levels of truth'.

About the mess and injustice of his contemporary society Howells had many penetrating things to say, but in his dealings with his characters he refused to see far beyond their conscious minds. It is the relative egotism or selflessness they exhibit in relations with other people which interests him more than their most private, most inward convulsions. As people moved towards the atypical, the excessive, the aberrational, the singular experience, Howells did not follow them. We should be cautious, however, of ascribing this simply to a failure of nerve. It was also a matter of where – for civilization's sake – he thought the emphasis of fiction could most profitably be put.

'If America means anything at all, it means the sufficiency of the common, the insufficiency of the uncommon.' Howells's words come strangely to our ears, for where his fiction tried to demonstrate this adequacy of the average, the literature we now most value tends to concentrate on departures from it. There is much less consensus of agreement about external reality now, and no available normative images of society. Our literature is drawn to the private, the isolated, the alienated, the disorderly, the violent – as though life becomes meaningful only in its extreme states. This was Trilling's point with reference to Howells. He noted that we now tend to exhibit a preoccupation with evil, chaos, and disintegration which in turn leads to a devaluation of 'moderate sentiments' and commonplace existence – a devaluation which is not only impoverishing but ultimately dangerous. It is as though we feel that ordinary life, as it stands, is too small, too trivial for art. He adds:

> When we yield to our contemporary impulse to enlarge all experience, to involve it as soon as possible in history, myth, and the oneness of spirit . . . we are in danger of making experience merely typical, formal, and *representative*, and thus of losing one term of the dialectic that goes on between the spirit and the conditioned, which is, I suppose, what we mean when we speak of man's tragic fate. We lose, that is, the actuality of the conditioned, the literality of matter, the peculiar authenticity and authority of the merely denotative.

Because we now feel that 'the mind's power of shaping is more characteristic of mind than its power of observation' our artists tend increasingly to devote themselves to the power of form, a devotion which 'is likely to be conceived in terms of hostility to matter, to matter in its sheer literalness, in its stubborn denotativeness'. Howells's strength was precisely his grasp of the denotative, the actual, the given.

Much modern art tends to solipsism, moving only in inward realms, seemingly trying to free itself from the objective world altogether. This is what Georg Lukács means by 'the attenuation of actuality' in modern western art: we are 'exalting man's subjectivity, at the expense of the objective reality of his environment'. This tendency towards 'the negation of outward reality' carries grave dangers in its train: neglect of the outer world finally leads to the disintegration of the inner self. As Lukács says, 'attenuation of reality and dissolution of personality are interdependent'. Now it is just this sane belief in the existence and value of external, literal matter which is Howell's strongest virtue. He had faith in the value of objective reality simply as it was observed: it did not first have to be refracted through the imagination, reshaped by the human mind. Inevitably this simple belief led him to underestimate the importance, the indispensability, of form, and this in turn prevented him from achieving any profound imaginative understanding of the reality he took so sturdily for granted. But his reverence for the commonplace gives his work a health, a humanity, an integrity which our predilection for the uncommon has led us, perhaps, to undervalue. What was it Dreiser called him? – 'one of the noblemen of literature . . . a wholly honest man'. As such, he deserves better than his current neglect.

8

Stephen Crane

Conrad said that *The Red Badge of Courage* burst upon the public with 'the impact and force of a twelve-inch shell charged with a very high explosive'. An apt image, not only for the book, but for Stephen Crane himself, who, by projecting his own inner warfares into a variety of fictional settings, exerted a decisive, and explosive, influence on the development of American literature – perhaps even on the innovations of twentieth-century prose. There had never been a book quite like *The Red Badge of Courage*. This is how H. L. Mencken remembers its effect on the literary atmosphere of the time. 'It gave the whole movement of the nineties a sudden direction and a powerful impulse forward. At one stroke realism was made its goal – not the old flabby, kittenish realism of Howells's imitators . . . but the sterner, more searching realism that got under the surface.' Mencken is not being quite fair to Howells, as we can learn from a letter written by Crane in 1894 in which he says:

> I renounced the clever school in literature. It seemed to me that there must be something more in life than to sit and cudgel one's brains for clever and witty expedients. So I developed all alone a little creed of art which I thought was a good one. Later I discovered that my creed was identical with the one of Howells and Garland and in this way I became involved in the beautiful war between those who say that art is man's substitute for nature and we are most successful in art when we approach nearest to nature and truth, and those who say – well, I don't know what they say.

Howells and Garland both gave great encouragement to the unknown Crane as soon as they saw his first work – *Maggie* – and Crane may well have learned something from such pronouncements as this by Howells: 'We must ask ourselves before we ask anything else, Is it true? – true to the motives, the impulses, the principles that shape the life of actual men and women?' Or the insistence of Garland that Art was a question of 'one

133

man facing certain facts and telling his individual relations to them'. It was a time when writers were doing a good deal of theoretical re-thinking about the novel, and, where Howells espoused 'realism' and Garland evolved his notion of 'veritism', Crane apparently accepted the term 'impressionism' for the particular sort of writing he aimed at. A friend reports this of Crane: 'Impressionism, he said, was truth, and no man could be great who was not an impressionist, for greatness consisted in knowing truth. He said that he did not expect to be great himself, but he hoped to get near the truth.' We are perhaps less happy nowadays with such confident abstractions but it is worth remembering that this was the time when Tolstoy was having a notable influence on American writers. While he was still a boy Crane was given a copy of *Sevastopol* – a study of war in which Tolstoy claims that the one hero of his tale is 'truth' – and Crane later stated that 'Tolstoy is the writer I admire most of all.'

However, Crane is certainly no Tolstoy, and his insistence on 'truth' will not serve to distinguish him from a large range of writers of the time who set themselves a similar aim. Nor will it help very much to attempt to differentiate impressionism from realism and veritism. Mencken was right to this extent: Crane had got at something which no previous American writer had managed to drag up into fiction. And to define and project this new material he had evolved a style which seemed quite unique, utterly personal and without precedent – a style which earned him the very real admiration and respect of writers as various as Howells, Henry James, and H. G. Wells, and which prompted the young Joseph Conrad into writing to him 'I am envious of you – horribly . . . Do you think I tried to imitate you? No Sir! I may be a little fool but I know better than to try to imitate the inimitable.'

What was so new, so inimitable about Crane? It might at first appear that his choice of subject matter was a major part of his originality. No American writer had previously attempted to write with such unmoralizing intimacy about the slum life of the Bowery before Crane. An enlightened contemporary review of *Maggie* gives us some sense of the step Crane was taking. 'There is unquestionably truth in it, the kind of truth that no American has ever had the courage (or is it bravado) to put between book covers. It is a question if such brutalities are wholly acceptable in literature.' Again, no American writer had ever written about war so unsentimentally and offered such vivid yet detached notations of its futile carnage and meaningless agonies. Crane's vision of war was unheroic, for the most part anti-heroic – and that again was new. And yet here we come upon a paradox. When Crane wrote the first draft of *Maggie* at the age of nineteen he had seen very little of Bowery life: he got the essentials down before he became a reporter in New York. Similarly he had never seen any war at all when he wrote *The Red Badge of*

Courage, thus prompting Ambrose Bierce to comment of Crane, 'This young man has power to feel. He knows nothing of war, yet he is drenched in blood' – a remark which was perhaps more penetrating than Bierce intended.

Of course Crane often did deploy actual experience in his fiction – *The Open Boat*, for instance, follows fairly closely his own experiences after surviving the wreck of the *Commodore* on New Year's day of 1897: but he started his career with two major studies of hitherto unstudied areas of life which he himself had never experienced. So much for any notions of documentary realism or reporting! True, he had had a few glimpses of the Bowery, and he had studied some articles on the Civil War in old periodicals, but the originating and shaping impulse for these stories came from inside Crane himself. These obsessive accounts of apparently social conflicts – slums, battlefields – are dramatizations of conflicts deep within his own psyche and temperament. In this connection his famous statement about *Maggie* that 'it tries to show that environment is a tremendous thing in the world and frequently shapes lives regardless' is misleading, for this suggests that Crane was some sort of naturalist or determinist whereas his most passionate concentrations were not on environment as a sort of 'given', shaping force, but rather on the individual's state of mind in certain recurrent situations. An extract from a letter corrects the balance: 'For the first time I saw the majestic forces which are arrayed against man's true success – not the world – the world is silly, changeable, any of its decisions can be reversed – but man's own colossal impulses, more strong than any chains, and I perceived that the fight was not going to be with the world but with myself.' There's a misleading touch of bravado in that, too, for the world is far from 'silly' in many of Crane's works; but the emphasis on man's inner battle with 'colossal impulses' is more accurate than anything which suggests that Crane's realism is primarily a matter of an accurate picture of social conditions.

Let us look again at *Maggie* – a book first published in 1893 at Crane's own expense and all but completely ignored. Subtitled 'A Girl of the Streets', it would seem to offer a coolly detached account of how economic and social forces reduce a basically decent girl to prostitution and suicide. So much is indeed in the book, but Maggie is in fact a purely romantic figure who 'blossomed in a mud-puddle . . none of the dirt of Rum Alley seemed to be in her veins'. She is precisely not a creature of her environment and her innocent passive helplessness and the relentless degradation which pursues her are pure melodrama. Where the book really does come alive is in its depiction of moods of primitive violence. Fear, and its concomitant rage, are the dominant emotions in the book. It starts with a picture of a small boy at bay in a street fight. 'A very little boy stood upon a heap of gravel for the honour of Rum Alley. He was throwing stones at howling urchins from Devil's Row, who were circling madly about the heap and pelting him.' Note that this situation is very similar to that of Henry Fleming in *Red Badge of Courage*, who also finds himself caught up in a terrible battle and who reacts with animal fear, and demonic anger, to the encroaching hostilities and threats. The little boy in *Maggie* is in fact Maggie's brother Jimmie, and it is this demonic, bemused fighter, and not the innocent and pure Maggie, who provokes the most interesting insights in the book. Jimmie cultivates a defensive belligerence in response to a world which seems bent on annihilating him.

> After a time his sneer grew so that it turned its glare upon all things. He became so sharp that he believed in nothing. To him the police were always actuated by malignant impulses, and the rest of the world was composed, for the most part, of despicable creatures who were all trying to take advantage of him, and with whom, in defense, he was obliged to quarrel on all possible occasions. He himself occupied a downtrodden position, which had a private but distinct element of grandeur in its isolation.

The world of the book is only nominally New York; as described it seems more like a jungle – people are compared to panthers, tigers, dogs, cats and so on – and at times like a childhood nightmare or phantasmagoria. The most threatening and terrifying figure of all, for instance, is Maggie's drunken, brutal mother, who is enlarged and distorted by the prose until she looms as a figure of repulsive horror who threatens to obliterate her children. Similarly the environment is seen as something which can devour or reject its children – 'The open mouth of a saloon called seductively to passengers to enter . . . The shutters of the tall buildings were closed like grim lips.' And the reactions of the threatened little figures who seem caught up in a nightmare of menace are deliberately rendered with grotesque and excessive touches. For instance, when Maggie breaks a plate and her mother rises up in howling wrath, Jimmie, understandably, runs away. But Crane adds a weird image to evoke this infant terror. 'The little boy ran to the halls, shrieking like a monk in an earthquake.' A bizarre image; and yet so much of Crane's work is concerned with running away, or not running away, from volcanic eruptions of violence, that we may note right away that a lot of his imaginative effort went into devising a new metaphoric vocabulary of fear. His main figures are continually being turned to 'grass' or 'bread' or 'glue', or their minds start to 'work like ketchup' as they find themselves undergoing a moment of pure panic.

A similar world is projected in *Georgie's Mother*, Crane's next long story. Again there is an ostensible social moral: a shiftless youth takes to drink, falls in with a gang of lay-abouts, and breaks his mother's heart.

But once again the recurrent vocabulary evokes the jungle, the battlefield, and a primitive world of barbaric savages. One member of the gang who has whipped his employer in a scrap is likened to 'a savage who had killed a great chief'. A room after a drinking party looks like 'a decaying battlefield'. And when George finally wins the battle with his mother (who is herself compared to a 'soldier' who 'remained at her post') her misery is described thus: 'It was as if she had survived a massacre in which all that she loved had been torn from her by the brutality of savages.' War was always Crane's theme – perhaps, as some have said, it was his only theme. The war of the child against parents; the war of man with other men; the war of the individual with society; the war of man against nature and the universe – and the war of man with himself. If war was his subject then panic was the moment of war to which he continually returned. His figures succumb to cowardice as often as they aspire to bravery.

In this connection it is worth mentioning another of his pieces of writing about the Bowery, called 'An Experiment in Misery'. Crane said of this story that in it 'I tried to make plain that the root of Bowery life is a sort of cowardice.' The interesting aspect of the story is that originally it started by showing a young man deliberately dressing up as a tramp and *temporarily* trying out the life of a Bowery bum before returning to his own level of society. Then Crane altered it so that the main figure – a youth who wanders into the Bowery – is in fact an outcast and not just an experimenter. The story ends with his lamenting his exclusion from good society and feeling 'his infinite distance from all that he valued . . . He confessed himself an outcast, and his eyes from under the lowered rim of his hat began to glance guiltily, wearing the criminal expression that comes with certain convictions.' Notice he feels himself to be guilty – not society. He has joined the ranks of the cowardly. This is scarcely what we would expect from any kind of social realism in which the economic factors would predominate. Here we have only a strange sort of psychological impressionism, so that the descriptions of various scenes, apparently impersonal and detached, actually reflect the boy's state of mind. Nowhere is this more remarkable than in the description of the dormitory of the doss house where he spends a night. 'He could see . . . the forms of men sprawled out, lying in death-like silence, or heaving and snoring with tremendous effort, like stabbed fish . . . For the most part they were statuesque, craven, dead. With the curious lockers standing all about like tombstones, there was a strange effect of a graveyard where bodies were merely flung.' The boy feels himself to be in communion with corpses. He is an outcast, and it seems as if he has stumbled into the ranks of the dead. It is an exact anticipation of the key scene in *The Red Badge of Courage*. When Bierce said that Crane's imagination was 'drenched in blood' he might have added – particularly the blood of mortal wounds; for Crane's imagination was more death-drawn, death-scared, death-haunted than that of any other American writer. When Hemingway located the 'moment of truth' in close proximity to the moment of possible death, he was taking up one of the central preoccupations of Crane's work.

Published only two years after *Maggie*, in 1895, *The Red Badge of Courage* is one of those miraculous books in which a writer seems to have found the perfect dramatic setting for an exploration of his most profoundly felt theme. In Crane's case this theme was a boy's encounter with the absolute reality of death. The setting is peculiarly suitable because the Civil War was that horrifying outburst of intra-familial slaughter which signified America's loss of innocence. Henry Fleming's bloody progress towards maturity coincides fittingly with America's own agonized coming of age. Thus the book strikes us as being at once a matchlessly vivid evocation of a significant historical moment, *and* a timeless archetypal ritual of initiation. Nevertheless, the prime emphasis is on certain major shifts and developments in Henry Fleming's state of mind, and it is here that we see Crane's most searching probing and revelation at work. As a child 'he had, of course, dreamed of battles . . . in visions he had seen himself in many struggles'. He never expected the dream to become reality – still, he is a human child and this means that his head is swarming with inherited or intuited violence. When the actual war breaks out his mother tries to keep him at home, but 'he had made firm rebellion against this yellow light thrown upon the color of his ambitions'. As so often in Crane the first act of rebellion is against the home, particularly the mother. But when at last he is about to go into battle, 'a little panic-fear grew in his mind'. He does not know and cannot know how he will actually behave in a real 'crisis'. 'He was an unknown quantity . . . He must accumulate information of himself.' And he realizes that 'the only way to prove himself was to go into the blaze'.

Here then Crane has arrived at that moment which was to prove so important for his contemporaries and for much modern fiction – the moment of 'the test'. This idea of 'the test' is of course absolutely central to Conrad's works, for Conrad too was interested in men who are 'tested by those events of the sea that show in the light of day the inner worth of a man, the edge of his temper, the fibre of his stuff'. Lord Jim dreamed of glory but failed the test of reality. (Conrad's art is his own, but his theme had been anticipated by Crane, whose influence on Conrad's work was perhaps more considerable than is usually realized.) For Henry Fleming too fails his first real test, and Crane is nowhere more brilliant and original than in tracing out the psychological states which are the prelude to flight. In his growing panic Fleming starts to feel 'alone in space' and 'separated from the others' because 'No one seemed to be wrestling with such a terrific personal problem.' His growing fear makes him feel like an alien – 'He was a mental outcast.' 'In the darkness he saw visions of a thousand-tongued fear that would babble at his back and cause him to flee . . .' Shortly after, he sees his first corpse – an omen of the reality he is going to meet. And immediately the whole environment becomes vibrant with invisible menace. 'He thought that he did not relish the landscape. It threatened him.' A house looks ominous; the shadows of the woods seem to be full of enemies. The panic grows – 'It was all a trap.' A preliminary skirmish gives him an illusory sense of having passed the test, but when the full onslaught of the enemy rushes at him, 'he was like a proverbial chicken. He lost the direction of safety. Destruction threatened him from all points.' Paranoia and pure panic take possession of him. He runs from the scene of the battle – 'he had fled, he told himself, because annihilation approached'. He is in flight from the idea of death. And this precipitates the great central scene of the book (which I mentioned earlier). In his flight he seeks out thicker woods, denser thickets, ever darker places. 'He walked on, going from obscurity into promises of a greater obscurity.' He is a real outcast now, a coward shunning his fellows and the searching light of day. He finds what seems the ultimate retreat, a place of absolute quiet 'where the high, arching boughs made a chapel'. But he is not alone.

> He was being looked at by a dead man who was seated with his back against a columnlike tree . . . The eyes, staring at the youth, had changed to the dull hue to be seen on the side of a dead fish. The mouth was open. Its red had changed to an appalling yellow. Over the gray skin of the face ran little ants. One was trundling some sort of a bundle along the upper lip.
>
> The youth gave a shriek as he confronted the thing . . . The dead man and the living man exchanged a long look.

Here is the core of the book. The youth has fled the battlefield only to find himself in a horrifying sort of natural charnel house. In running away from corpses he has run into a corpse. A man can avoid everything but death. But death is an absolute, waiting to turn its ghoulish stare on the living from all sides. The outcast finds himself where he least wanted to be – literally face to face with death. He flees again – but this time 'he began to run in the direction of the battle'. The way back is not easy or direct. The very trees and brambles seem to impede his return; more punishing and shaming yet, he finds himself involved in a procession of men returning from the battle, but returning with honour: 'he was amid wounds. The mob of men was bleeding . . . He wished that he, too, had a wound, a red badge of courage.' The wound, of course, is the badge of the man who has stood up to death and survived. Crane explored its symbolic importance in a separate story. 'An Episode of War', in which he wrote: 'A wound gives strange dignity to him who bears it. Well men shy from this new and terrible majesty. It is as if the wounded man's hand is upon the curtain which hangs before the revelations of all existence . . .' Here again we see Crane anticipating one of Hemingway's crucial tenets.

Before Fleming can rejoin his comrades, that is be re-accepted into the community, he has to undergo an agonizing ordeal with two dying men. He endures their company, which is biting reproach to his unscarred cowardice. He has to watch the 'tall soldier' do his terrible dance of death, which Crane makes truly appalling with his gift for combining cold details with grotesque impressions in a unique way. When the tall soldier dies his jacket falls open and Fleming sees that 'the side looked as if it had been chewed by wolves'. At this hideous spectacle he turns to curse the heavens, and then comes a very famous line. 'The red sun was pasted in the sky like a wafer.' This has been taken as the perfect example of his new impressionism, but we should note that it is impressionism containing symbolism. The wafer evokes the Christ who was mangled and sacrificed by his fellowmen – this in turn reminding us of all the massacred innocents in human history. The tattered man imposes a different ordeal for he keeps asking Fleming where he was hit, thus unwittingly exacerbating Fleming's guilt. 'The simple questions of the tattered man had been knife thrusts to him. They asserted a society that probes pitilessly at secrets until all is apparent.' The psychological anguish at being alone and unscarred among a community of the wounded has never been more subtly drawn than in these chapters. It is significant that the remainder of the book – in which Fleming returns to his comrades and becomes a hero in the subsequent battle – is far less convincing and interesting than the first half of the book. Fleming goes to sleep – it feels like for a thousand years – and Crane makes the ritual significance of this very clear. 'He had slept and, awakening, found himself a knight.' Fleming's former panic turns into a barbaric rage, a lust to kill all that previously threatened him. The psychological probing is less acute here, for Crane's notions of heroism were somewhat literary. Hence the inflated rhetoric of the conclusion: 'He had been to touch the great death, and found that, after all, it was but the great death. He was a man.' Hence also the final note of peace, which is all a matter of words and has little to do with what James called 'felt life'. 'He had rid himself of the red sickness of battle. The sultry nightmare was in the past . . . He turned now with a lover's thirst to images of tranquil skies, fresh meadows, cool brooks – an existence of soft and eternal peace.' A lyrical conclusion to the initiation ceremony – Fleming has achieved his manhood. Crane was only twenty-two when he wrote the book, and perhaps he is writing in his own hopes for a serene maturity. But there is enough in this book alone to show that eternal peace cannot be achieved by man – if only because nightmares can return and mankind as a whole has never rid itself of 'the red sickness of battle'.

A more subtle account of 'heroism' may be found in a later story called 'A Mystery of Heroism', in which a young soldier crosses a field under fire to fetch a bucket of water. Again, it is a test: the youth finds himself alone in a field of death. Yet he is really there out of a mixture of cowardice and bravado. 'He had blindly been led by quaint emotions, and laid himself under an obligation to walk squarely up to the face of death . . . He was mainly surprised.' Crane puts it beautifully: 'he was an intruder in the land of fine deeds' and, like many another intruder, he panics after the initial act of bravado. Having got the water he goes 'mad from the threats of destruction'. The fact that, in his panic, the youth nevertheless does pause to give a dying man a drink of water, justifies the title of the story. Heroism is a mystery – it is one of the strange things that can happen to a man undergoing the test. The fact that, marvellously, it can happen did not blind Crane to the fact that man is basically panic-prone in the face of death and this awareness is responsible for some of his most original and telling perceptions. I am thinking for instance of one his last short stories, 'The Upturned Face'. This is a war story which has nothing to do with history, but with a timeless moment in a war between mythical armies. It is simply about some men burying one of their friends who has been killed. Although they are under constant fire from the enemy, their main dread is of the corpse. They feel nausea at having to touch it, and the final moment of horror comes when they have to shovel earth onto its face. It is this and not the enemy fire that all but unmans them. The last sound of the story is a dreadful, meaningless 'plop' as the first earth lands on the still staring face.

The Red Badge of Courage is a masterpiece and was instantly acclaimed as such. The fact that Crane was so young when he wrote it justifies Hemingway's subsequent description of the book as 'a boy's long dream of war'. A dream which nevertheless struck its readers on account of its vivid realism, and prompted some veterans to compliment Crane on the accuracy of his account. Perhaps this apparent paradox can help us to discern what was so original and powerful about Crane's style. 'Impressionism' of course is a word with its own ambiguity. It can mean how you see a thing (a relatively objective matter), or how you feel about a thing (a more subjective concern). The amazing aspect of Crane's prose is its ability to combine perceptions and reactions in one image. A few examples:

> Tents sprang up like strange plants. Camp fires, like red, peculiar blossoms, dotted the night . . . From this little distance the many fires, with the black forms of men passing to and fro before the crimson rays, made weird and

> satanic effects . . . There was an occasional flash and glimmer of steel from the backs of all these huge crawling reptiles . . . The guns squatted in a row like savage chiefs. They argued with abrupt violence. It was a grim pow-wow.

Such images have a visual vividness; at the same time the notions of strange plants, satanic figures, crawling reptiles, and savage chiefs tell us a good deal about the various primitive emotional states Fleming is passing through. This attempt to find the right image to convey both perceptions and the reactions of his main figures means that Crane the author seldom intrudes directly. Garland was right enough when he said that Crane put 'his own psychology into his observations'. He seems to be suppressing his own emotions and to be concentrating on trying to get down the matter as it struck responses in those who were actually involved in it. Hence the famous detachment and impersonality of his style; hence the prevailing air of understatement, economy, and compression. He cuts out everything which is not being seen or felt. This tone has something in it of the dead-pan humour of Mark Twain at the same time as it anticipates the best of Hemingway. But the particular combination of conveyed intensity and apparent disengagement is Crane's own. Quite often it produces really grotesque effects so that we, the readers, start to experience a weird, estranged reality, in company with the characters. 'Arms were bent and heads were turned in incredible ways. It seemed that the dead men must have fallen from some great height to get in such positions. They looked to be dumped out upon the ground from the sky.' The sense of strangeness adds to the sense of horror without blurring it. In general we can say that Crane's details and impressions are never mere information. Even his famous preoccupation with colours (five in the first paragraph of *Red Badge*) is more than simply visual, and many of the particulars singled out by his prose tend to take on a symbolic status (like the wind-tower in 'The Open Boat').

Crane was subsequently a witness of actual battles. He went to report on the Spanish–American war; reports of his behaviour at the time suggest that he deliberately put himself in the line of enemy fire as though to experience in reality what Henry Fleming had been through in his imagination. After that he went out to Greece to report on that country's war with Turkey. It was there that he married the colourful Cora Taylor, a spirited and devoted woman who had at one time kept a brothel in Florida and who followed Crane out to the war. But these encounters with real wars, although they produced some fine work, did not provoke anything so profound and searching as *The Red Badge of Courage*. What Crane knew about fear, panic, and the sense of a menacing and malignant environment which threatens a man with his own death, he did not need to learn from any other battlefield than that of his inmost self. However, a real event did provide him with the subject for one of his greatest short stories – indeed one of the great short stories in western literature – 'The Open Boat'.

This does indeed transcribe with great fidelity what happened after Crane was shipwrecked after the wreck of the *Commodore* on 1 January 1897; yet it has a more than documentary significance, as Conrad recognized when he said of it: 'The deep and simple humanity of its presentation seems somehow to illustrate the essentials of life itself, like a symbolic tale.' Once again it focuses on what was Crane's main theme – men who survive a brush with death and gain some new understanding of life as a result of the encounter. The famous opening sentence – 'None of them knew the colour of the sky' – suggests that the men are all but buried alive, and the ludicrous fragility of the boat becomes the fragility of all human life, tossed and menaced by relentless waves of dissolution. But Crane avoids all portentous rhetoric and ostentatious allegory. The narrating tone is even, ironic, even comic; it is not laconic and pseudo-tough, but it holds on to an undismayed clarity. The prose itself seems to be making the necessary effort of balance and detachment in a dreadful situation to which the only alternative response would be the blurred convulsions of panic. Thus: 'A singular disadvantage of the sea lies in the fact that after successfully surmounting one wave you discover that there is another behind it just as important and just as nervously anxious to do something effective in the way of swamping boats . . . There was a terrible grace in the move of the waves, and they came in silence, save for the snarling of the crests.' The movement of the story is the painfully slow and continually endangered movement of the boat towards the land. The sea, with its waves 'most wrongfully and barbarously abrupt and tall' and its sharks, is the realm of death. In their extremity the men look to the land expecting help, a life-boat, some sign of imminent rescue – 'There was the shore of the populous land, and it was bitter and bitter to them that from it came no sign.' What they do see on the land seems either unaware of, or indifferent to, their plight. Thus the moment when they see a man on the shore and try to interpret what he is doing. Is he waving to them? Why is he taking his coat off?

> 'What's that idiot with the coat mean? What's he signalling anyhow?'
> 'It looks as though he were trying to tell us to go north. There must be a life-saving station up there.'
> 'No; he thinks we're fishing. Just giving us a merry hand. See? Ah, there, Willie!'
> 'Well, I wish I could make something out of those signals. What do you suppose he means?'
> 'He don't mean anything; he's just playing.'

And so they go on, eagerly trying to read the indifferent life of the shore. Another indication of this indifference is a tall wind-tower. 'This tower was a giant, standing with its back to the plight of the ants.' Finally, with the boat 'drunken' with the water that is now pouring in, the men have to make their own attempt to reach the shore. During this last stage of the struggle, the correspondent – in effect Crane himself – is caught in a current and wonders whether it can be possible that he is about to die. His meditation here goes to the heart of Crane's work. 'Perhaps an individual must consider his own death to be the final phenomenon of nature.' On this occasion the correspondent is finally helped by a figure from the shore – a naked saint who rushes to help them. But although the land proves hospitable the story also ends with a corpse. 'The welcome of the land to the men from the sea was warm and generous; but a still and dripping shape was carried slowly up the beach, and the land's welcome for it could only be the different and sinister hospitality of the grave.' For the survivors, however, something has been gained – 'the wind brought the sound of the great sea's voice to the men on the shore, and they felt that they could then be interpreters'. Interpreters of the sea to the land: by extension, interpreters of the experience of death to those who have never known what it is like to be beset on all sides by the forces of annihilation. Crane, who in his imagination seems always to have been standing at the edge of his own grave, was such an interpreter.

I have mentioned some of Crane's major work based on the violence and fear of slum-life, war, and ship-wreck. To complete this brief survey it is important to mention two of his best stories from one other segment of his fictional world – the West. Crane had spent some time in the West during 1895 (this included a visit to Mexico in the course of which he had an encounter with some Mexican bandits, which gave him the opportunity to make some more discoveries about his own capacity for panic and survival), but, as usual, his two most important stories with a Western setting were based on invented situations. And, as might be expected, both stories deal with a man confronting his own possible, or actual, death. 'The Bride Comes to Yellow Sky' opens with Jack Potter bringing his newly wed bride back to Yellow Sky, where he is town marshal. The comfortable Pullman coach in which they are travelling symbolizes 'the environment of their new estate' – a step away from the raw life of the West towards marriage and domestication. This step fills Potter with a curious feeling of guilt – he feels he has made himself a social outcast, a traitor. 'He had committed an extraordinary crime . . . he had gone headlong over all the social hedges.' This perhaps reflects Crane's own feeling about being involved with Cora Taylor: be that as it may, the point is that Jack Potter is now suffering from 'a new cowardice' – the central emotion in Crane's fiction. Back in Yellow Sky a drunken gunfighter named Scratchy Wilson is on the rampage, and when Potter returns to his house he runs straight into his old enemy. Potter has no gun, but still has the image of that Pullman coach in his mind, and all that it signifies in the way of his 'new estate', so he stands up to Scratchy Wilson unarmed. ' "I ain't got a gun because I've just come from San Anton' with my wife. I'm married" said Potter.' The very word literally disarms Wilson – he does not know what to make of that concept; and the story ends with his retreat. 'He was looking at the ground. "Married!" He was not a student of chivalry; it was merely that in the presence of this foreign condition he was a simple child of the earlier plains. He picked up his starboard revolver, and, placing both weapons in their holsters, he went away. His feet made funnel-shaped tracks in the heavy sand.' Wilson represents the frontier code based on pre-civilized violence. Potter overcomes his initial feelings of cowardice by standing up to the threat of this code and implicitly asserting the superior strength of a non-combative, more civilized commitment. In this brilliant little story Crane seems not only to make a further exploration of the varieties of men's cowardices and braveries, but also to distil an important truth concerning something that was happening to the West of America in the latter part of the nineteenth century. The psychological moment also symbolizes an historical moment.

Written in the same year – 1898 – 'The Blue Hotel' is an unforgettable story of an outcast figure who, in a state of pathological terror and rage, seeks out his own death. Three men from a train put up at a hotel in a desolate town isolated in the middle of an empty, wintry prairie. All the guests in the hotel remain quiet except a Swede, who seems in the grip of an irrational fear, perhaps precipitated by the alienness of the place and the vastness of the empty space around it. He is obsessed by the idea that Western towns are notorious for their high rate of murders and deaths, and he interprets every innocent question, every movement towards him as a threat, a challenge to fight, a movement in a conspiracy against him. 'Apparently it seemed to the Swede that he was formidably menaced.' He suddenly announces things like – 'I see you are all against me' and 'I suppose I am going to be killed before I can leave this house.' This phase of prolonged paranoia and repeated panic-retreats gives way to a manic phase of sneering belligerence. During a card game he accuses another man of cheating, a fight is duly arranged, and the Swede is as mad in his lust for violence as he was in his previous panic. 'Demoniac' is Crane's word for him. After a savage fight the Swede emerges victorious, but he has also made himself a complete outcast, loathed by the rest of the men. He leaves the hotel, plunging gladly into a storm of excessive harshness. 'The conceit of man was explained by this storm to be the very engine of life. One was a coxcomb not to die in it. However, the Swede found a saloon.' And it is in this saloon, once again amid an alien group of men, that the Swede picks his second fight, this time to be knifed by the local gambler. His corpse is left alone in the saloon, staring up at the cash-machine which carries the 'dreadful legend': 'This registers the amount of your purchase.' It seems to suggest that in some deep way the Swede wanted his death, and what he has discovered is that the price he has had to pay for it is – precisely – his life. Here indeed we have a quintessentially Crane story: the outcast and his deeply ambivalent feelings about the group, the community – panic, rage, violence, and a confrontation with death. This being so it is odd that he added a social moral in the last section, in which it transpires that the Swede was right and one of the men *had* been cheating at cards; thus, says one of the other men, 'We are all in it . . . every sin is the result of a collaboration. We, five of us, have collaborated in the murder of this Swede.'

This social moral is a fairly clumsy addition to a brilliant psychological study, but it indicates, perhaps, that Crane was turning away from the study of the isolated individual's encounter with panic and violence, and beginning to look at the society which surrounds these individuals and, as often as not, turns them into outcasts. 'The Monster', another story written at this time, is a terrible indictment of society's cruelty, stupidity, and persecution. A house catches fire; Henry Johnson, a negro, risks his life to save a child. But the flames reach him and his face is burnt off, leaving him a monster and an idiot. There are some bitter points in Crane's description of this horrifying fire. First of all, a print of the Declaration of Independence drops to the floor as soon as a flame touches it, 'where it burst with the sound of a bomb'. And when Johnson enters the fire for the child Crane says: 'He was submitting, submitting because of his fathers, bending his mind in a most perfect slavery to the conflagration.' When he survives in his mutilated state, not only does society shun him, but it ostracizes the doctor who chooses to care for the maimed negro. Whether or not one takes the negro as a mask for Crane, as some critics do, there is undoubtedly a deeply bitter hatred and fear of society at work here, as well as some rather complicated, self-punishing guilt feelings consequent upon that hate.

This story is set in Whilomville – in effect, 'the town where I once lived' – and his last book was a collection called simply *Whilomville Stories*, which are children's stories, or at least stories about children. It might seem strange for a maturing artist to return to studies of childhood – the school, the street, the playground. Yet we remember that the first paragraph of Crane's first book was about children fighting, and it soon becomes clear that what is drawing Crane in this book is his perennial interest in those archetypal emotions and instincts: panic, fear, cruelty, rage, occasional bravery, recurrent cowardice. Childhood is a jungle, just as war is. Crane displays the same animism and primitivism in writing of both: in both you can find the misery of the outcast, the savagery of the herd; and in both you encounter those situations of menace and violence in which an individual is forced to discover what he really amounts to, not in theory but in practice, in action. And these were Crane's central concerns. Crane had not been to war when he wrote *The Red Badge of Courage* but he had passed through childhood, so perhaps it is fitting that in his last book he should return to that phase of life which seems to have provided him with the impulses, the perceptions, the dreams and nightmares, which so richly nourished his rare powers of imagination. Crane laid bare so many nerves, fears, pretensions, and self-deceptions that had not been exposed in quite that way before, that we tend to forget that he had barely reached manhood when he died. For when Crane finally succumbed to TB in 1900 he was, incredibly, only twenty-eight. Yet he had already published fourteen books (including, incidentally, some very original modern American poetry), books which contained work of sufficient power and originality to exert a decisive influence on twentieth-century writers of the calibre of Conrad and Hemingway.

On hearing of Crane's death, Henry James wrote, 'What a brutal needless extinction – what an unmitigated unredeemed catastrophe! I think of him with such a sense of possibilities and powers.' The youth who started his literary career by enthralling the social realists William Dean Howells and Hamlin Garland, and who within a few years had won the very real admiration and respect of more inward-looking, symbolist writers like Conrad and James was clearly a very unusual young writer indeed. I have said something about the originality of his subject matter, but to give a more complete sense of his achievement I should end by saying something about his style, and here I can scarcely do better than quote the testimony of yet another major modern writer – H.G. Wells. Having praised Crane for 'the persistent selection of the essential elements of an impression . . . the ruthless exclusion of mere information . . . the direct vigour with which the selected points are made', Wells summed up by asserting that

> it seems to me that, when at last the true proportions can be seen, Crane will be found to occupy a position singularly cardinal . . . In style, in method and in what is distinctively not found in his books, he is sharply defined, the expression in literary art of certain enormous repudiations . . . It is as if the radical thought had been razed from his mind and its site ploughed and salted. He is more than himself in this; he is the first impression of the opening mind of a new period, or, at least, the early emphatic phase of a new initiative – beginning, as a growing mind must needs begin, with a record of impressions, a record of a vigour and intensity beyond all precedent.

9

The Bostonians *and the human voice*

A voice, a human voice, is what we want.

Olive Chancellor's cry for 'a human voice' comes just before Verena Tarrant is about to give her address in Miss Birdseye's apartment which will enthrall and captivate – in different ways – both Olive and her Southern cousin, Basil Ransom, and duly precipitate the action and struggles of the novel. The question of her 'voice' – its appropriation and development, its muffling and silencing – is central to the book, and this in turn opens up problems of rights and abilities of utterance, articulation, discourse, publication – speech and writing – in general, which are not only peculiarly pointed and relevant to the period of American history about which James was writing (the 1870s), but part – a central part – of a contestation and struggle which are endemic to our, and arguably any, society. It is a matter not only of who 'has a voice' – who holds the pen, who holds the floor – in society, but more searchingly of what *is* a voice, 'a human voice'? It is because this is a matter of profound and permanent importance that I think James's novel about a group of Boston feminists in post-Civil-War America is as alive and urgent (and instructive) for us today as it was for his (mostly unappreciative) contemporaries.

Concerns connected with speech and print are dominant throughout *The Bostonians*. Very simply, let me suggest that there are two series of linked phenomena which are visible, and opposed. On the one hand we find repeated references to lips, tongue, voice, the lecture-platform; on the other hand we have references to hands, pen, print, popular journalism. In both cases the concern is with various forms of publication, publicity, and – more generally – the relationship between private and public. The line leading to the lecture-platform is predominantly female, and that ending up as journalism, male. But not exclusively so. The battle – for it is a battle, the continuation of the Civil War in other spheres, by other means – is indeed between men and

148

women, Basil and Olive in particular, but it is not a straightforward battle. The sexes, sexuality, 'the sentiment of sex' (James's phrase), have gone somehow wrong – are awry, distorted, confused, deformed, 'perverted' (a word that recurs in the book). And the problem(s) can be traced to a malfunctioning, or breakdown, or perversion, of the operations of the hand and the mouth, not only as they work communicatively (writing and speaking), but as they behave erotically. In its prime expressive and reproductive functions, the body is well out of joint in *The Bostonians*. (Let me just quote here from Michel Foucault's *The Uses of Pleasure*, where he describes Aristotle's attempts to define *akolasia* – dangerous self-indulgence and excess in the legitimate pursuit of pleasure: 'self-indulgence – *akolasia* – relates only to the pleasures of the body; and among these, the pleasures of sight, hearing, and smell must be excluded . . . For there is pleasure that is liable to *akolasia* only where there is touch and contact: contact with the mouth, the tongue, and the throat . . ., or contact with other parts of the body.' Overt and direct genital contact is of course not depicted in James's novel – but the mouth and the hand, in their more or less sexual/appetitive roles, are very much to the fore and they are often the site, occasion, or instrument of an excess, an over-indulgence in power – manipulation, coercion, assertion, repression.)

Let me briefly consider the depiction of Verena's father, Selah Tarrant, a quintessential charlatan, perfect sympton and product of the post-Civil-War years, who peddles all kinds of false and debased modes of exploiting, manipulating, working on, a fathomlessly gullible public. He is a 'mesmeric healer' who was also an 'itinerant vendor of lead pencils' but cannot write (although he worships newspapers), and who 'always had tickets for lectures' though, here again, 'he didn't know how to speak'. He merely mongers the trashier cards and tools of publicity and mystification. But it would seem that he panders to more than crass credulity and superstition. When Doctor Prance, that succinct realist, is telling Ransom what she knows about Selah Tarrant, she says that he works on lots of ladies with his cures, though he is quite ignorant of physiology. She is of course entirely sceptical and dismissive about his so-called therapeutic gifts. 'All she could say was that she didn't want him to be laying his hands on any of *her* folks; it was all done with the hands – what wasn't done with the tongue.' That last clause could well serve to cover most of the activities of the book – indeed most distinctly human activities. But there us, unmistakably, a tolerably scabrous innuendo in the tart doctor's comments. Selah Tarrant has lived his life in various kinds of Bohemia, including the 'Cayuga community, where there were no wives, or no husbands, or something of that sort'. His only gift seems to be that he is 'very magnetic', as Mrs Tarrant feels. He is, disappointingly, hopeless with words, but 'Selah possessed as a substitute – his career as a healer, to speak of none other, was there to prove it – the eloquence of the hand. The Greenstreets had never set much store on manual activity; they believed in the influence of the lips.' The Greenstreets were Abolitionists and Mrs Tarrant's parents – and the 'influence of the lips' is to emerge in the strange gift of her own daughter, whose 'eloquence' is to be so remarkable and remarked upon. But that 'eloquence of the hand', that 'manual activity', of Mr Tarrant . . . no wonder that Mrs Tarrant is 'full of suspicion of the ladies (they were mainly ladies) whom Selah mesmerized'. In a book in which, in varying forms, the attempt to define and defend true 'eloquence' is constantly engaged on all levels, Selah Tarrant's furtive, unqualified, and concealed manual eloquence with dissatisfied ladies may act as a reminder of what debased roguery, or venal venery, may pass as a form of vendible competence in this distracted and disoriented society.

But there is another side to Selah Tarrant's abilities and aspiration, intimately related to his dubious mesmeric gifts. Whichever organ it might be that he manages to move to remuneration with his manual eloquence, his real desire is to obtain what is called 'the ear of the public'. For him the ultimate desire and reality alike is publication, publicity.

> In reality he had one all-absorbing solicitude – the desire to get paragraphs put into newspapers, paragraphs of which he had hitherto been the subject . . . The newspapers were his world, the richest expression, in his eyes, of human life . . . his ideal of bliss was to be as regularly and indispensably a component part of the newspaper as the title and date, or list of fires, or the column of Western jokes. The vision of that publicity haunted his dreams, and he would gladly have sacrificed to it the innermost sanctities of home. Human existence to him, indeed, was a huge publicity . . . The *penetralia* of the daily press were, however, still more fascinating . . . He hung about, sat too long, took up the time of busy people, edged into the printing-rooms when he had been eliminated from the office, talked with the compositors till they set up his remarks by mistake, and to the newsboys when the compositors had turned their backs. He was always trying to find out what was 'going in'; he would have liked to go in himself, bodily . . .

Here indeed is an aspiration to an extreme of ontological displacement, or perverse self-reification. Selah Tarrant is a comic-grotesque figure, but with his squalid manual eloquence combined with his wild desire to decorporealize into newsprint he illustrates how degraded and deranged a person's relationship to the private and the public, to the body and to society, can become. Seen from this point of view, and as the father, the progenitor, of Verena – who is the desired, ambiguous, body and voice around whom the book revolves and the struggles are waged – he is a central and, in an appropriately perverted and extreme form, a representative figure in the world of the novel.

Before considering his eloquent child, it is worth noting here the description of the professional journalist in the book, Matthias Pardon. He too is a devotee and proselyte of publicity. With this result: 'For this ingenious son of his age all distinction between the person and the artist had ceased to exist; the writer was personal, the person food for newsboys, and everything and everyone were everyone's business. All things, with him, referred themselves to print . . . His faith, again, was the faith of Selah Tarrant – that being in the newspapers is a condition of bliss . . .' He is also a somewhat effeminate character, sexually – or sexlessly – indeterminate, and here again we find a perverse erotic displacement – journalism as *jouissance*. But there is a further-reaching implication in this particular perversity-into-publicity. 'He regarded the mission of mankind upon earth as a perpetual evolution of telegrams; everything to him was very much the same, he had no sense of proportion or quality.' *Everything to him was very much the same* . . . here again we have in an extreme and comic (comic-ish) form a version of an ontological blight which is affecting the society of this book – a loss, a fading, a collapsing of difference, differentiation, distinction. In one sense a social homogenization (though of course there are the rich and poor), a cultural equivalizing, a downward levelling-out. In another, potentially more disturbing, sense, a loss of sexual difference, sexual identity. Not a society of inverts or perverts, though inversion is strongly adumbrated and 'perversion' is in the air; rather, the growing sense of a society in which gender-distinction is becoming blurred, confused, problematized in the wrong manner – a society in which people are losing their sexual way. Women, indeed, are often discerned as losing, or not having, their distinctive outlines, their form – as, for example Miss Birdseye – 'this essentially formless old woman who had no more outline than a bundle of hay'. It is not simply a matter of the blurring contours of old age; the formlessness of the female has penetrated the 'essence'. There is 'much vagueness of boundary' about the residence in which Miss Birdseye lives, and that boundary-vagueness not only afflicts the female form of many of the women (and men) in the book, it reaches to the cultural taxonomies and classifications, the conceptual clarifications and distinctions, on which society rests. The North–South boundary had just recently become vague even to catastrophe, and in the aftermath the identities of the liberated and the enslaved in these dis-united, re-united states had become endlessly problematized. It is perhaps small wonder that gender boundaries are becoming uncertain, a source of radical insecurity and a site of desperate definitional antagonisms. Here let me just cite another minor character who offers herself as a comic extreme of a condition which is more seriously prevalent – to varying extents – throughout the society of the book, Dr Prance. 'It was true that if she had been a boy she would have borne some relation to a girl, whereas Doctor

Prance appeared to bear none whatever. Except her intelligent eye, she had no features to speak of.' This is James's, or the narrator's, sense of humour, and we will come to him(?) later. But blurred, dissolved, effaced, erased – absent – features (or overemphasized and artificially enhanced and distorted ones) are much in evidence in this book, and a female who would have borne any resemblance to a girl only if she had been male may be said to be, in a suitably perverted way, an absolutely typical figure: it is entirely appropriate that it should be she who makes a statement that has reverberations and implications beyond the immediate context: 'Men and women are all the same to me . . . I don't see any difference.' This heralds, or threatens, not so much the dissolution as the disappearance of distinction altogether. Not equality but erasure.

Verena Tarrant herself, with her 'flat young chest', is somewhat sexually indeterminate, though of course on account of youth rather than any other thwarting, deflecting, or deformation of her sexuality. As yet imperfectly defined, formed, she is in her plasticity, vulnerability, passivity, docility, and unassertive openness something of a *tabula rasa* – a blank to be inscribed, a figure to be shaped, and of course would-be inscribers and shapers are duly drawn to her fair, young, promising presence. She poses many problems of interpretation – 'naturally theatrical', 'effrontery or innocence', 'schoolgirl', 'half-bedizened dam-sel', 'Mountebank', 'doll', 'human gazelle', 'moving statue', 'naiad', 'Arcadian', and so on; the attempts to define, to fix, and thus in a way appropriate her, proliferate around her. Yet she eludes, or fails, or perhaps exceeds the terms applied to her. Perhaps because she is, indeed, 'an odd mixture of elements', perhaps because of what Ransom sees as her 'singular hollowness of character'. Too full, or too empty? Or perhaps just very simple: 'she enjoyed putting on her new hat, with its redundancy of feather, and twenty cents appeared to her a very large sum'. One particular problem about her is the mystery of her origin, and by the same token, or *a fortiori*, the origin of her voice. Given her parents, it is a wonder 'how she came to issue from such a pair'. Olive Chancellor can hardly accept that she is the product of such 'trashy parents' and prefers to see her as having a transcendent or generic origin. She holds 'that no human origin, however congruous it may superficially appear, would sufficiently account for her'. Alternatively, she likes to think of her as emanating mysteriously from 'the people', emerging from 'the social dusk of that mysterious democracy' which she mythologizes. This way she can think that Verena's 'gift', her 'power', her 'eloquence' – in a word her voice – 'had dropped straight from heaven, without filtering through her parents'. The 'source' of her compelling fluency is, as it were, the heart of the mystery. The word 'source' is used advisedly, since Verena is 'a young lady from whose lips eloquence flowed in streams'. It 'irrigates', it 'gushes', it 'overflows'. The flow is indeed torrential and Tarrant can well sound like 'torrent' (as it contains 'rant' and suggests 'taunt' – I shall come back to that), and since near the end it is explicitly indicated that her spoken 'lubrications' will take second place, indeed be displaced by, Ransom's written 'lucubrations', I do not think it is fanciful or tasteless to detect something of a lubricious hint in that youthful female flowing. Verena is quite clear that the faculty/gift/voice is not her own, not her. 'It is not *me*, mother.' Indeed it is described at times as an almost involuntary physiological process, a kind of voiding. 'The voice that spoke from her lips seemed to want to take that form . . . She let it come out just as it would - she didn't pretend to have any control.' Whatever – 'It was some power outside – it seemed to flow through her.'

But we are not dealing here with inspiration, prophetic possession, tongues of flame, wood-notes wild, or the inexplicability of genius. The narrative gives some very clear clues concerning the nature of the determining environment of her early childhood.

> She had been nursed in darkened rooms, and suckled in the midst of manifestations; she had begun to 'attend lectures' as she said, when she was quite an infant, because her mother had no one to leave her with at home. She had sat on the knees of somnambulists, and had been passed from hand to hand by trance-speakers; . . . and had grown up among lady-editors of newspapers advocating new religions, and people who disapproved of the marriage tie. Verena would talk of the marriage tie as she would have talked of the last novel – as if she had heard it as frequently discussed.

The 'infant' is precisely without speech, and it is of course clear how crucial for her subsequent emergence as an amazing speaker this early conditioning is. Not only was she the recipient, the receptacle of incomprehensible lectures and modishly progressive (or morally subversive) newspaper talk, she was positioned and distributed. And by somnambulists and trance-speakers! She does indeed move through her later life with something of the gait of a somnambulist, in something of a trance, herself. Certainly she is peculiarly susceptible to 'mesmerization', and not only by her father. And being 'passed from hand to hand' is the very definition of her fate and destiny. I will come back to 'spells' and 'hands'. The point here is that she is very much a product of a particular milieu of post-Civil-War America, and in that sense her parentage does indeed extend beyond, transcend, the 'trashy' Tarrants. She is the child of a particular period – a period of peculiar derangements, dislocations, deformations, degradations, and destabilizations. And so is her voice. When she says to Olive, 'Oh, it isn't me, you know; it's something outside', she is in fact testifying to the fact that she does not speak but, as we now say, is spoken. Of her many passivities, her most total docility is to language. She is entranced and mesmerized by it, under its spell, in its hands. She is an open aqueduct to the flow of her verbal environment. She is first a slave to her father; she becomes Olive's slave, and will be Basil Ransom's. But perhaps most notably and profoundly she is, in Lacan's terms, a slave of language ('serf du langage'). Beyond emancipation. Though not beyond blocking and damning and the promise of a mutilating aridification. For there are other slaveries to be taken into account and to succumb to.

But she is not merely echoic. She may or may not be merely 'a mass of fluent catchwords'; her discourse may be 'full of schoolgirl phrases, of patches of remembered eloquence, of childish lapses of logic, of flights of fancy'; her 'enchanting improvization' may indeed be in large part a tissue of 'inanities'. But her voice is not identical and coextensive with, composed of, constituted by, the words it utters. The transcripts of the fragments of her speeches which appear in the book are not, to our ears, so utterly the 'balderdash' which Ransom defensively–aggressively insists they are. The expression is marked by somewhat vapid generalities but the sentiments are, or should be, quite unexceptionable, unarguable. Ransom reacts as a male under threat at a particular historic moment, and James is not a little prophetic himself in his book's discerning of tendencies and presagings of large cultural shifts. But the magic and mystery – Verena's own mesmeric power (for she too can cast spells) – is in that part or dimension of her voice which is not exhausted in the words it utters. We may say 'tone' or 'timbre' but I think James is focusing on something deeper than that. When Ransom first hears her, he is enchanted. 'It was not what she said; he didn't care for that, he scarcely understood it . . . the argument, the doctrine, had absolutely nothing to do with it. It was simply an intensely personal exhibition.' Near the end when Basil seeks out Verena in Marmion and overhears her practising her speech he exclaims, 'involuntarily, "Murder, what a lovely voice!"', though he persists in loathing 'the words'. (There is a comparable crucial split between voice and speech, or sound and word, in Conrad's *Victory*, in which Axel Heyst is under the influence of the semantic voice of his dead father – his written words; and is also 'enchanted' by the sheer sound of the voice of the woman, Lena, whom he rescues and takes to his island, but whom he can never 'read' or understand semantically. The struggle and divorce between voice-as-speech and voice-as-sound is differently distributed in Conrad's novel and a different drama ensues, but I think he is here working in the same area as James is in *The Bostonians*.) What I think James is examining and dramatizing is the complex relationship of the sexual body to language – a drama enacted in the figure and fate of Verena Tarrant with a particular, though not unique, intensity. She is depicted as being peculiarly susceptible to the manipulations and appropriations of sexuality and language, not least in their cruder, though compelling, forms. Her relationship to what she says is slightly strange – neither a seer nor a parrot, she is in an uneasy alliance with her words, a mixture of precocious intermittencies of mastery and a more durable and willing passivity, a sort of sincere enchanted servitude which at times takes on the grace of spontaneity and initiation. And so with her body. She seems very willing to give it – there is something hapless in her generosity of compliance; and yet it is so constantly and crudely taken that attempts at autonomy are always overtaken by powers of victimization. That is why it is right that the drama should centre on her mouth, that site and aperture of the body which is at once, as it were, erogenous and semantic – where sexuality and meaning meet and merge – or collide. It is the speaking mouth which Olive Chancellor wants to keep open, promoting her to the lecture platform and 'prompting her to infinite discourse'; it is the erotic mouth which Basil Ransom wishes to stop with a kiss (as Olive quite correctly sees), pulling her off into a life-long domestic silence and incarceration like all the other 'very voiceless . . . women of the South'. They both, for different and doubtless for mixed motives, wish utterly to control Verena's maiden 'flow'.

Verena figures, she *is*, the precariousness, the insecurity of the body as it attempts to mediate, control, coordinate those two powers 'outside' which work on, in and through her – language and sexuality. Part of her particular pathos and poignancy is that 'she didn't pretend to have any control'. She is an exemplary victim. This is one reason why there are so many references to hands on and around her. She is indeed massively handled, endlessly mancipated, from her father's exploitative charade (travesty or blasphemy) of laying on of hands (on her head), to Olive Chancellor's desperately possessive, icy, sterile (and perhaps perverted) embraces/enclosings/arrestings, to Basil Ransom's more brutal pullings, forcings, grabbings, and twistings (edged with sadism). It is he who, at the end, has 'the simple purpose of getting her bodily out of the place' and who 'by muscular force, wrenched her away'. It is indeed a purely 'bodily' and muscular matter, and we are made powerfully aware of just how ruthless and crude male 'manual eloquence' can be. Though if Ransom seems merely to be bringing southern plantation habits to bear on his relations with women, we should remember that Olive quite literally 'buys' Verena in a fairly illicit deal – on the black market, we may say. North and South; one way and another, Verena Tarrant is now the exemplary figure emerging in the foreground – on the platform – of social history: the helpless young woman as slave – to be 'passed from hand to hand', to be coerced, appropriated, disposed of. It is another token of Verena's vulnerability to outside forces of all kinds – not just the muscular – that we often hear of her coming under the 'spell' or the 'charm' of people – mainly Olive; but the proclivity, the hypnotizability, is clearly there. And in this chaotic, centreless, directionless, confused, crowded, and jostling society, there are many people eager to weave their more or less tawdry spells, exercise their charms for more or less squalid ends (Verena is not the only victim. Basil Ransom nearly falls under the 'spell' of the self-travestying femininity of Mrs Luna in New York; and of course other people come under the spell of *her* voice, whether it is the sound or the words). So many spells, so much susceptibility, so much more or less vulgar charlatanry, such a drift to the mesmeric − all this is surely symptomatic, where it is not constitutive, of a society in great disarray, with values and authorities and coherences in doubt or far to seek. The whips and the manacles may have gone, but in post-Civil-War America the social disorder and general lostness, uncertainty, cynicism, released self-aggrandizement, gullibility, and general, confused, collective effervescence, meant that all kinds of other debased and degrading power-plays and power-relations could take root and, perversely, flourish. Verena Tarrant is a singular but representative growth of this particular ground and climate.

   The struggle to appropriate Verena is most strenuously conducted by Olive Chancellor and Basil Ransom. Between them it is indeed another Civil − and not-so-civil − War. They are easily, and rightly, identifiable as extreme opposites − her neurotic feminism and his reactionary masculism each representing vehement, hysterical, 'perverted', and warped distortions and intensifications of contemporary splits and divisions concerning gender rights and responsibilities. It is now recognized that it is quite wrong to see Olive as the sick, half-repressed lesbian and Basil as the brave warrior fighting on behalf of embattled, heterosexual health and sanity. Each is as 'partial', blinkered, obsessional and bigoted as the other (though what the narrator's attitude to them is we shall have to consider separately). They are both described at various times as 'provincial' − indeed pretty well everyone in the book is 'provincial', as befits a society which has lost all sense of a centre. More to the point they have a comparable desire and determination to rob Verena of all autonomy and independence. This is well indicated by a gesture each of them makes in relation to Verena − a cloaking gesture. When Olive has drawn Verena out into the icey night from her parental home in order to make her promise 'not to marry' (it is also a literal dragging of her away from notionally eligible, interesting young males inside the house), she flings 'over her with one hand the fold of a cloak' and holds her in it while she extracts the promise to, effectively, renounce her sexual identity. Mr Pardon is more felicitous than he realizes in his warning to them − 'You ladies had better look out, or you'll freeze together!' When Basil 'wrenches' Verena away from the Boston Music Hall, he thrusts 'the hood of Verena's long cloak over her head, to conceal her face and identity. It quite prevented recognition . . .' In this case, Basil does not want to force her to relinquish her sexual identity; he wants to reduce her to it. But in each case, the cloaking gesture enacts a will to muffle and erase Verena's own emerging, or potential, full, human, complex identity. Indeed, Basil effectively bundles her out of the book into some permanent, extra-social, bedroom of his own, for his own use, pleasure, and disposition. Recognition of Verena – *as* Verena – is indeed effectively prevented. Terminally. Simplifying, we can say that Olive wants Verena to be the voice she thinks she lacks – and nothing else. Basil wants her to be the body he knows he wants – and nothing else. Verena's tears – which conclude the book, but continue forever beyond it – are a poignant comment on her sense of helplessness at her plight and doom.

Olive Chancellor is perhaps sufficiently adumbrated in her name. A female Cromwell – 'the regiments of Oliver' was one of James's ways of referring to extreme, aberrant Puritans – she is indeed a kind of morbid and ferocious chancellor (law or state official), whose most appropriate place in the church would indeed be the chancel, that area reserved for the (ideally celibate) clergy. And she is of course a 'cancellor': she wishes to cancel sexuality. Her frantic discomfort in a gendered world – it does not satisfy her to be considered 'unwomanly', since she 'hated this epithet almost as much as she would have hated its opposite' – enacts and expresses itself in her self-negating body ('she had absolutely no figure') and her passionate spinsterhood (she 'was unmarried by every implication of her being'). Indeed she is 'essentially a celibate': denial and disavowal of sexuality are part of her essence. Perversion of sexual essences is another diagnosis of the book. Her 'immense desire to know intimately some *very* poor girl' may be interpreted in many ways, according to how we read 'immense desire' (for her desires are rare indeed compared with her repudiations and militancies), and 'know intimately' (for what might, and might not, intimate knowledge mean for this febrile, Bostonian spinster?). The patronizing/exploitative class implications are notable as well, and they are amply borne out when she quite coolly 'buys' (or is it 'rents'? It is not contractually settled as to whether Verena is freehold or leasehold) her chosen impoverished specimen. Verena is her object, her doll to dress, her protégée, her supplement – ideally, her voice. This is all sufficiently bad, no doubt, and very unhealthy – though we should remember that Verena does acquire education, European travel, an enlargement of experience, and the possibility of at least some kind of public identity and a sort of recognition – albeit all on Olive's terms. It may fairly be said that this is all at a cost and that the price is too high, or – as it transpires – simply impossible to pay.

But the potentially perverse or sterile moulding (or warping, if you will) of Verena by Olive is, it seems to me, in terms of a threat to identity and relative autonomy as nothing compared to the total oblivion promised, guaranteed, by Basil. It should also be remembered that Olive is objectively described and recognized as 'distinguished' – no matter how she may deprecate and disparage some of the assets and attributes of her class, she clearly has some ineradicable tone and style which denote breeding. Her 'culture', restricted and thwarted and selective and polemicized as it is, is nevertheless one of the less spurious qualities in the spreading vulgarity and charlatanry of this society. (Her appreciation of the piano music at Mrs Burrage's little party – 'she came near to being happy' – is reluctant and short-lived, but it is clearly genuine and a sign of authentic taste.) And, compared with most of the figures in the book, she is genuinely intelligent, no matter that she misapplies or misdirects her intellections and acuities. She is also honest. She is lots of other things as well, of course – not least paranoid and possessive to the edge of madness. But by the end – in the remarkable scene of grieving and worrying while Verena is out in a boat with Basil and Olive begins to fear she is drowned – in the sheer intensity of her suffering she acquires a kind of stature and seriousness beyond, well beyond, that of any other character in the book. One quotation from the moving account of her anguish:

> Those hours of backward clearness come to all men and women, once at least, when they read the past in the light of the present, with the reasons of things, like unobserved finger-posts, protruding where they never saw them before. The journey behind them is mapped out and figured, with its false steps, its wrong observations, all its infatuated, deluded geography. They understand as Olive understood, but it is probable that they rarely suffer as she suffered.

At this point Olive is as tragic a figure as any of James's heroines helplessly contemplating waste, loss, and error in the irrevocable, irrecoverable, irremediable past. Basil Ransom is strong, handsome, magnetic – there is a lot of magnetism around – but he is never so finely moving as this.

But it is he who wins – or rather successfully abducts – Verena, and I want now to trace out some aspects and implications of his relationships with the tongue and the pen. At the very beginning when he is introduced, after descriptions of his 'magnificent eyes' (intimations of hypnotisms to come) and his 'leonine' hair (Mrs Luna bitchily but accurately predicts that Verena will 'run off with some lion-tamer' – she addresses the words to the very lion/lion-tamer himself), the narrator devotes some space to attempting to transcribe his voice, his accent as well as his speech. He writes – the words are interesting –

> the reader who likes a complete image, who desires to read with his senses as well as with the reason, is entreated not to forget that he prolonged his consonants and swallowed his vowels, that he was guilty of elisions and interpolations which were equally unexpected, and that his discourse was

pervaded by something sultry and vast, something almost African in its rich, basking tone, something that suggested the teeming expanse of the cotton field.

From the start we are exhorted to hear the voice while reading the word – in the interests of a 'complete image' – which is a fair admonition as we are being introduced to a figure, indeed a society, seemingly bent on confusing or separating the two, and aiming at very notably incomplete images. As we shall see, the African South is determined to stress and use 'the senses' and quash 'the reason', while the chilly Northern Boston is happy to promote the latter and severely restrict the former. Imbalance, distortion, and deformation are the order of the day in this America. New York is not a place of harmonizing mediations – rather an arena of colliding incompletions. Basil Ransom's voice gives us some forewarning with its 'elisions and interpolations', for he leaves (or rubs) things out, and puts (or thrusts) things in. He is – humanly speaking – an occluder and an intruder, and in the pursuit of the gratification of his 'senses' he is determined to 'elide' Verena's 'reason' altogether. And not just Verena's, but the reason (and reasonable claims) of her sex. Remember that the big speech which Verena is preparing to give in Boston is entitled 'A Woman's Reason', and it is just that, in its entirety, that he is determined quite ruthlessly to silence. The reason and reasoning of women must not have a hearing. Meanwhile, while thousands wait and wish to hear Verena's address, he is given the confidence to assert his superiority and unquestionable authority and invincible power by the acceptance of one of his misogynistic articles by an utterly obscure journal with the definitively unarresting name of *The Rational Review* (devoted, no doubt, to the support and furtherance of a Man's Reason). Male fatuity could not well be carried further. Certainly, it is his pen versus her speech, or his phallus versus her mouth (I am no cruder, I think than the almost primitive violence of the last contestation warrants). The pathetic nature of the evidence for the potency of his pen as against the enormous interest aroused by her imminent speech explains some of the desperation (and fear) motivating his final forcible abduction (a rape, really) of Verena. The extent of Verena's – and the narrator's – collusion with this assertion of brute force (more panic than heroic) is a matter I will return to. But I want to look a little closer at Basil's attitude to writing and speaking.

On entering a room his instinct is to pick up any book which might be to hand and indeed when we first see him he has just done that: having found a volume on a table in Olive's house he has 'lost himself in its pages' when Mrs Luna finds him. His vision of future bliss consists of a dream of 'leisure in which he saw himself covering foolscap paper with his views on several subjects' – a vision which almost tempts him to succumb to Mrs Luna and her promise of financial ease. He is very ambitious and, quite like most of the other characters, and very like the feminists he despises, he has 'a desire for public life'; though he wishes to privatize – intensely and definitively – the one person who seems destined for real public success. His efforts to achieve public recognition in the courts through the legal profession have got him nowhere. He has, simply, 'made a mess' of the few jobs that have come his way. He has also tried writing articles but his voice has brought him 'luck as little under the pen as on the lips', the two agencies or organs of self-promotion and self-assertion – self-publication – thus clearly set forward. (One candid editor suggests that his writing and ideas might have had more success in the sixteenth century.) His root conviction is that 'women were essentially inferior to men', and he can develop this into a critique of his age as too feminized, weak, and talkative – though, as the narrator indicates, 'he liked to talk as well as anyone'. He has, indeed, a 'primitive concept of manhood', is 'very conceited', 'very provincial', and, of course, very 'reactionary'. He likes to drink and keeps himself easy with 'a little variety-actress' with whom he established 'cordial relations'. A man's man, take him all in all. His 'immense admiration' for Carlyle is to be noted, since we might refer to what James wrote about Carlyle in another context. Carlyle's pessimism was 'not only deep, but loud' and 'it is one of the strangest of things to find an appreciation of silence in a mind that was, before all else, expressive'. James has some admiration for Carlyle's 'magnificent vocalization', but he clearly finds his style, which is at the same time his thought, more powerful than persuasive. 'It is not defensible, but it is victorious.' Apt words for Basil Ransom. What James fastens on is Carlyle's perverse relish for voicing his cynicism and pessimism: 'few men have rioted so in their disenchantment, or thumped so perpetually upon the hollowness of things with a view to making it resound'. (This from a review of the correspondence of Carlyle and Emerson written in 1883 – when James was working on *The Bostonians*. Olive is not an Emerson, but some of her vague aspirational, optative theories and transcendental terminology do have an arguably Emersonian tinge, and, while James was dramatizing the battle between Basil and Olive, he may well have had in mind the differences he had discerned between Carlyle and Emerson, whom he saw as radically opposite temperaments and types. Of course, they were friends – but then they were both men.)

Like Carlyle, Ransom is 'much addicted to judging his age', and, while he berates it as being 'talkative, querulous, hysterical, maudlin, full of false ideas', we can see that at least half of that indictment applies to himself. My point is only that he is as much a product as a scourge of his age. He is not so much the critic of the feminists as their rival. For all his 'gallantry' and pseudo-stoic rhetoric and his pose of patrician detachment and disenchantment, he is as much a competitor in this world of self-promotion and publicity as Matthias Pardon. He wants to get in, get on – by pen or lips. (At one point, his memory of Verena is described as unrolling itself in his head 'like an interesting page of fiction' – he has paper on his mind, or in his head, almost as much as does that aspirant to self-paperization, Selah Tarrant.) More than once he describes Verena's public talks as 'ranting and raving', indeed 'rant and rave' is a catch-phrase of abuse in the book, and we may note that there is 'rave' in Verena as well as 'rant' in Tarrant – Ransom wants to excise, amputate, 'elide' part of her constitutive identity; cut out the parts he does not like and simply crush them into oblivion. But not only are the terms quite excessive, at least on the strength of what we are given; Ransom is as given to ranting and raving as any of them, as his outburst to Verena in Central Park amply demonstrates. He wants to separate her body from her thoughts and speech. 'I don't listen to your ideas; I listen to your voice', he tells her, insisting that she has no real connection with what she says, thus in effect telling her that she has no real connection with language. In a word he literally wants to 'infantilize' her – take her back out of speech altogether. This is 'primitive' indeed. He not only wants to have the last word: he wants to have the only word. James's insight into the motivation behind the male resistance to feminist claims is here as profound as need be. It is the very right to speak – truly speak – and be heard that is at stake. Then and, one must assume, still now. Ransom simply maintains that women have 'no place in public', and he says, honestly enough, to Verena, 'My plan is to keep you at home and have a better time with you there than ever.' (But what kind of time will Verena be having, we may ask, echoing Jim's very pertinent question when Tom Sawyer explains that he wants to put him in a prison for his fun and games.) But the arresting and marginalizing or privatizing impulse with regard to Verena really goes deeper than a will to assert that a woman's place is in the home. Certainly he does want to restrict Verena to the house, and when she tentatively questions whether that would not be a 'waste' of her voice, he glibly answers that 'the dining-table itself shall be our platform'. But his most abiding intention is revealed in a transcription of his thoughts in indirect speech which states with ominous clarity – 'if he should become her husband he should know a way to strike her dumb'. There is real violence and aggression in his urge to ' "squelch" all that', all that being her public life, or, we might say, her speaking life, her life in speech. There is a distinctly sadistic streak in the way in which, the grim relish with which, he asserts his power over Verena, in the 'conviction he had that however she might turn and twist in his grasp he held her fast'. If she does express any resistance, make any gesture towards retaining some independence or asserting her freedom, he simply dismisses these as 'instinctive contortions', while he says 'to himself that a good many more would probably occur before she would be quiet'. And that is what he wants – Verena finally made dumb. As she explains his demands to Olive, she shall never 'open my lips in public'. The lips to be opened in private do not, of course, talk. Just how exclusively sexual his designs are is intimated by the way he takes up a metaphor which Verena employs in her New York address. She had spoken of women as being kept in a box by men through the ages, a box in which they themselves have never found, or placed, themselves. It is not a particularly arresting trope, but on their walk in Central Park, Basil 'kept talking about the box; he seemed as if he wouldn't let go that simile. He said that he had come to look at her through the glass sides, and if he wasn't afraid of hurting her he would smash them in. He was determined to find the key that would open it, if he had to look for it all over world.' One can only imagine that his relentless sexualization of the simple simile was little short of coarse.

It is on the walk in Central Park that Ransom really seems to cast his sexual spell over Verena. Interestingly, the narrative again notes a divorce between voice as speech and voice as sound, as when Verena finds herself succumbing to 'his deep, sweet, distinct voice, expressing *monstrous opinions* with *exotic cadences*' (my italics). It is here that his earlier resolution that Verena was made 'for privacy, for him, for love' begins to take effect. Whereas their first meeting in Harvard Memorial Hall had inevitably been compassed about with associations of the War and slavery, the Park setting is more auspicious. They 'lost themselves in the Maze' and thread 'the devious ways of the Ramble' – it suggests an atmosphere and a place conducive to deviation from paths of resolve and rigid pledges, deviancy, perhaps even errancy. There is the opportune passing of some children with their nanny, happily for Basil's cause since Verena 'adored children'; and there are all those 'statues and busts of great men' which they admire, suitable mute bystanders for Basil's tirade about male supremacy which is to be unleashed in this anomalous pastoral spot in the heart of the American city. I want to comment on only one of his assertions (you cannot call them arguments, let alone ideas), the one already quoted as to his plan to keep her at home, where all women belong. Verena raises that absolutely pertinent question: 'And those who have got no home (there are millions, you know), what are you going to do with *them*? . . . You can't tell them to go and mind their husband and children, when they have no husband and children to mind.' Ransom's answer is – well, sublime. 'Oh, that's a detail!' In fact, as beside his Carlylean 'vocalizing', Verena raises the important issues and asks the relevant questions. When she asks, simply enough, how far he has advanced in his ambition to achieve some sort of public position and platform, he registers it as a 'perfectly legitimate taunt', and he as little likes Tarrant taunting as Tarrant ranting. Again when she innocently asks, 'Why don't you write out your ideas?', he feels his masculinity impugned even though she has no knowledge of the rejection slips his essays in sixteenth-century ideology have earned him. 'This touched again upon the matter of his failure; it was curious how she couldn't keep off it, hit it every time.' How sensitive his male vanity must be, how precarious his sense of potency. No wonder he wants to make and keep her quiet! The confidence which the acceptance of one article fills him with has been alluded to and is the basis for his conduct and assurance in Marmion, to which I will return. But before moving from the Central Park episode I want to draw attention to a short descriptive note on the urban scene into which they emerge as they leave the park. 'Groups of the unemployed, the children of disappointment from beyond the seas, propped themselves against the low, sunny wall of the park; and on the other side the commercial vista of the Sixth Avenue stretched away with a remarkable absence of aerial perspective.' It was this period which saw the emergence of a large urban proletariat in the United States, and along with that a newly visible class of the permanently disaffected, if not exactly disenfranchised – namely, the poor and unemployed among whom would be immigrants of various colours. Among other things this is one of James's most ambitious (and to my mind successful) social novels. James does not have much to say about this class, but he is clearly aware of another developing division in America, the effects of which would be even more profound than the differences between the North and South – namely, between the financially successful 'corporate' America signified by 'the commercial vista of the Sixth Avenue' and the swelling ranks of the 'children of disappointment', stacked like refuse against the opposite wall. It is only a hint in this book, but it is against this background that we should judge Ransom's dismissal of the problem of the 'millions' of women for whom home and marriage was not a chosen or available 'career' as – 'a detail'. It is a truism now that the exploitation and suppression of the working classes, racial minorities, and women are all part of the same hegemonic syndrome. What is perhaps remarkable, given his reputation for a somewhat effete affiliation and allegiance to the leisured and privileged classes, is that James could see it, and the implications of it, so clearly.

When Ransom finally does 'write out' some of his ideas in a form which allows them to be printed, it seems to seal Verena's capitulation. She now defers to his speaking and writing, or, as we might say, his articulate pen. 'He speaks with his pen', she says admiringly to Miss Birdseye; and 'he is sure that in future his pen will be a resource', she explains to the, quite correctly, sceptical Olive. ('And this vision of a literary career is based entirely upon an article that hasn't seen the light? I don't see how a man of any refinement can approach a woman with so beggarly an account of his position in life.') There is no question, it would seem, as to the validity or intelligence of his ideas, nor of the quality of his style, nor, certainly, of any imaginative gift. (There is no imaginative writing in this book – it is all more or less journalism, polemic, and advertising or scandal. It represents the debasement of literacy into mass publicity which James was to excoriate with renewed urgency in *The Reverberator*, and indeed publicity and public interest are referred to as 'the reverberation' in this novel before James decided to use the word as the name of a fictional newspaper.) No, the only important thing about Ransom's writing's being published is that it seems to legitimate his claim to the exclusive authority and superior potency of 'his pen' over her 'voice', for the pen now usurps, appropriates, and dominates the domain of speech as well. He speaks with his pen. Which leaves, will leave, Verena with no rights or organ of articulation. Olive Chancellor is certainly extreme and hysterical in her presentation of what motivates Basil Ransom, but she is hardly all wrong. 'It was because he knew that her voice had magic in it, and from the moment he caught its first note he had determined to crush it. It was not tenderness that moved him – it was devilish malignity.' Ransom promises to 'support' Verena with his pen – just the pen. By the same token it is what he will silence her with. It is indeed a phallic victory of the crudest sort.

But it would seem that Verena colludes with her defeat and his ascension to power, and at least half wants, half welcomes it. The key moment, perhaps, occurs in Central Park when she begins to succumb to his charges of the 'want of reality' in her association with the feminist movement: 'she was sure, at any rate, it was her *real self* that was there with him now, where she oughtn't to be' (my italics). This is the beginning of a growing equation of her 'real self' with her sexual self – an identity which Ransom always, exclusively, insists upon and which Olive, hopelessly, strives to deny. The extent to which the narrator appears to collude with this tendency and corroborate this reading of Verena's 'real self' I will consider in a moment. But certainly the narrative recognizes, concedes, or celebrates the fact that Varena 'had succumbed to the universal passion'. It would seem that with the stirring of an undeniable, unnegatable sexual attraction, all her previous commitments, attachments, resolutions simply melt and fall away. 'She was to burn everything she adored; she was to adore everything she burned.' That such a fairly masochistic reversal of volitions can be exacted and accorded apparently so easily and quickly testifies, at least, to the awesome power of the sexual drive. Without too much difficulty, it would seem, 'it was simply that the truth had changed sides'. Just like

that. 'She loved, she was in love – she felt it in every throb of her being.'
This could be seen as selling the appeal of the feminist movement rather
short, or the irresistibility of male sexuality rather long. But perhaps
James is trying to look a little deeper than that. 'It was always passion, in
fact; but now the object was other.' It is an arrestingly simple and succinct
diagnosis but a very important one. We hardly need to consult Freud on
the varieties and vicissitudes of libidinal 'object choice' to realize that
James is suggesting that our attachments and dedications might be a good
deal more precarious and arbitrary than we know or care to consider. Just
how 'quickly truth changes sides for Verena is paradigmatic of how
worryingly abrupt can be the switch of passionate allegiances. Or perhaps
we should say, the collapse into unpreferred sexual enslavement. For
James, or the narrator, clearly privileges, however reluctantly, the
superior power of the physical over the cerebral, even, or perhaps
particularly, when there is detectable 'perversity' on both sides – a
savage, regressive carnality from the defeated plantations of slavery,
versus a sterile, innutriently abstract and theorectical intellectuality
holding its somewhat hysterical vigil in the chilly spinster interiors of
Boston. Physical sexuality triumphs, it would seem, by the end, both
effortlessly and irresistibly. Here is Verena going to meet Ransom for one
of those agreed afternoon meetings when he is so persistently courting
her in Marmion: 'she felt that his tall, watching figure with the low
horizon behind, represented well the importance, the towering eminence he had in her mind – the fact that he was just now, to her vision, the
most definite and upright, the most incomparable, object in the world. If
he had not been at his post when she expected him she would have had to
stop and lean against something, for weakness'. Pausing only to note that
this last observation is an exact anticipation of how Freud would define
'anaclitic' love (that instinct to lean against the man which is the alternative
to 'narcissistic' love on the part of women), I would suggest that seldom,
surely, has there been a more indirectly explicit description of a woman's
eager rendezvous with the phallus.

But it should be stressed that this triumph of physical sexuality is not
saturated with Laurentian gladness and positivity. It is certainly
registered as inevitable, but arguably as much a fate and a doom as a joy
and a liberation. There is indeed no liberation for Verena in this book.
She is simply passed from hand to hand – to hand. She capitulates to
varying charms, submits to different powers, comes under different
spells. Aroused sexuality is simply the most powerful spell that she has
come under, and Olive Chancellor is again not all wrong in characteriz-
ing it to herself as 'an atrocious spell'. We might remember that James
himself once gave (to Grace Norton in 1880) as one of his reasons for not
marrying that 'if I were to marry I should be guilty in my own eyes of an

inconsistency – I should pretend to think just a little better of life than I really do'. We must not forget how Ransom bundles Verena out of the book into an indefinite future of dumbness and weeping.

In connection with the ambivalence of Verena's capitulation to sexual desire, I would draw attention to an unusual moment in the narrative when Olive finds Verena sitting in her house in a darkened room, after her prolonged boating expedition with Basil which has driven Olive to distractions of worry and suffering. Olive takes her hand compassionately and Verena allows her own to be held. 'From the way it lay in her own she guessed her whole feeling – saw it was a kind of shame, shame for her weakness, her swift surrender, her insane gyration.' The phrase is repeated twice to powerful, cumulative effect as Olive waves away the lights and the women sit together, silent in the deepening darkness. 'Distinctly, it was a kind of shame . . . It was a kind of shame.' It is the most eloquent silence in the book, as the implications of the reiterated phrase spread. Sexuality – here a woman's helpless enslavement to it – is, involves, entails, 'a kind of shame'. For once, Olive has no rhetoric of reproach or exhortation but sits in silent sympathy in a recognition of woman's physiological lot – or doom.

I want to look a little closer at Verena's capitulation and Basil's victory, and this will involve a consideration of the narrator and the narrative voice and stance. As omniscient, or at least third-person, the narrator clearly has, or arrogates to himself, definitional responsibility and authority. When he describes characters (or actions) as intelligent, cultured, distinguished, courteous, or provincial, perverse, fatuous, etc., then it implies that he knows and recognizes those qualities, attributes, and defects. Occasionally he protests, with conventional self-deprecation or self-exculpation, that he is only a 'historian' or 'reporter'. But one of his first-person intrusions more accurately defines his role, and reveals his power. After ascribing a 'terrible regularity of feature' to Mrs Farrinder, he interpolates: 'I apply that adjective to her fine placid mask because . . .' As well as transcribing the story, he distributes and applies the adjectives. The autocracy-by-epithet is sometimes used quite blatantly. He may describe a woman as 'essentially feminine' or a manner as 'altogether feminine', as if he could speak with absolute assurance as to what that essence, if of course it is an essence and not an arbitrary cultural construct, actually is. He can refer, unambiguously and patronizingly, to Ransom's 'narrow notions', so he must know what truly broad ones are. He can suggest that a New York scene bespeaks 'a rank civilization', which would seem to indicate some acquaintance with a healthy one, and when he refers to the contemporary 'slangy age' as though it was an axiomatic and indisputable established truth, he speaks as one who knows what the higher discursive elegancies and decorums are, or should be. Certainly he can at times foreground his predilection for fairly gratuitous periphrasis to comic effect – 'garb of toil', 'obtrusive swain', 'peccant tissue' (a disarranged veil!). There is obviously a touch of mandarin self-mockery here, and it is not all patrician hauteur and disdain. Similarly, he somewhat ironizes his proclivity to insert odd French phrases into his writing (a tendency which James deprecated in Whitman by noting that 'we cannot but regret his too great familiarity with the foreign languages'). Thus having made fun of Mrs Tarrant's weak pretensions to metropolitan chic – 'she knew, in advance, just the air she should take . . . just the *nuance* (she had also the impression she knew a little French) . . .' – the narrator starts to sprinkle his text with obtrusively unnecessary French words in very visible italics: *portée, milieu, à la Chinoise* (and later, *bibelots, dénouement, improvisatrice, portière*, etc.). Perhaps we may say that this is all just part of James's almost inscrutably bottomless sense of the inherently comical strain in his relations with language.

But there is also the matter of the narrator of this novel and his relation to his material. At times he makes clear gestures of self-distancing and disinvolvement with fastidious disclaimers – 'I hardly know . . .', 'I must content myself . . .', 'I am forbidden to do more . . .', 'we need, in strictness, concern ourselves with it no further . . .', 'there is a certain propriety in averting our head . . .', 'a liberty we have not yet ventured on . . .', 'I must plead a certain incompetence . . .', and so on. As well as conventional narratorial informalities, they serve as small, discreet signals that our narrator is tactful, scrupulous, polite, modest (up to a point) and decorous – he, surely, knows the proprieties in a world in which the general sense of them seems sadly lacking. The voices in the book are all notably partial – meaningless and mechanically garrulous, for the most part, with even the two (arguably) most articulate contenders for the innocent ear (Verena) revealing their crack and bias, Olive coming at times to sound like a 'broken saw' even to Verena, and Ransom revealing himself for the second-rate Carlylean ranter that he is. In all this, the voice of the narrator certainly seems to bespeak more balance and sophistication, more tolerance and inclusiveness, more poise and detachment, more experience and wisdom; it is the tone, perhaps, of the centre. And yet, the voice sometimes betrays itself, a little, with uncharacteristic judgemental vehemences. Some of the comments on Miss Birdseye, for instance, are marked by an unmodulated tone of mockery which verges on asperity – 'a confused, entangled, inconsequent, discursive old woman'; 'the poor little humanitary hack'; 'her grotesque, undistinguished, pathetic little name', and – here the facile insertion of the second adjective (and their application is solely and self-confessedly the narrator's privilege) in the interests of a certain alliterative cleverness, is certainly cruel and arguably cheap – her 'delicate, dirty, democratic little hand'. These introductory derisions and diminutions are hardly compensated for by the mellow, elegiac mood which attends Miss Birdseye's gentle dissolution as something of an apologetic reparation. On the other hand, it could be said that the narrator at times seems to come a little under the spell of Ransom's unreconstructed and unregenerate 'manhood', his apparently irresistible virile charms. Trying to establish whether the narrator and/or James is actually a bit of a misogynist, or – on the other hand – a proto-feminist is, of course, a futile and pointless exercise. Arguably Olive Chancellor with all her frenzied sterility and hysterical paranoia is a more intelligent, more civilized, more truly cultured figure than Ransom; possibly a more heroic one, certainly a more tragic one. And the narrator's sympathies are manifestly with the plight and fate of the generous, pathetic, too-plastic, ever-appropriated Verena. What does seem to happen is that he, or his story, hand her over (for she is, after all, in his hands as well) to Basil Ransom at the end with suspiciously little struggle or, perhaps it is the same thing, in a state of almost implausibly extreme helplessness and abjection. Perhaps this is James's/the narrator's way of indicating his sense of the 'atrocious' power of the sexual drive. But is is worth looking a little closer at the collapse and effacement of Verena.

At one point even Basil is 'quite appalled at the facility with which she threw it over' – 'it' being her 'gift' in particular, but really her sympathy with feminism and indeed her claims to her own voice (her own identity) in general, so that we may fairly demur at that 'facility' as well. Immediately after this, when Verena asks whether her voice is to be wasted, Ransom makes the crude, patronizing and ominous rejoinder, 'the dining-table itself shall be our platform'. The narrator comments: 'This was Basil Ransom's sportive reply to his companion's very natural appeal for light, and the reader will remark that if it led her to push her investigation no further, she was very easily satisfied.' Well, yes – we *do* remark it. James himself, in his own voice, wrote in 1868: 'It seems to us supremely absurd to stand up in high places and endeavor, with a long lash and a good deal of bad language, to drive women back into their ancient fold.' In *The Bostonians* Basil Ransom explicitly states his determination to force Verena to 'return to the ancient fold', and we may infer that the lash will be as long, and the language as bad, as necessary. Now Verena, at the comparatively early point when Ransom uses the phrase to her, counters his easy male derision spiritedly. 'The ancient fold, you say very well, where women were slaughtered just like sheep.' And she more than holds her own. Yet at the end, she does seem to go very meekly to the slaughter. When she pleads to be allowed just to give her Boston address – "Oh, let me off, let me off – for *her*, for the others' – his almost sadistic refusal – 'You are mine, you are not theirs' – may be explained by his having made the occasion a crucial test of his power over Verena, and of his own virility. He regards the possibility of Verena's speaking in the hall as symbolic or representative of everything which 'challenged all his manhood'. But why should the author, as it were, collude with him and so utterly undermine Verena's powers of even this amount of more-than-reasonable resistance? It is a foolish question, I concede. A novelist tells his story; strengths and weaknesses ebb and flow in the most mysterious and unpredictable ways: in life and so in novels. Yet it is a cruelly total victory achieved at the cost of exacting and eliciting an indeed 'atrocious' state of paralysed abjection. (On Olive's part as well, as she begs Ransom just to allow Verena to speak – 'I'll be vile – I'll go down in the dust.' She asks Basil, 'Haven't you any soul', and of course there is her answer. He is just the body in determined, soul-less, pitilessly selfish, triumph.)

It might be suggested that the civilized and urbane narrator himself feels helpless before Ransom's crude sexual insistence and thus feels prompted to dramatize the totality of Verena's helplessness in the face of it. It is also fairly clear that James himself oscillated in his attitude towards the calls and claims for the 'emancipation' and rights of women, sometimes sympathetic, sometimes downright hostile. He is clearly ambivalent about male domination and oppression, and female subjugation and victimization, as any reading of his novels must bear out; so we will not be surprised to detect both real sympathy for Verena and some strange attraction to, fascination with, Ransom's magnetic and forceful physicality (not, I think with his 'ideas'). And there is another factor worth noting. Ransom's battle is not only for Verena; it is against – partly Olive, but he knows he's won – but by the end, the public, the Boston audience, the people of contemporary America. We know about his taste for Tocqueville and his scepticism as to the virtues and values of democracy, but in the last scene that scepticism reveals itself more as fear and loathing. What Mr Pardon regards as 'our Boston public' and the impresario Mr Filer refers to as 'a lovely crowd', Ransom hates as 'senseless brutes' with some uneasy thoughts stirred by 'a glimpse of the ferocity that lurks in a disappointed mob'. For post-revolutionary nineteenth-century republics it was of course a permanently unsettling – and unsettleable – question as to when the 'people' were a 'public' and when they were a 'mob', always being, of course, potentially either and actually both. Along with many other American writers of this time – Mark Twain no less than Henry Adams or Francis Parkman – Henry James himself was ambivalent, sceptical, pessimistic, and probably somewhat frightened, about the potentially awesome power and potentially awesome barbarity of the great American people/public/ mob. At the very end of the novel the narrator speculates, rather than asserts (which, in his omniscient role, he often does) what might have been Ransom's thoughts as Olive Chancellor desperately, bravely, 'rushed to approach the platform' to face the vast, agitated, angry audience (rising 'in waves and surges' – the sea being the absolutely central and recurrent image for the crowd–mob in nineteenth-century literature). It is an odd moment, because Ransom himself does not see Olive, busy as he is with man-handling Verena. The narrator sees her, but he then prefers to imagine Basil's possible reaction. 'She might have suggested to him some feminine firebrand of Paris revolutions, erupt on a barricade, or even the sacrificial figure of Hypatia, whirled through the furious mob of Alexandria.' The two allusions are apt, since it is unclear whether Olive will discover her voice and role as a leader (and the possibility is certainly there) or end up as a martyr to the crowd's fury. Either way, we may note, she seems to be approaching true heroic status at the end. But why does the narrator have to, as it were, deflect or detour his appropriate speculations and comparisons through a non-attentive and thus non-responding Ransom? Perhaps to indicate that his inflamed, anti-democratic, southern imagination would turn naturally to the violence of revolutionary mobs. But partly, I think, because the narrator shares some of that feeling, and fear, of the public-turned-mob. It allows him a flicker of apocalyptic dread without obliging him to abandon his own poised and unruffled, unhysterical tone. As he ends his narrative with the 'mob' of 'senseless brutes', now settled to listen to Olive Chancellor in a 'respectful hush', he simply registers that even Ransom has to recognize that 'a Boston audience is not ungenerous'. The narrator has indulged, but not betrayed, a latent fear and a defensive contempt – through Ransom. Ransom defines himself, precisely, against the crowd. 'He was not one of the audience; he was apart, unique.' It is of course the standard Romantic gesture and stance, the quest for, and insistence on, privileged ontological singularity and ineffaceable individual distinction. The narrator seems in part to sympathize with the aspiration and claim, but is also sophisticated enough to hint at both its clichéd conventionality and its posturing self-deception. Thus I think that the narrator reveals both his ambivalences and uncertainties about sexual and political power – just how 'atrocious' is the sexual spell? Just how potentially senseless and brutal are the 'people'? – and finds a narrative way of containing and distributing them so that his own poise is maintained to the end. If he is not exactly a 'complete image' he may be sensed as avoiding radical incompletion more than any of the characters in his story. If there is a truly 'human voice' in the book, then I suggest that his own would be the most persuasive candidate.

But of course an author's voice is never wholly his own – indeed any search for an original, originating voice is doomed, in writing as in speaking. To be more precise, there is much in *The Bostonians* which is a re-speaking of matters raised and dramatized in Hawthorne's *The Blithdale Romance* (1852), which was also much concerned with the women's rights movement in America (the first women's rights convention was held at Seneca Falls, New York, in 1848). Both in its general theme and in crucial characters and dramatic details, James's novel owes much to Hawthorne. Consider the crucial exchange or argument between the powerful proponent of women's rights, Zenobia, and the monomanical reformer (and male chauvinist), Hollingsworth. This is part of Zenobia's case:

> Thus far, no woman in the world has ever once spoken out her whole heart and her whole mind. The mistrust and disapproval of the vast bulk of society throttles us, as with two gigantic hands at our throats! We mumble a few weak words, and leave a thousand better ones unsaid. You let us write a little, it is true, on a limited range of subjects. But the pen is not for woman. Her power is too natural and immediate. It is with the living voice, alone, that she can compel the world to recognize the light of her intellect and the depth of her heart.

Here the central struggle of *The Bostonians* between male pen and female voice is clearly adumbrated, and while Zenobia is very different from Olive, being among other things unmistakably a sexually active and desiring woman, Hollingsworth at times can sound very like Ransom. Here are some of his notions of woman. 'Man is a wretch without woman; but woman is a monster – and, thank Heaven, an almost impossible and hitherto imaginary monster – without man, as her acknowledged principal! . . . if there were a chance of their attaining the end which these petticoated monstrosities have in view, I would call upon my own sex to use its physical source, that unmistakable evidence of sovereignty, to scourge them back within their proper bounds!' Here indeed is the long lash and the bad language which James referred to, and we can have no doubt that Ransom would have – indeed will – echo every word and sentiment. But more. There is a young girl, Priscilla, of mysterious origin who joins the community of Brook Farm. Like Verena she is a figure of poignant vulnerability, yielding docility, and susceptible hypnotizability. She also embodies a barely blossoming sexuality which is both troubling and tempting. She has one notable gift – making purses. 'Their peculiar excellence, besides the great delicacy and beauty of their manufacture, lay in the almost impossibility that any uninitiated person should discover the aperture; although, to a practised touch, they would open as wide as charity or prodigality might wish. I wondered if it were not a symbol of Priscilla's own mystery.' This seems almost obscenely prurient, either on the part of Hawthorne or his etiolated bachelor narrator, Miles Coverdale. But Priscilla's own not very mysterious mystery is Verena Tarrant's as well. Priscilla is also a pliant, dependent figure who is, like Verena, passed from hand to hand. At first she wants to submit almost abjectly to Zenobia's power and protection, but she then is taken over and away by the intransigently male Hollingsworth – Verena follows an analogous trajectory. And there are closer echoes. Priscilla is under the mesmeric influence of Westervelt, a dubious, charlatan hypnotist who seems like an early avatar of Selah Tarrant. He uses Priscilla as part of his show – she is 'pliant to his gesture' as Verena exactly is to her father's and, like Verena, is sometimes regarded as 'a mountebank' – in which she appears on the platform as the 'Veiled Lady' who 'through the potency of my art' holds 'communion with the spiritual world'. At the climax of one of the key performances in a 'Lyceum lecture hall', when Westervelt is boasting that she is completely and immovably under his spell and in his power, Hollingsworth bursts onto the stage and calls Priscilla to come to him. She rises, throws off her veil, and escapes from 'the jugglery that had hitherto environed her'. 'She uttered a shriek and fled to Hollingsworth like one escaping from her deadliest enemy, and was safe forever!' As can easily be seen, the dramatic configuration and setting which end James's novel are clearly laid out in Hawthorne's, albeit Olive is more in the position of Westervelt; Ransom uses brute force in place of Hollingsworth's summons; Verena is much less certain and happy about her 'escape' and is most certainly not 'safe forever'; and James may be said to be more ambiguous and searching about the 'jugglery' which 'environs' Verena – on all sides.

Zenobia is, it is agreed, based largely on the figure of Margaret Fuller, a formidable New England intellectual and articulate defender of women's rights who had been drowned in a shipwreck (with her child and Italian husband or consort) two years before Hawthorne's novel. Hawthorne was clearly made uneasy by Margaret Fuller and he wrote, repellently, after her death: 'Providence was, after all, kind in putting her, and her clownish husband, and their child, on board that fated ship . . . a strange, heavy, unpliable, and in many respects, defective and evil nature . . . she proved herself a woman after all and fell like the lowest of her sisters.' Hawthorne's defensive–aggressive attitude to women, particularly sexual–intellectual women, is not my subject here. But there are two rather interesting aspects of his treatment of Fuller in the figure of Zenobia. For one thing, he makes her much more attractive and frankly erotic and also allows her some very forceful arguments (even if her case is not so subtle and intellectually powerful as Fuller's work, *Woman in the Nineteenth Century*). And for another, it seems as if the excessively male Hollingsworth wilts into impotence after Zenobia's last blistering attack on his manhood. 'Are you a man? No; but a monster! A cold, heartless,

self-beginning and self-ending piece of mechanism . . . It is all self!
Nothing else; nothing but self, self, self!' We know what Hawthorne
thought of 'egotism' and we hardly feel that Zenobia's indictment is in
any way ironically undermined. Certainly it has an emasculating effect
on Hollingsworth, who turns 'deadly pale' and turns to his frail young
ward for support – 'Yes; the strong man bowed himself; and rested on his
poor Priscilla.' This reversal of role, which is almost a castration, seems
permanent, for when the narrator sees them years later, Hollingsworth
looks 'childlike' as he clings to Priscilla, while 'In Priscilla's manner, there
was a protective and watchful quality, as if she felt herself the guardian of
her companion.' It is an extraordinary defeat for the seemingly strongest
man, and something of a posthumous victory for the outspoken Zenobia
(who drowns herself shortly after that last speech). We can hardly
anticipate such a striking reversal in the relationship of Basil Ransom and
Verena Tarrant in the years after his rescue of her from the platform –
though of course, particularly in these matters, you never know. But it is
clear that for both writers the depicted triumph of the dominating
'macho' male is attended and surrounded by some far-reaching
ambiguities and uncertainties of outcome.

It would be possible to expand on the historical and social significance of
James's novel. Concern about all aspects of public speaking – 'eloquence'
– was particularly acute in America, a country which, as a commentator
put it in 1842, had been 'spoken into existence'. It was, indeed, more than
any other country, a linguistic construct, which, as Tocqueville put it,
'exists, so to speak, only in the mind'. And to the extent that America had
been spoken into existence, it had to be maintained and consolidated by
constant eloquence: hence the supreme importance of oratory – and of
lawyers – in the decades after the War of Independence. (Washington
Irving parodied America as a society ruled by a 'pure unadulterated
LOGOCRACY or *government of words*' in *Salmagundi* as early as 1807–8.)
As Robert Ferguson puts it in his *Law and Letters*, concerning the special
duty of lawyers and public orators in the first half of the nineteenth
century: 'There was a solemn obligation to speak and to speak often.'
The founders and guardians of the new republic were aware of the
crucial role to be played by public speaking; thus John Quincy Adams in
his *Lectures on Rhetoric and Oratory* (1810) notes that 'In the flourishing
periods of Athens and Rome, eloquence was POWER.' There was also,
from the start, a concern about what might happen to public speaking in
a democracy, a worry articulated by Tocqueville and James Fenimore
Cooper (who also stressed the dangers of the degradation of the written
word in the growing tyranny-by-newspaper of America). America and
public speaking were, then, coeval. It is hard for us to appreciate the

almost god-like status achieved by the great orator, Daniel Webster. And figures like the Duke and Dauphin on Huckleberry Finn's raft, or Melville's confidence man, are simply masters and manipulators of the American people working somewhat lower down on the spectrum of American rhetoricians. Certainly, as David Simpson shows in his book *The Politics of American English*, as the nineteenth century progresses 'we can see a developing concern with the demagogic potential of this privileging of the spoken word'. By the time James came to write *The Bostonians* in post-Civil-War America, public oratory – and journalism – seem to have been proliferating and, at least from the point of view of some of the more patrician American observers, becoming more debased. Certainly then, the issues James concentrates on in his novel were of particular importance in the America of his time. But I have preferred to suggest the more general and abiding relevance and importance of these issues, particularly the question of the problematics which attend the very notion of 'a human voice'. What, really, is a human voice? How do you know it when you hear it; how can you be certain when you speak with (in) it? To what extent can we transcend or control the degree to which, in all manner of ways, we are spoken? James can make us aware of the perversions, the aberrations, the delinquencies and derelictions, the appropriations and usurpations, of the human voice. He shows us the struggle to possess it, and suppress it. When Verena Tarrant says 'They tell me I speak as I talk, so I suppose I talk as I speak' we are made aware of possible teasing but important differences. What is the relationship between talk and speech? It is, perhaps, the difference between private and public, but then where do those ill-defined areas begin and end? Indeed, is there any true privacy left in the rampant publicity of the world of this novel? Selah Tarrant effectively public-izes his domestic interior by his absurd attempts at grandiloquence and formality at the dinner table. Ransom is not against publicity, he simply wants it all for himself. He does not silence Verena because he wants to save the sanctities of the private life, but simply because he wants to be the only voice. His idea of the private life is one involving an amenable, nameless, variety actress. There is, indeed, something touching about the tentative ways, we feel, in which Verena at times tries to start talking rather than 'speaking' – to find and identify and use her own voice. As opposed to being a conduit for language's own torrential flow. That struggle is a pain and a problem for her and her eloquence is at once dubious and doomed. In her complicated and poignant relationship to both the sound and sense of her own voice, and the various voices not her own both in and around her, Verena Tarrant dramatizes a predicament which may indeed be said to be exemplary. Before Heidegger so

explicitly stated it, Henry James knew of 'the confusion of the true
relation of dominance as between language and man. For in fact it is
language that speaks . . .'

Note. I have chosen not to subsume, or relate, this consideration of James's novel to the long history
of male valuing and privileging the silent woman (Cordelia etc.) and degrading, deriding,
deforming, and demonizing the 'garrulous' woman (shrew, termagant, scold, witch, mad
prophetess, etc.), since there has been a good deal of work on this ancient tradition in recent
years, particularly in feminist criticism, and I wanted to focus more closely on just what is
going on in James's novel. But of course, it has its particular place in that tradition, not least as a
subtle and fairly far-reaching critique of it.

10

Games American writers play: ceremony, complicity, contestation, and carnival

> But every now and then, players in a game will, lull or crisis, be reminded how it is, after all, really play – and be unable to continue in the same spirit . . . Nor need it be anything sudden, spectacular – it may come in gentle – and regardless of the score, the number of watchers, their collective wish, penalties they or the Leagues may impose, the play will, walking deliberately . . . say *fuck it* and quit the game, quit it cold.   (*Gravity's Rainbow*)

How do we read books which emerge from our own environment, which are part of our ongoing contemporaneity? If we address ourselves to works of the past, products of a different society, a different economy, a different historical matrix, we are reading not only those works but by implication the silent language of anticipations and expectations, permissions and prohibitions, which surround them and make up their context. Whatever else a book may do it records a series of choices from the available discourses at a particular time. It is a commonplace to say that the condition of meaning is exclusion, but it is worth remembering when reading a book from the past that we are indirectly reading or being exposed to the tacit social rules and conditions which governed the exclusions and inclusions which are as much a part of the book as any more ostensible subject matter. To put it very simply, when we read a book from the past we are in fact reading a book and a context, but in reading a book from the present we *are* the context.

Reading a contemporary work we should be aware, or better, we should be *made* aware, of the discourses within us which we bring to the text. For example, a book which attempts to do this quite deliberately, and successfully to my mind, is Robert Pirsig's *Zen and the Art of Motorcycle Maintenance*. The very title suggests the interaction or confrontation of discourses traditionally kept separate, and the book is based on the idea of giving new visibility to contemporary discourses by

176

just such confrontations and recontextualizations. They 'interrogate' each other. One quotation from the book: the narrator gives what he calls a 'classical' description of a motorcycle. He then comments: 'There's certainly nothing strange about this description at first hearing. It sounds like something from a beginning text-book on the subject, or perhaps a first lesson in a vocational course. What is unusual about it is seen when it ceases to be a mode of discourse and becomes an object of discourse. Then certain things can be pointed to.' A lot of contemporary American fiction, it seems to me, is working in this area of turning modes of discourse into objects of discourse, and a lot of its vitality is dependent on the reader's ability to recognize the shifting relation between discourse as mode and as object within the book and within himself. Then – 'certain things can be pointed to'. In the future different readers will point to different things – if only because they are inevitably reading through our readings.

What I want to point to in some recent American fiction can perhaps be most economically prepared for by the introduction of four words, each suggesting a different relationship between literature and society – thus we might consider literature as ceremony, complicity, contestation, or carnival. The first three words may be found in Sartre's *What Is Literature?* The first kind of writing is produced 'when the power of the religious and political ideology is so strong and the interdictions so rigorous that in no case is there any question of discovering new countries of the mind, but only of putting into shape the *commonplaces* adopted by the elite in such a way that reading . . . is a ceremony of *recognition*'. Whatever Sartre's intentions, ceremony suggests something positive, public, and based on shared beliefs and values. Complicity suggests a more covert activity, involving a degree of conscious or unconscious bad faith on the part of the writer as he simply confirms the public in its own image and its own selective perspectives on the society of the time. Bourgeois society in particular 'does not ask to be shown what it is, but it asks rather for a reflection of what it thinks it is'. (This crucial distinction could be amplified by considering Freud's essay on Fetishism and the tension between knowledge and belief that he diagnoses as being present in a 'fetishistic' relationship to reality; and by considering Lacan's notion of people who inhabit the realm of the 'Imaginary', living lives based on 'mirages and misconstructions'.) The bourgeois audience did not ask the writer 'to restore the strangeness and opacity of the world, but to dissolve it into elementary subjective impressions which made it easier to digest'. They wanted to 'buy with their eyes closed'. A writer attempting to resist this kind of complicity will find himself engaged in contestation, attempting to make society more aware of its own structuring.

> If society sees itself and, in particular, sees itself as *seen*, there is by virtue of this very fact, a contesting of the established values of the regime. The writer presents it with its image; he calls upon it to assume it or change it. At any rate, it changes; it loses the equilibrium which its ignorance had given it; it wavers between shame and cynicism; it practises dishonesty: thus, the writer gives society a *guilty conscience*.

Contestations become more radical as they increasingly refuse any complicity with what they are describing, just as the writer feels an increasing dissonance with his society as his own position becomes more problematical and his role in society has to be constantly re-invented. In such conditions, literature moves increasingly towards 'negation' until finally it turns on itself. 'In the end there was nothing left for literature to do but to contest itself. That is what it did in the name of surrealism.' Generalizing from Sartre's argument, we can say that unless a writer overtly accepts and celebrates the value system and reality picture of the society in which he writes, he must inevitably move towards complicity or contestation. These activities can obviously take many forms and may occur together in the same work; the question I wish to consider is where contemporary American writers situate themselves in this tension between complicity and contestation, and whether they have found an alternative way of being-in-society at the present time.

One obvious problem is that writers and readers alike are over-exposed to language, so that a gesture of revolt is easily transformed – by our present context – into a distraction for entertainment. Just what a writer might do in contemporary society is one of the problems implicit in Fredric Jameson's book *Marxism and Form*. He cites Marcuse and his contention that 'the consumer society, the society of abundance, has lost the experience of the negative in all its forms, and that it is the negative alone which is ultimately fructifying from a cultural as well as an individual point of view'. He describes Adorno's conception of the work of art and its relationship to its immediate historical situation, namely that it inevitably 'reflects' society but it should also 'refuse the social . . . the socio-economic is inscribed in the work, but as concave to convex, as positive to negative'. And Jameson's own contention is this: 'we begin to glimpse what is the profound vocation of the work of art in a commodity society: *not* to be a commodity, *not* to be consumed, to be *unpleasurable* in the commodity sense'. Here then are three possible prescriptions for the contemporary writer – to attempt to discover significant ways of reintroducing the experience of negativity to the reader; to reflect society by refusing it; to produce works which are non-commodities and thus somehow to violate the pleasure principle of the purchaser-consumer. We may add Sartre's injunction that a work of literature should be 'a task to be discharged', one implication of this being that it should turn

readers into active producers rather than passive consumers. In general it
would seem that what is needed is what Zamyatin called 'harmful
literature', which is quite different from any specific didactic, polemical,
or propagandist literature. 'Harmful literature is more useful than useful
literature, for it is antientropic, it is a means of combating calcification,
sclerosis, crust, moss, acquiescence' ('On Literature, Revolution, Entropy, and other Matters', 1970). What we find when we turn to some
recent American fiction is, I will contend, varying attempts to move
beyond complicity and contestation into an area which I will designate as
carnival. But let me start to be more specific.

Here are two quotations; the first is from Ishmael Reed's *Yellow Back
Radio Broke Down*: 'Whats your beef with me Schmo, what if I write
circuses? No-one says a novel has to be one thing. It can be anything it
wants to be, a vaudeville show, the six o'clock news, the mumblings of
wild men saddled by demons.' The second is from Jerome Charyn's *The
Tar Baby*. In this novel the main character, Anatole, loses his 'feel for
mapping': 'He wanted to clear his head of taxonomies, to quit being
reader of griddles and signs.' My preceding comments all ultimately
concerned the literary work as being some kind of mimesis – positive or
negative. What the quotations point to is an impulse to move beyond the
constraints of existing categories, so that in reading the work it is
impossible to stabilize it within any one genre. If category *per se* can be
seen as being connected to the different modes of discourse which
'systematize' us, then the impulse to confront, conflate, dissolve, or even
annul categories can be seen as part of an attempt to desystematize the
reader. (As Nietzsche reminds us in *Will to Power*, you can devalue
categories without devaluing the universe. Indeed it may be necessary to
devalue categories in order to revalue the universe.) Reed is euphoric;
Charyn's Anatole is melancholic, and his exhaustion with 'signs', his
desire to rid himself of taxonomies altogether, point to a possible
ambiguity in this thrust beyond contemporary modes of 'mapping'
experience. It may lead into an exhilarating circus of categories, or into a
taxonomic void. Thus a deliberate dis-orientation may lead to a new re-
orientation or a state of no-orientation; both are felt to open up the
possibilities of a new freedom which is unavailable within the existing
categories.

This is why, I think, there is a very discernible increase in the emphasis
on writing as a 'game' among contemporary American writers and
critics – Albert Guerard has written extensively of 'the sense of fun
writers take in the games they play'; Philip Stevick in his interesting
inquiry, 'Metaphors for the Novel', lists a collection of some fifty
metaphors he has found being employed to describe the novel and
concludes: 'Fiction in the Seventies is dream, prayer, cri de coeur, and

fingernails on a blackboard. But pre-eminently, as Fielding, Sterne, and Jane Austen knew, the novel is a game.' Ronald Sukenick's idea of a 'New Tradition in the Novel' is called, gamefully enough, Bossa Nova – which, 'needless to say . . . has no plot, no story, no character, no chronological sequence, no verisimilitude, no imitation, no allegory, no symbolism, no subject matter, no "meaning" . . . ' The general consensus among such writers and critics is that contemporary fiction should be anti-realistic, non-representational, non-referential, and attempt to 'present elements of its texture as devoid of value; new fiction . . . seeks this value-less quality not as an act of subtraction, or dehumanization, or metaphysical mystification, not as a gesture of despair or nihilism, but as a positive act in which the joy of the observer is allowed to prevail as the primary quality of the experience' (Stevick). John Barth's praise for Smollett's *Roderick Random* as 'a novel of non-significant surfaces' is representative of this way of thinking about new fictional possibilities. I think that all these descriptions of, and prescriptions for, the novel are problematical if taken literally. Even the metaphor of fiction as 'game' has its difficulties. As Stevick himself pointed out, it poses the question of whether the game is in the writing, the reading, or the book itself, or all three. Also, games have rules in a way that improvised play does not, and in some contemporary American fiction it would be difficult to maintain a distinction between 'game' and 'play'. Another problematical aspect of the metaphor is worth noting As Lévi-Strauss points out in the *Savage Mind*, 'Games thus appear to have a *disjunctive* effect: they end in the establishment of a difference between individual players or teams where originally there was no indication of inequality. And at the end of the game they are distinguished into winners and losers. Ritual, on the other hand, is the exact converse; it *conjoins* for it brings about a union (one might even say communion in this context) or in any case an organic relation between two initially separated groups'. In a highly competitive western society, the word 'game' is necessarily ambiguous, suggesting at once a temporary reprieve from work, and a disjunctive striving to establish winners and losers at all levels. Hence the use of such phrases as 'the games people play' and even 'war games'. If society itself is seen as a series of more or less vicious and exploitative games, then what kind of 'game' is the novel playing?

Perhaps a word which contains suggestions of play, game, and ritual would be useful here. It might therefore be helpful to invoke the word 'carnival' as defined by Michael Bakhtin in his monumental work on *Rabelais and His World* (MIT, 1968). In his terms, during carnival life is lifted out of its routines, hierarchies are dissolved, fixed models are unstructured, the closed world enshrined in official concepts and formulae is broken open. In addition, in carnival the existing forms of coercive socio-economic and political organization are suspended, in particular by games; games are 'extra-official' and 'extra-territorial' and involve a liberation *from* (not argument *with*) officially sanctioned laws and regulations and beliefs. Carnival inverts and fractures and demystifies prevailing ideologies, which are static, hierarchic, based on rigid categorical separations, and constituting the reification of *one* organized and power-sanctioned view of reality. Bakhtin sees the Renaissance as, 'so to speak, a direct "carnivalization" of human consciousness, philosophy, and literature'. And he notes a related phenomenon in the literature of the period – 'the carnivalization of speech, which freed it from the gloomy seriousness of official philosophy as well as from truisms and commonplace ideas'. Just such a 'carnivalization' of consciousness and speech can, I think, be detected in some recent American fiction. There is one important point about the word 'carnival': carnival is public, for all the people, originally connected with the market place as a central meeting place. Can the 'public-ity' of the carnival be recreated on the privacy of the page? There is, certainly, one important possible similarity between a carnival and a novel. It might not make much sense to ask what is carnival 'about', but you can ask, What is going on there? This is what Bakhtin did, and in his opinion carnival is an enactment of life freeing itself from old rigidifying forms, experiencing its own boundless potentiality for ever more life in ever more forms, none of them final, and releasing an energy of regeneration. Many contemporary novelists and critics abhor the use of the word 'about' in discussing contemporary fiction, one reason being that in asserting what a book is 'about' a commentator may in effect reduce the novel to the very thematic simplifications and conventional formulations which it set out to escape from. (Criticizing the 'about' approach in the classification of folk tales, Propp makes the crucial criticism of such an approach, namely that it offers 'no single principle for the selection of decisive elements'. However I think it remains an indispensable word and I will return to it at the end.) But if novels may be considered, metaphorically, as carnivals and games, we – the public – can at least ask, What is going on there? – even if any one particular game wishes to maintain that it is only 'about' itself, non-representational, against interpretation, and so on. And the claim that a particular work is disengaged from all considerations of meaning, referentiality, significa-tion, etc., may *itself* be a game, a strategy to enable the writer to be free to explore new ways of meaning (not just new meanings) and new aspects of our unavoidable conditions of living among significations. (Significations can of course cease to be registered as 'significant', though it seems hard to maintain a stable distinction between the two; or significations may be felt to drown out significance. We are becoming very aware of the complex shifting relationships between signal, sign, signification, and significance, and it is hardly surprising that some contemporary novelists incorporate the problem into their work in a variety of ways. Joyce is obviously a key influence in all this, but Joyce's own work, with its almost totalitarian ruthlessness and fanatical efficiency of ordering, albeit on his own unique terms, lacks the 'carnival' element which I am trying to identify in some contemporary American fiction.) That there are distinct possible advantages in this strategy of considering the novel as 'game' may perhaps be thrown into sharper focus if we consider briefly an avowedly 'serious' novel in which life itself, but not the book, is compared to a game, albeit a hard and mean one. I am referring to Joan Didion's *Play it as it Lays*, which has been compared to Eliot's *Wasteland* and the works of Nathanael West.

The problem with this novel, to put it very simply, is that it is too easy to read. It involves that kind of debasement of referentiality which other writers are trying to resist by asserting that their books are not 'about' anything in the conventional manner. I am not referring to the vocabulary, or the syntax, or the economic brevity of the chapters in Didion's novel; it is the descriptive conventions operating in the text which are too familiar. Tentatively borrowing an over-used word from linguistics, I would say that in its deep structure the book is almost completely cliché-ic. It offers a species of instant supermarket nihilism. What the words refer to is upsetting and disturbing enough – suicide, abortion, isolation, mental breakdown, etc. But the patterning of the words is ultimately undisturbing. To take two of Piaget's terms, the book does not require accommodation (which involves struggle or work); it can be assimilated, which is a comparatively effortless, automatic process.[1] This is commodity nihilism which involves us in no new experience of negation, no real refusal of society, and in itself offers no evidence of struggle against being a commodity. The test is not in what the book appears to refer to (in which case every daily paper would be another *Wasteland*), but in what the book does to us as readers. It sets us no tasks, it does not drive us back into our own discourses to discover there the accumulating clichés and stereotypes which we mistake for thinking. It seems to imply that while life may be all problem, the language in which it is re-presented is no problem. But in a contem-

---

[1] This is perhaps a too simple adaptation of Piaget's terms, which he applies to stages of sensory-motor development. This is how he makes the distinction:

> Now all such behaviour that has innate roots but becomes differentiated through functioning contains, we find, the same functional factors and structural elements. The functional factors are *assimilation*, the process whereby an action is actively reproduced and comes to incorporate new objects into itself (for example, thumb sucking as a case of sucking), and *accommodation*, the process whereby the schemes of assimilation themselves become modified in being applied to a diversity of object. (*Structuralism*)

My contention would be that serious fiction in one way or another modifies our mental 'schemes of assimilation' and it is this which Joan Didion's novel fails to do.

porary work of *fiction*, if language is not a problem *nothing else is*. ('Problem' is not meant here to be synonymous with 'the difficult'; it is intended simply to refer to that which makes of the reader an active participant rather than a passive consumer.) Didion's novel is a quick 'wasteland' assembly kit (think by contrast of the *work* initially required to read Eliot's *Wasteland*, or the real sense of strangeness released by West's books, which contemporaries also found hard to read), and as we automatically assemble it as we read we experience not 'a strangeness and opacity' restored to the world, but a familiarity and transparency unrevoked from the words.

In this chapter I wish to look at three recent American fictions which have been regarded as 'games'[2] and try to answer the question: What is going on there? Let me turn first to a work which visibly offers itself as a game, or a sustained piece of play, *Willie Masters' Lonesome Wife* by William Gass. We may note immediately that a lonesome wife is already a potential paradox suggesting both solitude and connection, a lapsed contract, a failed union, and the text concerns itself with those things which both join and separate us – lips, sexual organs, dances, words. There is a hovering parallel between semen given and taken away (in a contraceptive) and semantics, meaning which we own and lose. The pages seem to unite us to the writer; they even carry images of the stains of a coffee cup as if to put us in the position *vis-à-vis* the page which the writer was in while penning it. But it is an illusion of course, and tells us that we are not where the writer was. It is not our coffee cup, not our stain. The paper divides us where we seem to meet. In the middle of the book there is a reference to Bottom's playing at being the wall (in *Midsummer Night's Dream*). The text is both the wall and the crack through which Pyramus and Thisbe have to try to make contact. But the wall and the crack are also illusory and we the readers are also left lonesome.

In attempting to describe the book it is impossible to invoke the usual categories. It is an assault on our customary orderings. Typographically it is a kind of game. The print varies constantly, lines inflate and grow smaller, tumesce and detumesce; footnotes crowd out the text and corner us; the text divides into two, into three, into more – it cannot be read in a linear way. Clusters of words murmur or shout at us from unexpected places in the margins; asterisks begin to proliferate like some rapidly

[2] Of course it would be possible to choose many other novels. In particular, Robert Coover's *The Universal Baseball Association Inc.* not only explores games, and the instinct to create games; it also, as far as I can make out, brings the language of game theory into the text so that it too is changed from a mode to an object of discourse. But Coover's work would require a whole separate essay. My choice of these three works is necessarily arbitrary and I can only hope to justify it by the end of the paper.

reproducing organic life until they fall around the pages like stars. There are headlines and placards, even bursts of music. The pages change colour. In every way the texture of the text is constantly transforming itself; it is chameleon, protean, metamorphosing – whatever else it does, it is constantly unstabilizing us as conventional readers. The book also pretends to be a body, with photographs of breasts on the cover and buttocks on the back. This is not incidental, for orifices, nourishment, and excrement are central concerns of the book. We are, it reminds us, constantly taking things in and as constantly secreting or excreting them, as excrement, saliva, dirt, semen, and words. There are intermittent allusions to pipes, tunnels, corridors, intestines – world and words flow through us: we swallow objects and disgorge signs. On the title page there is a photograph of a hand reaching out – and we are after all always trying to 'mancipate' things and people who in turn e-mancipate themselves from our grasp. There is also perhaps a cultural echo of Michelangelo's Adam. But there is no answering hand of God, or anyone else. The wife is lonesome. The book begins with body and ends with words, or rather, they seem to come together – the text corporealized, the body verbalized. It is a monologue of a woman dreaming to herself; it is a monologue of language dreaming to itself.

As we read it seems to be the reverie of a woman, a former burlesque actress and stripper, thinking about the men who have entered her and left her. 'Empty I began, and empty I remained.' Just so, many voices have entered the language, used it, and departed, from Shakespeare to the crudest vernacular lout. By an unstated inversion or reciprocation, a woman becomes a language used for different occasions in different ways, and language is a woman used for different occasions in different ways. At one point the text announces: 'A distinction is usually made between adherence and adhesion. The tendency prevails to confine adhesion to physical attachment, adherence to mental or moral attachment.' Perhaps a fragment from philosophy? As the text has no one original author but is instead a nexus for fragments of a multiplicity of discourses, it does not matter where the words *come from*. What they *do* is remind us that we are creatures of ever-attempting, ever-failing modes of attachment. We try to adhere ourselves to other bodies through embraces and holdings and adhere to the world through words and concepts. Yet the text constantly touches on the dread involved in the sense of the failure of all our adhesions and adherences. Throughout there is a sense of loneliness, lovelessness, emptiness, fear, the coldness of frost, the dark Africa of the night sky. It is a recognizable American geography, perhaps the Midwest, but more generally a geography of intense solitude. It is also a lexical geography, language itself in a reverie over its past.

We start by hearing a woman musing over the growth of her own body, but soon the interplay between body and language starts. The voice in the text says, 'I dream like Madame Bovary. Only I don't die, during endings. I never die.' Men die, sexually and corporeally. Language does not. Thus she goes on: 'Travel, dream. I feel sometimes as if I *were* imagination (that spider goddess and threadspinning muse) – imagination imagining itself imagine.' The echoes are of Beckett, of course, and all those spiders of the American imagination, Walt Whitman and Emily Dickinson included. As she says: 'I used to write the scripts myself. I stole from the best, from the classiest greats . . . They laughed just the same.' Then there is a sudden change in tone: 'she felt the terror of terminology. Why aren't there any decent words.' And the mind/voice turns to words, just words, turning them over, playing with them as a sort of non-epistemic pigment, sounds to cuddle up with – 'catafalque', 'crepuscular', 'dirigibility' – 'but catafalque is best'. Catafalque, perhaps not entirely coincidentally, is the structure on which the coffin rests which holds the body. The body dies: language, which to a large extent sustains and constitutes the body throughout its life, remains. Like a catafalque. Dryden, Flaubert, Hardy, Joyce and many other dead writers linger on in fragments in her drowsy monologue. Similarly the voice is a woman, but also 'I'm only a string of noises, after all, a column of air moving up and down.' Noncorporeality is both death and a kind of immortality, like the literature which continues to move around inside this 'string of noises'. People die – how often we are reminded of it – but, 'I, on the other hand, made so luckily of language – last .... even in a row of dots .... in silence .... in nothing .... I am. Back now, of course, composing myself again, full of liberty, creation and my claw.' Thus we keep encountering in different forms the interminglings and separations of the wastings of the body and the preservations of the word. And one thing that does emerge as transcending the seedy Midwest existence bespoken at one level of the text is this: 'the whole of literature lies before us . . . like a land we live in, once we've moved there, in the purest figure of our former life . . . only here in this sweet country of the word are rivers, streams, woods, gardens, houses, mountains, waterfalls and the crowding fountains of the trees eternal as it's right they should be . . .'

After all kinds of mockery and teasings of the conventional reader – the crude 'literalist' who, like a bad lover, can think only of plunging straight ahead in a crude monolinear manner – the text moves to a beautiful conclusion in which the woman and language speak together:

> When a letter comes, if you will follow me, there is no author fastened to it like the stamp; the words which speak, they are the body of the speaker. It's just the same with me. These words are all I am. Believe me. Pity me. Not even the

> Dane is any more than that. Oh, I'm the girl upon this couch, all right, you
> needn't fear; the one who's waltzed you through these pages, clothed and bare,
> who's hated you for her humiliations, sought your love, just as the striptease
> dancer does . . . Could you love me? Love me then . . . then love me . . . Yes. I
> know. I can't command it. Yet I should love, if ever you would let me, like a
> laser, burning through all foolish ceremonials of modesty and custom . . . My
> dears, my dears . . . how I would brood upon you: you, the world; and I, the
> language . . . . . . I am that lady language chose to make her playhouse of . . .

The idea of the 'playhouse' of language might be set beside Nietzsche's idea of 'the prison house of language' to give some idea of the sense of release experienced by reading Gass's text. Indeed the transformation of that prison house into a playhouse through the use of all kinds of techniques of eruption, displacement, decategorization, and everything implied in the word 'carnivalization' could be seen as the motive force behind the 'games' American writers play. The ultimate aim may indeed be to escape from the prison house altogether, just as a character in one of Gass's stories tries to 'drive himself into wordlessness' and the speaker/writer of his present work in progress, 'Tunnels', seems bent on burrowing out of language itself. But if we can never finally avoid being to some extent 'creatures at the mercy of language' (Lacan) then at least – let the game go on. So Gass's text ends with the lady-language exhorting herself . . .

> Then let us have a language worthy of our world, a democratic style where rich
> and well-born nouns can roister with some sluttish verb yet find themselves
> content and uncomplained of. We want a diction which contains the quaint,
> the rare, the technical, the obsolete, the old, the lent, the nonce, the local slang
> and argot of the street, in neighbourly confinement. Our tone should suit our
> time: uncommon quiet dashed with common thunder . . . Experimental and
> expansive . . . it will give new glasses to new eyes, and put those plots and
> patterns down we find our modern lot in. Metaphor must be its god now that
> gods are metaphors.

It is as though language itself is seeking for the conditions of its own carnivalization. Gass's text takes us into the heart of the heart of the desolations of our corporeal existence, but it also takes us into 'the sweet country of the word' – writer and reader talking and dying alike, the lonesome self losing and recreating itself in language, the prison house turning itself into the playhouse before our very eyes.

One of John Barth's key works is entitled *Lost in the Funhouse*, and in his subsequent novel he continues to explore the problematical position of the writer in the playhouse. We are named before we name, spoken before we speak, told stories before we narrate; given a hyper-awareness of this condition, what is a contemporary narrator to do? Barth's *Chimera* can best be read, I think, as his projection of various aspects of the situation of the American writer now.

Barth is a narrator; he has all of world literature available to him and to varying extents internalized within him, so that it is doubtful if he can ever tell an original story, for all the narrative structures and patternings have been explored. By the same token he is a voice, but is that voice his own? Thus the narrating voice on the page – and the subsuming of voice into page is an important aspect of the whole book – says/writes: 'I wonder how many voices are telling my tale . . . I'm full of voices, all mine, none me; I can't keep straight who's speaking as I used to . . .' But if he cannot tell an original story in an individual voice he can attempt to explore the origins of story and try to lay bare all the ambiguities of using a narrative voice which both is and is not his own. The title itself points to both the structure and the ambiguity of the book. The Chimera is a three-fold monster – lion, goat, serpent – it is a taxonomic freak, an ironic challenge to orthodox taxonomy. It is also an apparition, an illusion. Within the book there are three contiguous but discontinuous stories, as in the parts of the beast: 'Du nyazdiad', which effectively is concerned with the position of the story-teller; 'Perseid', an authentic hero; and 'Bellerophoniad', a 'phony' or inauthentic hero (Barth himself pointed out the pun in the name). In the original legends both these heroes killed monsters with the aid of magic and divinely given aids. These aids include Pegasus, the winged horse now associated with poetry. Pegasus also defies taxonomy in being a magic synthesis but is a transcendence of natural forms and human categories, whereas the Chimera is an anomalous and counter-transcendent assortment – not a super-real synthesis but a sur-real, or unreal, botch. The opposition between these two is somewhere at the heart of Barth's book, which is itself a kind of Pegasus/Chimerical entity.

The book engages the phenomenon of heroes, figures who through *action* created a distinct pattern in their own lives, then a distinct pattern in oral *legend*, and thence a distinct *narrative* pattern in printed words. This movement from life into words is an ambiguous one, and it is one which is confronted in the text as the heroes/voices/pages discuss how life is transformed into legend, reality into myth, archetype into stereotype, action into print – transformations which also involve a move from time into relative immortality. This points to another central preoccupation in the book – what lasts? An aspect of this is, what is the relationship between narrating and time? 'Perseid' opens in this way: 'Good evening. Stories last longer than men, stones than stars, stars than stones. But even our stars' nights are numbered, and with them will pass this patterned tale to a long-deceased earth.' Perseus threatened with the Gorgon's head finally becomes a star and, putting it very simply, one problem the book keeps returning to is how to achieve the good immortality of estellation and avoid the bad immortality of petrification. Or as Barth himself put it in an interview, the thing is to find the narrative trick of turning stones into stars. And he also said that he likes the idea of himself as a writer using a pencil like a lance, 'riding the horse of inspiration to kill the chimera which has become a synonym for fictions, illusions, and hallucinations'. In this way he hopes to avoid the petrification which threatens him as a fiction writer, and he attempts to do this by piercing through all the layers of legend – text, voice, life – to confront and contest the very origin of the narrating impulse. To put it very simply, here is the question the modern writer asks himself: 'What can I say that's new?' One answer: 'I can say "What can I say that's new"', thus putting the problem in a larger context in which it can be approached and probed from as many angles as the writer cares to explore. The old stories can only be retold as meta-stories, stories commenting on themselves in a variety of other languages including modern vernacular and computer-programming terminology.

At this point let me give two quotations from the endings of the two tales about the ancient heroes. At the end of the 'Perseid' Medusa asks Perseus if he is happy with the way this story ends. He answers: 'My love, it's an epilogue, always ending, never ended . . . which winds through universal space and time . . . I'm content . . . to have become . . . these silent, visible signs; to *be* the tale I tell to those with eyes to see and understanding to interpret; to raise you up forever and know that our story will never be cut off, but nightly rehearsed as long as men and women read the stars . . .' This is the satisfactory resolution of life into tale and print. Bellerophon, on the other hand, who was thrown from Pegasus while trying to fly up to the gods directly and who wandered wounded and alone into utter obscurity, has a different conclusion. While falling he has a conversation with his teacher Polyeidus, and asks: 'Can you turn me into this story?' to which Polyeidus answers in the emphatic negative, adding: 'What I *might* manage . . . is to turn *myself* from this interview into you-in-Bellerophoniad-form: a certain number of printed pages in a language not untouched by Greek, to be read by a limited number of "Americans", not all of whom will finish or enjoy them.' To which Bellerophon replies with a complaint to the world: 'I hate this, World! It's not at all what I had in mind for Bellerophon. It's a beastly fiction, ill-proportioned, full of longueurs, lumps, lacunae, a kind of monstrous mixed metaphor . . .', and he trails off into silence and we are left with the incomplete book in our hands. How will our modern fictions end – integration and synthesis at a higher level (Pegasus) or the collapse into a heterogeneous mess? What Barth is doing to us as readers is expose us to, and engage us in, the problematics of narrative utterance and writing in our present age. At one point he includes in the book an amusing account of someone who tries to program a computer to compose 'not hypothetical fictions, but the "Complete", the "Final Fiction".' Everything from magic to myths to masterplot summaries is fed in, and out comes an alphabetical chaos. With so much available disparate data, what chance is there for an innocent fiction any longer? What Barth seems to be insisting is that if fiction seems to have exhausted its possibilities (and his text includes some weary enumerations of all the different devices used by novelists in the past either to mystify or demystify their readers), then it must find its future in the centre of that exhaustion. What is at stake is active survival amid over-abundance of inert material – or a new approach to estellation among increasingly threatening modes of petrification.

At one level this is a book which makes the critic or commentator completely redundant. Barth puts his sources into his text, he includes letters and statements revealing his ideas about the writing of the novel, he lists his pet motifs and favourite themes. There is very little for the critic to trace, interpret, or decipher. The only secret in the book is that it keeps no secrets. It gives them away at a rate which does indeed make the book difficult to read in any conventional way. All a commentator can do is to step back into a different frame of reference and, once again, ask, not what is the book about so much as, what is going on here? A certain amount of arbitrariness in the ordering of any comments offered by way of an answer is justified by such a text and I propose to isolate just three aspects of the book. The first concerns the false hero Bellerophon. As represented by Barth he is a figure obsessed with pattern, the heroic pattern is this case, which occurs in various forms and diagrams in his story. There is in this the idea of a man deliberately trying to sacrifice his self-hood to a pattern, which means that the pattern takes precedence over life, pre-forms it, indeed petrifies it in advance, since the individual with such an aspiration can only ever become an imitation, not the thing itself. As Bellerophon realizes near the end: 'I saw the chimera of my life. By imitating perfectly the Pattern of Mythic Heroes, I'd become, not a mythic hero, but a perfect Reset . . . it's hardly to be imagined that those patterns we call "Perseus", "Medusa", "Pegasus" . . . are aware of their existence, any more than their lettered counterparts on the page.' One problem being explored here is that of excessive self-consciousness, and the over-abundance of *schema* and models. Barth is fond of Borges's comment that God doesn't study theology, any more than saints study the lives of saints or (as Barth said in interview) birds study ornithology. But we are reading and encountering stories, forms, patterns all the time, so how can we *be* the original story of our life and not a simple retelling of one gone before, and how can a writer *tell* an original story rather than merely repeat one that has already been told? One answer is to be found in the second aspect of the book I wish to mention – namely, what is going on in the first section of the book called 'Dunzadiad'?

This is apparently a story told by the younger sister of Scheherazade and is obviously related to the situation of the novelist today, since Dunyazade has to listen to all the stories Scheherazade tells and then at the end has to face the problem of what story *she* will tell. *The Thousand and One Nights* would seem to be an abiding obsession for Barth, with its intimate connection between narration/copulation and survival. In this tale, through the auditor Dunyazade, he images Scheherazade, exploring the possibilities of story-telling, trying to get at its secret power so that she can prolong her life. She has given up expecting salvation by a genie, knowing that the only magic is in words. 'The real magic is to understand which words work, and when, and for what: the trick is to learn the trick.' Scheherazade refers to all the stories about treasure to which no one can find the key and adds that she has the key but can't find the treasure, the key being the pen and ink she doodles with. What she suddenly realizes is that 'the key to the treasure *is* the treasure', at which point a genie does appear, the genie of her imagination. Between them they go into all the problems of fiction, its future and origins, as he remembers stories she has yet to tell. Two or three key points in this story are worth isolating. The genie – and now think of this as, say, the contemporary American novelist's imagination – explains the situation he was in until those words – 'the key to the treasure is the treasure' – came to him.

> There's a kind of snail in the Maryland marshes – perhaps I invented him – that makes his shell as he goes along out of whatever he comes across, cementing it with his own juices, and at the same time makes his path instinctively toward the best available material for his shell; he carries his history on his back, living in it, adding new and larger spirals to it from the present as he grows. That snail's pace has become my pace, but I'm going in circles, following my own trail.

The shell is not a statement about the material it is made of, though without that material it could not exist. What it adds to the world is its own spiral shape. The spiral is an open-ended form; the circle is closed. This is important – the contrast between the circle and the spiral turns up repeatedly in this book, and while the 'Perseid' is based on the spiral, the 'Bellerophoniad' is organized on the circle. It would seem that one way of putting the problem for some contemporary American novelists is how to break out of the circle into the spiral: in going round in a circle, narrative degenerates into cliché and language disintegrates into a purposeless jumble of letters and empty spaces, the remnants of a code no longer transformable into messages. The spiral shell is purposive, a thing assembled, an extension of the code which at the same time both permits and *is* a new kind of message. (Of course the spiral shell of Daedalus is somewhere behind this, but it touches on a much larger problem, namely that of the very idea of a 'new' piece of writing.) To put it in simple terms, there are two impossible extremes when it comes to writing a novel – total repetition and total innovation or novelty. The first is precluded by temporal considerations so that, as Borges has reminded us, *Don Quixote* written now using exactly the same words in the same order would be a different book. The second is precluded by conditions governing communication. No one can invent a completely new language which can also be used for purposes of communication, so any novelist must to some extent traffic in the familiar. In between these two impossible extremes there are varying degrees of what I will call here 'imbrication'. The extent to which a novel (say) overlaps with what is known and familiar can vary enormously, and it would be impossible to establish any metric by which to measure degrees of imbrication. Yet we can clearly register works which seem to try to reduce the degree of imbrication to a minimum, and others which rely heavily on a high degree of imbrication, merely changing or modifying a little so that the reader is teased but not taxed. (These problems of imbrication and modification point to the basic problems of repetition and difference in language itself which have concerned French writers such as Deleuze. This is outside the sphere of my competence, but for a very lucid and helpful assessment of the subject see Edward Said's article, 'An Ethics of Language', in *Diacritics* (Summer 1974).) One example where a change in the degree of imbrication affected a writer's reception can be seen in the changing response to Melville's work. The earlier books were popular as they seemed to be recognizable as belonging to a familiar genre of travel writing. Imbrication was high. In *Moby-Dick* the imbrication is drastically reduced as the familiar genre spirals out into new areas of fictional exploration. The result was that the book was much less popular than Melville's previous work, and from this point his career as a writer declined as far as readership was concerned. For the writer imbrication is involved with survival.

For the writer to go round in a circle is to engage in repetitions of increasing probability, which may be said to contribute to fictional entropy. To open the narrative circle to the spiral, then, would be to counteract this entropic tendency. And for Barth the way out of the circle into the spiral seems to lie in the realization that the key to the treasure is the treasure. We may think of that proposition applying to fiction in these terms. According to older epistemologies reality was the treasure and to get at it you had to find the right key – right representational mode, appropriate verbal procedure, etc. To say that the key *is* the treasure is to reject that kind of dualistic model; indeed in a way it rejects the idea of any pre-existent reality waiting to be opened. The key is language, and if the key is the treasure, language is the treasure of reality. This extreme conclusion does not, I think, imply some kind of complete solipsism, nor any idealist denial of material existence (though it may preclude the fictional engagement of historical, political, and social problems). Barth's work is very aware of the body, of sexuality, of love and loss, of death. The emphasis, I think, is on the contention that the only reality we can do anything about is language, not how the world appears but how it reappears in words and how words reappear in new contexts. In every sphere man is a creature who engenders re-presentations, and interest in fiction has increasingly shifted from the 'what' of presentation to the 'how' of representation. This is the point of one exchange between Scheherazade and her genie in which they are discussing the relation between framed and framing tales, and Dunyazade comments: 'This relation (which to me seemed less important than what the stories were *about*) interested the two of them no end, just as Sherry and Shahryar were fascinated by the pacing of their nightly pleasures or the refinement of their various positions, instead of the degree and quality of their love.' The answer of Scheherazade is notable as it contains implicitly a whole theory of the aesthetics of the novel. 'That other goes without saying . . . or it doesn't go at all. Making love and telling stories both take more than good technique – but it's only the technique that we can *talk* about.' This is very different from an autotelic theory of art; it does not deny subject matter, but rather asserts that you can only talk about how you talk about it. Which is literally metalanguage – a statement about making statements. This conclusion is in line with William Gass's well-known observation that increasingly 'the forms of fiction serve as the material upon which further forms can be imposed. Indeed, many of the so-called anti-novels are really metafictions.'

The whole debate concerning whether fiction ought to be, or can be 'referential' or can only be 'meta' is probably both too familiar and certainly too large to be addressed here. Some of the problems can be resolved by recognizing that all usages of language involve both, as Jacobson pointed out, but that will go almost no way towards explaining why Joyce Carol Oates writes the kind of novel she does and William Gass writes the kind of novel he does. It is quite clear that they think that words within a fictional text are to be arranged in very different ways to very different ends. To see the issue from another angle, it is interesting to note some of the comments of Henri Lefebvre in *Everyday Life in the Modern World*, in which he diagnoses a 'decline of referentials' as part of the malaise of modern life, since it leads to an 'uncoupling of signifiers and signified'. 'The decline of referentials had generalized the uncoupling' in the absence of a referential and code providing *common places* (*topoi* and *koina*, social topics) the link between the two signs is insecure; we are already familiar with the floating stock of *meaningless signifiers*.' One result of this is 'the fascination of signs': 'floating in swarms and clouds they are free for all, ever available and, taking the place of action, they appropriate the interest formerly involved in activity'. Thus 'language and linguistics relations become denials of everyday life'. We live in the age of 'metalanguage'. Here is a very clear statement of his position.

> There is *contradiction between referential and metalinguistic functions*, the latter eroding the former and supplanting them; the vaguer the referential the more distinct and significant grows metalanguage . . . metalanguage becomes a substitute for language by assuming the attributes of referential-endowed language; the disappearance of each referential liberates a signifier and makes it available, whereupon metalanguage promptly appropriates it, employing it for jobs 'at one remove', which contributes to the decline of referentials, while metalanguage reigns, detached and 'cool'.

This is almost to hypostatize metalanguage, or to make of it an independent force taking over society in an almost Burroughs-like manner, yet one can see what Lefebvre is getting at. I have not, of course, done justice to his whole argument, but two comments on his position occur to me. If the situation is as he describes it, then can a writer still use language as though it still had the kind of referential function and potency which Lefebvre says has in fact been pre-empted by metalanguage? Or might he or she, recognizing that something has happened along the lines of Lefebvre's diagnosis, rather not confront this increasing predominance of metalanguage and, in one way and another 'lay it bare' in their own texts in such a way as to make the reader more aware of this metalinguistic take-over, so that he will perhaps be less vulnerable to the manipulative and coercive abuse of signs in other metalinguistic areas of life (such as advertising) which is one of Lefebvre's concerns?

Lefebvre also writes about the 'death of the ludic spirit' in contemporary everyday life and laments the decline of 'festival, of which play and games are only one aspect'. He hopes for a 'resurrection of the Festival' but for him it must be social, actual. There can be no other form of festival. 'Art can replace neither Style nor the Festival in a society dominated by the quotidien, and is an increasingly specialized activity that parodies the Festival, an ornament adorning everyday life but failing to transform it.' I can respect this point of view, but would still want to propose that the parodies of festivals (and festivals of parodies) offered by some Art can have a positive 'transforming' effect on everyday life.

However I must record that my own experience of other people's readings of the works I am discussing in this paper does not do much to sustain my contention. Thus on the one hand I have heard a philosopher who is very aware of problems of language praise Didion's work very highly, and, on the other, heard an expert in the field of cognitive development admit that after a few pages he couldn't be bothered to go on with *Gravity's Rainbow*. Outside of students, who are the readers I am referring to?).

The final aspect of Barth's book I wish to touch on concerns the figure who in many ways is a key to the whole enterprise – Polyeidus, the seer of many forms, the protean counsellor whom Barth reminds us he has always been interested in. As a tutor to Bellerophon he speaks of 'ontological metamorphosis' with a contemporary weariness of such over-familiar terminology. In Barth's terms he is a version of the figure who, as he becomes more aware of his art, loses his potency as an artist. At first he could turn into other people, then places, but later he mainly turns into documents – a kind of précis of the writer's changing attitude to the power of his own words. On one memorable occasion he finds himself in prison and tries to turn into the cell itself so that the guards will think he has escaped and go away, leaving him to go free. But he has lost his power in three dimensions and turns, not into his dungeon cell, but into a 'magic message spelling out that objective: *I am a chamber*'. This does give him a kind of freedom, but he now finds himself a firebreathing monster with a lion's head, goat's body, and serpent's tail – a chimera. The idea of a writer turning himself into the prison he is in is already very suggestive. The further suggestion that, since this cannot be managed literally, he turns himself into a message which stands in lieu of the prison by naming it, is even more so. And the unexpected development whereby in his liberation he finds that he has turned into an enormous fiction, or a fictional enormity (the inversion is Barth's own), is a very telling piece of wit. At the very least it suggests some of the ambiguities involved in trying to break out of the prison house of language (and all the patterning determinants it contains) through the playing of fictional games. As the book nears its end Polyeidus is plotting how to turn into the pages we are reading, finally permeating the whole work, the ultimate metamorphosis which will prolong his existence through pagination. Polyeidus becomes the book we are holding: there are no monsters, no heroes, not even any voices, for even they remind us that they are 'all mere Polyeidic inklings, written words'. There is a curious feeling here of the narrative plenitude which is our past suddenly dissolving into ink and paper, becoming apparitional, chimerical. We do not even actually have the novel. As Barth has said, what is a novel, where is it? Its ontological status is uncertain. What we hold is only one copy. Of a copy. Barth's quest for the origins of narrative, through the strategy of a continuous displacement of myth into modernity and vice versa, has brought him close to the point at which the quest discovers its own futility and the writer finds that there are no origins, only 'inklings'.

Perhaps there is a state of contemporary consciousness, felt with particular acuteness by a writer of fictions and stories, when a repletion of material and motif suddenly feels like an emptiness, and with all the stories of the world in his head he is suddenly thrown back into himself, alone, in an empty room, self-ejected from the fictions he may hitherto have played with, as all the narrational wonders of the world resolve themselves into mere arbitrary marks on the page. And if pages have their longevity they have their pathos too. It is perhaps at this point that the writer transforms himself into a statement about his cell in order to escape from it. But I think there is an even more central concern in everything I have mentioned. It emerges very directly once in the shortest possible sentence, when the author is characteristically discussing his main thematic concerns. One of these is 'the mortal desire for immortality . . . and its ironically qualified fulfillment – especially by the mythic hero's transformation, in the latter stages of his career, into the sound of his own voice, of the story of his life. I am forty.' I am forty. This suddenly brings before us the mortal narrator, half way into life, half way into death. What is going on here is, I think, a game of mid-passage, the very existence of narrator and narrativity alike in the balance. It shows signs at times of being a quite desperate game, and it is always a dangerous one, since at any moment the Pegasus flight may give way to the chimerical condition.

Of all the works of recent American fiction which have been referred to as 'games' by one critic or another, the strangest would seem to be *Gravity's Rainbow*, yet there is no doubt that the book offers some sort of dark carnival of discourses which undermines all our habitual modes of apprehension as we confront it. Pynchon's concern has always been related to problems of decipherment and what Lukács described as 'the incommensurability of . . . interiority and adventure – in the absence of a transcendental "place" allotted to human endeavours, particularly as this incommensurability manifests itself in a permanent instability in the relationship between the interpreting mind and the varying fields of signification which it must negotiate'. His first novel, *V*, can be seen as a modern repetition and distortion of the paradigm novel for western fiction, *Don Quixote*. Stencil is the figure (also the copy) who attempts to apprehend and pattern reality according to his single 'ideal', obsession with 'V'. In Lukács's terms his consciousness is much 'narrower' than the world through which he moves, and everything either has to be 'translated' into terms consonant with his one interpretative scheme, or screened out. (His obsession with 'V' is the clue with which he attempts to find his way through the labyrinth, but in the process he transforms the labyrinth into clues.) At the other extreme is Benny Profane, whose consciousness seems to be so wide and unselective that he experiences no *gestalt* at all in his perceptions of the world around him. For Stencil everything signifies too much and, taken to its logical extreme, his mind would conflate the whole of existence into a single sign − 'V'; all differences would finally vanish as the over-integrated world resolved itself into one undifferentiated clue. That it would be a clue to itself indicates the ultimate danger of such a quest, for if V can mean everything it means nothing. For Benny Profane there are more signals than significances; he detects no clues anywhere and is a motiveless wanderer up and down the generic street of the twentieth century, going nowhere and seeing only separate objects in a disintegrating world. The contrast is between a mind which sees everything as interconnected and over-determined and one which sees no connections and experiences only randomness, contingency, and indeterminacy. Is Stencil a lunatic, or a man with creative vision? Is Benny Profane a realist, or a figure of dulled and impoverished perceptions? Between them these two figures point to the question which worries so many of Pynchon's characters. Are we surrounded by plots − social, natural, cosmic; or is there no plot, no hidden configuration of intent, only gratuitous matter and chance?

This of course is the problem which takes hold of Oedipa Maas in *The Crying of Lot 49*. She is named the executrix of a will and in trying to discover its meaning she feels plots starting to take shape around her and clues starting to multiply, so that out of necessity she becomes a desperate cryptologist. The problem becomes a matter of where to look for meaning and of what to regard as significant. It is as if she were reading a book but whereas in a stable text the words stand out against the blank paper as figures against ground, in the book she is reading words and blanks, figure and ground, exist in a very unstable relationship and at times seem to become interchangeable. If there is no significance in the word or the figure then the reading mind starts to search in the spaces around and between them. Putting it very simply, if the sign turns into a blank, then, the feeling goes, perhaps the blank will turn into a sign. In the case of Oedipa Maas the book is called America and what she has to try to decide is whether there is a strange ambiguous system or conspiracy at work, a second America hidden but operating in the interstices of the visible social structure?[1] Or whether she is hallucinating, 'in the orbiting ecstasy of a true paranoia'?

I am stressing this aspect of Pynchon's work because whatever else *Gravity's Rainbow* is, or does, it provides an exemplary experience in modern reading, so that you do not proceed from some ideal 'emptiness' of meaning to a fullness, but instead find yourself involved in a process in which any perception can precipitate a new confusion and an apparent clarification turns into a prelude to further difficulties. The novel does indeed have a recognizable historical setting – unlike the other 'games' I have discussed. It is engaged with Europe at the end of the Second World War and just after. In choosing to situate his novel at this time Pynchon is concentrating on a crucial moment when a new trans-political order began to emerge out of the ruins of old orders which could no longer maintain themselves. At one point he describes the movements of displaced people at the end of the war as 'a great frontierless streaming'. The sentences that follow mime out this 'frontierless' condition in an extraordinary flow of objects and people and conclude: 'so the populations move, across the open meadow, limping, marching, shuffling, carried, hauling along the detritus of an order, a European and bourgeois order they don't yet know is destroyed forever'. A later passage suggests what is taking the place of this vanished order: 'Oh, a State begins to take form in the stateless German night, a State that spans oceans and surface politics, sovereign as the International or the Church of Rome, and the Rocket is its soul.' The Rocket is specifically the V-2 which was launched on London, and, because it travelled faster than sound, crashed before the sound of its flight could be heard – a frightening disruption of conventional sequence and cause–effect expectations. (Hence the famous opening sentence – 'a screaming comes across the sky'.) But it also becomes the paradigm product of modern technology, and in making it the central object of the book Pynchon is clearly addressing himself to the socio-political implications of contemporary trends in history. But he refuses to do this in a conventional narrative way because conventional narrative procedures were themselves products of that vanished bourgeois order and it is no longer possible to 'read' what is going on in any conventional manner. Thus

---

[1] In defining the position in society of various minority groups or sub-cultures, sociology sometimes applies the idea of 'marginality' or 'peripherality'. The point about such metaphors is that they imply a stable and locatable area for the minority group – the margin is that clear demarcated area which is not part of the text, the periphery is that part or boundary furthest from the centre. It might be more appropriate to the times to introduce the notion of 'interstiality' as a mode of existence for all kinds of people and groups who do not feel themselves to be part of the established social structure but find their way of life in various gaps. Just as any language depends on spaces, pauses, intervals, so even the most monolithic society must contain some gaps. Between the paving stones, life persists in the crevices.

Pynchon's characters move in a world of both too many and too few signs, too much data and too little information, too many texts but no reliable editions, an extreme 'overabundance of signifiers', to borrow another phrase from Lévi-Strauss. I stress this first because, before attempting to indicate what the novel is 'about' in any traditional sense, I think it is important to consider how to read it, for more than anything else this book provides an experience in modern reading. People who expect and demand the traditional narrative conventions will be immediately disoriented by this book.

There is one phantasmagoric episode in a 'disquieting structure' which is a dream-version of some contemporary hell. We read: 'It seems to be some very extensive museum, a place of many levels, and new signs that generate like living tissue – though if it all does grow toward some end shape, those who are here inside can't see it.' Now this is not only applicable to all the dozens of characters in the book itself – drifting in and out of sections, participating in different spaces, finding themselves on different levels; it is both their *dream* and their *dread* to see an 'end shape' to it all, though of course, being in the book, they never will. But, and I think this is very important, nor do we as readers. One of the things Pynchon manages to do so brilliantly is to make us participate in the beset and bewildered consciousness which is the unavoidable affliction of his characters.

As we read the book we seem to pass through a bewildering variety of genres, behavioural modes, and types of discourse – at different times the text seems to partake of such different things as pantomime, burlesque, cinema, cabaret, card games, songs, comic strips, spy stories, serious history, encyclopaedic information, mystical and visionary meditations, and scrambled imagery of dreams, the cold cause-and-effect talk of the Behaviourists, and all the various ways that men try to control and coerce realities both seen and unseen – from magic to measurement, from sciences to séances. At one point, one character is reading a Plasticman comic; he is approached by a man of encyclopaedic erudition who engages him in a conversation about etymology. Here is a clue for us – we should imagine that we are reading a comic, but it is partly transparent, and through it we are also reading an encyclopaedia, a film script, a piece of science history, and so on. There is only one text but it contains a multiplicity of surfaces; modes of discourse are constantly turning into objects of discourse with no one stable discourse holding them together. This is not such a bizarre undertaking as it may sound. We can all read and decode the different languages and genres Pynchon has brought into his book. Modern man is above all an interpreter of different signs, a reader of differing discourses, a servant of signals, a compelled and often compulsive decipherer. In Henri Lefebvre's use of the word, we do live in a 'pleonastic' society of 'aimless signifiers and disconnected signifieds' on many levels, so that we can see evidence of hyper-redundancy in the realm of signs, objects, institutions, even human beings. Wherever we look there is too much to 'read'. But never before has there been such uncertainty about the reliability of the texts. One character in the novel, making his way across the wastelands of post-war Europe, wonders whether it does contain a 'Real Text'. He thinks that such a text may be connected with the secrets of the Rocket – but perhaps the 'Real Text' is the desolate landscape he is traversing, or perhaps he missed the Real Text somewhere behind him in a ruined city . . . Reading Pynchon's novel gives us a renewed sense of how we have to read the modern world. At times in his book it is not always clear whether we are in a bombed-out building, or a bombed-out mind, but that too is quite appropriate. For how many of those rockets that fell in London fell in the consciousness of the survivors, exploding in the modern mind? And, looking around and inside us, how can we be sure how much is Real Text, and how much ruined débris?

In all this it is impossible to say with confidence what the book is 'about', but constantly we have the sense of many things that it seems to be about. We may take a phrase from Lévi-Strauss, admittedly out of context, and say that for the reader there is an 'overabundance of signifiers' in the book just as, for the characters, there is comparable overabundance in the world they seem to inhabit. But the Rocket is always there. It is phallic and fatal, Eros transformed into Thanatos, invading 'Gravity's grey eminence' only to succumb to it, curving through the sky like a lethal rainbow then crashing to the earth. Does it strike by 'chance' or according to some hidden design, some 'music' of annihilation which we will never hear but is always being played? Around the rocket and its production Pynchon builds up a version of war-time England and post-war Europe which is staggering both in its detail and its fantasy. In addition the novel, as if trying to reach out into wider and more comprehensive contexts, extends back into colonial and American history, down into the world of molecules, up into the stars, back even to Bethlehem when men saw another kind of burning light in the sky. In all this certain abiding preoccupations may be discerned. Pattern, plots, and paranoia – these are familiar in Pynchon's world; add to those paper, plastic, preterition, and Pavlovian conditioning, and some of the main themes have been listed (the alliteration is not of course accidental – Pynchon, as author, knows that he is engaged in an activity related to Stencil's search for V. Unlike Stencil, however, he is constantly breaking up the gathering pattern of echoes, clues, and similarities). What emerges from the book is a sense of a force and a system – something, someone, referred to simply as 'They' – which is actively trying to bring everything to zero and beyond, trying to institute a world of non-being, an operative kingdom of death, covering the organic world with a world of paper and plastic and transforming all natural resources into destructive power and waste – the rocket and the débris around it. 'They' are, precisely, non-specific, unlocatable. There is always the possibility of a They behind the They, a plot behind the plot; the quest to identify 'Them' sucks the would-be identifier into the possibility of an endless regression. But whatever Their source and origin, They are dedicated to annihilation – this is a vision of entropy as an extremely powerful world-wide, if not cosmos-wide, enterprise. From Their point of view, and in the world of insidious reversals and inversions They are instituting, the war was a great creative act, not the destruction but the 'reconfiguration' of people and places. They are also identified with 'the System' which 'removes from the rest of the World vast quantities of energy to keep its own tiny desperate fraction showing a profit . . . The System may or may not understand that it's only buying time . . . [that it] sooner or later must crash to its death, when its addiction to energy has become more than the rest of the World can supply . . . Living inside the System, is like riding across the country in a bus driven by a maniac bent on suicide.' The ecological relevance of this is all too frighteningly obvious.

Inside the System everything is fixed and patterned but its organizing centre – its 'soul' – is the Rocket. To the extent that the System, and everyone inside the System, in one way or another converge on the Rocket, they are converging on death. Outside the System, and one of its by-products as it were, is the Zone in which nothing is fixed and there are no patterns or points of convergence. There are 'no zones but the Zone', says one voice. This is the area of 'the new Uncertainty' – 'in the Zone categories have been blurred badly'. In the Zone everything and everyone is adrift for there are no taxonomies, and no narratives, to arrange them. If all the concepts are blurred, can the people in the Zone have any knowledge of reality, or are they perhaps nearer to reality by living in a deconceptualized state, fumbling around among the débris left when the prison house of language itself seems to have been destroyed? In the Zone there are only 'images of Uncertainty'. This involves a release from feeling that one is living in a completely patterned and determinate world, but also a panic at being outside any containing and explaining 'frame' (in his review Richard Poirier wrote at length on the significance of the 'frame' throughout the book). Those outside the System seem doomed to go on 'kicking endlessly among the plastic trivia, finding in each Deeper Significance, and trying to string them all together . . . to bring them together, in their slick persistence and our preterition . . . to make sense out of, to find the meanest sharp sliver of truth in so much

replication, so much waste . . .' Figures in the book inhabit either the
System or the Zone or move between them (or do not know whether
they are in either or both, for of course System and Zone have no
locational as well as no epistemological stability), and this in turn elicits
two dominant states of mind. Paranoia and anti-paranoia. Paranoia is, in
terms of the book, 'nothing less than the onset, the leading edge, of the
discovery that *everything is connected*, everything in the Creation, a
secondary illumination – not yet blindingly One, but at least connected'.
Of course, everything depends on the nature of the connection, the
intention revealed in the pattern, and just *what* it is that may connect
everything in Pynchon's world is what worries his main characters, like
Slothrop. The opposite state of mind is anti-paranoia, 'where nothing is
connected to anything, a condition not many of us can bear for long'.
And as figures move between System and Zone, so they oscillate
between paranoia and anti-paranoia, shifting from a seething blank of
unmeaning to the sinister apparent legibility of an unconsoling
labyrinthine pattern or plot. 'We are obsessed with building labyrinths,
where before there was open plain and sky. To draw ever more complex
patterns on the blank-sheet. We cannot abide that openness; it is terror to
us.' Those who do not accept the officially sanctioned 'delusions' of the
System as 'truth', but cannot abide pure blankness, have to seek out other
modes of interpretation. Thus 'those like Slothrop, with the greatest
interest in discovering the truth, were thrown back on dreams, psychic
flashes, omens, cryptographies, drug-epistemologies, all dancing on a
ground of terror, contradiction, absurdity'. This is the carnival of
modern consciousness which the book itself portrays.

All this is related to our situation as readers. To put it very crudely, the
book dramatizes two related assemblings and disassemblings – of the
rocket and of the character or figure named Slothrop. Slothrop is
engaged in trying to find out the secret of how the Rocket is assembled
but in the process he himself is disassembled. Similarly the book both
assembles and disassembles itself as we try to read it. For just as many of the
characters are trying to see whether there is a 'text' within the 'waste' and a
'game behind the game'; that is what we are having to do with the book as
it unfolds in our attention. There is deliberately too much evidence,
partaking of too many orders of types of explanation and modes of
experience for us to hold it all together. In seeing some possible
connections we are missing others. Reading itself thus becomes a
paranoid activity, which is, however, constantly breaking down under
the feeling that we will never arrive at a unitary reading, never hold the
book in one 'frame': the sense of indeterminateness is constantly
encroaching on us. We fluctuate between System and Zone, paranoia
and anti-paranoia, experiencing both the dread of reducing everything

to one fixed explanation – an all–embracing plot of death – and the danger of succumbing to apparently random detritus. Behind all this is the process of nature itself, working by organization and disorganization. The rocket is described as 'an entire system *won*, away from the feminine darkness, held against the entropies of lovable but scatter-brained mother Nature'. It engorges energy and information in its 'fearful assembly', thus its 'order' is obtained at the cost of an increase in disorder in the world around it, through which so many of the characters stumble. But in its fixity and metallic destructive inhumanity it is an order of death – a *negative* parallel of the process of nature, since its disintegration presages no consequent renewal and growth. That is one reason why at the end the rocket is envisaged as *containing* the living body of a young man (Gottfried), for this is the System *inside* which man is plotting his own annihilation. If we as readers try to win away one narrative 'System' from the book we are in danger of repeating mentally what They are doing in building the rocket. To put it in its most extreme form, they are trying to reduce all of nature's self-renewing variety to one terminal rocket; we must avoid the temptation to reduce the book to one fixed meaning. That is why our reading should be paranoid and anti-paranoid, registering narrative order and disorder, experiencing both the determinate and the inderminate, pattern and randomness, renewing our awareness of our acts and interpretations as being both conditioned and free, and of ourselves as synthesizing and disintegrating systems.

In this way we can to some extent be released from the System–Zone bind which besets Pynchon's main characters, in particular the figure of Slothrop. What happens to Slothrop is in every sense exemplary. One of the earliest events in his life is being experimented on in a Pavlovian laboratory (which is related to the obsession with all kinds of control and 'conditioning' which the book also explores). He is last seen, if seen at all, on a record cover. In between he has been the Plasticman and Rocketman of the comics he reads, played a variety of roles for English and American intelligence, been involved in the distorted fantasies and plots of dozens of figures in post–war Europe, all the time approaching the centre, the secret of the Rocket, which is also the absolute zero at the heart of the System. He knows that he is involved in the evil games of other people, whether they are run by the army or blackmarketeers or whatever, but he cannot finally get out of these games. Indeed, leaving all the games is one of the hopes and dreams of the few people with any human feeling left in the book. But it remains a dream. Reality has been pre-empted by games, or it has been replaced by films so that people can be said to live 'paracinematic lives'. As he moves through different experience-spaces he suffers a loss of emotion, a 'numbness', and a growing sense that he will never 'get back'. Along with this erosion of the capacity to feel, he begins to 'scatter', his 'sense of Now' or 'temporal bandwith' gets narrower and narrower and there is a feeling that he is getting so lost and unconnected that he is vaporizing out of time and place altogether. Near the end of his travels Slothrop suddenly sees a rainbow, a real one, and he has a vision of it entering into sexual union with the green unpapered earth; it is the life-giving antithesis to the rocket's annihilating penetrations: 'and he stands crying, not a thing in his head, just feeling natural . . .' After that he effectively vanishes. There is a story told about him. He 'was sent into the Zone to be present at his own assembly – perhaps, heavily paranoid voices have whispered, *his time's assembly*, and there ought to be a punch line to it, but there isn't. The plan went wrong. He is being broken down instead, and scattered.' The disassembling of Slothrop is, as I have suggested, in some way related to the assembling of the Rocket – the plan that went right – and it has far-reaching and disturbing implications.

The last comment on the possible whereabouts of Slothrop is this: 'we would expect to look among the Humility, among the gray and preterite souls, to look for him adrift in the hostile light of the sky, the darkness of the sea . . .' This idea of 'the preterite' is very important in this book and, I think, central to Pynchon's vision; as he uses it, it refers to those who have been 'passed over', the abandoned, the neglected, the despised and the rejected, those for whom the System has no use, the human junk thrown overboard from the ship of state (a literal ship in this book, incidentally, named *Anubis* after the ancient Egyptian God of the Dead). Set against the Preterite are the Elite, the users and manipulators, those who regard the planet as solely for their satisfaction, the nameless and ubiquitous 'They' who dominate the world of the book. It is one of the modern malaises which Pynchon has diagnosed that it is possible for a person to feel himself entering into a state of 'preterition'. But, and once again Pynchon's erudition and wit work admirably here, the idea of humanity's being divided into a Preterite and an Elite or Elect is of course a basic Puritan belief. In theological terms the Preterite were precisely those who were not elected by God and, if I may quote from a characteristically chilling Puritan pronouncement, 'the preterite are damned because they were never meant to be saved'. In redeploying these terms, which after all were central to the thinking of the people who founded America, and applying them to cruelly divisive and oppositional modes of thought at work throughout the world today, Pynchon once again shows how imaginatively he can bring the past and present together. One of Slothrop's ancestors wrote a book called *On Preterition*, supporting the Preterite as being quite as important as the Elect, and Slothrop himself wonders whether this does not point to a fork in the road which America never took, and whether there might not be a 'way back' even in the ruined spaces of post-war Europe? – 'maybe for a little while all the fences are down, one road as good as another, the whole space of the Zone cleared, depolarized, and somewhere inside the waste of it a single set of coordinates from which to proceed, without elect, without preterite, without even nationality to fuck it up . . .' This then is the organizing question of the book. Is there a way back? Out of the streets 'now indifferently gray with commerce'; out of the City of Pain, which Pynchon has taken over from Rilke's Tenth Duino Elegy and offers as a reflection of the world we have made; a way back out of the cinemas, the laboratories, the asylums and all our architecture of mental drugging, coercion, and disarray (derangement)? Out of a world in which emotions have been transferred from people to things, and images supplant realities? Where, ultimately, would the 'way back' lead to, if not some lost Eden previous to all categories and taxonomies, election and preterition, divisions and oppositions, 'griddles and signs'? Can we even struggle to regain such a mythic state? Of course the book offers no answers, though the possibility of a 'counter force' is touched on. It moves to a climax which is deliberately a sort of terminal fusion of many of the key fantasies and obsessions in the book – the note is comic-apocalyptic, or, perhaps we can now simply say, Pynchonesque. The opening page evokes the evacuation of London, with a crucial comment – 'but it's all theatre'. On the last page we are suddenly back in a theatre. We are waiting for the show to start – as Pynchon comments, we have 'always been at the movies (haven't we?)'. The film has broken down, though on the darkening screen there is something else – 'a film we have not learned to see'. The audience is invited to sing, while outside a rocket 'reaches its last unmeasurable gap above the roof of the old theatre'. It is falling in absolute silence, and we know it will demolish the old theatre – the old theatre of our civilization. But we do not see it because we are in the theatre trying to read the film behind the film; and we will not hear it because, under the new dispensation, the annihilation arrives first, and only after – 'a screaming comes across the sky'.

If these three books are 'games' they are, I think, games trying to break the games which contemporary culture imposes on us at all levels. They are games to 'quit the game' to the extent that this is possible. They are games, if you like, in line with the prescription laid down by the Russian critic Dobrolyubov when he wrote: 'It is necessary to work out in our soul a firm belief in the need and possibility of a complete exit from the present order of this life, so as to find the strength to express it in poetic forms.' Such exits can only be temporary and in this sense the books themselves are, and offer, limited periods of such an exit. Inasmuch as what Lacan calls the master-words of the city ('maitresmots de la cité') may tend to reify into a dominant 'privileged' discourse, these games may challenge and disturb this mastery and simply make readers aware of new possible ways of being in language. But from another point of remove they are games very much *about* important matters, for one is about the future and survival of language, one is about the future and survival of the narrator, and one is about the future and survival of the planet itself. They are games in the sense intended by Adorno when he wrote that 'The unreality of games gives notice that reality is not yet real. Unconsciously they rehearse the right life' (*Minima Moralia*).[1]

---

[1] In the context the translation seems to make no distinction between game and 'play'. Adorno is writing about how children use play as 'a defence'. 'In his purposeless activity the child, by a subterfuge, sides with use value against exchange value. Just because he deprives the things with which he plays of their mediated usefulness, he seeks to rescue in them what is benign towards men and not what subserves the exchange relation that equally deforms men and things.'

11

Toward an ultimate topography: the work of Joseph McElroy

Topography. *The science or practice of describing a particular place, city, town, manor, parish, or tract of land; the accurate and detailed delineation and description of any locality.*

Terminus. *The deity who presided over boundaries or landmarks . . . The point to which motion or action tends, goal, end, finishing point.*

Smuggle. *To convey (goods) clandestinely into (or out of) a country or district, in order to avoid payment of legal duties, or in contravention of some enactment; to bring in, over, etc., in this way.*

It is not accidental for the object to be given to me in a 'deformed' way, from the point of view [place] *which I occupy. That is the price of its being real. The perceptual synthesis thus must be accomplished by the subject, which can both delimit certain perspectival aspects in the object, the only ones actually given, and at the same time go beyond them. This subject, which takes a point of view, is my body as the field of perception and action* (pratique). (M. Merleau-Ponty, *The Primacy of Perception*)

Then, on the surface of being, in that region where being wants to be both visible and hidden, the movements of opening and closing are so numerous, so frequently inverted, and so charged with hesitation, that we could conclude on the following formula: man is half-open being. (Gaston Bachelard, *The Poetics of Space*)

'Are we ever far from smuggling?' asks a character in Joseph McElroy's first novel, *A Smuggler's Bible* (1966), and in his fictional exploration of this question McElroy added a major new metaphor to contemporary literature. The answer, in brief, is obviously no, but we can hardly begin to comprehend the ramifying implications of the metaphor. For boundaries create smuggling, boundaries of every kind – national, physical, conceptual – and man, that moving system of penetrable surfaces, barriers, and gaps, that 'half-open being', is a perpetual smuggler in every realm. How could we begin to estimate the million stares, glances, and glimpses, the myriad engorgements and incorporations, gross and subtle, which make up our day? They are clandestine in the sense that they are conducted in secret, in silence, obeying no law other than the procedural logic which governs our fierce and tender sensory appropriations, our swift and elusive mental manoeuvres by which an endless stream of material is constantly being shifted across the frontiers which organize our thoughts, and that awesome neural activity which makes man, among other things, a continual synaptic drama. We smuggle the past into the present through memory, objects into images through metaphor, ideas into books through print, and ourselves into other people through who knows how many mesmeric and penetrative magics. A 'smuggler's bible' is a facsimile of the sacred book which contains nothing but can carry anything. Instead of being a sacred text, it is a cunning device which offers an opportunity for unusual assemblage and devious conveyance. It is the modern novel, but we did not see it in quite that way before McElroy's brilliant first novel, which is just such an object as is described inside it: 'Inside the Bible's cover is pasted a bookseller's label identifying the article; "A Smuggler's Bible. Used by smugglers on both sides of the Atlantic in the early nineteenth century to conceal small objects of value. Actually a mere box, this 'Bible' could be used to contain any assortment of goods the smuggler could get into it."' Only McElroy's bible-box has its label on the outside. What did he put inside?

A screwdriver among other things. 'It is a "seven-level" screwdriver, so-called by electronic technicians, who use this plastic-handled tool with the two-and-a-half-inch blade for so many purposes – chipping, hammering, as a low-voltage shortening bar, prying – that they rely on it constantly.' I single this out to start with because one of McElroy's notable interests is in all the kinds of man-made hardware which we constantly encounter and with which we endlessly extend our capacities; to this he affords an unromantic, demystifying, appreciative attention which opens up new possibilities for the way fiction can itself operate in the modern world. Other writers – Bellow, for instance – can give us the talk of our time in all its incredible variety; McElroy is rare in giving us some of the tools of our time in all their wondrous ingeniousness. I will return to this aspect of his work later on. For now I will temporarily purloin that seven-level screwdriver (as David, a character in the book, steals it from someone else) to pry open McElroy's seven-levelled book (as David uses it to open the actual smuggler's bible in the book which contains his manuscripts). There is a clear narrative situation. On board a ship making a transatlantic crossing an American named David Brooke, travelling with his English wife, is trying to organize a series of manuscripts he has brought with him. These consist of eight different 'memories' which he has accumulated at different periods in his life by an effort of intense empathetic projection – at what cost to his own identity and his relations with others is one of the recurring problems of the book. This, if you like, is his loot, a sort of experiential contraband which he has smuggled out of other people's lives. His principal concern is the matter of connection. 'Here's what he is thinking: Are the manuscripts one manuscript simply as they now stand? After all, they're crawling with links. Words in one manuscript recognize words in others, intransitive, transitive. There must surely be one substance the eight memories together make. And if not? If not, then David has barely a week to join them.' Just what is connection, separation? What fits into a system, what makes a pattern, what constitutes a form? McElroy and his character share this preoccupation with other modern writers, of course. He has obviously appreciated Lowry's *Under the Volcano* and Gaddis's *The Recognitions*, and obviously read Nabokov, Borges, and Beckett, as who has not? He must likewise be well aware of what Pynchon has been doing from the start, and no writer has made more out of the very concepts of plot, pattern, frame, etc. than Pynchon. He has read lots of other things, too, but the matter of degrees of influence is irrelevant. McElroy's interest is in the very structure of perception – how do you see the coherent field of objects, *if* you do? If not, what is it to perceive incoherence? We are constantly moving from spreading clarifications to inchoate confusions – things fall together and fall apart at the same time – and McElroy follows that movement. Being a writer, he is obviously concerned with the structure of a book, but he can clearly see this as part of a much larger matter – namely, what is the nature of the structure of systems? His interest is phenomenological and technological as well as literary. How do you assemble a book? How do you read a map? How is a ship put together? How do we see, how do we move; how do we make love? How do we use screwdrivers?

David is sitting with his file of manuscripts on board ship. 'David feels the ship's infinitesimal roll weight one buttock then the other. What about stabilizers? Which direction is forward?' It is an important part of the book that we are made aware that David is as much in a ship as he is in his memories; for of course there are certain available potential parallels, homologies, or analogical echoes precipitated by this kind of double, or multiple, habitation.

> David doesn't really understand the plan of the ship, but he can move from one part to another with a strange rapidity. The ship grows smaller day by day. Moving from one lounge or level to another, he is struck . . . by the lack of transitions . . . First he was in one place; then he was in another. He forgets, when he is below, which way is forward and comes to doubt the relation of the barbershop to the stateroom, his and Ellen's dining room to the children's playroom, the bridge to the pool.

This of course exactly describes his situation in his manuscript fragments (or forms), and I use the preposition advisedly because his mind does

move around among the various cabins which are his compartmental-
ized memories, now in one place, now in another, and often struck by the
lack of transitions, the memories undoubtedly and locatably there but
the relationship between them uncertain. And this is not, as it were, a
decorative or playful analogy, but a functional one, inasmuch as it brings
home in a novel way the kind of reciprocal influences which flow
between the structured spaces we move through and the kind of shapes
we make. And this kind of analogy is not fixed and closed, but open and
generative. For example, in the last section in which David has smuggled
himself back inside his father – it is his supreme feat and in some ways
constitutes 'a release' – he re-creates or appropriates his father's
experience in a church in Bergen.

> Looking upward you thought of a ship's hold. You were peering up through
> antique superstructure into a vortex of night. The door rattled open, a mote of
> blindness came into the corner of your eye from the light admitted by the
> newcomer. Then the door closed. You cared nothing for the newcomer. You
> felt calm captivity in this inside-out ship – the shingled forest organism of its
> hull outside enclosing the masts and levels and catwalks of its superstructure,
> enclosing even the night through which it passed.

As the church is an inside-out ship, so the book is an outside-in world.
What is inside and outside? We live at a constantly changing interface
and that is where McElroy is doing his work. The excitement triggered
by such passages as the one I have just quoted is not just a matter of
intellectual appreciation of an unusual and vivid metaphor (I necessarily
can only speak for myself), but the result as well of something firing in
our 'neural neighborhood' (the phrase is McElroy's) in recognition of a
new way of reading our possible sense of things.

The book contains the eight distinct 'memories' joined and separated,
sequentially if in no other sense, by short sections which are lettered A to
z, and then again A to z. These are concerned with David himself and the
whole operation of assembling the book. In the last sentence on the first
page marked z, David is described as removing the letters t, u, v, w, y, z
from the 'alphabet soup' of a boy he once knew. It is a memory, of
course, and anticipates the next section, which records the experience of
that boy and his relationship to his father. Does it constitute a link? Is it a
neat bridge-passage concealing a gap? Is it a bit of a Nabokovian game? It
does not matter, of course, but it is indicative of something the book
seems to be doing which is worth taking notice of. That old aesthetic
problem – does art 'forge' a form, or does it discover one which is already
there latent in its material? – occurs in various versions in the book, but
more particularly it focuses on the operations of memory. Memories we
certainly have, and just as certainly they never take on a fixed and final
form or sequence. It is as though we have within us a kind of meta-
memory which can endlessly arrange and rearrange memories in

configurations of varying degrees of complexity, and it would be both pointless and impossible to say at any one point in time whether a particular memory or memory cluster was a form or a fragment.

It is part of the originality of McElroy's book that it includes and explores these matters as they affect the art of written narrative, which, just to restate the obvious but crucial fact, involves the linearization of memory in one way or another. And where McElroy's book may be said to differ from *Under the Volcano*, in particular, and *The Recognitions*, is in its periodic resistances to the solicitations of form. They can only be periodic, of course, and symbolic – David's separate memories have a very clear narrative form and there McElroy's book stands, well architectured and firm, shipshape as we might say. But the book does contain as it were, instructions for its disassemblage, and warnings against trespassing into too much order. 'David found data forming too plain a pattern . . . David had to take out details that made the memory too schematic. Perhaps: impose *dis*order on one's memories.'

One figure in the book, himself a narrator, can reproduce drawings from the dictionary, including triskelions and tesserae. A triskelion is 'that lonely figure of three legs or arms joined at one imprisoning center', and the suggestiveness of that description speaks for itself. Tesserae, on the other hand, are 'unfairly easy to draw, for instead of creating a mosaic out of pieces, all you do is draw your shape and then throw over it a cross-hatch of lines, the resulting cell-like pieces being, of course, the tesserae'. The pattern must not be made too easy, just as things must not be overexplained. 'In an age of explanation a veritable chaos of elucidation is possible.' Another character, Jaro, a brilliant Czech-Jewish student, owns 'an Andean quipu, a mnemonic device, a kind of abacus the Incas webbed by knotting bits of rope or string in many different ways'. In the event, he hangs himself with it. It is a harsh irony, and a cautionary one since David is precisely knotting together a rope of memories. But it is followed by another irony. The person who tells the story of Jaro is bitterly reproached by his auditor. 'You reduce your friend's last days to a printed dated summary – able, straight, without mistake and unmistakably yours. I bet you even remembered to make a carbon. What'll you do if someday after you've typed one of your monstrous chronologies you discover that the carbon reads differently from the original.' I think it significant that the reproach comes from a woman; later I will try to explain why. 'Mosaic' seems to be an acceptable word for the provisional forms that experience takes on. One encounter is described by a friend as 'one more tile in a gathering mosaic of excitements'; but against that we can set the phrase David uses to describe his mental condition prior to a kind of breakdown he experienced – 'the gathering incoherence was already great'. Perhaps the key word is 'gathering', for it suggests not only a centering accumulation but an ongoing process which may be experienced as amplification and clarification, or over-loading and confusion. The mosaic is moving, movable. To quote from a later essay by McElroy on his own work, 'my story in *A Smuggler's Bible* was designed to fracture'. It fractures while it is being put together, and vice versa.

A central problem in all this, and not of course a new one, is that it is possible to remember too much. Anthropologists use the phrase 'structural amnesia' in describing how oral tribes and societies transmit certain information (of all kinds) selectively from the past and, as it were, forget the rest. In this novel, David records his attempt to bring everything together in his mind – he calls himself 'a kind of epistemo-logical reuniac' – even writing letters and establishing a kind of communications network among the various people in his life. The attempt brings him to a kind of mental breakdown in which, for a period, he suffers from total amnesia – in part simulated, in part real, thus both a strategy and a sickness. It came partly from a blow on the head with a book administered by his angry wife, and partly from a realization that his attempt to establish a sort of community among all the people he knew, even if only via letter and in his own head, had in fact isolated him from everybody. Thus in a letter to his wife:

> And I knew my memory was one reason I'd failed to bring them within the circle of myself. Can you understand that? Finding myself cut off from other people (excised from their lives) and also cut out in part because I was letting reliance on memory let me preoccupy myself with matters other than those immediately confronting me, I thought I would choose to act in a way consistent with this excision . . . Maybe still the highest life demands the most ruthless and even *amorous* memory; yet everyone . . . practices the art, or if you will, takes daily doses of the milk of, amnesia.

How much must a writer remember to forget? Obviously there are problems and processes here which are impossible to formulate. But as there are and must be gaps in the memory, as there are gaps between people and languages and countries and creeds, so – I think McElroy was implying – let there be gaps in the book. And respect the unordered for what might be its precious unamenability to order.

'(All right for *you*, Davey B. Have you ever thought what'd happen if I left you? If the salt lost its saviour – if the mad world's heterogenii were to be left unordered and unlaid by our homogenius?)' This is spoken by a voice which starts the book – 'He doesn't know what I am, but he knows I'm in him and behind him. His name is David Brooke, and he and his meddling English wife are aboard the Arkadia bound east.' It isn't exactly his alter ego, but it is involved in his creative or ordering mental activity and can be identified as that very compulsion to write and arrange and connect which haunts and obsesses part of David. This spirit of hectoring intentionality is not so much the ghost in the machine as the machine in the man, for not only does it speak with an arrogant, mandarin, misogynistic, possessive, jealous, and thoroughly tiresome voice, it is made to sound mechanical. Again:

> He still hears that intimate mechanical voice – my voice; it spoke to him from one of those experimental weighing machines in the exhibit at the New York Coliseum; it said words to him that seemed impossibly important: 'One hundred sixty-five pounds; project yourself into the lives of others. Project, reorient-ate' – an electronic quiver made the voice seem all the more certain – 'analyze, synthesize, assimilate; project yourself.' And David decided to do just that.

As I have noted, McElroy is far from being antipathetic to machines, but here it does seem as though the shrill reiterated imperatives from this voice have a potentially dehumanizing effect on David. The other key figure in the book is David's wife, Ellen, though she says very little. But that is part of the point; for Ellen, and this seems to be true of most of the important women in McElroy's work (particularly the wives of the protagonists), seems to be beyond the need of narrative (hence my earlier point), and it is the narrating drive in David which threatens to separate him from Ellen. Thus, in the sections between the main chapters, we usually find the voice struggling to retain possession of David's consciousness and volition, to preempt his loyalty and come between him and Ellen. At the end of the second page marked z, i.e. the final interlude prior to David's final attempted projection into the mind of his father, the voice is finally vanquished and goes out in a Joycean sputter of parenthetic protest: '(please! Don't you know me? I'm Yore Old Eeyore Yore Ol' Gay Donkey egomorphosed so as to pass unnoticed in that low-lit stable tableau. David! David! Aieee! DB—) "Ellen." ' Thus the last word David speaks, in terms of the actual narrative time of the book, is his wife's name, presumably signifying some kind of release from a mechanical urge to arrange and a return to a human ability to 'connect'.

Nevertheless the advice given by the machine-voice is responsible for the book that David assembles. The vocabulary of projection and penetration recurs constantly in differing contexts as David, as it were, 'collects' parts of other people's lives, or inserts himself in some way into their consciousnesses. He is called a 'snooper' and of course this is in part a continuation of that sense of the ambiguous status of 'the observer' which has vexed or engaged writers as various as Thomas Mann, Henry James and Hawthorne, and Charlotte Brontë. For David this attempt to project and penetrate is in part a search for material but, perhaps more important, it is a quest for some form of community, and in truth he engages with a marvellous variety of characters who emerge very impressively as quite distinct consciousnesses in the course of the book:

male and female, English and American, lonely eccentrics (e.g. an old forger – a gesture to Gaddis? – 'The coins are all he cares for in the whole world, and I'm participating in his life by getting him to tell me') and close family. But there is also another aspect of this urge to project himself into other people, best illustrated by the feeling ascribed to David when he once saw a suicide already falling from a building: he 'saw with utter clarity that somehow he should have been able to enter the man's mind and tell him to live – to live'. The idea of using one's mental power to in some way reprogram the thinking of another person seems to hold great interest for McElroy, and I do not think he is talking just about telepathy. That it would be a highly ambivalent power goes without saying, but McElroy returns to it often enough to indicate that it is a serious matter to him. In this book he concentrates more on the ambiguous nature of the attempt to enter, really to penetrate though not necessarily to change, another person. Some words David says to his father: 'Get finally into the heart of another person and you risk an explosion. Only reach the center of a person, break into the rock-central blindness and desire, the utter elements of the person, and you risk a blow-up. Avoid the risk and you settle for epistemological impotence.' Epistemological impotence is something which neither David nor McElroy will settle for, so there is a constant reengagement with the impossible project of some ultimate annihilating penetration. Between impotence and blow-up all kinds of strange dilations and contractions of the self take place as it either tumefies, and displaces or diminishes the existence of others, or recedes toward a condition of omniscient weightlessness, a condition which seems to hold a particular interest for McElroy. This, I think, is something which happens not only to many of his main characters but to McElroy's prose as it at times distends in a detectably self-gratifying exercising of its quite extraordinary resources ('parthenogenetic proliferations', to borrow again from his box), and at other times quite selflessly deploys itself in the service of the most intricate and respectful and responsible accuracies concerning the visible and tangible and constantly to-be-moved-through world, and the people moving through it – toward, away.

Robinson Crusoe is mentioned in the book:

> Onto the sparsely imprinted sands that had seemed his fate, Crusoe brought eighteenth-century London, self and place cohabiting: each of them both the city and the man. But if he could have thrived on those domestic sands – and he *did* thrive – whence came the roots that made him firm? From that London he never left? From that self that was different from London? From outside? Surely from outside. Or from within?

Robinson Crusoe and Sinbad the Sailor, whose strange adventures are also alluded to, are two figures who offer a paradigm of the problem for the writer, as it is explored so richly and from so many angles, and with so many tonal changes, in McElroy's book. Is he to be a Crusoe on his island or a Sinbad on his voyages? One part-answer – and of course there are only part-answers to a question composed of emblematic extremes – is that he can be a Crusoe on the voyages on his island, and a Sinbad on the islands of his voyages, as McElroy's novel so impressively demonstrates.

In 1968, McElroy published a short story called 'The Accident', which touches on what we might call the problematics of pity and, though this is barely explored, the relation they have to narration. A young city man has moved into the country. On the road that he uses to go into town lives a very old woman with her even older husband – poor, infirm, but in some ways ruthless. He gives the old woman lifts and helps her in odd little ways on the principle that, as he says, 'People *must* be kind to one another.' Her response to his help is a colloquial remark which, due to ellipsis, strikes him as oddly ambiguous: ' "If I can ever do anything for you, Mr. Ephraim, you been good to us." Such simple illogic: he must work it out. If she could ever do anything for him, he had been good to her .' In the event, she does not do something for him when she has the chance. Swerving to avoid her on the road one night, he drives his car into a ditch. The police threaten to charge him with drunken driving and he knocks on the old woman's door asking her to tell the police that it was a genuine accident which was not his fault. But she will not come out and seems to be quite indifferent to his plight, and it is this apparent failure of reciprocity which hurts, rather than the police threat:

> Alec had felt he would gladly be locked up for the night rather than be shat on by the woman he had pitied and helped. What was wrong with pity? Never pity people, it's cruel: he'd heard that said . . . But now he thought he saw the accidental logic of Mrs. Paul's parting words that first Saturday: 'If I can ever do anything for you, you've been good to us.' She'd had the chance tonight, and hadn't taken it. Did that mean he *hadn't* been good to her. Of course she hadn't meant precisely what she'd said. The interpretation of her error had been his logic, *his* wit. Yet even for her that accidental logic worked. For after all, what good was Alec to her?

Waiting for him in his cottage is a local girl whose persistence is matched by his disinclination to get very involved with her. To 'amuse' her and at the same time to distance her, he narrates. 'I want to tell you a story, "I want to tell you something . . . I've had an accident", he began.' Accidents ('anything that happens: an event: an unforeseen contingency: a disaster', *OED*) precipitate narrative ('a poetry of accident' is a phrase used in *Ancient History*), but what role does narrative play in relationships? What are some of the implications of our impulse to pity and our impulse to tell? And are they interconnected?

This short story hardly ventures far into these matters, but McElroy's next novel, *Hind's Kidnap* (1970), centres on a man who wants to help people or, as we say, to lend a hand. The colloquialism is particularly apt since it suggests the basic ambiguity in our mancipating and e-mancipating relationships with the world around us. What really is it to hold and let go? What is collection and what protection? Where does release fade into abandonment? What is 'possession'? McElroy chose for his organizing metaphor the idea of 'kidnapping' in all its possible aspects. Kidnapping is obviously related to smuggling, with a specific human reference. You do not nap things, you nap kids (though in the earlier use of the verb you could 'nab' anything), but in doing that do you thereby turn the person into an object? Do you do the same if you try to rescue that person? Jack Hind goes through this novel with his hands out. He wants to 'protect', be a 'savior', support, 'shepherd' others, be a 'moving watchman' in the city (an idea developed at length in *Lookout Cartridge*), a 'guardian'. Hind has indeed been brought up by a guardian and developed that specific protofamilial role into a stance *vis-à-vis* the world, thus developing, as his wife sardonically puts it in her section of the book, a 'huge holy supersympasocial hand'. He is initially not concerned to try to find out who his real father was, seeing in such an attempt an inturned self-interest; rather, he thinks it is better to try to help other people. To this end, he becomes obsessed with an unsolved kidnapping which took place years ago. The original parents are dead, the kidnappers unknown, the police uninterested, but Hind feels that a child should not be allowed to 'disappear' in such a way, and for much of the book he identifies any possible significance his own life might have with trying to solve the kidnap and find the boy. 'If the kidnap case didn't matter, neither did he.' In fact this distinction between his own family origins and the search for an unrelated other turns out to be mistaken, since the child he ultimately finds is himself, in the discovery of his real father (the guardian, who for reasons made clear in the book had concealed the fact of his paternity). The guardian, who, among other things, is a self-appointed guardian of the precisions and embodied meanings of language ('Language is what you build on, Jack, so best get it right'), says to Hind at one point in an etymological discussion, 'Get your roots right, and rich vocabularies open to you', and the book explores with really quite marvellous originality some of the possible connections, parallels, and significant echoes between etymology and genealogy, or the very notion of 'roots' and derivations.

To give just one example, the book is pervaded with the names of trees. The characters Hind is involved with include Hershey Laurel, Maddy Beecher, Ivy Ash, Oliver Plane, Dewey Wood. To which one person says, 'do you expect anyone to believe those names?', and another exclaims, 'the *names* you populate your life with, your heartfelt beneficiaries', and Hind – 'names made you think'. Hind, a giant of a man whose childhood was notable for his 'insatiable growth', once played the part of a tree in a play and liked 'the swaying protectiveness he imagined he conveyed'. Because of his gangling, proliferating body, children would climb on him – 'Hind was an object'. His friends are 'trees or possessed of tree connections', and there is a reference at one point to an Indian bachelor tree ceremony in which the man marries a tree first. His wife is 'Sylvia'. At the very end of the book, Hind has started to write the *Life* of his guardian, with the opening words: 'This is a man who, possessed by a dream of freedom which he never, hence, possessed, thought himself a shepherd but found himself a tree.' (The novel is subtitled *A Pastoral on Familiar Airs*, 'pastoral' literally meaning, of course, pertaining to shepherds.) What is going on in all this? A Nabokovian game in which McElroy flaunts the novelist's imperial powers of gratuitous and unlikely nomination? Perhaps unavoidably that, but I think there is something more. He himself offered an explanation in his essay 'Neural Neighbourhoods', which I found a shade cryptic but which referred to the names as being not only 'pollutions' but 'revelations'. As I read it there are first of all the enriching ironies available to McElroy by writing a *pastoral* about the *city*, for this is very emphatically a novel of the modern city. Then there is the original perspective in which it puts one of the main concerns of the book. When the children crawl on Hind he becomes an 'object', but this is not the kind of reification which we associate with, say, the dehumanization of the factory assembly-line worker. For a tree is beautiful and alive, and it may be 'used' as an object in a spirit of gratitude, affection, even admiration, as the child avails himself of its proffered protectiveness and its inviting shadowy entanglements and aerial declivities. It is simply not human, though not thereby less than human. To the extent that Hind sees his friends in terms of trees (and we are allowed the feeling that in some odd way the names are *his* names for them) and turns his life into a kind of movable forest, as it were, he is in some way 'using' them, no matter how apparently selflessly, displacing them from their own unique human otherness onto some metaphorical terrain of his generous imagination. But then there is the further consideration that some aspect and actuality of a man (or woman) can be rediscovered in the figure of the tree – an enhancing, not a reifying, vision. Hind wanted to be a shepherd, wandering single, unmoored; he has to discover that he is a tree, with roots and spreading obligations – a father, a wife, a child. In doing so, rich vocabularies open to him – of writing, of perception, of living.

From the core idea of kidnapping, the fictional inquiry branches out into interrelated actions and deeds: smuggling, abducting, collecting (like David, he 'collects people's lives'), rescuing, adopting ('confusing enough to be adopted by your own father'), catching (glimpses, objects, people), possessing. The ambiguities of this last are suggested by the guardian when he picks up a rock and announces that 'this chunk of feldspathic rock is in possession of my hand'. How this may operate on another level is indicated when Hind tries to involve a girl in his narrative about the kidnap which he is tracking down and building up, following clues in every direction (clues which are planted, deceptive, illusory, imagined – and real, for there was an actual kidnap, no matter how much Hind makes it over into his personal obsession – and discoveries are made). The girl, he speculates, may already know something relevant which she is unaware of, 'so she was possessed *of* by being possessed *by* the shrouded, running tale'. McElroy is extremely aware of the crucial role played by prepositions in the attempt to define in what relationship, in a given context or configuration, a person stands to what (whom) ever else in that context, and to what a shifting extent we may be owned by the things we own, the ideas we form, the stories we tell. Hind's motives for starting the 'hunt' are obscure because overdetermined; he sees it as a self-validating quest though it is also of course a form of flight. Whatever it takes him toward, it takes him away from his wife and daughter. There is no point in attempting any summary of the many accidents and incidents, neighbours and neighbourhoods, the hunt involves him in; as in the short story, each new episode precipitates a need to 'tell'. 'He must tell somebody. He would tell how each alarming diversion, as you retreated from it and looked back, began to be alive and independent, a subcounterplot thriving in a style its very own.' McElroy does fill his book with a rich variety of 'subcounterplots' and they do indeed thrive in their own styles – again, his narrative and lexical resources reveal themselves as being prodigious. More to the point is just to note that the compulsion to 'tell', which involves composing, connecting, plotting, can be a separating drive which devalues the other into an auditor, an adjunctive but nonessential presence. Like David Brooke, Hind is 'at the mercy of his memory' and, like David, there are times when he has been ready to forget the data accumulating exponentially in his head.

All this leads to the anagnorisis and reversal in the novel, whereby Hind comes to recognize that he must embark on a 'dekidnaping policy'. This involves the resolve and the attempt to 'unthink' people, to emancipate them like the uncaged nightingales in the fairy story he remembers, to 'erase' his 'use' of them as clues and leads in his gathering plot, to give each individual who has been deployed in his narrative the 'chance to unwrap and let go as accidental organic personal end, as non-means'. Versions of the Kantian imperative that we should use people as ends and not means – an imperative which has informed much (most?) great fiction of the past – appear so often in the concluding part of McElroy's book that he runs the risk of that devaluation-by-repetition which is as present in fiction as it is anywhere else. However, he offers a novel account of that impulse toward disburdening, unlearning, and forgetting; that complex desire to somehow 'give back' the unbearable bounty which simple existence bestows on the privileged self – which are no doubt universal feelings but which seem to occur in American literature in unusual and acute forms. What Hind wants to do is to press 'through the dekidnap toward a luminal surface afloat somewhere ahead, a last light emanating from a free life with Sylvia and May'. It is not of course as easy as all that, and cannot be effected by a simple change in policy. For one thing, 'people quite simply refused to be dekidnaped'; for another, you cannot 'unsee' what you have seen any more than you can 'give back' the 'nonreturnable gift of place with its landscaped encumbrancies'. And how do you treat a *place* as an 'end in itself', apart from the passions and the purposes of the people moving through it? It is as if, by way of recoil and recompense, Hind is embarking on the impossible project of de-intentionalizing the self! But as any phenomenologist – and Joseph McElroy – very well knows, every act of consciousness demands a certain object because every conscious act intends something. Hind wants to somehow un-story his world and let everything return to its previous randomness and uncollected otherness, but – what he has seen, he has seen. Of course, then the problem is just what has he seen, and it is in his charting of the rich ambiguities of our perceptual processes that McElroy achieves some of his most original effects. I can barely allude to some of these but will single out three objects in the book: a map, a jigsaw puzzle, and a Dürer woodcut.

The map is of New York's subways and Hind peruses it carefully; it is defaced, deteriorating, and crosshatched with the cryptic scribblings of the 'preterite' of the city (I use Pynchon's word, as it is a rather Pynchonesque map), but 'even in its present state, [it] could probably be read'. 'On it he hardly knew his own city . . . Initials and dates clustered at all angles; the eye, making its own smooth stroke, might if it tried divine a whole clock face inlaid with intimations of rectangular forms . . . a painfully slow map, if you studied it. On the other hand, using it you could really make time around the city.' Hind's difficulty in finding the city in the map is related to his difficulty in hearing the city in its name, and both are specific instances of the problematical relationship between map and ground, word and thing, which have been much discussed in recent years in a number of contexts. The important factor in the experience as described is that the map changes according to the intention with which you study it, what you are looking to see. In this case it changes according to whether Hind looks at it for some kind of model or projection of the city, or as a display of encoded information which would enable him to avail himself of the city's transport system. The jigsaw, which is a 'Jesus-puzzle picture', exemplifies this experience of ocular oscillation another way.

> You looked, and maybe all you saw was abstract landscape rather like the
> ruined subway map, with no perspective to speak of, just flat, waving black
> and white; then, what Maddy Beecher and Cassia were crowing about, and
> ridiculing you for not perceiving, came clear: in the whole tangle was Christ
> looking out, the pale, rather Northern Christ – but not exactly looking out of:
> indeed, rather, the tangle *was* Christ.

We are all familiar with such optical-illusion pictures which can be read
in more than one way, often as focus shifts so that figure and ground seem
to change places. McElroy is clearly fascinated with the implications of
these strange visual shifts in everyday life. The vocabulary of 'perspective' is very prominent in the book, and there are various speculations
about what is called 'anti-perspective' or seeing things in their 'flat
reality', devoid of depth.

During a spell of teaching, Hind tries to develop this latter theory of
vision and urges his students to see a Dürer woodcut as 'an exquisitely
jumbled flat surface' apart from the 'alluring illusions' which the
employment of perspective offers to the eye. Which provokes the
following response from one student:

> You try to make us unsee degrees of depth in Dürer's *Flight into Egypt* so we can
> see truly the quote unquote ultimate topography scratched by the man's hand
> in a wood block that remains a wood block. Yet the picture's story . . . well,
> you couldn't begin even to *tell* us this story if Dürer's modeling and depth and
> perspective did not make you see what you dare to dismiss as illusion. What are
> you trying to do, break us? What good is it to say, Unsee all this and even if you
> have to dilate your eye to do it see only surface sections of hatchings and blanks
> . . . You change back and forth, Mr. Hind, because you don't know yourself.
> You say it's all background – us too – there is no foreground, we are part of a
> flat design. Maybe you want to disappear into your background. But I see
> myself *against* mine . . . there *is* space between us, and each has his own
> perspective.

If we merely assessed this as a contribution to the study of the mechanics
of vision, it is not particularly startling; but context is all, and appearing
in McElroy's novel some of these basic ambiguities, or multiplicities, in
our perceptual processes are enlivened and vivified. By the same token,
in introducing such phenomenological concerns into his fiction,
McElroy energizes our sense of the multiple possibilities in the focusings
of the novel. The move toward an 'ultimate topography', with the
scrupulous delineation of the surfaces and lines and intersections which
make up the perceptual field, or simply the particular 'place', for some
person at some point in time, and which McElroy himself I think is
attempting, is not incompatible with the power of narrative. You can
study the map synchronically or travel by it diachronically; 'old hard
perspectives' may 'vanish in new sweet (plain ungrounded) si-mul-ta-

ne–ities of time place side by side', whence again we may see things again in freshened and less rigidified perspectives.

All these considerations bear on the significance and epistemological, even ontological, status of Hind's 'kidnap' venture. 'There was in the end more to your abortive re– and de– kidnap than an April to X–mas tour of salient wood, stone, steel, or synthetic points, wasn't there?' Which is to say that there was something to be narrated as well as something to be studied topographically. The verdict of the book seems to concur with that, and I will quote at length from a late passage, partly to give an example of McElroy's style and the ambitious range of phenomena it seeks to enlist. (There are only two sentences, and the style throughout is marked by a calculated distension which can put a strain on the reader who begins to lose the *gestalt* of the sentence but which does involve him in some of the complexities of the processes of perception. There are precedents.)

> And it will not do to recant under pressure these varieties of familiar pattern lingering in your upper gums and the middle mass of your mind – in favor of random data today fourteen years later, the random close smell of roto-chickens fresh-spitted after lunch turning all afternoon behind the butcher's window in whose moving surface you see not only a pair of thick female eyebrows but across this random upper West Side street an old movie marquee billing prices of cabbage, carrots, tomatoes, beets; any more than it will do to lose yourself in, so to speak, the undertaker's man Carmen La Branche's sight, no the sight of Carmen La Branche, as he stands, knees very slightly bent, in line at Kold Kut City: or, right around your corner, in a neighbourhood you must admit is recognizable, to lose yourself in the sound of a can of calorie-free pop which in answer to your coin bangs down to the lower opening where your hand, like a mind (of its own) waits to grasp. No, the patterns of adoption, of possessed and possession, of male purpose, female laurel, filial paternity, of fore and aft, of illusory deep and delusory flat, wait for you as steadily as the greasy-haired woman (ostracized from Phyllis's genial fountain though never originally appected there) whom you see here at your corner, whom you may chalk on your score slate as another pitiable breast in the pitiable mass of accidents but who cannot help telling you much more than that pastoral chaos of random data wound in naked tape: look at her trudging across Second: with her cigarette in hand, which thus scores the act with a stroke of white against her linty black coat, she crosses herself again coming across the cobbles before the waiting, idling cars, one of which guns heavily as she passes for she is oblivious of her very own, though transitory, red light.

Dreiser is somewhat behind this[1] (though McElroy aspires to a higher degree of phenomenological accuracy in tracing the way the eye scans a field), and, as I noted earlier, this is very distinctly a city novel. As Hind

---

[1] 'Dreiser's coming back . . . These kids want accuracy' – a quotation from his next novel.

starts on his 'hunt', the city seems to lose its name, become simply a part of the 'coastal density', a 'placental city', impingingly and perceptibly there but as a shifting kaleidoscope of phenomena no longer stable within their conventional nominations. It is as Hind makes his saving return to the surfaces of things that the city seems to be 'shifting back into the old markings' and 'insisting on its names' (there is quite a bit of toponymy in the book as well). Here again McElroy's unusual ability to describe changing perceptual relationships to the environment is clearly in evidence, so that the city is not given as mere background, but as it is seen, as it is traversed, as it is thought.

In this connection I want to note one particular oddity or apparent idiosyncrasy in McElroy's writing in this book. Hind is said to feel that in embarking on his hunt 'he entered a new and necessary range, terrain, plot, tract which only he entered and where nothing could follow'. At another point, a remembered voice can be heard 'in another track, branch, line, lane, road, deadend of Hind's brain': later 'Hind felt his own role, part, assignment, relation, intervalence, interception, in all this was not worth weighing.' I could multiply numerous examples of other triplications (or sextuplications!) and in fact the 'habit of releasing triune verbal extensions of your private insights' is mocked by the guardian in the book. It can be irritating, like a mannerism, and we can all reach for dictionaries of synonyms. But what I think McElroy is foregrounding is the phenomenon of the multiplication of terms, whereby we have many different ways of mapping words onto similar things, each of them making us register the things in a slightly different way. We are, as it were, endlessly translating and retranslating the world according to vocabularies of the discourse within which we happen to be operating, and I think McElroy wants to get into his fiction. One other quotation in connection with this:

> And you thought of the soft mass of Cassia's insides, unknown to her, and bubbling away, different from the outside skeleton of membranes, hair, crust and polish, each with untamed intersections of message while behind and below were dark bubbling insides loved but almost never seen.

Such a passage makes you realize that if, in one vocabulary, man is (was) the measure of all things, in another he is, and no less wonderfully, a 'wet computer'. And what McElroy is doing seems to me to be one of the very important things that modern fiction should do. In more general terms the main achievement of this remarkable novel, for me, is the particular way it brings together surfaces and deeds, places and people, topography and narrative, along with a meta-awareness of the perceptual problems involved and an understanding of the necessity of the attempt. The result is a very particular kind of what the social anthropologist Clifford Geertz calls (borrowing the term from Gilbert Ryle) 'thick description' (see his

'Thick Description: Toward an Interpretive Theory of Culture', in *The Interpretation of Culture*, London, 1975), which is a major extension of the achievements of contemporary fiction.

In *A Smuggler's Bible* there was a character suspiciously like Norman Mailer called Duke Amerchrome, and I need hardly point out just what is being synthesized in that surname. He indulges in a kind of visionary autobiography while mocking at 'self-advertisement' (*sic*) and is given to instant metaphysics which come out in 'foaming formulas'. He says things like 'My mind is America' and mythologizes himself, and David 'half suspected Duke didn't really exist – that he was the product of a concatenation of sounds . . . the product of the liturgy of hearsay, that he was the reputation implicit in his name, that the public world had conspired to assemble him before my eyes but there was no Duke'. McElroy's next novel, *Ancient History* (1971), seems, in part, even more to emerge from an obsession with, or at least an interest in, Norman Mailer, or that type of American public teacher–preacher–social diagnostician who aspires both to be and to make 'history'. The figure in question in the novel is called Dom and is described as 'a prophet in the present in a superland of plans', regarded by many as a 'hero ideologue' and who says things like 'America's an only child'. He engages in 'Americanolysis', makes a tolerably spectacular leap from a window at an institute in Santa Barbara, and is said by a less than sympathetic student to want 'the Nobel Prize for Ubiquity'. But the narrative situation of the novel indicates that McElroy is interested in more than the phenomenon of Mailer.

The first-person narrator describes himself as having slipped into Dom's empty 'living room' shortly after, so we gather, Dom has committed suicide. It is there that he sits furtively writing, not only musing over the possible meanings of Dom's life and death but also considering how those meanings are related to the more modest memories of his family and friends. This secret and somewhat illicit entry into the room parallels the equivocal instinct to penetrate his consciousness, an instinct familiar from McElroy's previous novels. 'I was one of those only children who go into other people's lives.' He regards himself as the 'Unknown Survivor': 'every suicide demands a survivor who foots the loss and breaks or bricks up the code'. He 'fills up' the space left by Dom's death, and it is as though he is constantly drawn to preempting and occupying the private space of others: there is some guilt at this and he even wonders if he did not in some way help to bring about Dom's suicide (used once as a transitive verb – 'Leave your lock off and someone's going to come in and suicide you'). His musings and inscriptions in Dom's 'evacuated' space include the confession that he is indeed 'using' Dom. 'I have used you during what was tonight, Dom,

but in order to dig away at less spectacular puzzles.' I will try to outline
one or two of those puzzles, but in general they concern the geometrics
and physics of relationships, or, as the narrator puts it, 'the anthro-
toponymy of friendship'.

He has the familiar problem of remembering too much; he speaks,
rather nicely, of 'my memory's growing refrigerator' and is indeed
sufficiently avid of detail to keep a file on Brooklyn Heights hors
d'oeuvres! This precipitates the also familiar desire to be capable of a
releasing forgetfulness. 'I wish I could be Forgetorix the First, and leave
behind me a mass of Past.' In his head he is endlessly arranging different
memories in private patterns, or we might say writing, or drawing,
history on his own terms, and he gives an interesting reason for this:

> I must tell what I see for the First Time Ever about my old ancient history: I see
> that whether from an only child's insulation or some other costive formula, I
> was overconfident in fact about the *lack* of bearing all that stuff had upon my
> life: so I could and would in my expatiations blithely abduct from context and
> casually charm contraband into my locus: for I was Utmosis the last.

I am not sure I can do 'Utmosis' unless it indicates the utmost in osmosis (I
find some of McElroy's neologisms keep their secrets, but then he is
clearly more erudite than I am): but 'abduct' and 'contraband' nod
tactfully enough back to the previous two novels and we can see
McElroy is making another imaginative exploration of the, at times,
monstrous collating powers of the memory, this time employed as a
consolation and compensation for a sense of singleness – to fill up the
spaces of solitude.

The narrator uses a special vocabulary in the course of his meditations,
but it can be said that in general he sees the problem as one quite as much
of separations and distances as connections and transitions. He keeps the
memories of his friends Al and Bob separate (as he kept them separate in
his life) and both in turn separate from Dom, even though in a sense of
course they all cohabit in his head. There are possibilities for triangulation here, to go no further into geometric forms, and in fact with this
book we move well into mathematics. He speaks of maintaining
necessary 'equidistances' and attempts to resist what he refers to as the
'hardening of polyconnective tissue in me'. But of course in some ways
everything is 'polyconnected' ('We share life, even our attempts not to'),
so he has to find ways of charting phenomena composed at once of
distance and relationship. Although this leads him into contortions and
distensions of discourse which are at times comical, at times desperate,
and at times just plain insane, he does point to some important problems
– perceptual problems which imply related problems in the writing of
fiction.

The narrator is interested in the application of field theory to what goes on among people and inside the head. He ascribes the source of this interest to Dom, who, however, drew some extreme speculative inferences from it:

> 'Field' as in your 'Neutraline Equatics': a mode that lowers, eases, even coolly ousts ancient hectic hierarchies that set the mass of us or our parts discretely off from each other or from the mass of our setting. Yet my eyes cry out, 'Can all that other life I know about subside into some rankless field and lose its poignant fussy orders?'

In the processes of perception, as in the processes of thinking and writing, there has to be an ordering of data, and to that extent it could be said to be 'hierarchicalized'. In a body there is the distal and the ventral; in space the remote and the proximate; in time there is primacy and recency. A 'rankless field' would simply be an unperceived one. It is a matter of preserving differences without letting these turn into patterns of dominance. In terms of memory it entails, on the narrator's part, an egalitarian respect for the most apparently modest detail – a drenched sneaker, white-knuckled fist – along with the notionally more significant and more public ones – Dom's life and death, while trying to preserve their distinctness even as they tend to conflate within him. He certainly is a fuss, a solipsistic fuss bustling round the furniture in his head, but 'poignant fussy orders' may be said to be the very stuff of life as we see it, write it, live it, and this book gives us a new sense of how this is so, and of some of the fuss and some of the poignancy that it entails.

As a child, the narrator was both learning 'ancient history' and acquiring his own, and for a time the two seemed to be parallel. No longer, though they are still both in his head: 'I know the two histories, one verbatim in the graceful English of Herodotus, the other poly-vectored in my doomed memory.' I will come to vectors in a minute, but it is clear that the book is engaging the phenomenon of different kinds of history somehow existing alongside each other in the mind. 'Para' means 'by the side of, beside', and the subtitle to this novel, 'A Paraphase', implies a phase or phases (of memory, of text, of consciousness, of life?) existing by the side of the more accustomed modes. McElroy wrote about this in 'Neural Neighbourhoods', and I would not think of encroaching on his explanation of his own intentions. In the novel, the narrator, by moving into Dom's room for his own purposes, thinks he has turned it from a site into a para-site (he likes his wordplay), and from there he develops his idea of paraphase, describing 'this night of time that seemed urgent one way when I came in your locked door but now spreads like an inestimably charged field ever, yet, within the coordinates of this room, to a mode like time, but solute – a paraphase'. 'Solute' means dissolved in solution, and you can take it from there. But it is clear that there is some drive toward a new dimension of time or consciousness, or writing. 'I'd hoped that my paraphase would be a break-through. Into the unimpeded field beyond the sway of ordinary light.' I am not very good at new dimensions, so it is not for me to assess the success of this aspiration – in one sense every book is a paraphase, indeed a para-site, if that is how one chooses to think about it. Where the book manifestly is successful is in evoking the intricate and effortful manoeuvres which are involved in the remembering–writing project which is going on. Many suggestive references are made to particular typewriters in the narrator's life; one in particular he was given as a youth which had a back-spacer'. So too has the mind, another kind of type-writer, and it too can go forward into message, and then go back over it. Another equivalent in the object world is the boomerang, one of which is thrown off a bridge in this book, and 'It came *back*! it came *back*!' It is with such pregnant correspondences, homologies, parallels, echoes that McElroy provokes us to rethink the mind.

The language and tone he uses to achieve this vary a great deal. They can certainly have the effect one of the characters says the narrator's words have on him – they 'show up as if before an electric field old images sleeping on the inside of his head: a room filling with salt water, a church filling up with winter boats'. But he has also extended his vocabulary in the quest for new accuracies and exactitudes. Since the narrator (and certainly McElroy) is absorbed in finding ways to plot or chart how people are distributed in changing configurations both through time and in space, he has drawn on terms from mathematics and field theory and physics in general. Thus in addition to more customary terms like 'veerings' and 'velocities', he uses 'valencies', 'vertices', and 'vectors'; there are axes and coordinates, pyramids and parabolas, radial lines and intersections. There are even a couple of diagrams illustrating the relation of locus to focus and directrix and 'parabola as conic section' which seem entirely sound and clear as far as my primitive mathematics can judge. These are not gratuitous importations; McElroy really wants to know what happens in terms of mass and energy when, say, you dive off a board into a pool or when, say, two people move into each other's orbit and fall in love. ('Great distances at which forces in a field occultly but exactly work – aren't they, Dom, like those silences love knows it does not have to fill?') Exact measurements *do* matter, as the narrator insists, and since man is as much a creature of mathematics as he is of metaphor, there is no reason to exclude its terms from the discourse of fiction as if in dread of some gruesome numerological or mensural contamination. I find it refreshing rather than the reverse to come across passages like the following in a work of fiction: 'I was trying to phrase in my head the fresh equation – something about how one coördinated (a) one's field contact with the distal and (b) one's actual contact with the immediate, and I couldn't quite work it into triangulation.' Of course some of this kind of thing has been done before – by Robbe-Grillet, for instance. But McElroy's range of fictional discourse is far wider and his attempt to amplify that discourse with terminologies of exact measurement and field theory rather than substitute one for the other seems to me more interesting. But there are one or two problems.

One is the demon of repetition which seems to haunt McElroy's enormous talents, and the 'fields' and 'vectors' are just too thick on the ground, or rather page. But more centrally there is the matter of the tone of the narrator. There is no doubt that what he is attempting is entirely serious and it represents a real problem and challenge for the writer, any writer, who must realize that no matter what he does, ultimately all the distances and dimensions of our corporeal existence, 'all interruptions and rates of time and spaces of lapse collapse into even script'. Within that inevitable limitation the narrator does achieve some novel chartings. But the tone varies a lot. It can be defensive ('my petty focus'), and comic and ironic ('the vectoral elite, of whom I must have been the sole representative there'). I quite like his 'secret Centrifuge' in which things and ideas are 'subjected to certain separations and simulated gravities', and I do not mind the 'vectoral muscle', which I will not attempt to explain here. We know that he is a lonely, obsessive fuss and can take that as an essential part of the book. Even he suspects that what he is attempting to do might be taking him toward the edge of madness. But at times he sounds like a real maniac. I can just about understand passages like 'how your theory of Welcomed Interruption sprang from your sense that our state is now a Field-State of InterPolyforce Vectors multimplicitly ploding toward Coördinate Availability and away from the hierarchical subordinations of the old tour-de-force anthropols' and so on, though it does not do a lot for me, as Matthew Arnold used to say. And of course it could be a joke on Mailer. But in passages like this – 'In the anthrochron of friendship those are big questions, though in the field of probabilities – which is trying to engross my already smudging parabolas and my dystrophic dialectic of anthronoiacly keeping apart Al and Bob – these misgivings spread into tacit maturity' – I get the feeling that the vocabulary is wagging the man and wagging him into self-parodying incoherence. Which may of course be deliberate, but what then of the seriousness of the undertaking? I have the sense that McElroy had some uncertainties about what he was doing and so makes the narrator periodically undermine his own proceedings (his name, incidentally, is Cy, which may be a wink at cybernetics). Nevertheless, though less magical than the previous two novels, probably because it was deliberately more theoretical and abstract, the book is a remarkably interesting phenomenological novel about a very discernibly American spatial and temporal terrain.

> Whatever else my imagination gropes for, it is neither easily familiar with nor easily insulated from structural steel, violent combustions and printed-circuit electronics. But in fiction – and I don't mean science fiction – how does one write about technology and its relation to people? Perhaps not directly at all, but rather in accord with some virtue of vision to be found in technology.

Thus McElroy in an article called 'Holding with Apollo 17'. Before commenting on this aspect of his imagination let me quote from a different kind of book:

> work nowadays is never done by men, nor is it done by machines, it is always done by man–machine systems . . . and interface is an imaginary plane across which information and power are exchanged. In the case of the man–machine interface, the exchange is predominantly of information . . . The dynamic problem of interface design is the problem of fitting together these two systems, human and hardware, one obeying the principles of biology and the other the principles of physics.   (*Man–Machine Systems*, W. T. Singleton)

And this:

> As the gap between man and machines has narrowed – not by degrading man, let me repeat, but by enriching our conception of a machine – the question (i.e. what is the relation between men and machines) has moved from the philosopher's study through the scientist's laboratory and the industrialist's factory and on to the desks of our national planners.
>
> ('Computers, Communication, and Cognition', George A. Miller)

And on to McElroy's desk too. We have for too long allowed ourselves to be terrorized by technology; we have romanticized it, vilified it, reified it, demonized it; we have found various ways of bracketing it out of what we think of as the truly human part of our lives. One of the most interesting and important aspects of McElroy's work is his growing attempt to demystify that man–machine relationship which, in fact, pervades our lives in every conceivable way. He is against the 'liberal–intellectual bias against the manned-space programme', for instance, and in a number of short pieces concerning that programme he outlined the necessity to see the NASA systems in their own terms and not through older rhetorics which give ontological priority to the privileged Self. This does not involve a capitulation to technology with gasps of wonder but rather 'lucid attention': what are there to be seen are 'exact and explicable mazes of sequence so finished in their power that their even beauty transcends conflict and perhaps transvalues boredom'. At the moon-launch, 'everywhere measurement and vista conjoin', and McElroy carefully surveys what he describes as 'a non-narrative field of collaborative functions'. Elsewhere ('The Skylab Cluster') he wrote, 'At NASA, a mystery tends to contain itself in operational problems', and again he urges a new kind of attention: 'contemplate the crystal as an emblem of the kind of attention I am urging: for crystallinity is the extent to which the outward and visible form of this solid has been controlled by its atomic structure. Let true imagination grow from truth.' This seems to be admirable, and McElroy's interest in man–machine systems and interfaces, like his interest in phenomenology and physics, architecture and engineering (the pyramids, Stonehenge, Chartres, Brooklyn Bridge, Clifton suspension bridge, the Vehicle Assembly Building at Cape Kennedy),[1] so far from being distinct from his interest in fiction, actively nourish it in ways which I think are necessary if contemporary fiction is to be fully 'operative' in the world today, just as I think it is as important for the literary critic to read, say, Gregory Bateson's papers collected in *Steps to an Ecology of Mind*, or the papers from *Scientific American* collected in *Perception: Mechanisms and Models*, as it is for him to read the latest theoretical work from Paris.

There is one aspect of McElroy's interest in the spacecraft which I think is worth noting because it may be influencing the way his fiction is going or will go. He ends the essay on 'Holding with Apollo 17' with the reflection that the physical details of the project (i.e. special considerations for the astronaut's body) may be necessary 'in order quite possibly to translate us toward forms more cerebral. Not necessarily a good thing, by our old standards. But the next thing.' And he returns to a related speculation in 'The Skylab Cluster' when he writes that 'its studies in weightlessness . . . may help to show us some way toward longer journeys'. There is in McElroy's work a perceptible reaching for, journeying toward, 'forms more cerebral', a condition of 'weightlessness' more metaphorical and psychological as yet but perhaps presaging other modes of experiencing. 'The next thing'.

But McElroy is a novelist, not a science correspondent, and he wants 'story'. It might be thought that science fiction would be the obvious genre, but, he writes, 'the trouble I've often had with science fiction was the fiction not the science. I could more often accept the story's future-facts than find in its human or non-human lives a clear reality (however fabulous) to match the mad clarity of hardware.' Nor can you simply 'technologize' narrative, so there is the problem of what kind of story to tell and how to tell it. Here is a clue to McElroy's sense of his position

---

[1] In an article on 'The Art of John Willenbecher' (*Art International*, 20 March 1975), McElroy wrote, 'words come to me in a pressure ready to try the capillaries of the structure', and the statement could be extended out of that specific context and applied to many other structures as well. The article, incidentally, also reveals McElroy's fascination with all kinds of shapes and 'relations among shapes'. Thus, on Willenbecher's labyrinths: 'The real action is in the movement that inheres in relations. While the mind's eye works along the ruled paths, it also slides more freely back and forth through boundaries as if the maze were of two minds. The mind's eye here feels shapes change, feels change as shape, and even for instants of shifting speculation feels shape as energy and shape as change.' These words could be applied fairly exactly to the experience of the central figure of *Lookout Cartridge*.

from an article which appeared as 'Growing Up Embooked' (not, I gather, his own title):

> Since in the grown up novels I write I have tended to fracture or submerge the storyline, I am all the more haunted by stories I love. They have a speed and wholeness, and they effortlessly obscure the question of just what it is in us that makes us want stories. Whatever it is, and whatever effect it may be having on me right now, as I try to move my characteristic mazes of reflection and modern discontinuity back toward some mode of heart-gripping mystery-thriller, it is a need that my child and I share.

That 'mystery-thriller' was to be *Lookout Cartridge*, but before coming to that novel, let me briefly glance at one or two of the stories he loves.

Of course he admires Nabokov, as he has stated more than once; as clearly, and also self-confessedly, he found aspects of Butor's work of use to him (Butor, incidentally, finds Nabokov's work of no interest). But I want to fasten on three works which he himself singled out as giving him special pleasure (in 'Neural Neighbourhoods'). He 'loved the patterns' in Isak Dinesen's 'The Roads Round Pisa'. I will not summarize here the strange encounters and characters and coincidences that make up the somewhat hallucinatory adventures of Count Augustus von Schimmelmann, but simply note his reaction to finding himself involved in all these mysterious incidents. 'With the happy wonder of a searcher for gold who strikes a vein of the metal in the rock, he reflected that he had come upon a *vein of events* in his life' (my italics). Certainly everyone and everything seem both stylized and bizarre as though acting out some kind of marionette comedy, but, thinks the previously accidic Count, 'if I have now, at last, come into a marionette play, I will not go out of it again'. The hunger to be in some way involved in sheer eventfulness is a need and desire which clearly interests McElroy and influences the kind of narrative he writes. Italo Calvino's wonderful *Invisible Cities* is another of his favourites, with those marvellous descriptions of fantasy cities which keep giving one new glimpses and senses of one's own experience of city-ness. (E.g. Tamara: 'Your gaze scans the streets as if they were written pages; the city says everything you must think, makes you repeat her discourse, and while you believe you are visiting Tamara you are only recording the names with which she defines herself and all her parts. However the city may really be, beneath the thick coating of signs, whatever it may contain or conceal, you leave Tamara without having discovered it.') For a writer as interested in the city as McElroy, the following words would clearly attract his attention. 'With cities, it is as with dreams: everything imaginable can be dreamed, but even the most unexpected dream is a rebus that conceals a desire or, its reverse, a fear. Cities, like dreams, are made up of desires and fears, even if the thread of their discourse is secret, their rules are absurd, their perspectives deceitful, and everything conceals something else.' The city as rebus is, I think, a notion which would appeal to McElroy. There is also the cartographic consideration of how one can or should 'map' a city. For instance, Esmeralda is made up of networks of canals and streets on different levels so that 'the most fixed and calm lives in Esmeralda are spent without any repetition', since there is always a new way of getting from one point to another. 'A map of Esmeralda should include, marked in different colored inks, all these routes, solid and liquid, evident and hidden.' How do you 'tell' a city, as Marco Polo in his book tries to tell all the fantastic cities he has seen to his employer, Kublai Khan? As he says of Zaira, he could count the steps and give the degree of the arcades' curves and so on, 'but I already know this would be the same as telling you nothing. The city does not consist of this, but of the relationships between the measurements of its spaces and the events of its past'. Telling the city requires a new kind of mapping involving measured relationship between spaces and events. Fiction as a kind of new cartography – and indeed cartography as a kind of fiction – are clearly important considerations for McElroy. (For more details of what he likes in Calvino's work, see McElroy's own review in the *New York Times* of 17 November 1974.)

Perhaps most revealing is his comment that 'my favourite work of fiction might be Kleist's novella *Michael Kohlhaas*', in which, in McElroy's words, 'the simplest chain of momentums shifts one small degree into another track entirely, in which the energy released by the determined rebel expands geometrically and his chosen power joins larger collaborative powers not his own'. It is indeed an amazing work about a man who, in seeking redress for one local injustice, sets into motion a train of events which rapidly involves an increasing area of Europe and more and more august and powerful personages until at last his case becomes a concern of the Holy Roman Empire, to be commented on by Luther and ruled on by the Emperor. Michael Kohlhaas is an exemplary citizen who yet brings turmoil to medieval Europe: 'posterity would have had cause to bless his memory, had not one of his virtues led him into excesses. For it was his strong sense of justice that made of him a robber and a murderer.' It is as if he is a small locus of energy applying itself in entirely prescribed and convention-governed ways, which is suddenly given a shove in a different direction and proceeds to disrupt the increasingly complex hierarchy of power systems which make up the society of the time. After that initial shove – the gratuitous insulting act of injustice by a local aristocrat – it is as if nothing and no one can really control the ramifying events precipitated by that displaced energy. This, if you like, is history as physics in a fictional mode, and it comes very close, I think, to what McElroy was

trying to do in his next novel. Here is a comment on Kleist's novella by
John Gearey:

> By the middle of the action, the background has become the foreground. The
> sheer number of persons and interests threatens to overwhelm the essential issue
> with extraneous concerns. That, however, is also a point the story wished to
> make. History, with its burden of detail, its necessary bureaucracy of events,
> rather than hampering Kleist in the development of his initial idea, actually
> seems to have helped educate him to its ramifications, and rather than working
> against him in the genre he had chosen to express the idea, extended the scope
> of the genre itself. Yet this abundance of persons and motives is significantly
> confined to limits, for the resulting concentration, or density, of action in the
> objective world is the very thing against which the hero struggles.

The lure of eventfulness, the city as rebus, history as physics – these three
aspects of just a selection of the fiction McElroy particularly likes point us
nicely toward his next novel, *Lookout Cartridge* (1974).

The novel opens with an explosion in New York seen from a
helicopter which will be given explanatory context only in the
concluding pages of the book. The narrator, Cartwright, then ponders
the question 'Was there a beginning?' and reverts to an incident when he
received a violent blow in the back which pushed him down an escalator
that happened not to be working. Whatever degree of malign intention
there may have been in the thrust, it sets Cartwright into an uncertain
precipitous movement, half falling but managing to turn that motion
into a kind of volitional striding more under his control, which in fact
adumbrates his movement throughout all the fields, patterns, sequences
of events which ensue. Another shoved Michael Kohlhaas is on the
move.

This alerts us to the problematical origins of momentum, which are
not only linked to the no less problematical origins of narrative but to the
larger question of who initiates action and who suffers it – or how can
you tell the victim from the aggressor? Cartwright returns to the
incident on the escalator about halfway through the book.

> Yet when I began this story did I think this momentum mine? I think I did. But
> it was my pusher's first, then mine, which I see now is like what I, if not . . .
> Dagger, saw us doing in the film, taking other energy in process and using it for
> our own peaceful ends. But was not the end there that of my pusher? . . . I saw
> that the pusher had pushed me because I must have in some way pushed him
> . . . I saw that the way to survive the pusher's push was to use its force to move
> on.

These somewhat Newtonian speculations are absolutely central to the
drive of the novel, which is concerned with energy and thrust – physical,
interpersonal, political, narrational – of all kinds. Cartwright and his
friend Dagger have made a film, and unknown people for unclear

reasons want the film destroyed, Cartwright's diary of the film destroyed, and quite possibly Cartwright himself destroyed. Hence that initial mysterious push. From that moment Cartwright wants to find out who and why, and this produces the 'mystery-thriller' McElroy had said he was moving toward, for it transpires that, as Cartwright only half-speculatively put it, 'I said I had been launched down a dead escalator as part of an international power struggle.' But, being by McElroy, it is a mystery-thriller in a new mode, and to give some sense of this mode I want to quote, apparently inconsequentially, from quite another realm of the book. It concerns the Yiddish word *shtip*.

> For my *shtip* exemplifies the multiple and parallel sorties which raise our brain above the digital computer to which it is akin; the digital computer works its yes and no operations faster than the brain yet is confined to serial single-file-one-quest-at-a-time circuit-seeking; but the human natural Body Brain . . . sends countless of these single files not one at a time but all at once circulating down the deltas, through the gorges and moving targets and (like parties of Indians – Brooklyn, Hindu, Maya, Hollywood or, as the English call the American, *Red*) athwart the axes of all pulsing fields.

Shtip, explains a character shortly after, 'means first of all a push', and Cartwright's shtip is his 'sense of other people's lives' which leads him to make 'multiple and parallel sorties' into an increasingly complex network of people of all kinds in many countries, just as his 'Body Brain' can make multiple mental sorties. Internally and externally this drives him 'athwart the axes of all pulsing fields', just as charting this multiple motion takes McElroy's style athwart ('transversely . . . in an oblique direction', *OED*) a wide variety of differing discourses. That's *his* shtip, and very original fictional results it produces.

If the book is precipitated by push, it is organized around catch – in particular a specific catch, just as there was a specific push. When Cartwright was a boy in Brooklyn, his friend Ned threw an autographed baseball from the street up to his fourth-floor apartment as a gift. Cartwright leaned out dangerously far and caught it and 'it came to rest in a moment of equality that I'll never forget'. Some kind of energy was 'transferred' to him in 'my act of snatching the ball at its interval between thrust and fall'. It gave him a sense of 'having sluiced between gravities'; also 'Ned had acted, and the act had a velocity greater than any memory of its origin.' The intermittent sensation of 'free-floating between gravities' recurs to Cartwright and would seem to produce that sense of weightlessness mentioned earlier, a feeling of perfect poise in that infinitesimal 'interval between thrust and fall' which gives the sensation of having momentarily transcended gravity, or of having found some magical space in between all thrusting and falling, from where he can see everything and suffer nothing. Any mystery-thriller is concerned with thrusters and fallers, usually at a very basic level. It is a mark of McElroy's originality that he can see the isomorphic relations between the familiar shovings and tumblings of conventional conspiracies and killings, and the physics of being pushed down some stairs or of catching a ball, and make us experience these relationships in a new and exciting way. For they *are* related, and eventually Cartwright does 'catch' those who tried to 'push' him and who stole his film. To catch a thief. To catch a ball.

From the start he feels that he has been 'inserted into a situation', as, presumably, one inserts a cartridge into some kind of chamber in a system. The question then becomes what kind of chamber or vacancy or slot (and McElroy seems obsessed with slots of every kind), in what kind of system, has he been inserted into? He tends to assess or experience things in terms of distances and encroachments and either introduces his 'motion into a field' or feels involved in greater powers around him ('we are in the grip of forces – but also of their absence'). At the beginning things happen to him: as the action progresses he 'makes things happen'. From 'looping inside someone else's plan' and being 'in someone else's system' (that prevailing feeling in contemporary American fiction), he moves toward a kind of autonomy and, sometimes simply by unpremeditated plunges in unexpected directions, or uncalculated interventions and interruptions in other circuits of activity, a feeling of godlike power. He is some as yet not fully stated message in a complex code; he knows that he has his 'place in a multiple system' and moves 'between blind coghood and that sinister hint of godhead or godbody in me issuing from my place in a field of multiple impingements'. Sometimes he feels he has achieved, or inserted himself into, some new kind of space in which he feels 'weightless in a giant wheeling field where distance and duration decay into fresh equation'.

As I mentioned earlier, that move toward a kind of new dimension in which a state of weightlessness is experienced is discernible throughout McElroy's fiction, which is perhaps his own distinct version of that aspiration to get beyond all systems that is also a profoundly American yearning. At the same time, or by instant oscillation, the god recalls his coghood. 'I had once more in recent days found myself poised weightlessly mighty like a god, held in a field of my own generation or finding, in a space between impingements of other fields like the short moment between forces when I snatched the autographed ball flung up by Ned' – which immediately yields to 'Yet no: . . . Fields impinge. You must build yourself into the life around you.' But the sense of, and desire for, that mysterious privileged space recurs (as in McElroy's other books, it is potentially damaging to the protagonist's family life), and to inquire into it a bit more curiously, I want to fasten on the word 'between'.

Cartwright himself constantly uses the word as he moves between different countries: 'I was between two groups and two languages'; 'I was between many people in many directions'; and so on. Understandably it seems to take on a kind of nontopographical existence of its own so that there are intimations of what we might call prepositional or adverbial space, and Cartwright feels he has, at times, 'inserted himself into a dimensionless place Between', and from another quarter there are expatiations on 'the age-old mystic In-Between carved like a moat of insulation . . . to guard a Jewish self prior to actual territory'. The book explores this curious psychic state of feeling somehow both prior to territory and beyond topography with great imagination and originality. And it is discovered to be far from unequivocal sensation. 'Unfortunately, to be between does not necessitate being constantly connected with what one is between.' So, disconnection through displacement. But worse – 'There are times when your sense of being between here and there, between people, between one thing and another, fades not even into absurdity but into something else, death or revelation, more likely death, as you sense that whatever they are (whom you are or were between), they are not near after all, not holding, don't know you, or just don't know.' It is one of the exciting aspects of McElroy's prose that in addition to moving toward some form of 'ultimate topography' – and the vivid evocation of differing terrains, American, English, Scottish, Corsican, Welsh, is one of the most notable features of the book – it reaches out to explore states of moated consciousness in which the sense of place (and other people) begins to fade altogether. Among other things, what this involves is a kind of liquefaction of consciousness in which boundaries – the very condition of all our organizings of experience of every kind – lose their stability. As in a moment in the helicopter, when

> Lower Manhattan bulges, or bulges in some inflationary sign to me that weightlessness may make those canals come unplugged and Terminus the god of boundaries and property may be subject to mercurial delusions because of insecurity arising from the fact that his post was created to take some of the work-load and even responsibility off Jupiter's back but the liquid stir of that city aggregate there below may be my post Terminal sense that I'm at the center but overcommitted and underconnected.

The canals, I think, refer to the intricate structurings of the ear which 'compute my balance' and which he has been describing in detail with characteristic respect and accuracy, and we may say that McElroy, himself a master if not quite a god of boundaries at times, reaches for (and achieves) a post-terminal style which is unique in contemporary fiction.

I use the term 'reaches for' advisedly because of a curious recurring image in the book which offers, I think, an unusual insight into what McElroy is doing. Two quotations, one from the beginning, the other near the end:

> I have in my head things I may not have exactly seen, just as you who read this have me. A hand enters a lab's glass wall through large elastic lips seeking a glove port. You have seen this, don't think you haven't. Once the hand is into the sleeve it feels its way into a thick lightweight glove in order to get at pieces of who knows what on the other side of the glass – cans of bacteria, say.

And

> . . . even if mine had been a gloved hand at last programming its way through a deep transparent wall to handle dangerously contaminated substances much less administer justice, bring peace, or transform my own oscillations into something more fixed (that would nonetheless then demand motion in the observer to be understood), I would still feel short of that direct current I had envisioned if not dreamed of.

The image is repeated in at least seven other contexts with variations – Cartwright reaching for things he does not know he knew, for substances he cannot identify, into situations dangerous but unclear, with occasional intimations that the gloves might come off though it would seem that such unmediated contact is not really possible (perhaps that is the 'direct current' he had envisioned). The book has much to say about filming and the camera, but 'the camera is like a pure glove reaching untouching to the thing it takes'. We reach to touch and thus in a sense to 'have' (see, know, remember – any number of nontactile modes of appropriation and possession), as Cartwright finally has both his information and his would-be killers through action, McElroy has his material for his fiction through writing, and we – he keeps reminding us – have him through reading. And, he implies, we all 'have' much more than we think we have, both outside and inside. Reach around and see.

The reaching hand introduces itself into another environment or field. This relates it to a cartridge which, as Cartwright explains to an old man in a record shop, is like a cassette inasmuch as 'you inserted both into solid state systems'. (It is nice that cartridge comes from cartouche and thence *carta*-paper.) Cartwright is 'a lookout between forces' but a lookout on the move. 'A lookout stays in one place. But what of a moving lookout with a stationary trust?' He also has a 'lookout dream', and this of course is connected with his sense of moving in the realm of In-Between. But he is a lookout cartridge and this poses one of the problems the novel explores. 'Cartridges stayed hard when out of touch with other cartridges but when in touch opened and shifted.' Thus Cart-Wright is a soft cartridge (*cf.* wet computer), or rather he alternates between being hard and soft, so that the lookout cartridge swells and contracts, 'narrows from the walls of its slot' but 'enlarges too so that that which lies between, crowds that between which it lies'. This double sensation has been explored before by McElroy, and it is, I think, related to a basic tension between a drive toward a pure (weightless) monadic ocular relationship to the world, and a consciousness of, and conscience for, not only the

unavoidable impingements of everyday life but in particular the trusts
and loyalties and reciprocities entailed by the family. You may say that
this is an old subject but that is nothing to the point. What matters is that
McElroy has reexplored and revivified this tension in terms of modern
life, computers, cartridges, cameras, and all. Cartridges also go off and, as
I said, the book starts with a detonation. (I do not know if any allusion, or
debt, to Julio Cortázar's story 'Blow-up' was intended, but there are
certain similarities in the idea of a camera registering potentially
disturbing or dangerous phenomena – and hence information – which
the cameraman neither knew nor intended to catch. Add the explosion
and 'blow-up' is a very appropriate pun.)

Cartwright's film – the one he *intended* – was to be about power:
'Power shown being acquired from sources where it had momentum but
not clarity'. It has no specific political context, though it may be about
revolution or at least it could be 'lurking on the margins of some
unstable, implicit ground that might well shiver into revolution'. It
consists of a number of different, apparently quite random episodes or
partial episodes, taken in various countries. It has a theme of displacement
which is also its technique, since it decontextualizes the episodes from
their setting and shifts from one to the other – at least that was the idea. It
was also going to appear to be a 'documentary daydream' which would
nevertheless indirectly 'express some two decades of America': it would
show 'America and England in some dream of action and peace', but
'through all the scenes mingling England and America and deliberately
unplacing the scenes, there was a cool theme of America itself'. Of course
there are other possible films on the film – it depends on what you are
looking to see, and this triggers the plot. All this allows the use of the
vocabulary of filming, speeding, splicing, looping, zooming, montage
(linkage and collision), etc., which McElroy freely avails himself of, just
as he draws extensively on computer terminology (once again quite
excessively, and so repetitiously as to weaken some of his effects).
Chapter titles can be 'Printed Circuit Cut-In Flash-Forward', or
'Vacuum Insert', or 'Slot Insert'. ('Witness a different cartridge: not a
thing solidly instated in a slot, rather a slot inserted in a thing .' Think
about that.) It may sound somewhat reminiscent of, say, Burroughs or
Pynchon, but McElroy makes unmistakably original use of it, and it is all
part of a wide range of interests which really do operate within the
ongoing thrust of the narrative quite dazzlingly. And he does not just
dump (insert) chunks of data from disparate areas of study and
technology into his book. His concerns are interrelated whether he is
comparing Mayan calendars to analogue computers, examining ord-
nance survey maps and Mercator projections, considering the 'strangely
intentional arrangements' of the Standing Stones of Callanish ('It was all

meant. No question there . . . Meant, however, by who knew what overlapping desires?') and at Stonehenge (is it a 'message' or does it mean 'simply the distance and the work in moving those stones'?), or engrossed in the strange processes which occur in the forming of peat.

I think the narrative sometimes loses itself in its own entanglements and I gave up trying to differentiate a number of minor characters with eccentric names. Also I found the book unnecessarily long. (*Gravity's Rainbow*, say, is necessarily long, but McElroy endangers his marvellous achievements with repetition and thus, I am sure, restricts his readership; the long book and the plight of the modern reader is a topic I would like to say more about another time.) But all the fields of multiple impingements are held together in the book, not in a static unity but in a series of changing moving constellations. There is an abiding interest in 'power in process' and how people tie into other people's energies in every conceivable way – not registered with the melodrama of vampirism but with more of the measured accuracy of physics: and behind it all there is that basic concern with the relationship between narration and family. ('I wanted to take home a tale to my family they could understand. But it might be too late. They were dispersed.') And through it all – 'a cool theme of America itself'.

This has been simply an introductory consideration of some aspects of the work of Joseph McElroy, which should be far, far better known than it is. Eulogistic epithets tendered by critics are not particularly necessary, but more readers are. For McElroy is a very important writer working with extraordinary energy and imagination right at the very boundaries of contemporary fiction; indeed, he is redrawing some of those boundaries, and at times going beyond them – post-Terminal.

12

Frames and sentences

A story first – from a newspaper. In connection with the Pope's planned visit to England in 1982 the Royal Mint produced 'an object called a plaque in precious metals which features medallions of Her Majesty and His Holiness vis-a-vis'. The then Protestant Conservative MP, Enoch Powell – whatever else, a formidable intellectual and forensic logician – did not like the look of this at all. He wrote: 'The political overtones of the Royal Mint striking a medal in commemoration of a papal visit of the United Kingdom, bearing Her Majesty's effigy at all, let alone in conjunction with the papal effigy, are obvious. Whose then is the responsibility?' He went on to record how he tried to find precisely whose responsibility it was to give 'permission to use representations' of the Sovereign: tracking this responsibility to its source proved to be curiously difficult. Chancellor of the Exchequer? He denied responsibility. Try the Lord Chamberlain; he referred him to the 'Comptroller', whoever that Dickensian figure may be. He was directed to the Exchequer for the Royal Mint – well, he said, if he got clearance, it was 'no concern of mine on what, and for what purposes and in what context that effigy (representation) is used'. Enoch Powell is surely right in asserting that 'a politically charged decision' had been taken, and I take it as something of a parable that he could not finally trace the power which issues the 'permission to use representations' to its source. The story concerns only representation of the Queen – the primary site of Majesty, symbol of the highest power. But the story raises directly or by implication far-reaching questions. Who or what has the power to issue – or withhold – the 'permission to use representations' in general, not just of the Queen but of any of her subjects – or indeed, any 'subject' at all? And the answer seems to be that nobody, quite, seems to know. Yet Powell is right. The question of what may or may not be 'represented',

238

and in what context, is always potentially a political question. I am not
thinking now of manifest attempts at censorship – the legal difficulties of
Joyce or Lawrence etc. I am, rather, suggesting that now when we perhaps
think that anything can be written, anything can be represented, with no
politics or law or power involved, we might do well to recall that
something, somewhere – no matter how subtly – is always impeding or
encouraging, prohibiting or facilitating, what may or may not be
'represented'. Though who or what forbids or permits representations
may be as hard to discover as Enoch Powell found out. Or harder.

I now want to move to a quotation from Derrida, from his long essay
'Living On: Border Lines'. The essay concerns Blanchot, but contains the
following generalization. 'The narratorial voice is the voice of a subject
recounting something, remembering an event or a historical sequence,
knowing who he is, where he is, and what he is talking about. It responds
to some police, a force of order or law . . . In this sense, all organised
narration is "a matter for the police".' Now what can that mean? It
would seem to imply that any 'organized' narrative is in effect
responding to a tacit interrogation – who? what? when? how? why? etc.
That is – narrative in the traditional sense is always acting under the law.
We might question at what point an 'organized' narrative gives way to a
dis-organized one, a question of some moment for post-modern fiction.
And what about a book like *Tristram Shandy*: it certainly has its own kind
of organization – is that a matter for the police? However, Derrida's
point is related to a more general concern with what he calls 'the
problematic of judicial framing and the jurisdiction of frames'. The
implication is that most of us are, at one level or another, 'framed'. It is
perhaps no accident that in English the word 'frame' can refer both to the
apparently neutral activity of supplying some kind of line of demarcation (as in framing a picture), and the less innocent activity (which may
be judicial or criminal) of arranging things so that someone appears in a
false and imprisoning position or context, as in a 'frame-up'. Partridge
also gives as a definition for the slang use of 'frame', 'to effect a
prearranged conspiracy'. Some of Derrida's statements would seem to
imply that to varying extents we are all 'framed' in this less innocent sense
– i.e. held in a false position beyond our control, whether as writers,
readers, or citizens ('subjects', as we say in England). But who or what is
policing us or 'framing' us? Not the Lord Chamberlain or the Chancellor
of the Exchequer – as Enoch Powell found out. Perhaps we could say
'the Law', though beyond certain clear interdictions, that can be as
difficult to locate both in its sources and its operations as Kafka so
comically and terribly demonstrated. Another answer might simply be
'language' – not this or that discourse, but language itself. A well-known
extreme example of this proposition may of course be found in *Leçon* by

Barthes in which he writes: 'Mais la langue, comme performance de tout langage, n'est ni réactionnaire, ni progressiste; elle est tout simplement: fasciste; car le fascisme, ce n'est pas empêcher de dire, c'est d'obliger à dire.' A less extreme version of this position may be found in Heidegger: 'Man acts as though he were the shaper and master of language, while in fact language remains the master of man. When this relation of dominance gets inverted, man hits upon strange manœuvres. Language becomes the means for expression . . .' The important point to note is that Heidegger envisages possible situations in which 'this relation of dominance gets inverted'. Man starts to speak instead of being spoken. Perhaps the 'fascism of language' can be resisted. Perhaps 'expression' can overcome, bypass or dismiss the 'police'. Let me remind you of Barthelme's story 'And then'. It starts: 'The part of the story that came next was suddenly missing, I couldn't think of it, so I went into the next room . . .' As he tries to think up the next part of his narrative, the room starts to fill up with policemen – I wondered 'what kind of "and then" I could contrive which might satisfy all the particulars of the case . . . and rid me of these others, in their uniforms.' By sufficiently twisting the narrative he manages to ' "open up" the situation successfully'. Such attempts to 'open up' the situation, get rid of the police, and let in new narrative possibilities we might take to be symptomatic of a post-modern aspiration; as we might the apparent 'moral' of the story. 'Goals incapable of attainment have driven many a man to despair, but despair is easier to get than that – one need merely look out of the window . . . But what we are trying to do is to get away from despair and over to ease and bliss, and that can never be attained with three policemen, with bicycles, standing alertly in our other room.'

All this may involve exploding known modes of representation, or twisting them in new ways. In this connection I want to quote again from Barthes, this time from 'Diderot, Brecht, Einstein', where he makes an important assertion which supplements what he wrote in 'L'Effet de Réel'. 'Representation is not defined directly by imitation: even if one gets rid of notions of the "real", of the "vraisemblable", of the "copy", there will still be representation for so long as a subject (author, reader, spectator or voyeur) casts his *gaze* towards a horizon on which he cuts out the base of a triangle, his eye (or his mind) forming the apex.' We note the reference to the crucial position of the subject, who, as a homogenizing element, acts as the essential guarantee of the 'representational' space he commands. To the extent that the subject is de-composed, so will that fixed representational space – or space of representation – also be de-composed. And indeed this has happened in a lot of recent fiction – mimetic expectations are often frustrated or assaulted; the author's voice seems to have lost its authority, and it sometimes becomes impossible to answer the questions, who is speaking, who is telling, who is seeing? We might also add that it can also become difficult to answer the question, who is reading? The 'destruction', decomposition, or simply the discomposure of the reader is manifestly the aim of a good deal of recent fiction. In the words of the greatly underrated Don DeLillo: 'There's a whole class of writers who don't want their books to be read. This to some extent explains their crazed prose . . . What you want to express is the violence of your desire not to be read . . . If you're in this class, what you have to do is either not publish or make absolutely sure your work leaves readers strewn along the margins.' One danger of course is that in 'destroying' the reader, the author may go some way to destroying his own text. You can perhaps erase the reader by profferring an 'unreadable' text – but what then? An example – *JR*, by William Gaddis. It is a book (by a major author) which almost wilfully defies reading. It goes out of its way to make no concessions to the reader – no breaks, pauses, chapter divisions, no marked differentiation of character or scene. Just before the end of the novel a composer (Bast) is talking to a writer about their work in general: 'I mean until a performer hears what I hear and can make other people hear what he hears its just trash isn't it Mister Eigen, its just trash . . .' What Bast is saying is that until an artist finds a listener/reader, his work does not preserve its intrinsic value in lordly unappreciated solitude but may be just another form of – trash. Gaddis ends the book with a characteristic joke. I take it to be a fragment of a phone call or tape of JR's voice as it forges ahead into new commercial possibilities: 'So I mean listen I got this neat idea hey, you listening? Hey? You listening . . .?' At this point no one is listening to JR and it is a question how many readers are still listening to Gaddis. And if he has lost (destroyed) his readers, must he then in a gesture of perverse self-mortification classify his own work as trash? Trash it most certainly is not. But a problem begins to define itself. There is a kind of narrative which works under the Law. It answers all the tacit questions of the 'police'. But what if you avoid the Law, utterly defy the 'police'? Can the result only be unreadable, inscrutable, un-interrogatable? What can there be between the Law – and trash? (Or the too-readable and the unreadable.) Does it have to be a matter for the police or for the dustbin?

Of course not, though, as I intimated, I think that the line between an 'organized' narrative and a dis-organized – or anti-organized – narrative is now hard to draw. The 'police' must be finding it increasingly difficult to decide which narration is or is not 'a matter' for them. But to return to the frame. Of course in one sense novelists have always 'framed' their characters, not just by putting them in a book, but within the book itself.

Take that incomparable moment in *The Wings of the Dove* when Milly Theale is shown the portrait by Bronzino at Matcham by Lord Mark. She looks at the portrait through helpless inexplicable tears.

> Perhaps it was her tears that made it just then so strange and fair – as wonderful as he had said; the face of a young woman, all magnificently drawn down to the hands, and magnificently dressed; a face almost livid in hue, yet handsome in sadness and crowned with a mass of hair rolled back and high, that must, before fading with time, have had a family resemblance to her own. The lady in question, at all events, with her slightly Michaelangesque squareness, her eyes of other days, her full lips, her long neck, her recorded jewels, her brocaded and wasted reds, was a very great personage – only unaccompanied by a joy. And she was dead, dead, dead. Milly recognized her in words which had nothing to do with her. 'I shall never be better than this.'

Milly in the novel is indeed 'framed' by London society – used and placed this way and that, subject of a 'pre-arranged conspiracy'. Here she has what is almost an epiphanic vision of her own situation – beautiful, framed, unaccompanied by a joy, and – prospectively – dead, dead, dead. That, she sees, is the 'sentence' which has been pronounced upon her. She experiences to the full the extreme possible pathos of being 'framed'. Milly, then, is doubly 'framed'. Why do I make this point? Writers have indeed always known about frames – and 'breaking frame' is as old as the novel. What I think we have seen in a lot of what is called post-modern fiction is an attempt to submerge the frame, to call in question the lines of demarcation, to render problematical what is, as it were, inside a text and what is outside it: edges, borders, limits, frames, have been in various ways questioned, redrawn, undermined – un-privileged or re-assessed. Think, for example, of John Barth's festive playing around with framework, endless recessions of 'frame tales'; or of some of Robert Coover's fictions exploring the origins, limits, terminations of narrative; or of Pynchon's central concern with the power of film to 'frame' reality, producing 'paracinematic' lives and 'movie children' so that Poirier can rightly say of *Gravity's Rainbow*, 'everybody is to some extent framed' and the only escape from this condition seems to be by death – e.g. John Dillinger – or diffusion and dispersal – e.g. Slothrop (see in this connection Erving Goffman's work on 'frame analysis', which in large part confessedly arises from a major article by Gregory Bateson entitled 'A Theory of Play and Fantasy'). Sometimes we no longer know how to read what we read. It is, to all intents and purposes, 'unframed'. And so, by the same token, are we. It can be liberty. It can mean confusion. The 'police' may leave us alone, but we may be radically dis-orientated – or just non-orientated.

　　If 'frame' is one word which is both neutral yet potentially 'loaded', so is 'sentence'. Yes, a sentence is a sentence – capital letter to full stop. But it is also what a judge metes out in court. *Sententia* can mean both a statement and a verdict. An example where both senses are crucially present comes in *The Prelude*, Book XI (1194–5), in which Wordsworth, in a rather low mood, thinks that all the old great poets are done with – superseded. 'Their sentence was, I thought, pronounced: their rights / Seem'd mortal, and their empire pass'd away.' There it is: yes, their sentence(s) have indeed been pronounced, on stage, in books, whatever. They have uttered and been heard to utter. But also – judgement has been passed on them. The two processes seem curiously indistinguishable. As a writer is 'pronouncing his sentence' so, in some way, sentence is being pronounced on him. To make a 'statement' is to invite, inevitably, a 'verdict'. If I want to focus some attention on frames and sentences it is partly because I think there has been too much emphasis on a struggle or opposition between referentiality and reflexivity – referentiality, so the notion goes, involves using words to refer to things and is, in the event, more representational, more in touch with history and politics, more 'realistic', and thus more humane. Reflexive writing is often regarded as 'aesthetic', mandarin, too self-regarding, too concerned with language and a display of its own devices. And thus less humane. This seems to me something of a false and arid antinomy. All words are referential – they refer to concepts. If we wanted apparently constant referentiality and conventional representation, we could hardly do better than go to the newspapers. I am really saying that I am not too interested in discussions of differing degrees of referentiality – they invariably become pseudo-moral or pseudo-political arguments and you can end up with the crude if honest polemics of a John Gardner, or the more sophisticated, somewhat priestly and sententious reproaches of a Gerald Graff. Walter Abish's impressive book, *How German Is It*, is manifestly concerned with Nazi Germany and – among other things, what does 'it' matter to our contemporary state of mind ultimately – the different ways in which the Nazi past is buried, suppressed, disavowed, covered over with the rich cake of contemporary Germany. William Gass's *The Tunnel* – not yet complete – approaches its material in a wholly different way – through a narrator who is a historian of Nazi Germany and who ultimately seems bent on, or driven to, 'tunneling' down to the 'fascism of the heart'. Very different works – yet who is really to say that one is more 'referential' than the other? They *refer* in different ways.

But it is in general that I think we might consider the new emphasis on, and awareness of, the sentence. Ian Hacking concludes his excellent book *Why Does Language Matter to Philosophy* by suggesting that after the 'heyday of Ideas' and the 'heyday of meanings' we have moved in this century into the 'heyday of sentences'. Among other writers, he quotes Quine, who affirmed that 'knowledge is a fabric of sentences' and via a number of other writers (including Foucault) he arrives at his own conclusion: 'knowledge itself has become sentential'. Certainly I think in the literature of this century the sentence has come into new prominence. There is a new kind of consciousness about the sentence and sententiality. Remember Faulkner's often-repeated ambition to get 'all human history into one sentence', while at the same time Hemingway seemed to want to *exclude* as much as possible from the sentence so that only the smallest unit of sense remained. In 'Projective Verse' Charles Olson says that the sentence has started 'jumping all over the place and growling' and if it has not always been doing that it has been doing some unusual things. Two examples: first, from Beckett's *The Unnamable*: 'The fact would seem to be, if in my situation one may speak of facts, not only that I shall have to speak of things of which I cannot speak, but also, which is even more interesting, that I shall have to, I forget, no matter. And at the same time I am obliged to speak.' Utterance here all but grinds to a halt from its own hesitations, indecisions, forgetfulness. And yet it has to go on. And this from *Lord Jim*: 'but the power of sentences has nothing to do with their sense or the logic of their construction. My idiotic mumble seemed to please him.' Here the power of communication comes not from sentences as we understand them, but from an 'idiotic mumble' which generates them. Again the traditional authority of the sentence is called into question – yet the sentences continue.

A very clear attack on the traditional sentence may be found, not surprisingly, in Barthes (*Pleasure of the Text*). 'The sentence is hierarchical: it implies subjections, subordination, internal reactions.' Barthes sees the sentence as another weapon of the dominant cultural police. By way of a contrast he describes a reverie he had while dozing and imagining he was in a bazaar in Tangiers:

> I myself was a public square, a *sook*; through me passed words, tiny syntagms, bits of formulae, and *no sentence formed*, as though that were the law of such a language. This speech, at once very cultural and very savage, was above all lexical, sporadic; it set up in me, through its apparent flow, a definitive discontinuity: this *non-sentence* was in no way something that could not have acceded to the sentence, that might have been before the sentence; it was: what is eternally, splendidly, outside the sentence.

As opposed to the illusory 'referential plentitude' he referred to in 'L'Effet de Réel', Barthes offers this image of a buzzing non-sentential bazaar – which might seem to be a form of heaven for many so-called post-modern writers if you listen to all their statements in favour of discontinuity, randomness, fragmentation, absence of syntax, improvisation, openness, etc., etc. As Alan Wilde shows in a *Boundary 2* article, whatever many post-modern writers might do when they actually write, they theoretically – if you can call it theory – espouse 'chaos', the buzzing of Barthes's non-sentential bazaar. But we must recognize that it really *is* – semantically – chaos. It is not that it makes the approved sentences of the official culture impossible (inaudible) – it makes *all* sentences impossible. This seems to me as much of a concession or submission to the official cultural forces as would the most conventional text – because it challenges nothing, and offers nothing new. There must be – there is – a lot between Barthes's dominating cultural sentence and the chaos of his non-sentential bazaar. What many of the important writers of this century have done is to challenge the hierarchy of the sentence – open it up, render it problematical (as in the Beckett and Conrad examples). But they go on uttering – making sentences even while the old type of sentence seems to fall to pieces in their hands. I suggested that many writers of our period have sought to challenge and disrupt the tyranny of established frames which not only can hold characters in false positions but can also place and hold readers in false positions too. So also I believe that many writers have sought to challenge the hierarchy of the traditional sentence (which may also hold characters and readers in fixed and false positions). Which does not mean that there will be – or could be – no more frames and sentences. Impossible. What it does mean is that we have seen and will doubtless continue to see all kinds of stretching and reshaping of the traditional forms, or indeed writers opening them up and leaving them open – we have seen a good deal of *aposeopesis* (i.e. breaking off into silence) and *anacoluthon* (i.e. sentences not considered grammatical by orthodox grammar) and many other kinds of deviation, transgression, disruption, perversion if you like, of conventional forms. But these things do not take place in a void. Somehow we recognize the ghost of an old sentence structure – or the inchoate birth of a new one. Somewhere we know there is a frame.

It is unimaginable to me that before our own period we would have had a story simply entitled 'Sentence' (Barthelme) on a sheet. It is if you like the autobiography, the confession, the lament, of a sentence. It ends: 'a disappointment, to be sure, but it reminds us that the sentence is itself a man-made object, not the one we wanted of course, but still a construction of man, a structure to be treasured for its weakness, as opposed to the strength of stones' – and there the sentence gives another twist and vanishes into silence (*aposeopesis*) – but that is the point: whatever its weaknesses and however it disappoints, it is 'a construction of man'. We can, and do, and even must, live within the fallible constructions of sentences. We cannot live in stones. This from William Gass in 'Gertrude Stein and the Geography of the Sentence': 'Every sentence is a syntactical space (a room) in which words (things, people) act (cook, clean, eat, or excrete) in order to produce quite special and very valuable qualities of feeling.' It is his assertion that Stein 'did more with sentences, and understood them better, than any writer has'. Let me remind you how closely Gass – and Stein – see the relationship between recombining words and rearranging items of living: what we get are 'new sentences of behaviour, new paragraphs of life'. If, when I say, 'we live in sentences' you say 'come now, you cannot mean that literally. You do not open the door of a sentence when you enter your house at night.' I would answer – very well, but that is an impoverishing literalness. In a way I *do* open a sentence as I open the door. If that sounds foolish or wilful, think of a world without sentences – not Barthes's non-sentential bazaar, but a sentential void. For a start, there would be no doors to walk through – no frames to hold them up . . . That is one reason why I think that the opposition between 'rendering' a world, and 'making' a world is ultimately a sterile if not a false one. This is not to say that there are no problems in the word–world relationship, and Alan Wilde has managed to point to some apparent contradictions in Gass's work on this point. I would maintain that all writing is representational in some sense – and the ultimate source of the permission for all representations, sovereigns and subjects, walruses and carpenters, beauties and beasts (to take up my little opening parable) is of course ultimately the language itself. What the writer has to do is to force the language to allow him to write new sentences. You can find a person's politics, as you can find his ethics, in his sentences; as Conrad very well knew when he said that a writer's morality is implicit in every sentence that he writes. So that, I suggest, is where we must pay attention until we experience what Wittgenstein called 'the dawning of an aspect'. And having mentioned Wittgenstein (and Jean-François Lyotard is surely correct to make him a key figure in his book, *La Condition Postmoderne*), I would remind you of just one thing he wrote about sentences: 'But how many kinds of sentences are there? . . . There are *countless* kinds: countless kinds of use of what we call "symbols", "words", "sentences". And this multiplicity is not something fixed, given once for all; but new types of language, new language-games, as we say, come into existence, and others become obsolete and forgotten.' (I note in passing that this emphasis on 'language-game' avoids a lot of the problems encountered by the French with their transcendent notion of a 'langue' – but that is another story.) That potential multiplicity of new language-games is one of the phenomena behind the amazing plurality of fictions of this century – modern and post-modern. As long as you can find someone to share the rules with you – i.e. an interlocutor, a reader – then any new fiction game can be played. Our fictions will vary according to 'the way we choose and value words', as Wittgenstein puts it; by the same token we may all 'choose and value' different fictions. A post-modern consensus would not only be an impossible dream: it would be a contradiction in terms.

Our language is never complete, a fixed totalitarian system. You remember Wittgenstein's famous image: 'Our language can be seen as an ancient city: a maze of little streets and squares, of old and new houses, and of houses with additions from different periods; and this surrounded by a multitude of new boroughs with straight regular streets and uniform houses.' And, we might add, boroughs of crooked streets and some highly idiosyncratic houses. But they are all additions to the city. And whatever we want to build in this city of language-games, there will always be some kind of frames and some kind of sentences. As critics I think we should try to be as alert to these as possible – in all their ambivalence and ambiguity, always aware how sentences may be verdicts, and frames may be conspiracies.

A last word from William Gass, from an essay appropriately called 'The Ontology of the Sentence':

> We must take our sentences seriously, which means we must understand them philosophically, and the odd thing is that the few who do, who take them with utter, sober seriousness, the utter sober seriousness of right-wing parsons and political saviours . . . are the liars who want to be believed, the novelists and poets, who know that the creatures they imagine have no other being than the sounding syllables which the reader will speak into his own weary and distracted head. There are no magic words. To say the words is magic enough.

13

William Gass's barns and bees

William Gass was born in 1924. In his own words: 'I was born in Fargo, North Dakota, but my family left there when I was six months old and moved to Warren, Ohio, where I grew up. Then I had three-and-a-half years in the Navy in World War II, attended Kenyon and Cornell, partly on the GI Bill, and I started right out teaching philosophy at the College of Wooster, Ohio. I was there for four years and then went to Purdue, where I have remained ever since.' (That was in an interview in the *Chicago Daily News*, 1 February 1969. Since then he has moved to Washington University in St Louis, where he is currently a professor of philosophy.) In that same interview, Gass answered questions about his childhood very frankly.

> I had an awful home, I think it could be described as a childhood of absolute misery. I suppose everybody tends to think this way up to a point, but it was really a wretched household. It was not dramatically bad, it was self-contained within the four walls, and the people in it were rotting, and I really mean rotting. My mother ended up an alcoholic who died in an insane asylum . . . They [his parents] were both hiding from themselves all the time, hiding their misery. They needed one another as someone needs the person he hates because these are all the emotions he has left. They didn't hate in a dramatic way, nobody beat anybody else up, none of that. It was a subtle self-disintegration, both murdering the other in their subtle ways. And they succeeded in doing it . . . I grew up in the Depression, but my father was a high school teacher, and we didn't suffer economic deprivation, never discomfort materially. It was emotional . . . death . . . I got to the point where I just said, 'hold it', and I left. It was a matter of self-preservation. I . . . had . . . to . . . get . . . out!

By his own account, Gass turned from this life to writing – 'I think that in my case writing was an escape from the world in which I was trapped to this fanciful world, this world of my own, that I could control and construct. And then, as I grew older, and I wanted to write seriously, I

248

realized that was a tremendous handicap, because what I'm doing now is building a world of words in which you are trapped. And you want to go out of that world, but still you're afraid of it.' A deep sense of the attractions, and dangers – the glorious possibilities and the potential deprivations – attendant upon living in a self-made 'world of words', and the ambiguous instinct to get out (back?) into the wordless world, or world without words, are clearly in evidence in nearly everything that Gass has written. And the 'characters' in his fiction – to use a conventional term which is of dubious validity, since the main 'character' in all his work is simply Language itself – are, surely, among the loneliest, most self-sealed, self-absorbed figures in contemporary fiction. This remarkably candid interview ended with the – somewhat fatuous – question 'Is it important to remain unhappy to write?' Gass's answer is worth quoting in full, since it provides a clue, a figure, for much of his creative work.

> There's a marvellous poem by Rilke, one of my favorite authors, and I suppose it expresses what I'm after more than anything else. It's about a torso of an archaic Apollo, a little statue, ruined, its head and legs and arms are gone. And the poet is looking at this and he describes it as if the eyes of the missing head were still there, looking down at the body, splashing the torso with light. And Rilke draws a contrast between the reality, the beauty, the sense of existence, in that ruined broken stone, in contrast to the whole body of the observer who is, nevertheless, less real than the statue. The work of art is a challenge in its own beauty and reality despite the fact that it is smashed, to the reality and way of life of the observer. This is another reason I think lots of works of art antagonize people, because they challenge their lack of existence. Here is an inanimate object, some paint on canvas, a piece of stone, words on paper, that has more value, more significance, than they have. And the poem ends with this marvellous line: 'You must change your life'. That's what the statue says. And this is what I want my work to say to people who are reading it, and to myself.

(The poem is 'Archaïscher Torso Apollos', translated as 'Archaic Torso of Apollo' by J. B. Leishman.)

In approaching Gass's work it is important to remember that he is a dedicated – and brilliant, by all accounts – teacher of philosophy. Important, not because he uses fiction to 'illustrate' or 'dramatize' particular philosophical problems, but because he regards fiction as capable of doing things which philosophy cannot – perhaps should not – attempt to do. But his awareness of philosophy, and philosophical issues, is always there. As far as I can make out, his first published piece of work was a philosophical essay (for *The Philosophical Review* – vol. LXVI, 1957; reprinted in *Fiction and the Figures of Life*), though according to his own testimony he started writing 'serious' fiction in 1951–2 (parts of *Omensetter's Luck*, and 'The Pederson Kid'), and the (now discontinued) periodical *Accent* devoted a whole issue to his fiction in 1958. His philosophical essay was entitled 'The Case of the Obliging Stranger'; since it is his first and probably only piece of 'straight' philosophy, it is worth quoting from it at some length, since it reveals, among other things, his dissatisfaction with the kind of 'proofs' and 'evidence' which philosophy tries to educe when dealing with ethical problems. The essay begins:

> Imagine I approach a stranger on the street and say to him, 'If you please, sir, I desire to perform an experiment with your aid.' The stranger is obliging, and I lead him away. In a dark place conveniently by, I strike his head with the broad of an axe and cart him home. I place him, buttered and trussed, in a ample electric oven. The thermostat reads 450°F. Thereupon I go off to play poker with friends and forget all about the obliging stranger in the stove. When I return, I realize I have overbaked my specimen, and the experiment, alas, is ruined.
>
> Something has been done wrong. Or something wrong has been done.
>
> Any ethic that does not roundly condemn my action is vicious. It is interesting that none is vicious for this reason. It is also interesting that no more convincing refutation of any ethic could be given than by showing that it approved of my baking the obliging stranger.
>
> This is really all I have to say . . .

But then he goes on to demonstrate how difficult it is to prove or demonstrate, by laws, generalizations, theories, that such an act is wrong.

> Moralists can say, with conviction, that the act is wrong; but none can *show* it. Such cases, like that of the obliging stranger, are cases I call clear. They have the characteristic of moral transparency, and they comprise the core of our moral experience. When we try to explain why they are instances of good or bad, or right or wrong, we sound comic, as anyone does who gives elaborate reasons for the obvious, especially when these reasons are so shamefaced before reality, so miserably beside the point.

He accepts that 'principles' are employed in moral decisions, but then how reliable are 'principles'? 'Principles state more or less prevalent identifying marks, as cardinals usually nest in low trees, although there is nothing to prevent them from nesting elsewhere, and the location of the nest is not the essence of the bird.' Note how Gass moves away from the usual methods of argument into a vivid and exploitable metaphor, to point to the varieties and unpredictabilities of reality which philosophy's laws cannot contain or cope with. It offers us a glimpse of philosophy turning into poetry – a strategy of discourse which Gass has since developed into a remarkably powerful mode of statement. He concludes his essay thus: 'Ethics, I wish to say, is about something, and in the rush to establish principles, to elicit distinctions from a recalcitrant language, and to discover "laws," those lovely things and honored people, those vile seducers and ruddy villains our principles and laws are supposed to be based upon and our ethical theories are overlooked and forgotten.' To put it crudely, Gass is more interested in, or concerned with, the specificity of 'vile seducers' and 'ruddy villains' than with 'principles' or 'laws'. He knows the principles and laws perfectly well, but he also knows about all the actual concrete contingencies that escape them. He does not, like a Moralist, want simply – too simply – to *say*: he wants, as a fiction writer, to *show*. In one of his later critical essays Gass wrote: 'The advantage the creator of fiction has over the moral philosopher is that the writer is concerned with the exhibition of objects, thoughts, feelings, and actions where they are free from the puzzling disorders of the real and the need to come to conclusions about them.' And in a more recent interview (see *The New Fiction – Interviews with Innovative American Writers* (Urbana, 1974), conducted by Joe David Bellamy) Gass stated this:

> I see no reason to regard literature as a superior source of truth, or even as a reliable source of truth at all. Going to it is dangerous precisely because it provides a sense of verification (a feeling) without the fact of verification (the validating process) . . . Philosophy ought to spend more time than it has showing how little we need it – it and other foolish sets of opinions. I believe much of what has passed for philosophy, theology, etc., in the past is nonsense. Sometimes beautiful nonsense, if you enjoy myths of the mind as I enjoy them. Beliefs are a luxury, and most of them are wicked gibberish.

It is important to bear in mind Gass's radical scepticism concerning philosophy, or any system of ideas or beliefs, when reading his fiction. For, whereas one might expect the fiction simply to be a vehicle for the exposition of philosophical ideas, it tends rather to *dissolve* ideas, and any pretensions to conceptual fixity and abstract rigidity, in an extraordinary flow of language – breathtakingly unpredictable, iridescent, hyperbolic, baroque. What Gass the writer shows, ultimately, is language itself, at the fullest reach of its energy, all its potentialities and resources seduced into self-exhibition.

His first novel, *Omensetter's Luck*, was finally published in 1966 (New American Library). It has a rather strange history. According to Gass, the first manuscript was stolen when it was almost completed. He wrote a second version, then dropped that for a third version. As Gass said in the first interview referred to, 'One major character in the book, Jethro Furber, doesn't appear at all until the last version, and he really makes over the whole book.' Indeed it is hard to imagine what kind of book it would have been without the figure of Furber. Gass set his book in an

Ohio river town called Gilean, at the turn of the century. By his own account, apart from looking through such things as etiquette books and family home-books of the period, he simply invented a place and time 'sufficiently removed in the past so I could build a *mythological structure*' – 'I know nothing whatever of Ohio river towns and care less.' So although there is a detectable, indirect Faulkner influence at work in the novel, it is in no sense about the Midwest as Faulkner's work in a very profound, if oblique sense, *is* about the South. The main influence is James Joyce ('a great deal, very certainly and consciously' in his own words) and after Joyce, Gertrude Stein. Gass retains a great admiration for Gertrude Stein; he wrote an important introduction to a reissue of Stein's *The Geographical History of America* (New York, 1973), from which I take this revealing statement:

> Life is rearrangement, and in a dozen different ways Gertrude Stein set out to render it . . . Almost at once she realized that language itself is a complete analogue of experience because it, too, is made of a large but finite number of relatively fixed terms which are then allowed to occur in a limited number of clearly specified relations, so that it is not the appearance of a word that matters but the *manner of its reappearance*, and that an unspecifiable number of absolutely unique sentences can in this way be composed, as, of course, life is also continuously refreshing itself in a similar fashion . . . Gertrude Stein did more with sentences, and understood them better, than any writer ever has . . . she thought of them as *things in space*, as long and wriggling and physical as worms . . . By the time I understood what she means, *I* have been composed.

The interior monologue, with all its free-associations, its word play, its sexual and scatological murmurings and eruptions – and the sentence, the disciplined rearrangement, the controlled reappearance, of words, which may move out flat into space like the prairie, or writhe and wriggle in the air like a worm: these are the central features of Gass's style. His mentors, as he says, are indeed Joyce and Stein. But the combination and the unique resultant effects are Gass's own.

As a story, *Omensetter's Luck* could be summarized quite simply. Omensetter, a large, powerful, simple, 'natural', unself-conscious (if not *unconscious*), man arrives one day in Gilean with his wife and children and dog. He seeks and obtains work in the local forge, rents a house from an initially suspicious and unwilling inhabitant (Henry Pimber), and would be content doing his work, playing with his family, swimming with his pregnant wife, skimming stones on the river. He seems to be careless, dirty, even *foolish* – like an animal, some think. But mainly he is *oblivious*. He is intimate with the earth, the body – in them, of them. He seems to have the knack, the gift – the luck – of living without thinking, participating without introspection. Things always seem to fall out well for him because he is, as it were, on easy terms with things, with nature, with the elements. Yes, he is lucky . . . but there is something about him, and his luck, which in various ways disturbs the inhabitants of Gilean. His appearance in their midst – his serene, careless, even sloppy unawareness and ease-in-Being – awakens envy, admiration, and suspicion and antagonism. Himself an unreflecting inhabitant of existence, he unwittingly causes the fantasies and fears of the more morbidly conscious local population to come to the surface. They *watch* him – is he a magician (or is it witchcraft), as when he cures Henry Pimber's lock-jaw? What is *his secret*? What does he *mean* by being what he *is*? But Omensetter (and you can break the name up so that he is a setter of omens, signs portending good or evil, which other people try to read and decipher – but the sign never tries to decipher itself) is not a watcher, an observer: 'Omensetter lived by *not* observing – by joining himself to what he knew. Necessity flew birds as easily as the wind drove the leaves, and they never felt the curvature which drew the arc of their pursuit. Nor would a fox cry beauty before he chewed.' In some people – all of them living narrow, suspicious, emotionally arid lives – he stirs aspirations of emulation. To Henry Pimber, for instance, he becomes 'more than a model. He was a dream you might enter.' Pimber has lived a barren, negative life with his shrewish wife for years but the figure of Omensetter seems to bring him back, reluctantly, ecstatically, into life. This figure suggests to Pimber 'the chance of being new . . . of living lucky, and of losing Henry Pimber'. He had managed to reduce himself to the sentience of a stone, but the appearance/apparition of Omensetter affects him like that Archaic Torso of Apollo of Rilke's – he wants to 'change his life'. One representative quotation:

> Once to petrify and die had been his wish; simply to petrify had been his fear; but he had been a stone with eyes and seen as a stone sees: the world as the world is really, without the least prejudice of heart or artifice of mind, and he had come into such truth as only a stone can stand. He yearned to be hard and cold again and have no feeling, for since his sickness he'd been preyed upon by dreams, sleeping and waking, and by sudden rushes of unnaturally sharp, inhuman vision in which all things were dazzling, glorious, and terrifying. He saw then, he thought, as Omensetter saw, except for the painful beauty.

Pimber cannot live with this new disturbing vision, and, after a last meeting with Omensetter (when he says to him 'You knew the secret – how to be'), Pimber hangs himself – but high, high in a tree, not wishing to die as low as he feels he has lived. Indeed he hangs himself so high that his body is not found for many months – his disappearance becomes a mystery, with suspicions gradually turning towards Omensetter. And it is he who finally sees the body. The people seem to be turning vindictive – but at the end he simply packs up all his belongings and, with his family and dog, moves away. His luck holds.

So much for Omensetter, and the story of his sojourn in Gilean. But some three-quarters of the book concerns itself with the interior life of the Reverend Jethro Furber, that late arrival into the manuscript who effectively takes over the book. Omensetter, in whom nothing seems to be repressed or hidden, is not presented as having any inner life. Furber, who is a tight physical box of repressions and concealments, has a very vivid inner life indeed. And this is what Gass so brilliantly conveys – shows. Furber is a type of 'fierce Puritan intensity' and, in line with that religion, he is suspicious of nature, earth, the body. He sees nature as 'destructive', something to be fought against, as he intermittently fights against – and fails to control – the weeds in his barred, garden grave-yard. So much could be stereotypical, rendering the book simply schematic – Furber's battle against Omensetter (for is it Furber who tries to poison the inhabitants' minds against Omensetter with all the wiles of his perverse, insinuating rhetoric) would then be a battle between the gifts of life and the forces of death, between nature and anti-nature, between the physical and the mental. But Furber is opened up and the book is certainly not a simple Manichean melodrama. His mind, it is clear, was drawn to, and became obsessed by, the images of violence and sexuality in the Old Testament – 'only the wild time and his own terror attracted him'. His is not a truly religious mind, or, if it is, it offers us a powerful insight into the phantasmagoria of infantilism, aberrant sexuality, and sadism, which can seethe beneath the reiterated orthodoxies of that kind of religious mind, not to mention all the evidence and traces of displacement, distortion, and the endless return of the repressed, which constantly imperil lucid consciousness. Furber's mind works by perversion, inversion, but – more to the point – his mind never *stops* working, or playing; perverse paradoxes, foul fantasies, sadistic fancies, resentful envies, and deep self-loathing echoing around in his head to create a continuous inner cacophony. 'In the theatre of his head, in the privacy of Philly Furber's Fancy Foto-Cabinet – what thrilling horrors were enacted, what lascivious scenes encranked. Come to the skull show, honey.' In Furber, consciousness, mind, knowing, are excessively over-dominant, at the expense of the body, which is why he feels, with Omensetter, 'this was a contest he didn't dare lose' (needless to say it is his postulation, projection, that it *is* a contest – Omensetter is unaware of any opposition or oppugnance). When the people seem to be drawn towards Omensetter he uses all his powers to turn them away from him. For a time they resist, complain – 'whine' in Furber's terms. Because, as he sees it, 'They'd have to give up their hope of living like an animal and return to an honest, conscious, human life. The prospect was hard.' But Furber's is not honest, human consciousness, but consciousness gone mad, or consciousness *as* madness. His view of man's position in the world is one with a number of recognizable Existentialist precedents. In his own words: 'None of us wanted this world to begin with. We were orphaned into it . . . We are here – yes – yet we do not belong.'

But there are various ways of reacting to this sense of being-yet-not-belonging. Furber's way is almost hysterically to emphasize the not-belongingness, the separation between mind and nature. Man, for him, is the observer, the knower – 'the wondrous watchman'. His reproach to Omensetter is, 'you know nothing of the life you live in', and his hatred of this apparently felicitous absence of consciousness is based on its implicit threat to his own completely mentally oriented way of life – or death. By the end he has, he knows, made himself a monster – and at the end he is effectively terminally insane. Among his last words, these: 'love was never taught to me. I couldn't spell it, the O was always missing or the V, so I wrote love like live, or lure, or law, or liar.' And of Omensetter: 'I lied and lied. I spread hatred against him – all by lies . . . And after my lies, he spelled love: luck.' Omensetter's body – with his family – moves on: Furber's mind – in extreme isolation – caves in. Yet, as I shall stress, we must not read this as a parabolic struggle, an allegory, with love-life-nature-health triumphant over the sterile perversities of a diseased cerebration. There *is*, after all a vacancy, a blankness, about Omensetter. For all his lumbering size, in some ways he is not there at all – not being present to himself, he is not really present to others. Rather, he is the occasion of their dreaming, the site of their fantasies. Furber is more complex and more interesting. In particular he is a man gripped by, in the grip of, language – with all the ambiguous results which Gass knows attach to that state. He is constantly trying to use language to control and order his thoughts, and constantly failing, as language itself rebels against the inward speaker's intentions. An example:

> Through his head, to the tunes of children's songs, his pitiful beliefs, his little sentences of wisdom, danced foolishly as he dozed, the meters they were forced to skip to reducing them to a vulgar gibberish. He tried to rally his thoughts and form them in unassailable squares, but not a line would hold, they broke ahead of any shooting, and the Logos wandered disloyally off, alone, rudely hiccoughing and chewing on pieces of raw potato, looking surly and dangerous. No book but Nature is the word of God. Logos. No ghost. Whirled. Screech. Hisssst.

He is an actor, an orator, even – particularly – to himself. He lives in words: 'yes, words were superior; they maintained a superior control; they touched without your touching . . .' His feeling for and relationship to words is almost physical. 'All these words. Ah, I'll heel them home and make myself loved like a stray. A miracle, Pike – life out of ink.' His sexuality becomes verbalized: 'he made love with discreet verbs and light nouns, delicate conjunctions . . . Smooth and creamy adjectives enabled them to lick their lips upon the crudest story.' But 'fearless in speech, he was cowardly in all else': his comfort is his desolation. In touch with words, he touches nothing. 'He'd kept everything at a word's length, and it was words he saw when he saw her . . . all his speeches . . . his beautiful barriers of words', and – near the end – 'once again, in place of feelings – speeches'. Gass was to refer later to the 'sweet country of the word', but he also knew it could be an arid desert, an endless empty plain, an unreachable, impenetrable apartness. Perversely, perhaps, we are more involved with, even more in sympathy with, Furber because of his struggle with the word – not the Word of God, just the word in general – and the word's struggle with him. In him, in an extreme form, we see being worked out some of the paradoxical results of man's immersion in 'linguicity' – a master of words and a slave 'at the mercy of language' both. Marvellously, hopelessly, horribly – both. As for Omensetter – well, two comments by Gass himself, from the second interview already cited, will serve. 'Omensetter is a reflector. People use him the way they use their gods or other public figures – and upon him they project their hopes and fears. Who cares to know Omensetter? And when their hopes were dashed, they blamed the image in the mirror. So of course Omensetter is a mystery and he had to be left, in a sense, blank.' But this does not mean that we should romanticize or sentimentalize Omensetter, disappearing over the horizon like an anachronism from some lost Golden Age. Gass again: 'America never had its Omensetters. There aren't any such human felines. Such creatures are a part of the American myth. What we are losing is our belief in such things. Beliefs lost are minds cleansed. I applaud the development.' For Gass, as for many writers, to 'interpret' a work is to rob it of his meaning. In his case in particular, the meaning is absolutely inseparable from the texture of the text. It is not 'about' nature and Puritanism, Omensetter and Furber, or any other such facile binary oppositions. It is deeply concerned with – and is itself an exemplary product of – the imagination, consciousness, and the word. It is not about Ohio, or the American past. It is a great gesture of style. To be sure, such a style can make use of anything, like the heaps of odds and ends, the detritus from the past, at the auction with which the book opens. In that frame chapter an old man, the town storyteller called Israbestis Tott, is talking to a young boy. Here is a piece of the dialogue:

> I want it to be a long story.
> It is a long story.
> Put everything in it.
> I always put everything in it.

And so it is with the style and telling of William Gass, as was apparent in this amazingly original, really quite dazzling, first novel. He always puts everything in it.

His next published book of fiction was a collection of stories entitled *In the Heart of the Heart of the Country* (New York, 1968). Some of these stories had been written much earlier ('The Pederson Kid' – his first serious attempt at fiction, as early as 1951). When the book was re-issued (New York, 1977), Gass added an introduction which contains some revealing comments. He raises the question of who is the putative reader of such stories now: 'where is that second ear? No court commands our entertainments, requires our flattery, needs our loyal enlargements or memorializing lies. Literature once held families together better than quarreling.' But now, it seems to serve no social purpose, holds no-one together, has no identifiable audience. So, this: 'The contemporary American writer is in no way a part of the social or political scene. He is therefore not *muzzled*, for no one fears his bite; nor is he called upon to compose. Whatever work he does must proceed from a reckless inner need. The world does not beckon, nor does it greatly reward. This is not a boast or a complaint. It is a fact.' The contemporary American writer, then, can write only for himself: so there is no reason for the existence of these stories ('these litters of language . . . amazing . . . unimportant . . . both'), 'except that in some dim way I wanted, myself, to have a soul, a special speech, a style'. While other American writers struggle, none too successfully, with the vexed problems of relevance and 'literature as intervention', Gass candidly admits that he writes from, and for, himself. (It is worth noting, in case the impression is given of an ivory-tower academic writer, privileged and protected from history, that Gass the individual was much involved in many political issues during the turbulent 1960s. It is part of his honesty that he maintains that none of his writing emerged from that kind of political engagement, though his attitude to this has changed in recent years – as will be explained later.) The longest story, 'The Pederson Kid', Gass has described as a technical exercise, influenced by Stein. One example of a very Stein-like sentence:

> It was good I was glad he was there it wasn't me there sticking up bare in the wind like a stick with the horse most likely stopped by this time with his bowed head bent into the storm, and I wouldn't like lying all by myself out there in the cold white dark, dying all alone out there, being buried out there while I was still trying to breathe, knowing I'd only come slowly to the surface in spring and would soon be soft in the new sun and worried by curious dogs.

The story, taut and compelling, concerns a family that discovers a neighbouring child frozen near their door. They decide – after much intra-familial strife and antagonism – that three of them must go and see what has happened on that farm which caused the boy – the Pederson Kid – to run away in fright. Once there – it is in the depths of a terrible Midwest winter – it is not clear exactly what happens, only that some unidentified presence seems to be lurking around and that two of the party are shot, leaving the young narrator as a survivor, curiously happy in his new, ambiguous, 'freedom'. Of this story Gass wrote: 'the problem is to present evil as a visitation – sudden, mysterious, violent, inexplicable. All should be subordinated to that. The physical representation must be spare and staccato; the mental representation must be flowing and a bit repetitious; the dialogue realistic but musical.' The story achieves all these effects: its almost ritualistic prose achieves a haunting, even a frightening, effect. And where Gass had, apparently, initially planned the story to end with the rescue of the young narrator, the final version leaves things in doubt. Gass again: 'Though I dropped the rescue, I did not so much depart from this conception as complicate it, *covering the moral layer with a frost of epistemological doubt*' (my italics – it sums up what Gass often does). As he said in that later introduction – 'All stories ought to end unsatisfactorily.'

The four other stories are centred upon lonely observers ('wondrous watchmen'), obsessed, prurient, passively curious, isolates of the eye, and mind, and word. It is worth noting that, in interview, Gass admitted: 'I haven't the dramatic imagination at all. Even my characters tend to turn away from one another and talk to the void. This, along with my inability to narrate, is my most serious defect (I think) as a writer and incidentally as a person. I am (though I wasn't especially raised as one) a Protestant, wholly inner-directed, and concerned only too exclusively with *my* salvation, *my* relation to the beautiful, *my* state of mind, body, soul . . . The interactions which interest me tend to be interactions between parts of my own being.' Just so, the generative characters, or narrators, or meditative observers, in his stories, likewise seem to live along, and down, the lines of their own most private thought processes – Furbers, not Omensetters. The story 'Mrs Mean' Gass describes as 'a story of sexual curiosity translated, again, into the epistemological', and while the narrator gives his detailed account of the behaviour of a harassed, mean-minded, suburban housewife, we realize that it is the strange movements of his own mind we are tracing, as he devours and digests his neighbours with his passive, predatory watching: 'I take their souls away – I know it – and I play with them: I puppet them up to something; I march them through strange crowds and passions; I snuffle at their roots.' The basic situation – to be repeated in other works by Gass – is that of a watcher, inside himself, his mind, his body, his house, and a life outside – between them a window (crucial in Gass's work) or a space which both permits and prohibits contact, a medium or gap which cannot be penetrated or traversed. Thus a problem is posed: 'is there any reason for us to suppose that life inside is any better than the life outside we see?' Like other Gass narrators, this one turns away from social contact. 'My wife would strike up friendships, too, and so, as she says, find out; but that must be blocked. It would destroy my transcendence. It would entangle me mortally in illusion.' The compelling drive of the narrator is to somehow penetrate the 'house' (inwardness) of the 'other' without being involved in relationship. It is a fine, fomenting, perversity. Thus the story ends:

> The desire to know, and to possess. Shut in my room as I so often am now with my wife's eyes fastened to the other side of the door like blemishes in the wood, I try to analyze my feelings. I lay them out one by one like fortune's cards or clothes for journeying and when I see them clearly then I know the time is only days before I shall squeeze through the back screen of the Means' house and be inside.

What does it mean to be 'outside'; how to get 'inside'? These are central concerns in all of Gass's writing.

'Icicles' is, like much of Gass's subsequent work, based on 'an exploration of an image'. Fender is a failing property salesman; he withdraws more and more into himself, his house, his lonely bachelor habits, his watching from behind his window. He is told that *property owns people*, and has recognized that 'His little house possessed him, it was true.' He starts to attach value to the slowly, beautifully growing icicles which hang from the houses in winter; they become a source for his fantasy life – 'He would frequently rest to watch his icicles, the whole line, firing up, holding the sun like a maiden in her sleep or a princess in her tower – so real, so false, so magical. It was his own invention, that image, and he was proud of it.' Driven through failure into increasing isolation he feels that he, and his body, have become like 'an undesirable property for sale', with no likely buyers. It would seem that he would like to complete his withdrawal from the 'outside' (where thoughtless boys break icicles for fun – to his great pain), aiming even to occlude himself from language entirely: 'he tried to drive himself into wordlessness'. When the 'world of words' becomes a nightmare of isolation, this can be the desire, or dream, of many of the figures in the fiction of William Gass – who is himself the creator of the world of words they live in, privileged and hopelessly trapped. In 'Order of Insects', a housewife, compulsively intent on neatness and cleanliness, is initially horrified to find, each morning, heaps of dead insects (or 'roaches') on the carpet of the newly rented house she lives in with her family. But her terror turns into a strange aesthetic appreciation – 'it isn't any longer roaches I observe but gracious order, wholeness, and divinity'. It is as though she finds herself turning from the seemingly rich chaos of family life to the fascinating orderliness and clean fixity of death. Thus:

> I had always thought that love knew nothing of order and that life itself was turmoil and confusion. Let us leap, let us shout! I have leaped, and to my shame, I have wrestled. But this bug that I hold in my hand and know to be dead is

beautiful, and there is a fierce joy in its composition that beggars every other, for its joy is the joy of stone, and it lives in its tomb like a lion. I don't know which is more surprising: to find such order in a roach, or such ideas in a woman.

There is one order, the suburban one, 'tidy and punctual, surrounded by blocks', and there is another – 'the order of insects'. To have perceived the latter is to call into question the former. And Gass knows that his art shares the ambiguous beauty of the dead insect – 'there is a fierce joy in its composition that beggars every other'. If the fierce beauty of art 'beggars' every other, then it is doomed to live – or die – alone. But it 'lives in its tomb like a lion'. Or perhaps like the Archaic Torso of Apollo, radiant if petrified, showering and shedding a sense of the poverty and incompleteness on what is merely notionally, contingently, inadequately, 'alive'.

The title story, 'In the Heart of the Heart of the Country', is one of Gass's most remarkable achievements and one of the most distinguished American short stories written this century. It is unusual among his works in that it is based as closely as possible upon actual places and actual people. The opening sentence – 'So I have sailed the seas and come . . . to B . . . a small town fastened to a field in Indiana' – refers ironically, of course, to Yeats's Byzantium, but also literally to Brookston, Indiana, where Gass lived for four years. By his own admission, most of the people are 'modeled after actual people', and the names of clubs and organizations listed in the story are as he remembers them. But of course, though his data was rigorously factual, he recalls that, 'as I started to distribute my data gingerly across my manuscript, a steady dissolution of the real began . . . I knew that when I'd finished, it wouldn't be Brookston, Indiana, anymore, but a place as full of dream and fabrication as that fabled city (i.e. Byzantium) itself. Inside my cautious sentences, as against Yeats' monumental poetry, it would become an inverted heaven for man's imagination' (from a preface he later added). But it is also a modern *Walden*: where Thoreau's account of his deliberate exile is divided into chapters with headings such as 'Economy', 'Reading', 'Sounds', 'The Village', 'Brute Neighbours', 'House-Warming', Gass's story is divided into brief sections with headings such as 'A Place', 'Weather', 'My House', 'People', 'Vital Data', 'Education', 'Household Apples', and so on. In itself this would merely be a structural echo, but, like *Walden*, this is a prolonged meditation on the mystery of place, with an isolated, single narrator steadily, scrupulously, scrutinizing the composition of his locale, the surrounding environment which he is *in*, but not *of*. They both register and record things with the apparently detached eye of an uninvolved visitor. In both cases the house becomes an image for the narrator, his body and his presence in the place. But in Gass's story there is no Thoreauvian ritual of rebirth, or the seasonal cycle which brings

spring after winter, and draws butterflies out of bugs. Thoreau wrote
mainly in wonder; Gass – or his narrator – writes mainly out of
controlled rage and a barely concealed disgust and horror at the bleakness
of the life around him – indeed within him as well. Thoreau's work
celebrates renewal; Gass's story records entropy. Everywhere there is a
sense of desolation, growing waste, increasing vacancy – of places and
people – life running down. The narrator says, 'I did not restore my
house to its youth, but to its age.' Of another person: 'there's simply no
way of knowing how lonely and empty he is or whether he's as vacant
and barren and loveless as the rest of us – here in the heart of the country'.
Of the population at large: 'Where their consciousness has gone I can't
say. It's not in their eyes.' Of the town in general: 'Everywhere . . . the
past speaks, and it mostly speaks of failure. The empty stores, the old signs
and dusty fixtures, the debris in alleys, the flaking paint and rusty gutters,
the heavy locks and sagging boards: they say the same disagreeable things
. . . Here a stair unfolds toward the street . . . and I always feel, as I pass it,
that if I just went carefully up and turned the corner at the landing, I
would find myself out of the world.' The narrator is 'in retirement from
love' – he is 'out of job and out of patience, out of love and time and
money, out of bread and out of body'. His observations about the town
and its inhabitants are mixed with his memories of his love, vivid flowers
of rich nostalgia blooming in the entropic rubble. As usual, he is a
voyeur, intimately involved with his window, and his house. He lives
'*in*'. Yet he does not live 'in' as his cat lives so easily in his catness. 'You,
not I, live in: in house, in skin, in shrubbery.' Again, what is 'inside'? 'My
window is a grave, and all that lies within it's dead . . . We meet on this
window, the world and I, inelegantly, swimmers of the glass; and swung
wrong way round to one another, the world seems in.' If the world is 'in'
what, then, is the poet-narrator – out? Out of touch with the world,
perhaps out of the world, his house a coffin, his life a death. Only
memories of the soft contacts of love bring back intimations – and
aspirations – of life. 'A bush in the excitement of its roses could not have
bloomed so beautifully as you did then. It was a look I'd like to give this
page. For that is poetry: to bring within about, to change.' He must
change his life. But meanwhile, his pages often bloom in the excitement
of his style. The vision of the story is bleak, some of the satiric comments
are savage, and the evocation of a sense of utter desolation and almost
terminal loneliness is as powerful as in any piece of American writing.
But the words live, rise, take flight, breaking away from the degree-zero
state which the narrator seems to be approaching. One example from a
key section of the story, 'Household Apples'. The apples from his trees
have fallen all over his yard, making walking difficult, so he decides to
take on the 'Herculean' task of cleaning up – a task made more difficult

because of the swarms of flies attracted to the rotting apples ('Flies have always impressed me; they are so persistently alive' – another 'order of insects'). What to most people would be distasteful is transformed into a rich, climactic moment.

> Deep in the strong rich smell of the fruit, I began to hum myself . . . There were streams of flies; there were lakes and cataracts and rivers of flies, seas and oceans. The hum was heavier, higher, than the hum of the bees when they came to the blooms in the spring, though the bees were there, among the flies, ignoring me – ignoring everyone. As my work went on and juice covered my hands and arms, they would form a sleeve, black and moving, like knotty wool. No caress could have been more indifferently complete. Still I rose fearfully, ramming my head in the branches, apples bumping against me before falling, bursting with bugs. I'd snap my hands sharply but the flies would cling to the sweat. I could toss a whole cluster into a basket from several feet. As the pear or apple lit, they would explosively rise, like monads for a moment, windowless, certainly, with respect to one another, sugar their harmony. I had to admit though, despite my distaste, that my arm had never been more alive, oftener or more gently kissed.

The echo from Leibniz ('windowless monads') is worked effortlessly into this extraordinary kind of perverse pastoral. There are no windows in the world of flies – to that extent they, like the cat, live *in*. But there are no words, either, and it is in and through words that the narrator must, and can, bring life to his own living death.

Gass's next piece of fiction was entitled *Willie Masters' Lonesome Wife* (first published in *TriQuarterly*, 1968, then by Knopf, New York, 1971). Since I have discussed this work at some length elsewhere (see 'Games American writers play', ch. 10 this volume), I will pass over it here.

On Being Blue was Gass's next major work (Boston, 1976). It is subtitled 'A Philosophical Inquiry' but it is hardly philosophy in any traditional sense. Gass simply takes the one word 'blue' and broods, creatively, upon it. He explores and evokes all the connotations of the word, the different uses to which it has been put, the company – for words do keep company – it has kept. 'Blue' is sexual, of course; it is also sadness – of course. But the word has worked, and been given employment, in an amazing range of contexts. So the meditation starts:

> Blue pencils, blue noses, blue movies, laws, blue legs and stockings, the language of birds, bees, and flowers as sung by longshoremen, that lead-like look the skin has when affected by cold, contusion, sickness, fear; the rotten rum or gin they call blue ruin and the blue devils of its delirium; Russian cats and oysters, a withheld or imprisoned breath, the blue they say that diamonds have, deep holes in the ocean and the blazers which English athletes earn that gentlemen may wear; afflictions of the spirit – dumps, mopes, Mondays – all that's dismal – low-down gloomy music, Nova Scotians, cyanosis, hair rinse, bluing, bleach . . .

William Gass's barns and bees

And so he goes on, digging deeper, and wider, into the archaeology of the word, sounding it for all its varying associations, teasing the etymology and examining the contexts in which it has been used. It is almost as though Gass had said: 'give me a word and I will give you the world'. From one word, his meditations spread and spread until, once again, it is as though language itself can be seen ostentatiously demonstrating its polysemic dexterity, its infinite variety, its hopelessly democratic aptitudes as it moves so effortlessly through disparate realms of feeling, action, and classification.

The book starts with 'blue' and ends with 'gray' – the life of language versus the death of everything. This is part of the concluding paragraph:

> so shout and celebrate before the shade conceals the window: blue bloods, balls, and bonnets, beards, coats, collars, chips, and cheese . . . while there is time and you are able, because when blue has left the edges of its objects as if the world were bleached of it, when the wide blue eye has shut down for the season, when there's nothing left but language . . . watered twilight, sour sea . . . don't find yourself clergy'd out of choir and chorus . . . sing and say . . . despite the belly ache and loneliness, new bumpled fat and flaking skin and drunkenness and helpless rage, despite mumps, mopes, Mondays, sheets like dirty plates, tomorrow falling toward you like a tower, lie in wait for that miraculous moment when in your mouth teeth turn into dragons and you do against the odds what Demosthenes did by the Aegean: shape pebbles into syllables and make stones sound; thus cautioned and encouraged, commanded, warned, persist . . . even though the mattress where you mourn's been tipped and those corners where the nickels roll slide open like a slot to swallow them, clocks slow, and there's been perhaps a pouring rain, or factory smoke, an aging wind and winter air, and everything is gray.

When there is nothing left but language – there is everything left, as Gass demonstrates in this unique text in which language seems, veritably, to lyricize and, most articulately, lament itself.

Through the last two decades Gass has been writing essays and reviews – many of these are collected in volumes entitled *Fiction and the Figures of Life* (New York, 1971), and *World within a Word* (New York, 1978). In the former volume Gass makes his idea of what fiction is, and can do, very clear, though his position does change from time to time. The emphasis, as might be expected, is on the primacy of language – it would seem that Gass has no time for any conventional notions of referentiality. It is 'the release of language' which he celebrates and he goes out of his way to stress that, for him, fiction is simply 'about' the words it contains. It is a record of a series of choices that a writer has made among the available words. If we ask: but to what end did he make *those* choices, Gass is disinclined to answer. He seems resolved not to involve himself with problems of 'intentionality'. 'The concepts of the philosopher speak, the words of the novelist are mute; the philosopher invites us to pass through his words to his subject; man, god, nature, moral law; while the novelist, if he is any good, will keep us kindly imprisoned in his language – there is literally nothing beyond.' He sometimes qualifies the extreme implications of this assertion – as, for instance, when he detects a 'fear of feeling' in the works of many writers (whom he admires) who sometimes seem *only* to be playing with language – Hawkes, Barthelme, Coover, Barth, Nabokov, Borges. But for Gass in fictions – and in 'metafictions', as he identifies many modern novels – the word is the name of the game. As he insists: 'the novelist now better understands his medium; he is ceasing to pretend that his business is to render the world; he knows, more often now, that his business is to *make* one, and to make one from the only medium of which he is a master – language'. It is as though he wants to insist that the novel in no way impinges on – or is impinged upon – by the 'outside' world: 'I have argued that words are opaque, as opaque as my garden gloves and trowel, objects which, nevertheless, may vividly remind me of spring, earth, and roses. Or Uncle Harry, Africa, the tsetse fly, and lovesick elephants. On the other side of a novel lies the void.' But on this side of the novel is the living reader, still capable of being moved in any number of ways by the 'vivid reminders' which those opaque words of the novel arouse in him. In his contempt for simple notions of 'realism' Gass does sometimes take up an extreme position regarding the autonomy of language, and indeed some critics have found his work to be solipsistic. Yet if we consider the piece of fiction he has been working on since the middle 1960s, provisionally called *The Tunnel*, we can see that Gass as a writer is very much *in* the world of history, even while he is still inside his world of words. Gass himself has said for a long time that this is to be his most serious piece of work, and has himself described its proposed and prospective subject and theme. It is to be about – and narrated by – a middle-aged historian whose speciality is Nazi Germany. At the beginning of the novel he has just completed his great work concerning the Nazi treatment of the Jews and different aspects of German and Jewish guilt. He sits down to write an introduction to this work and finds that he cannot. Something is blocking him, something has gone wrong. *The Tunnel* is what he writes instead of the introduction. He realizes, or feels, that he is caught in what Gass calls 'the concentration camp of his own life', and he is trying to dig himself out of that entrapment by writing – hence the title. In general what is to be explored is his own latent, or not so latent, fascism amid the small, and not so small, fascisms of everyday life. In the simplest terms it is, says Gass, 'about the fascism of the heart'. He admitted – all this in the interview referred to – that this overt and deeply serious 'intention' marks a change in his work.

Whether Gass still feels the same way – eighteen years later! – and just when the book will appear, are currently imponderable questions. But from the extracts published in various magazines, there is no doubting the seriousness of the work (parts have appeared in *New American Review*, *Iowa Review*, *Granta*, and in *TriQuarterly 20* and *TriQuarterly 42*). What is not new is that Gass is once again concentrating on a man trapped inside his own head, trying and failing to find a way out ('You'll never get out of that mind', Gass promised, adding that he really wrote about the 'difficulty of getting out . . . all the time'). The first *TriQuarterly* extract is entitled, significantly enough, 'Why windows are important to me', and this establishes the position, and plight, of the narrator. 'I've two eyes, and walk; yet it's always a window which lets me see.' As he says, windows 'provide the frame, proscenium to stage, and everything is altered in them into art . . . or history . . . which seems, in circumstances of my kind, the same'. Looking out of a window – like hiding in a tree, which Gass reveals he did as a child – is to place yourself in a position in which you can see but not be seen. It is, already, a power situation. For the narrator, the window is like a tunnel, a hole, a cupboard, a space of retreat, where he can be 'a true self-by-itself, and so a self-inside-itself like Kant's unknowable knower'. He seems positively to enjoy this sensation: 'To enter yourself so completely that you're like a peeled-off glove; to become to the world invisible, entirely out of touch, no longer defined by the eyes of others, unanswering to anyone', so that he can experience 'a wholly unpressured seeing', 'a powerful out of the world feeling', 'safe from the haze of human shuffle'. But of course such a sealed-off life is intensely claustrophobic, and the narrator, Kohler (German for 'miner' – an intended allusion), is also a desperate digger in the tunnel, trying to 'get out'. How the work will resolve itself, we cannot yet infer. But it is clear that the narrator must, like Malory's Guinevere, 'amend my misliving' (a favourite line of Gass's). The solipsism is not in Gass's work but in his characters. And the basic thrust behind all his writing is not simply the invitation – 'you may enjoy my words' – but more urgently the exhortation – 'you must change your life'.

I will conclude this introductory consideration of the work of William Gass by offering a response to, an appreciation of, the most recently published (at the time of writing) extract from *The Tunnel*, entitled 'The Sunday Drive' (published in *Esquire*, August 1984). It is the narrator's account of a picnic, or rather two picnics, which he is remembering, and remembering himself remembering. A picnic. As a topic, a topos, it is at once simple and inexhaustible. It is the festive gathering of teddy bears in a children's song: it is the incongruous group and equivocal, obscure occasion evoked in Manet's *Déjeuner sur l'herbe*. It is the mellow enigma of Titian's *La Fête champêtre*, which is surely one of the great generative 'picnics' in western art. It is William Gass's 'Sunday Drive'. Even a glance at – a thought about – Manet's (or Titian's) painting will suggest how many themes and ideas can converge in the picnic; how many ambiguities and contrasts, meetings and oppositions, boundaries and interfaces it can convene and contain. Labour and rest; contrivance and indolence; tending and neglect; conviviality and separation; harmony and discord; consummation and loss; permanence and transience; ripeness and rottenness; gratification and melancholy; sociability and loneliness; sexual abandon and decorous civility; in two words, nature and art – their mutual encroachments and exclusions, blendings and oppugnacies, consonances and dissonances. The naked and the clothed, the raw and the cooked (and fermented), the wild and the cultivated, the Dionysiac and the domestic; and – you do not have to look too hard to find them – joyous intimations of fertile renewal and fecund abundance, shadowed by more sombre, autumnal premonitions of mutability, decline and death. All this – it simply amounts to every aspect of life – may be found, touched on, alluded to, glanced at, provocatively foregrounded or dimly marginalized, in the resonant, modest occasion of the pastoral picnic. And so they may be in Gass's version of suburban pastoral. He always puts everything in it.

   It is, of course, a specific version of pastoral. To be sure, the bears are there (if not the teddy bears, the Three Bears), or rather there are bears as barns (or barns metamorphosed into bears), as is a whole range of European art and literature in specific allusions or echoes and traces. But there is also a temporal, historical reference and locating – the Depression years in America. Indeed, the complex sense of time, of times, is one of the marked characteristics of the piece. Apparently stable references to fixed points of historical, biographical time are merged with, unmoored by, the flowing extensions, digressions, regressions, projections, of memory, imagination, anticipation, meditation. Consider the deceptive ostension of the opening statement, repeated in the body of the text, and in the closing sentence – 'This was years ago.' What does 'this' refer to: when was 'years ago'? We expect what follows to amplify and clarify this proleptic statement, but when by the end we read 'all of this was years ago now' we are scarcely more securely situated though we are certainly more richly informed. For 'all this' has comprised many different times and time scales, and 'now' (a notorious deictic) could refer to the time of writing (but then it should read '*is* years ago now'), the time of the Sunday Drive (but which one?), or even our time of reading. The relationship between 'this', 'was', 'ago', 'now' is an endlessly teasing one which cannot be disambiguated (such teasing can be found in Beckett of course), but which produces provocative uncertainties, duplicitous blurs, disorienting conflations, in our habitually more tidy, discrete, treatment of thens and nows. Gass, or the narrator as I should say, draws attention to what has been going on just before the end. 'I see I am standing three times in three times – mine, theirs, the weeds – now. It is utterly awful and confusing and I don't mind.' 'Theirs' refers to the barns, and he is referring to the conjunction, the co-presence, of the distinctly finite time of the single human life, the more imponderable longevity of man-made artefacts, and the eternal, cyclical time of nature's proliferating replacements. All there 'now'. And three more times. The time of the drive, the time of the remembered drive the narrator went on as a child, the time of his writing about all these times. Now. This pastoral confuses and introduces a sense of awe into our awareness of the ramifying complexities of our relationship to time(s). We should not mind.

It *is* confusing, though humanly so. The narrator is remembering a Sunday Drive he took with his family; he is also remembering an earlier drive (and drives) he was taken on by his family as a child. But he is also remembering remembering the earlier drive on the later one – all memories surrounded, linked and separated, fused and amplified in, and by, the remembering, narrating now. Preoccupations, pleasures, regrets, nostalgies, recriminations, shocks, epiphanies, resolutions, all begin to merge in, emerge from, his writing and re-collecting. Like the Rainbow ice-cream which gave him such delight as a child ('like having a noise melt in your mouth', a marvellous and not gratuitous simile), the result is an immensely pleasurable 'accidental and chaotic benevolence'. Like having the sights and sounds and feelings of multiple times melt in our minds. Pleasure is an important concern, as befits a meditation on what is intended as a pleasure excursion. There is a distinct, though subtly dispersed, sense of the tensions (dialectic) between authority and freedom, wayward impulse and firm control, relaxation and repression, wants and rules – more largely, between weeds and barns. Indeed, a whole politics of dominance and desire is intermittently sketched out and explored. The narrator, like his father, is only a 'Czar' in metaphor, and his wife's instinct for the 'regimental' manifests itself in oppressive furniture rather than military force, but problems of power gust around, and we are reminded that authoritarian regimes (monarchies, dictator- ships, totalitarianism – they are all dimly present, remembered by occasional adjectives, revived in unexpected nouns) can take many forms and appear in various guises. Not least – certainly not least – the family. And as the picnic is often seen as, and intended to be, the family outing *par excellence*, an occasion when the disparate members of a family can re- experience and celebrate their familiality in a shared pleasure excursion (or excursion into pleasure), it is hardly surprising that the piece becomes, among other things, an excursion – 'a drive' – into matters and problems related to and generated by desire and the family. And if the narrator's picnic is in some ways a disappointment and a failure, like the one organized by *his* father which he most notably remembers, it is because all pastorals are – in some ways – failed pastorals. Because death – literal or metaphoric, experienced or adumbrated, in large things or small (of the body, of the year) – is always there. ET IN ARCADIA EGO.

A family on a picnic can, should, form 'a familial consciousness', but, as the narrator recalls about his earlier outings, 'we generally didn't talk, and didn't join, and didn't form'. As it was then, so it is/was 'now'. The family on a picnic reveals, discovers, enacts, its fissile properties, its centrifugal tendencies – its inherent disposition to scatter (like the wind-borne seeds). 'Wandering' – errancy, divergence – tends to prevail over coherence and formation: disaggregation rather than aggregation, though of course the family – as families one way or another, through affection, dependency or coercion, usually do after such temporary, 'sabbatical', ventures into nature – comes home together. On the narrator's picnic (to distinguish it from his father's, though they constantly merge as the tenses shift and mix, forcing strange synchronicities, unmarked discontinuities, odd realignments) soon 'the wrangling is intense', between fractious children, imperious mother, silently resistant, oppositional and withdrawn father–narrator. The inflexible, autocratic maternal imperatives and strictures of Martha – 'You don't want *that*' . . . 'you *love* your brother' – tend to promote discord even as they seek to impose concord, as such orders and orderings often do. But clearly, if mutedly, the rifts in the family run deeper, particularly between the narrator and Martha, whose irritated, clipped exchanges – 'We stick these short words like tacks into one another' – seem like the recurrent skirmishes of a larger, longer battle. Recurrent fantasies of driving the family into the 'liquified shit' of the river and jumping clear at the last moment – 'bye bye', flickering dreams of annihilation and abandonment, suggest that this family is something of a time-bomb on a tolerably short fuse. Like all too many families, as one supposes. The last sentence opens up wider, even global, perspectives: 'we are waging other wars'. In this context 'wars' might suggest that the intra-familial war has moved onto another plane, escalated exponentially, in line with (or on the model of) the larger wars abroad – the Second World War, Korea, Vietnam (wars proliferate like weeds). To what extent this may serve to tie the piece into the larger intentions of *The Tunnel* it is, of course, impossible to say. But, as it is, it is an appropriate enough, or suggestive enough, point of termination. Memories of the soiled, spoiled picnics and pastorals of two generations can serve admirably well to suggest the seeds and growths of embryonic tendencies to violence and conflict, the smouldering, imperfectly suppressed rages of sadistic manipulation and dissatisfied desire, to be found in the microcosm, heterocosm of the family.

Let me comment on the interplay between desire and art – one of the many issues which, compressed and teeming, are growing, working, playing, in the rich undergrowth and blossom of Gass's prose in this piece (which can affect a sensitive reader much as the 'embrace of bushes' appears to the narrator in memory – 'flowered, fruitful, and blazing' – though, like the 'difficult' grasses he remembers, Gass's prose, in unsuspected places, may be as poison as ivy, as barbed as wire, as nervous as bees). I am thinking of the extraordinary passages concerning the ice-cream cones, and the barns. Near the end, after the part concerning the barns, the narrator writes: 'sometimes I know what I want, but I'm not on that account allowed to have it. DeeDeeDeeDeeDee.' The slight ambiguity of 'on that account' (*precisely* because, or *merely* because) reminds us of the joyless prohibitions of the negating matriarch that Martha has become. (Once they would have made love, but now everything in the relationship is dry, like the weeds they collect to serve as house decorations. There is a Freudian dictum to the effect that where there is love, there is usually wetness. On some of their picnics ('it's years ago now') the narrator recalls that 'our eyes sought not the moist but the dry'. So it is. So it has become.) The quintupled 'Dee' refers to the ice-cream cones at Daisy's Dairy Stores, which were, for the narrator as a child, the climactic, often deferred, pleasure of those bygone Sunday drives. Gass's recreation of this primal scene of pleasure is masterly. But more than than, the narrator effectively reveals the difference between the relative simplicity of his childhood wants and satisfactions and the far greater complexity of their adult manifestations. The difference is, crucially, a matter of the relationship between desire and language. 'At first I thought Daisy was a girl, then a flower, finally a cow; but Daisy was only a name.' Daisy, the source and locus of pleasure. At first, it must have been another person, or at least something flowering, or lowing. But 'Daisy' is only a signifier. The narrator knows that now. Thus we lose the world as we grow in language (in every sense).

But it is not all loss. A bit later, remembering his ecstasy at the colour and taste of the Rainbow cone, the narrator (now) adds a retrospective commentary. Four times he writes 'Later I could have compared (extolled) . . . ', and he gives the possible comparisons – stews, batiks, northern lights, mixture of nations, etc. But that is later. Now. 'Then I could only confess my wants.' The child has its wants, and its satisfactions, and very intense they are. But something is missing, or, more accurately, not yet present (the addition might not be a completion, but a supererogatory supplement, an excess): 'the youthful mind is a barren plain: there is no range of reference'. Range of reference is the result of accumulated language in the head. 'Could have' is an impossible tense – the past conditional, a time we can inhabit only in language. But, living in language, there is no limit to the possible range of references. The barren plain of a youth's life is, among other things, the relative absence of any mental obstacle looming between the feeling and formulation of 'wants'. But the dense lexical vegetation of the adult mind (this adult, but really any), while it increases the range of reference to (theoretically) infinity, also serves to defer, divert, long-circuit, desire interminably. The enrichment also entails a loss. 'You don't know what you want.' The placing of these words in the text makes the source of their utterance or inscription undecidable – the narrator's father to him as a child? the narrator to himself? to us? No matter – uncertainly originated, it is a certain truth. Living in a Rainbow richness of language, the narrator can no longer simply reach out and take hold of the bouquet, the bloom of a five Dee cone. But he can cup and relish the thought of that cone *as* a bouquet or a bloom, or whatever else he chooses to select from the infinite range of possible comparisons/flavours which are on offer in the great Dairy Store of language. And this the youth cannot do. He or she is limited to real cones with real ice cream in them. There is no point in attempting to adjudicate between the two states, the two Stores. In suggesting that Gass is – effectively – dramatizing something of the loss and gain involved in our inescapable linguicity in these refracted memories of childhood visits to an ice-cream parlour, I am not being frivolous nor, I hope, precious or fatuous. Gass unmistakably has a gustatory sense of language – he really tastes his words and invites us to do so too. It is, of course, a very basic gratification, since we first begin to grow, sucking and being suckled. To the extent that the adult state seems to deflect or debar us from the site of actual gratifications, the chances (the dangers? the compensations?) are that the adult will solace him or herself on a cone of words. Daisy is only a name. But there is a pleasure of, and in, the name as well. It is a pleasure which, as Gass's prose continuously demonstrates, can be very considerable indeed – weeds, poison ivy, barbed wire, frigid wife, and all.

But they will tend to be lonely pleasures, as the narrator indicates: desires denied, wants disallowed. Which brings me to the barns. 'Just over the hill is heaven', says the narrator, trying to amuse the children. They are not amused, but just over the hill are the barns, and 'the barns are beautiful'. Even Martha looks pleased. Perhaps they offer a visual point of extra-familial peace and rest. But note that the first sight (as remembered) of the barns triggers an apparently unrelated memory of what might have been a childhood love – Lois. However, what the narrator remembers about this episode is 'stomping' fiercely on some rather disgusting mud pies which Lois had made and somewhat sickeningly decorated. First love – nauseating, embellished little constructs – revulsion, anger, violence: in little, it could be the pattern of a life. It is all that the barns are not. Or better, the other way around. The barns are like ships, like 'good monumental sculpture' which gives the same sort of pleasure 'by the force of its immediate mass and the caress of its eventual texture' (not for the first time a description of the aesthetic, kinaesthetic effect of something in the world offers, at the same time, a perfectly apt description of the effects to which Gass's prose aspires – and achieves). The barns remain, retain. They hold. Hold together, hold and 'store' 'whisps of nostalgia', a rich darkness which the present may defeat but cannot destroy. One barn has an 'undeniably solid presence' which nevertheless seems to recede into 'the past perhaps, into never-never land', as if it contained its own 'vanishing point from which it might not choose or be able to return'. A satisfying, solacing, solid presence which contains the principle and possibility of its own absence – in which the gaps and holes seem to be actively gazing voids. Wondrous, enduring artefacts, sailing in and on time, cargoed and freighted with the rich absences and occlusions of the past, memory, and imagination, these barns are not only like works of art for the narrator, they activate the creative, metamorphosing, dreaming faculties in him – effectively solicit and inspire, indeed create, the artist. The barns, as transcribed and *in the transcribing*, become the site and venue of sombrely exuberant metaphysical and aesthetic speculation and epiphany.

But: 'Although at home, they are lost, alone, alive.' A way a lone a last a loved a long the . . . yes, Joyce is present at this foregathering, and such an echo and evocation make us realize that the narrator sees some of his own pathos in the barns, for he too is lost, alone, alive. Immediately another apparently unrelated memory follows. This is of the car crash he experienced and witnessed on that earlier picnic drive, or drives, which ended both in ice creams and, on this occasion, violence and destruction. DeeDeeDeeDeeDee – and Death. The mercy and mortality of the pastoral. After the crash the narrator is covered with purple berry juice, stained indeed with his first horrified experience of the reality of death. This memory extends into a more general recollection of the decay and decline of his family – his mother's drinking, the spreading pain. Family outing – a fatal collision – family disintegration: it is another pattern of life. It could be a continuation of the previous one – the love which generates hate, the family which shatters on violence and death. Once again, the narrator's memory swings round to the barns, for consolation. They are the cause of a 'calm elation'. They now seem to offer a point of exit – retreat – from the 'ordinary world', where, indeed, three barns can become three bears, and the mind can begin to play. The tenses go in all directions – I liked, I shall, I am, I was. Thoughts and things can run and jostle together – like licking the Rainbow. That, indeed, is life. But it is not art – at least not pure art, or an art of purity. Not Mondrian. 'Only in a painting or a poem can you find true purity . . . Never in a man or woman.' The barns seem to stir and awaken a dream of, a longing for, some unattainable realm of purity, transcendence really, beyond the messy entanglements of our creatural condition. Certainly one of the things the narrator finds 'pleasing' about the barns is 'the difference between what is natural here, and what is man made'. After the mixed pleasure of the Rainbow cream, and the more painfully mixed pleasure of love and family (hate and death), the only pure pleasure would seem to be in the artefact – the vacated, unused and useless, man-made structure. The uselessness is important – the barns have receded beyond utility. The narrator remembers his father's car, kept shining in the garage when he could no longer drive it. He remembers 'an old gas pump' which, 'dressed in rust', has become 'a work of art'. Note that it was not of course conceived or constructed as one. Through 'neglect' it has been liberated beyond function, and become what some aestheticians would call an object of intransitive contemplation. And thus and thereby – art. Neglect and rust mark the narrator's own habitation, indeed his life. It would seem he has some sympathy for these processes of letting things go, rot, stagnate, rust, fragment as the bread crumbles to bits as he cuts it. Certainly the barns have been liberated by being freed of tenants and purpose, by becoming, as it were, un-barned. 'These barns have been abandoned, but they have been abandoned to beauty. They are no longer barns. They are themselves . . . they have been left alone to breathe.' This beautiful passage contains a whole implicit aesthetic, which would seem to be close to Gass's own – at least in part. There are ambiguous implications in it concerning the relationship of art to human community and intentionality. For if the barns are most beautiful when least being barns, wherefore should and shall they be built? We cannot rely on art based on the fortuitous felicities of neglect. The man made is always made for some kind of purpose, even if that purpose be just play. There is something potentially non-human in the abandoned beauty of the barns. And indeed, that seems to be a major attraction for the narrator. He imagines emptying his house, his life – of furniture, of children – and living alone in the cherished vacancy. 'My life shall become barns. In one barn of me – the blessed barn – lonely as a rented room – I shall keep one light lit.' It is a dream of a distanced, lonely vigil in a rich and hallowed vacancy, some precious, purely illuminated space beyond the mess of family, the greater mess of war, beyond, perhaps, the rainbow multiplicity of the 'ordinary world'. It is one of the dreams of, and in, art. But it remains a dream – a barn dream. By the end, 'we are waging other wars; and now none of these conditions obtains'. It suggests a barn-less, as well as a love-less, world.

The narrator is not untouched by the world – insects rise and swarm about him, as they have done for other Gass narrators. He feels 'the embrace of bushes'; weeds and grasses 'engulf' him; bugs 'brush' him. Such caresses and cradlings are not conventionally pleasant. They derive from the rank, the rotting, the rampant aspects of nature – there is a 'perfume' of putrescence, and a somewhat perverse *frisson* of what may be called erotic entomology. And there are bees, 'nervous' and 'fierce persistent bees'. What does not, any longer, embrace the narrator – what he no longer embraces – is the human world. It is as if he is more aware of, drawn to, the barns and the bees. In an essay entitled 'Culture, Self, and Style' from his last book of essays entitled, characteristically one might say, *Habitations of the Word*, Gass writes as follows:

> It is simply not enough to live and to be honest – happy, to hump and hollar, to reproduce. Bees achieve it, and they still sting and buzz. To seek the truth (which requires method), to endeavour to be just (which depends on process), to create and serve beauty (which is the formal object of style), these old 'ha-has,' like peace and freedom and respect for persons, are seldom aims or states of the world these days, but only words most likely found in Sunday schools, or adrift like booze on the breath of cheapjacks, preachers, politicians, teachers, popes; nevertheless, they can still be sweet on the right tongue, and name our ends and our most honorable dreams.

Gass stresses and marvellously demonstrates continually the supreme importance, value, responsibility, and creative reach and possibility of language. He seeks to so use it that it will have the force and caress of the mass and texture of the barns; the hum and sting of the bees. He wants us to taste the sweetness and pungency of words. For it is in that realm of the extra, the surplus, the supplement, the over-and-above which is the gratuitous buzzing of bees, the unusable loveliness of unused barns, and – for man – simply language, that we discover and create meaning and beauty. A truism, to be sure. But to read Gass is to re-experience the quite immeasurable significance and excitement of that truism. In 'Sunday Drive' the narrator recalls and evokes the autumn in almost extravagantly rich and allusive prose. Then adds: 'Flamboyance and poetry aside, it's how this season goes to its death that is finally entrancing, and one feels compelled to "get out in it" . . . ' Flamboyance and poetry aside, there is always – and only – the undeniable real world and the undeferable reality of death. It is precisely in the flamboyance and poetry – the whole 'aside' of style and language finely used – that we find our fun, our dignity, our point. It is one of the great merits and energizing joys of Gass's writing that he constantly makes us realize that it is the 'aside' which *really* matters. Matters, really, quite as much as, if not more than, the given world and its decline – no matter how often, and from what urges and urgings, we are compelled to 'get out in it'.

Index